THE PERSIAN SPHINX

Amir Abbas Hoveyda and the
Riddle of the Iranian Revolution

A BIOGRAPHY BY
ABBAS MILANI

MAGE PUBLISHERS
WASHINGTON, DC
2001

Copyright © 2000–2001 Abbas Milani
Designed by Mohammad and Najmieh Batmanglij

All rights reserved. Printed in the United States of America. No part of this book may be used or reproduced in any manner whatsoever without the written permission of the publisher. Mage® and colophon are registered trademarks for Mage Publishers Inc. For information, address Mage Publishers 1032-29th Street, NW, Washington, D.C., 20007

Library of Congress Cataloging-in-Publication
Milani, Abbas.
The Persian sphinx: Amir Abbas Hoveyda and the riddle of the Iranian Revolution / a biography by Abbas Milani.--1st ed.
p. cm.
ISBN 0-943211-61-2 (alk. paper)
1. Huvaydā, Amir ʻAbbās, 1919–1979.
2. Prime ministers--Iran--Biography.
3. Iran--Politics and government--1925-1979. I. Title
DS316.9.H88 M55 2000
955.05'3'092--dc21
[B]

First edition
Second printing
Printed and manufactured in the United States

Hardcover ISBN 0-934211-61-2
Mage books are available through better bookstores, or directly from the publisher; toll-free 1-800-962-0922 or 202-342-1642
e-mail: info@mage.com
Visit Mage online at www.mage.com

To my son Hamid
"the light of my eyes"

Contents

Perils of Persian Biography

'I did that,' says my memory. 'I can't have done that,' says my pride. In the end, memory gives way.

—Nietzsche

The *Persian Sphinx* began in 1996. It was to be a 2,500 word project. In early July of that year, I had received a letter from the editors of *Encyclopedia Iranica*, asking me to write entries on five modern Iranian politicians. Amir Abbas Hoveyda's name immediately caught my attention. His entry, I surmised, would be the easiest. Here was a man who had been under the glare of the media for some thirteen years as Iran's prime minister; his trial at the hands of the Islamic Republic's "Hanging Judge" had been no less a public act. A spate of post-revolutionary memoirs, the existence of two major oral history projects—one at Harvard, the other at the Foundation for Iranian Studies—were all promising indications that the assigned task would be easy to manage. Furthermore, I had been a student of Iranian politics for almost all the years of Hoveyda's tenure. On the day Iranian newspapers announced his resignation, I was serving time in Tehran's infamous Evin Prison. I was there as an opponent of the Pahlavi regime and, along with other political prisoners, I had discussed ad nauseam the political significance of his dismissal.[1] Writing his life, or as the editors suggested, a 2,500 word redaction of it, would be, I imagined, fairly easy. Now, four years later, I am happy to report that I was agonizingly and blessedly, wrong.

It has been blessed because in the pursuit of the riddle that was his life, I have had a chance to revisit some of the same landscape that I had mined earlier while writing my own memoir. The experience was not unlike revisiting, as a guest, a landscape that I had toiled in earlier. My experience, as it turns out, was not unique. Even if we do not concur with Yeats that, "all knowledge is biography," we must, I think, accept the more common notion that all biographies are, at least in some sense, autobiographical. By comparing ourselves, and our times, to the agonies and choices others made, we may well arrive at self-cognition and possibly shed some light on the choices we face now. Biography, they say, "is an exalting baptism," since "burrowing into a life the reader experiences clarity and purpose by proxy."[2]

Early in the process of this "exalting baptism" I realized that nearly all of my preconceptions about Amir Abbas Hoveyda had been wrong. He was a far more complicated and interesting a character than I had ever imagined. He was a true intellectual, a man of cosmopolitan flair, a liberal at heart who served an illiberal master. He lived at the height of Iran's historic struggle between modernity and tradition, Western cosmopolitanism and Persian isolationism, secularism and religious fundamentalism, and ultimately between civil society and democracy on one hand, and authoritarianism on the other. He embodied the hopes and aspirations, the accomplishments and the failures of a whole generation of, usually Western-trained, technocrats who were bent on pulling Iran out of its cycle of poverty and repression and freeing it from the clutches of tradition. Pondering his life could also, I realized, shed light on serious questions about individual moral responsibility for acts within a political system, and the possibilities of reforming that system from within. I soon realized that much of what I had known about Hoveyda was a caricature of the man. *The Persian Sphinx* is an account of my attempt to find the man behind the mask, the self behind the caricature.

Biography, as a genre, has had a tortured history in Iran. While the Achaemenid kings of some 2,500 years ago were unabashedly self-assertive (the inscriptions they left behind gave detailed descriptions of their past deeds, and personal wishes), with the advent of Islam, the self was gradually eclipsed, and the individual was no longer directly described or revealed to the reader.³ Scholars have attributed this to the common Islamic belief that the human soul is composed of three faculties, two seeking the sublime and the divine, while the third, the "bestial" faculty, is caught in the vagaries of sin, and is prey to the temptations of the devil. Such sins and temptations are also, needless to say, the common threads that weave together, at least in part, the best biographies.

The New Testament and the Koran also tell us about each religion's views on biography. The Gospels, as the fount of Christianity, are essentially composed of four, sometimes conflicting, biographical narratives. Not only is Christ, as the son of God, the center of the narrative, but the world, and the word, have been created from God's love for his children. More importantly, implicit in the very structure of the four Gospels is the acceptance of a kind of biographical pluralism, the idea that a man's life looks different when viewed from different perspectives. In the Koran, on the other hand, the world, and the word, are created to show the glory of God. The prophet Mohammed, about whose life very little is offered and no ambiguity is tolerated, enters the narrative only to carry out the commands of his lord.

As late as the nineteenth century, when the self-assertive individual "I" finally reentered Persian personal narratives, this functional, ultimately self-effacing view of human life was still evident. Indeed, nearly 95 percent of some 250 Persian memoirs written in this period may be characterized by their focus on political, social, and cultural events.⁴ In other words, the eclipse of the self continued.

The same elements that parched the landscape of Persian biographies seem to have also impacted the history of Persian painting. Portraits are to painting what biographies are to historical and literary narratives. In the history of Persian painting there is a decided dearth of portraits. Islam, like Judaism and early Christianity, forbade portraits. Arabs refused to depict Mohammed and it was "the sacrilegious brush of a Persian painter" that first dared to draw him.⁵ With the absence of portraits, Persian miniatures became the predominant form of representational art, and in them the concrete individual was forfeited in favor of an attempt to capture the perfect form, the Platonic Idea of a human. In the nineteenth century, however, just as personal narratives became more prevalent in Persia, portraits too became more common.⁶

Even though personal narratives became more fashionable in the nineteenth century, biographies remained, for a variety of reasons, a rarity. Poverty of archival material makes writing Persian biography particularly perilous. When, for example, I can read about the details of the taxes William Shakespeare paid in 1595, but twenty years after Hoveyda's death, I still cannot get my hands on the minutes of his cabinet meetings, I develop what can only be called "archive envy."[7]

The Islamic Republic's approach to the archival material it has inherited from the previous regime has only darkened the picture. The government has made no attempt to systematically offer any of these documents for scholarly scrutiny. Instead various government agencies have doled out selected documents to fit their own immediate political exigencies.

In contrast to this shortage of reliable archival material, there is a surfeit of rumors and conspiracy theories, each accorded the status of revealed truth by their adherents. For any biographer, the treacherous waters of these hints and innuendoes are as hard to ignore as they are to navigate. And in modern Iran few Iranians have been the subject of as many rumors as Hoveyda.

With the absence of reliable archives in Iran, Western government archives and the mercurial memory of Hoveyda's friends and foes became my indispensable source of information about his life. While many British, French, and U.S. government documents have not yet been declassified, tapping into the recollections of those who knew Hoveyda also proved to be particularly difficult. Memory is always selective and it becomes more so when hued by the mandates of ideology, and the pride and prejudices of politics. Furthermore, at least two ponderously long decades of exile have lapsed since the time many of the events recounted here first took place. Time is the nemesis of memory, and thus the passage of these years could have only skewed the inherently supple and plastic contours of memory.

But a lack of archives and the tenuous threads of memory were not the only problems in attempting to reconstruct Hoveyda's past. Some of those who were present during crucial moments of his life did not, for a variety of reasons, wish to speak with me. A few have fashioned a new identity for themselves, altogether away from the realm of politics, and thus they either claimed total ignorance or amnesia. A handful of this group still live in Iran. They rightfully prefer to be forgotten by the Islamic authorities. A mere mention of their name in a book of this sort could solicit undesirable attention. Others were reticent because they are under the illusion that they are still players in the arena of Iranian politics; they harbor hopes of a royalist restoration and are worried that anything they might say could be held against them. A few of them still seem to rely on the patronage of the royal family for their very livelihood and could hardly be expected to risk it all for the sake of historical veracity. Then there are those who seem reticent to talk out of a sense of shame for the role they played in the arrest of Hoveyda. Silence, they hope, affords them plausible deniability.

Furthermore, many of the interviews in the two oral history projects were of little use for this biography, because the oral historians had often failed to ask the questions that are most relevant to Hoveyda's life. Thus a surfeit of pseudo-facts, a shortage of reliable documents, the reticence of those still alive to talk, and finally the specter of conspiracy, all haunted *The Persian Sphinx*, as I suspect they would haunt any biography of an Iranian.

To overcome these obstacles, I chose a method that was simple in principle, but difficult in practice. I tried to rely primarily on archival materials. Where such documents were not available—either because they had not yet been declassified, or because no records existed—I relied on interviews. I have talked to close to 130 people; many are Hoveyda's friends and foes; some are simply informed sources about Iran. In deciding whom I should talk to, I ignored the political pieties of both the left and the right, as well as those of the monarchists and their opponents. They each seem to have a litany of "kosher" and "tainted" sources. I was willing, and anxious, to talk to anyone who had a story to tell and was somehow involved in Hoveyda's life.

Nearly every story recounted here has been corroborated by a second independent source. Lest the endnotes become longer than they already are, I decided to eschew, as a rule, citing the second source. In a few instances where such corroboration proved impossible, I pondered the overall reliability of the source of the statement, as well as the nature of the claim itself, and then chose to either include it or leave it out. In other words, if most of a person's claims turned out to be accurate, then their one uncorroborated story could, I thought, be included in the narrative. Only in the future, when all archives are opened and the pertinent documents available, will we know whether my trust in these isolated cases was indeed warranted. In a few cases when reliable archival documents are silent and competing accounts of an event were hopelessly in conflict, I decided to offer both renditions, hoping to thus provide the reader, and posterity, with a feel for the sensibilities of the elite of the Pahlavi era.

I decided against using anonymous sources. I also refused to relay the words of those who did not want to be interviewed but were willing to send, through an intermediary, some invariably self-serving statement or anecdote.

The Persian Sphinx is a biography. It is a not a history of the Pahlavi era. Nor is it an attempt to appraise or underscore the accomplishments and the failures of the Pahlavi regime. I have dealt with these issues here only to the extent that they interface with Hoveyda's life. It is the hope of every serious biography to fuse the forensic rigors of academic scholarship with a novel's piercing gaze into the life and mind of one individual. Biography hopes to fuse what critics call the "interiority," or the inner life of the character, with the formative influences of the outer social surroundings. Every biography wants to creatively weave character and context into a narrative appealing to a wider readership than those afforded academic tracts. *The Persian Sphinx* is no exception to this rule. The Pahlavi era, and the pathos and pathologies of Iran's socioeconomic development, are no more than the context for the evolution of a man called Amir Abbas Hoveyda.

Writing is at once a solitary, and a social, act. It is social in its inevitable debts and dependence on others, and it is solitary both in the nature of the act of writing itself and in the fact that the ultimate burden of responsibility for any error of fact or judgment rests with the writer. In this sense, while I bear sole responsibility for all of the book's faults, its accomplishments, if any, have surely been the result of the kindness and the generous help of numerous friends and strangers. Many people, too numerous to all be named here, have kindly given of their time, their books, and their sometimes painful memories to make this book possible.

As always, I find it hard to do justice to my debt to Parviz Shokat. He was indefatigable in his search for Hoveyda's published writings in the pages of old Persian magazines and newspapers. He seems most happy in the mildewed stacks of libraries; even his political activism of the past was, in my mind, a closet in which he tried to hide his deep affinity for the world of research and scholarship. He read the entire manuscript twice, and with his legendary sense of political fairness, lassoed the narrative away from rash judgments. Ruth Shokat also read the book and had many interesting suggestions and ideas.

Many biographers lament the difficulties of dealing with the family of the characters they write about. I was blessed with having, in Hoveyda's family, a remarkably accommodating and non-intrusive cast of tolerant characters. Foremost amongst them were Amir Abbas Hoveyda's brother, Fereydoun, and their cousin, Dr. Fereshteh Ensha. She was the person who had the most contact with Hoveyda in prison (she was also his doctor). She kindly shared many of her painful recollections of those dark hours with me. She also provided me with hitherto unpublished, but crucial, letters and documents pertaining to Hoveyda's prison experience.

Fereydoun, too, has not only been a constant and gracefully patient source of information, but the magnanimity of his approach to the whole project has been nothing short of inspiring. Over the course of the last four years, he has gone out of his way to make every document, every book, and every source of information, not all of them favorable to Hoveyda, available to me.

But the true nature of his commitment was, in my mind, best captured in his actions when I visited him about a year ago. I was there hoping to find some photographs of Amir Abbas. Sitting in Fereydoun's dining room, under the gaze of a boldly-colored portrait of him by Andy Warhol, he pulled out a couple of old family albums, one ornate and silver-rimmed, the other simple and without frills, both worn by time. As we began leafing through the pages, he asked me to tell him which pictures I wanted. And then as soon as I pointed to one I liked—a tender photo of him and his brother, holding hands, with the faint yellow gloss of age casting its shadow over the two young boys (p. 46)—Fereydoun tore away the entire page where the picture was, and put it aside. Before long, some twenty-five pages of often dusty sheets of heavy, black paper were sitting on the corner of the dining room table.

Yet in the four years since I began working on *The Persian Sphinx* Fereydoun Hoveyda never tried to change the tenor of the book. Never once did he suggest that I include a word of approbation in, or exclude a critical comment from, the narrative. "All I want," he often told me, "is that the wall of silence around my brother be broken." A celebrated writer and critic himself, he knows and respects the sanctity, and the power, of words. The friendship I have developed with him is one of the greatest rewards of writing this biography.

The Persian Sphinx bore other fruits of friendship. Early in the course of my research, I spoke with Cyrus Ghani, and it did not take long to discover that he is truly a man of myriad talents and boundless generosity. He talks as passionately and as knowledgeably about Shakespeare and the history of nineteenth-century French literature as about films and fifteenth-century calligraphy in Iran. He read the entire manuscript twice and has used his lawyer's ear for the finer nuances of words, his scholar's eye for both the minutiae and the panorama of history, and his encyclopedic command of the many sides of modern Iranian politics—faculties that are all evident in his masterful book, *Iran and the Rise of Reza Shah*—to point out many errors in the early drafts of the book.[8]

Ebrahim Golestan also kindly agreed to offer his critique of the entire manuscript. He too is an erudite visionary who is famously candid in his opinions. He has been at the center of Iran's intellectual life for almost half a century; furthermore, he knew Hoveyda well and had often seen him operate, at close hand, in various political arenas. Golestan's copious notes pointed out some of the lapses and errors in my story, for which I thank him.

Ahmad Ghoreishi was instrumental in making some of the most important interviews for this book possible. Without his intervention, I suspect, many of the people who talked to me would have remained silent. It is a sign of the generosity of his soul that though in the last couple of years, some of his friends tried to dissuade him from helping me with this project, he was unfailing in his support.

My siblings were, as always, a constant source of guidance, encouragement, and help. My older brother, Hossein, who has lived in Europe for much of the past forty years, was a helpful companion in each of my trips to that continent. Without his help, it would have been impossible to do all I had to do in the short time I was in each city. Another brother, Hassan, took time out of his busy life to read the book and offer his words of encouragement and advice. My sister Farzaneh's sororal trust in my abilities was an always dependable source of intellectual and emotional support. Her commitment to the dispassionate language of scholarship was a reliable signpost for keeping the narrative free from the excesses of ideology. She not only read the entire manuscript, but she also patiently heard many of the chapters over the phone, only moments after I had written them and needed some immediate feedback. My younger brother, Mohsen, himself an accomplished political scientist, also read the book and used his own unique combination of wit and wisdom to help alleviate some of the book's shortcomings.

Two of my students at the College of Notre Dame, Alan Cheung and William Tse, were helpful in corralling and copying some of the original sources for the book. Alan, with his precocious sense of scholarly discipline and acumen, spent many long hours copying documents from the National Security Archive housed at Stanford University's Hoover Institute. William was helpful in finding many references to Hoveyda in U.S. newspapers and magazines.

I owe special debts of gratitude to Isabelle Nathan of the Archive Diplomatique at the French foreign ministry, in Paris, Regina Greenwell, senior archivist at Lyndon Baines Johnson Library in Austin, Texas, and Ibrahim Pourhadi at the Library of Congress.

I would also like to thank a number of colleagues and friends who read parts or all of the manuscript and offered often useful advice: Ervand Abrahamian, Ali Alikhani, Iraj Aryanpour, Ahmad Ashraf, Fakhreddin Azimi, Iradj Bagherzade, Ardavan Davaran, Dick Davis, Kasra Ferdows, Ali Ferdowsi, Mohsen Gharib, Hormoz Hekmat, Daryoush Homayoun, Habib Ladjevardi, Kevin Maxwell, Hassanali Mehran, Farrokh Najmabadi, Bahman Sadr, Irv Schneiderman, and Farrokh Shahabi. At Mage Publishers, thanks are also due to Harry Endrulat, who copyedited the manuscript, and to Tony Ross, who wore many hats, one of which included reading the proofs and making valuable comments.

Writing *The Persian Sphinx* has been a shoestring operation. Except for two small Faculty Development Grants from the College of Notre Dame, and a small advance from Mage Publishers, I have received no grant or financial help from any other individuals or organizations. The trips I made to Europe for this project were all made possible by unrelated invitations from different cultural groups and universities in Europe. Once there, I would lengthen my stay to allow time to work on the book. I thus owe a special thanks to Gardoon publishers in Koln, Germany, Dehkhoda Cultural Center in Berlin, the Idee Cultural Group in Stockholm, the Department of Asian and African Languages at Uppsala University in Sweden, and Khavaran Publishers in Paris.

Doris Nyland generously gave me access to her sublimely beautiful house at Salishan on the Oregon coast, where a good part of *The Persian Sphinx* was written.

Important as all these groups, places, and people have been, their help and contribution pales in comparison to the role two other people played in bringing this project to life. Mohammad Batmanglij is all one can hope for in a publisher and editor. He combines his refined sensibilities with a contagious passion for the world of letters and ideas. His wit and wisdom, his daring and his true dedication to his art and craft are all delightfully at odds with the crass commercialism that has turned much of the publishing world into the backwaters of what has been called the "culture industry." From the moment he heard of my intention to write a biography of Hoveyda, he spared no effort, financial, intellectual, or aesthetic, to shepherd the project to completion. On a couple of occasions, when I was overwhelmed with the apparently insurmountable obstacles that lay in the way of finishing the project, it was only his steady, patient, and unwavering support that finally brought the project back on track. Every time I visited Washington, I enjoyed not only the hospitality of his family and home, but also the kindness of his wife, Najmieh, who is herself a world-class culinary maestro, an aesthete, an astute publisher, a doting mother, and a dear friend.

This book's debt to Jean Nyland can truly not be measured in words. She has read, and heard, every word more times than I dare count, or she probably cares to remember. The catholicity of her erudition, her unfailing sense of justice, her judicious way with words, her knack as a psychologist for shedding light on the wonders and vagaries of the human mind, have always been a compass by which I have tried to navigate my way through the sometimes turbulent waters of this project. Her selfless patience in sharing, for almost four years, our life with the sphinx made writing this book far less emotionally draining than it might otherwise have been.

A.M.

March 2000

I beseech you, what manner of man is he?
...They say he has been fencer to the Shah of Persia.
　　　　　　—Shakespeare, *Twelfth Night*

CHAPTER ONE

Bridge of Sighs

*...On the Bridge of Sighs
A palace and a prison on each hand.*
—Byron

All his life, books had been his solace and passion, his sanctuary from the ordeals of the mundane. When he was free, history was the map by which he navigated the treacherous waters of what he once called the "Byzantine" world of Iranian politics.[1] Now imprisoned, a captive of the Islamic Revolution, the past would become a portent of his future.

By March 28, 1979, Amir Abbas Hoveyda, who had served the shah of Iran as prime minister for almost thirteen years, had been in jail for some five months. On November 8, 1978, in an attempt to appease the rapidly rising tide of revolutionary fervor, the shah had ordered Hoveyda's arrest. There was no appeasing the tide, however, and fearing for their lives, the royal family fled Iran on January 16, 1979, with little realistic hope of ever returning. They took with them much of their personal belongings, including the royal dog. Their long-trusted prime minister, however, they chose to leave behind.

On the morning of February 11, 1979, when the revolutionary tide—or squall—finally swept to power, Hoveyda was left all but unattended in his royal prison. In the chaos of the early hours his guards—all agents of the much-despised secret police, known by its Persian acronym of SAVAK—had fled, fearing for their own safety. Rather than risk an escape attempt himself, Hoveyda chose to surrender to the new Islamic victors. He thus gained the ill fortune of being the highest-ranking official and the only prime minister of the *ancien régime* to fall into the hands of the Islamic revolutionaries. Five other former prime ministers—Ali Amini, Jafar Sharif-Emami, Jamshid Amouzegar, Gholam-Reza Azhari, and Shapour Bakhtiar—succeeded in fleeing the country on, or around, the eve of the revolution.

Hoveyda spent most of his jail time reading, but on that cold March day, the only visible cot-side volume was an ornate, gilded copy of Islam's holy book.[2] He used the Koran not so much for spiritual guidance but as a source book to prepare his defense for what he had been led to believe would be his public trial in an Islamic court of law.[3]

Sometimes Hoveyda read *romans policiers*, as well. Since his youth, he had been an avid mystery reader. He preferred the French Série Noir, a specialized imprint in the tradition of American "hard-boiled" detective fiction by writers like Dashiell Hammett or Raymond Chandler.[4] Recently, Hoveyda had asked his cousin, Fereshteh Ensha, for books about the French and the Chinese revolutions. The dreaded "revolutionary terror" he read about in those books, a terror at once self-righteous, unbending, and vengeful, was no longer a mere abstraction. Since the fateful day when he had surrendered to the new revolutionary forces, that terror, this time in an Islamic guise, had been shaping, and haunting, his daily life.

IN HIS SALAD DAYS, AMIR ABBAS HOVEYDA wore an orchid on the lapel of his dapper tailored suits. Francesco Smalto, an Italian couturier and tailor to the shah of Iran, was also Hoveyda's tailor for many years. Lest he appear impertinent to the shah, who in the words of one observer suffered from "narcissistic grandiosity,"[5] Hoveyda remained discreet about his use of the royal tailor.[6] Less discreet were his colorful ties, chosen usually to match the color of the orchid he wore.

Now he was mostly bald and wore a dark Nelson cap from which some strands of white disheveled hair escaped. He sat in a dark, rumpled shirt and matching pants. Over the shirt, he wore a yellow worn-out sweater. A pair of white, ankle-high athletic socks covered his feet, exposing his shin-bones when he sat down. His cane stood next to the cot. He had first begun to use the cane in the summer of 1964, after a car accident left him with a damaged knee and fractured hip.[7] He continued to carry it long after his rehabilitation. In the often-cynical world of Iranian politics, many saw the cane as more form than function,[8] although since the accident, Hoveyda was often worried about losing his balance according to his physician.[9]

His critics said Hoveyda always had an eye for his place in history and he knew that in modern Iran all notable prime ministers had some idiosyncratic trademark. An opera hat, a fur cap, even pajamas and a blanket had served as ministerial trademarks in the past. Hoveyda's cane, along with a pipe, and an orchid had become his emblems.[10] But that was all in the past. Now weak, battered, though not defeated, he needed his cane to maintain his upright, some thought defiant, gait.

By late March, Hoveyda was being held in Qasr Prison, where he had been an inmate for about two weeks. Before his transfer to Qasr, he had been incarcerated for a few days in the Madreseh-ye Refah (Welfare School), which was both Ayatollah Khomeini's place of residence and headquarters for the incipient revolution. The school had been built as a bastion of religious training, a refuge from the secular education championed by the Pahlavi dynasty. Its founders included Shiite clerics like Ali-Akbar Hashemi Rafsanjani and Ali Khamenei, two of the Islamic Republic's most powerful politicians today. The Refah School was established in 1968, just three years after Hoveyda had been first appointed Iran's prime minister.[11]

The school's location, next to two of Tehran's most symbolically significant buildings, was full of historic ironies. On one side stood the Majlis building, on the other the Sepahsalar Mosque. The Majlis was the country's House of Parliament and had come to symbolize the Constitutional Revolution of 1905–06 and its incumbent secular turn in Iranian politics. Hoveyda's tenure as a prime minister had begun in 1965 when Hassan Ali Mansur, his close friend and Iran's premier at the time, was shot by Islamic terrorists as he was about to enter the same parliament building. The gun used in Mansur's murder had been provided by Rafsanjani.[12]

Next to the parliament was the Sepahsalar Mosque, a grand religious monument, which had served a role akin to Westminster Abbey in London. For more than half a century, the mosque had been the scene of every important, and official, religious rite or ritual held in the capital. The mosque had been built as an endowment by Hoveyda's maternal great-uncle, from whom it also took its name. As one of the many beneficiaries of the endowment, Hoveyda's mother received a monthly check from the mosque of 100 tomans.[*13]

With the collapse of the Pahlavi regime, the Majlis, which had for many years been a mere rubber stamp to royal decrees and only a hollow shell of its constitutional mandate, now stood empty, almost derelict. The political center of gravity had switched to the school that for two decades had remained—literally and metaphorically—hidden in the shadow of its grand neighbors, quietly offering its strictly religious curriculum to a small and select body of students. During the first hours of the revolution, prominent figures of the old regime were rounded up and brought to the Refah School, tributes from a jubilant crowd to their new masters.[†] The arrival of the prisoners at the school created a strange cohabitation of the jailer and the jailed, a forced communion between the victor and the vanquished.

Ayatollah Khomeini lived in a room overlooking the schoolyard. Prisoners were kept in another wing, across from the ayatollah's temporary residence. In those feverish first weeks of the revolution, the small schoolyard was regularly filled with people who filed in, dutifully chanted their enthusiastic devotion to the new regime and their hatred of the old, and then filed out. It is not hard to imagine the terrible impact those angry, exuberant, and menacing voices must have had on the men and women held captive in the building.

In the frightening turmoil of the revolution's first hours, and shortly after his arrival at the Refah School, Hoveyda received his first visit from two high-ranking members of the new regime: Khomeini's son, Ahmad, and Abol Hasan Bani Sadr, a French-educated sociologist and one of Ayatollah Khomeini's closest advisors. Moments earlier the two men had been summoned by the ayatollah. "I've heard that some of those arrested have been badly beaten by mobs," he had said. He then had enjoined Ahmad

---

* Before the revolution, 100 tomans was about thirteen dollars. In 1999 after two decades of sharp decline in the value of the Persian currency, the same 100 tomans would bring no more than ten cents.

† In a larger historical context, one can compare the scene to images carved on the walls of Persepolis, the 2,500-year-old ruins of Iran's capital during its days of glory and empire. The bas-reliefs depict supplicant subjects offering their tokens of submission to the Persian kings who ruled Iran.

and Bani Sadr to act as his emissaries and visit the prisoners. "Reassure them," the ayatollah had said, "that Islam does not condone such cruelties; tell them that henceforth they shall be treated fairly and that they will be tried according to the rules of Islamic law."[14]

The two ambassadors of hope stopped first at a large classroom that had become a jail for many of the Imperial Army's top generals. Some of the prisoners remained bravely defiant at such "reassurance," while others broke down and wept. There was also a civilian in the room, Salar Jaf, who had gained infamy in the Kurdish regions of Iran as an alleged operative of SAVAK. It was said that Jaf had obtained his seat in parliament as a reward. He waxed philosophical about his fate, saying in a sardonic tone, "For a while it was our turn to pillage; now the tables have turned."[15]

After conveying the ayatollah's words of assurance to the prisoners, Bani Sadr and Ahmad Khomeini crossed the hallway to the room where Hoveyda was held in solitary confinement. He was the revolution's trophy prisoner, and his private room was a token of this portentous status. There was a bed in one corner, a small, gray metal desk in the other. A thread-bare Persian carpet, some twelve feet long, covered much of the floor. On the desk was a tiny tricolored flag of Iran; the lion and the sun—a reminder of the country's pre-Islamic glories and, since the mid-nineteenth century, a symbol of the institution of monarchy—had been cut out of the center of the flag.[16] A single window facing the yard was now locked and clumsily covered with old newspapers.[17]

Hoveyda was reading when the two men walked in. He seemed to Bani Sadr surprisingly composed, even stoic.[18] The prisoner greeted his visitors with the kind of cordiality that had long been his forte. He had known them both when he was a man of power and they were but minor figures of opposition to the Pahlavi regime. In 1965, not long after becoming the prime minister, he had helped the young Khomeini obtain a passport to join his exiled father. The relationship with Bani Sadr had begun earlier, in 1959: Hoveyda was an official of Iran's National Oil Company and Bani Sadr was a leader of the student movement against the shah.[19]

All his political life, Hoveyda had survived partly on account of his unfailing willingness to help others. Many of the beneficiaries of this largess, including some in the royal family, had felt indebted to him.[20] Even some members of the Iranian opposition, particularly several prominent clerics who were emerging as key figures in the new Islamic regime, had

been recipients of Hoveyda's patronage in the past. But could the moun-
tain of debts and favors he was owed, including "payments of about eleven
million dollars a year in governmental funds to the Islamic clergy," according to Hoveyda's brother, save him now?[21]

In remembering his earlier meetings with Hoveyda, Bani Sadr, usually
reticent in his praise of others, was surprisingly loquacious. "He impressed
me as a decent man, as someone who meant well, someone who could
bear to hear criticism. I was usually frank and ruthless in my criticism of
him and the regime he served. He bore it all with a grin. On more than
one occasion, I asked him to help free friends who had fallen into the
hands of the secret police, and he usually did what he could. I grew to like
him; his problem was that he had no religious faith at all. Nevertheless,
when I left Iran to continue my education in France, he was the only official of the Pahlavi regime to whom I paid a courtesy farewell visit."[22]

Now, a little less than two decades later, they met again, this time in jail,
and their conversation began with banter about what Hoveyda had been
reading when the two men walked in. It was Jean E. Charon's *L'Esprit, Cet
Inconnu,* a neo-Gnostic treatise on the poverty of spiritual life in modern
times and the promise of a new more spiritual millennium. With little
effort at subtlety, Bani Sadr said, "Isn't it too late to be reading this kind of
book?" Hoveyda demurred, saying, "It is never too late to read anything."
Then the conversation turned serious, and the two emissaries reiterated
the ayatollah's words of reassurance.[23]

For many of the prisoners, the ayatollah's words of comfort proved
shockingly ephemeral. Less than a week after that visit, twenty-five of
them, nearly all generals, were executed by firing squads on the rooftop of
the Refah School. Indeed, the first round of executions that included four
generals, Nematollah Nasiri, Reza Naji, Mehdi Rahimi, and Manouchehr
Khosrodad, took place only hours after the purported visit of reassurance.
Their trials had each lasted no more than a few minutes. They had been
found guilty of "spreading corruption on earth." On the day of the first executions, bold headlines and blood-bespattered pictures of the four generals' bullet-ridden bodies, and their vacant faces, were all that appeared on
the front page of *Kayhan,* Tehran's daily newspaper. The next day, another
twenty-one people were sent to the firing squad, and a new galaxy of
haunting pictures, of deformed bodies and faces caught in the "Jaws of
Death," once again filled the pages of the newspaper.[24] In retrospect, the

obscene violence of those morbid pictures, their prevalence on the pages of Tehran's newspapers for many weeks, is a sad, and poignant, reminder of the frenzy of terror unleashed by the revolution. Many of the secular and religious radicals, who in those early days praised the rush of executions as the cherished embodiment of swift and sanguine revolutionary justice, were, themselves, before long consumed by the same terror.

For the early victims, there had been no jury, no defense attorneys, and no right of appeal. Revolutionary tribunals claimed infallibility. Those guilty of the nefarious crime of "spreading corruption on earth" were immediately executed. When the Western media began to criticize the spate of summary trials and executions, Ayatollah Khomeini's response was at once defiant and chillingly dismissive of what in the West is called the due process of law. The victory of the revolution, he decreed, was the best proof of the prisoners' guilt. The only "due process" they deserved, he said, was for the court to establish their identities. To prolong their "sinful" lives even for a moment was itself a sin and sacrilege. "We should have killed them all on the first day," declaimed the patriarch.[25] Hoveyda was near the site of the executions and could not have missed the sound of the firing squads.

Bani Sadr, who in those days waxed eloquent about the benevolence of Islamic justice, heard about the first round of killings on the radio.[26] He rushed back to the school to confront his mentor. In their long and hitherto affectionate relationship, this would be their first major confrontation. "I could not believe," Bani Sadr said nearly twenty years later with bitterness still evident in his tone, "that the old man would so easily lie to me."[27] Within a year, the relationship would turn even more difficult. Eventually, the septuagenarian patriarch of the revolution dismissed the young Bani Sadr from his post as the elected president of Iran. Fearing for his life, Bani Sadr fled the country.*

---

* Today, Bani Sadr lives in exile with his family, on the second floor of a modest, but heavily guarded, house in Versailles, a suburb of Paris. Before I was allowed to enter, a French gendarme, machine gun in one hand and dressed in blue battle fatigues, frisked me, as two other similarly attired and armed policemen watched. The room we met in was on the first floor. Bani Sadr wore a light gray suit, a yellow knit sweater, with matching yellow socks. His famous smile, stern and static, seemed still etched on his face. A couch, three divan chairs, and a coffee table, all withered by age and use, were the room's only furniture. A threadbare carpet, machine made with a poorly replicated Persian design, covered the floor. The walls were bare, but on the mantelpiece stood a line from a famous poem written in the elegant style of old Persian calligraphy: "Good tidings, the times of sorrow shall not last."

Upon reflection, in spite of many obvious differences between Hovey-da and Bani Sadr, there is at least one striking similarity in their fates—both men related as sons to powerful father figures that eventually turned against them. For Hoveyda one such figure was the shah*—often referred to as the nation's "crowned father"—and for Bani Sadr it was the ayatol-lah, who on more than one occasion had referred to his young advisor as "my son." In the classic Western Oedipus myth, the son kills the father. Perhaps patricide is a metaphor for the historical price societies must pay for progress. In Iran's archetypal story, in the *Shahnameh*, it is the father, Rostam, who kills his son, Sohrab. The story, considered by many as one of the keys to the riddle of Persian history, is a metaphor for the victory of the patriarch, for a system in which fathers devour their sons in order to maintain their own power.[28] As the shah had proved willing to sacrifice Hoveyda, the ayatollah soon proved no less willing to sacrifice his surro-gate son, Bani Sadr.[29]

That day, when Bani Sadr confronted the patriarch about the summary execution of the four generals, the ayatollah's reply was supinely pragmat-ic. The executions had become necessary, he said, because leftist groups had been distributing libelous leaflets in the city, contending that the new Islamic government had made a secret deal with the American govern-ment. The leftists claimed that the U.S. would give the new Islamic regime diplomatic recognition and help avert a royalist coup, and in return, the new government would spare the lives of 100 men and women at the top echelon of the Pahlavi regime.[30] The executions, according to the ayatol-lah, had been necessary to disprove the rumors.† As further justification, the patriarch went on to add that in the brief moments when Nasiri, one of the four executed generals, had been shown on television the night before, he had sent secret hand signals, covertly ordering his SAVAK agents to begin a campaign of terror.[31]

---

* Another figure who played a similar role in Hoveyda's life was Abdollah Entezam. See chapter 6, "The Wandering Years."

† In recently declassified U.S. government documents, there is some evidence of a possible deal. For example, we read that "On January 27 [1979], Khomeini sent a personal message to the U.S. recommending that, in order to avert disaster, it advised the army and Bakhtiar to stop intervening in Iranian political affairs. Khomeini appeared not only to be challenging the legitimacy of their involvement, but to be criticizing specifi-cally their closure of Iranian airports which prevented Khomeini's return. Khomeini concluded his message by asserting his preference for solving the problem peacefully." U.S. Department of State, "The Evolution of the U.S.-Iranian Relationship, A Survey," NSA no. 3556, 63.

Not long after that conversation, partly in response to mounting international pressure and partly as a result of efforts by Mehdi Bazargan, the prime minister of the Provisional Revolutionary Government, the bloody work of the tribunals was temporarily suspended. New strict guidelines, it was decided, would henceforth determine the work of all courts.[32] Consequently Hoveyda's trial was delayed. To the great relief of his family, he seemed to have received at least a reprieve. When he was moved to Qasr Prison, they even dared hope that his life might be spared.[33]

Qasr is the Persian word for "castle." Here, too, the many ironies implicit in his place of captivity could not have escaped Hoveyda's attention. The prison's name bore no literary allusion to Kafka. Qasr was called so because in the nineteenth century Qajar kings had built it as a summer resort. The Qajars ruled Iran for 128 years before their dynasty was overthrown in October 1925 by Reza Khan, a charismatic officer of the Persian Cossack Brigade, who by 1921 had become Iran's prime minister.* With the sometimes reluctant help and approval of the British, Reza Khan declared himself shah and founded the Pahlavi dynasty.

Early in his reign, the Qajar castle was turned into a prison. The compound eventually became a study in architectural dissonance. Its gracefully domed gateways and their ornate curlicues chipped by the neglect of many years, the handsome ochre-colored, bricked walkways, the shapely pond set in the spacious yard like a jewel—all remnants of the palace and reminiscent of the compound's leisurely past—were in sharp contrast to the purely functional annex, added to accommodate a surge of prisoners. Some of the same people who held Hoveyda in prison had once, not so long ago, themselves been prisoners at Qasr.

IT WAS COLD IN THE EARLY AFTERNOON OF MARCH 28, only a week past the celebration of the Persian New Year, when the door opened to Hoveyda's small solitary cell in Qasr. Six people were at the door: two French journalists, Jean-Loup Reverier and Christine Ockrent; a French cameraman, Jean-

---

* An elite brigade of Persian soldiers, usually commanded by Russian officers, was created by tsarist Russia to safeguard its colonial interests in Iran and protect the shah as well. Reza Khan joined the brigade in 1893–94 and soon rose in its ranks. For a detailed account of his rise to power, see Cyrus Ghani, *Iran and the Rise of Reza Shah: From Qajar Collapse to Pahlavi Rule* (London, 1998).

Claude Luyat; a young female interpreter, Ladan Boroumand; and finally, the warden of the prison and the prosecutor general of the Revolutionary Tribunal. Ockrent attempted to dissuade the two officials from attending the meeting. Their presence, she said, would be against the Geneva Convention. They refused to heed her advice, and she was too eager to score *the* scoop of her journalistic career to allow those spurious and, in her own words, illegal circumstances to deter her from continuing the interview.[34]

The journalists' saga had begun some three weeks earlier, when they had first arrived in Tehran to make a documentary about the Islamic Revolution that would be, in Ockrent's words, "free from Occidental clichés and prejudices."[35] The centerpiece of the report was to have been an interview with Hoveyda, but every politician they had approached had told them that such a meeting would be impossible to organize.[36] Apparently it had been Bani Sadr who finally promised to help.[37]

Relying on that promise, the journalists had arrived at Qasr Prison, hoping to tape the interview. After the requisite body search, they had only made it past the first gate, when they had been rudely turned away by angry guards brandishing their Russian-made Kalashnikovs. As with all revolutions before the rise of a consolidated central authority, power was still fluid in Tehran. No center held absolute sway, and a disgruntled guard with a gun could easily ignore the commands of the most powerful political leader.

Even on their second try on March 28, the reporters and crew had initially met with resistance and were refused access to Hoveyda. A call had been put through to Bani Sadr's office, and finally after more negotiations, after another bag and body search, the troop had arrived inside Hoveyda's cell, still in the ominous company of the warden and the prosecutor.

The warden's name was Hadji Mehdi Araghi; for his part in the assassination of Prime Minister Mansur in 1965, he had spent fourteen years of his life in prison. He repeatedly reminded the visitors that he, too, had once been a political prisoner. The prosecutor, Hadi Hadavi, had an ogreish disposition and a face ravaged by skin disease that worked together to give him a menacing look.[38] After leaving the prison compound, the journalists talked about the eerie physical resemblance the prosecutor bore to Antoine-Quentin Fouquier-Tinville, the notorious henchman and one of the chief prosecutors of the French Revolution and its bloody revolutionary tribunals.[39]

Congenial to a fault, Hoveyda exchanged French and Persian pleasantries with each of the visitors. "We are French journalists," Ockrent said by way of introduction. "We have received permission to interview you. A lot of people are concerned about you in France." With a wry smile on his face, Hoveyda answered, "France...so they've not forgotten about me in France."[40]

By then the group had arranged themselves on the floor of the tiny rectangular cell in the jail's hospital wing. Before the camera could begin to roll, the rules of the interview had to be negotiated. The prosecutor and the warden insisted on prohibiting any direct discourse between the prisoner and the French journalists. They distrusted foreign journalists. To them the Western media were only extensions of their governments and agents of their sinister designs. They were concerned that the interview, particularly if conducted in French, might be a ruse, a pretext to exchange secret messages. They had been against the meeting from the outset. No foreign journalist had bothered to visit *them* in prison.[41]

But the prosecutor and the warden were not the only members of the visiting group who had limited, and limiting, linguistic abilities. The two reporters, dispatched by French television to cover Iran at the time of a historic revolution, spoke not a word of Persian.[42] To remedy the journalists' handicap, and to allay the suspicions of the Islamic officials, it was resolved that Persian would be the mandatory language of the interview, but the two journalists would be allowed to ask their questions in French. The sibilant whisper of the translator, incomprehensible but always audible on the tape of the interview, affords the whole conversation a sinister air.*

---

* I searched for months for a copy of this interview. A friend found it by accident. It appears, incongruously, on the end of a tape entitled "Flames of Persia." The box cover claims the title film to be a documentary produced by the government of the shah, showing highlights of the controversial desert party given to celebrate 2,500 years of monarchial rule in Persia. Orson Wells, in the twilight of his career, and long after the artistic glories of *Citizen Kane*, narrates the film of this new Xanadu. Immediately after the scene depicting royal guests departing Tehran, the tape goes momentarily dark and silent; then a French broadcaster announces the Ockrent special and the interview. Bewildered by the juxtaposition of a jubilant royal bash and the sad sight of a prime minister in jail, I decided to call the producers and see whether a sadly sublime sense of irony—a conscious, albeit cruel, design—had dictated their strange choice of companion pieces. The receptionist who answered the phone was suspicious. "Why do you want to know?" she asked. I told her I was writing a book, and that, apparently, only added to her suspicion. She asked for my name and phone number, and promised to have the person in charge call me. A week passed and I heard nothing. I called again, and this time, eventually, a gentleman introduced himself as the one "in charge around here." I repeated my question. With no hesitation, he said, "No sir, no sir, there was no design. We had some empty space at the end of the tape about the celebrations, and somebody suggested we fill it with the tape of the interview." Here, too, it seemed, Hoveyda had become only an afterthought.

The arrangement proved immediately untenable. The interpreter, Ladan Boroumand, had, by her own admission, no prior experience in this kind of work. She had met Jean-Loup Reverier six months earlier, and on March 28, when he and his associates had not been able to find a professional translator for the interview, he had asked her for help. The solemnity of the moment, the sight of machine guns, the sea of prisoners walking about aimlessly, the clamor of some inmates for permission to use the toilet, the sour smell of sweat that wafted in the air—all had her flustered.[43] No sooner had she begun translating than Hoveyda found fault with her choice of words. "This is serious," he said, "the translation has to be precise."[44] He refused to continue unless he was allowed to speak French for himself.

Was he hoping for more sympathy in a Europe impressed with his lucid command of the French language? Was he trying to use his own agile French to send a subtle message to his friends outside? Was he genuinely concerned about the exactitude of the young woman's translation? While we may never know the answers to these questions, it is clear that there was a faint glimmer of hope in his eyes at the mere sight of the foreign reporters.[45] Maybe his wager to stay in Tehran had paid off; maybe he had been right all along that his many influential friends in Europe and America would not leave him at the mercy of a new Mahdi.*

But by the time the camera began to roll, Hoveyda's initial sense of hope had dissipated. Maybe the tone of the discussion, or the continued presence of prison officials, contributed to his new somber mood. Even before he uttered a word, as the camera zoomed in for a close-up of his face, his body language, and his eyes, told of his new anguished disposition.

The video shows him slumped on his mattress, cornered between the cell's barren walls and the troop of journalists and jailers. His head is sunk deep in his shoulders, his hands are clamped tight together near his groin. There was always a quality of melancholy, a mix of resignation and irony, in his deep-set eyes. If ever there was a man whose facial morphology was a metaphor of his character, Hoveyda was that man. That day his cheekbones, nose, forehead, bushy eyebrows, and cloudy eyes all seemed unseasonably aged. Both his crumpled pants and ill-fitting sweater accentuated

---

* In Shi'a Islam, the Mahdi, from the Arabic meaning "divinely guided one," is a Messianic deliverer who will bring justice and equity and restore true religion.

his corpulence, which in the past had usually been camouflaged by a trim, tailored suit.

Famously unaffected in the past, Hoveyda was no less well known for being exquisitely polite and deferential. But throughout this interview, he not only indecorously kept his cap on but also stretched his legs in a defiantly indifferent pose. The poker face by which he was known as a politician was replaced by the agitated, angry look of cornered prey. More than once, responding to Ockrent's pointed queries, he shook his head in disbelief and dismay. It had not taken him long to be roughly disabused of any notion he might have held about her intention to help him.

Hoveyda's posture, and his every expression, later became the subject of much controversy and conjecture. Even the position of his two hands turned out to be enigmatic. He sat with his fingers woven together and his two thumbs twiddling aimlessly, usually deemed a sign of anxiety or restlessness. But unbeknownst to the two journalists, in the secret language of Freemasonry, twiddling one's thumbs is the standard sign of distress, a call for help.[46] Hoveyda was indeed a Freemason, and in Iran this affiliation was a matter of considerable controversy. It is hard to tell if Hoveyda was beseeching his Masonic brethren to help him that day, but it is clear from the tape that he made no effort to hide his frustration and disdain for the journalists in his cell.

As soon as the camera was recording, Ockrent commandeered the interview and commenced a diatribe against the old regime. Jean-Loup Reverier is conspicuous only by his absence. The very first question she asked was spoken sharply, in an accusatory tone: "Do you think that your plight as a victim can be said to be a metaphor for the nature of the old system?" With a truculent look on his face, the prisoner shook his head. Had he expected a more sympathetic question that would allow him to talk about his plight? He remained silent for a long moment and then with anger on his face, he responded, "Don't you see my condition? What kind of question is this?" Ockrent's tone, more prosecutorial than journalistic, not only rankled Hoveyda that day but also caused a public uproar three weeks later when the interview was finally shown on French television.

Throughout his thirteen-year tenure as prime minister, Hoveyda had developed a complicated relationship with the Western media. Though the shah often talked tough against the West, he and his regime were sensitive to every word of the foreign press.[47] Hoveyda, with his cosmopolitan flair, his reputation as a polyglot and a liberal, his quick wit and affable style, his delight in clever repartee with journalists, was frequently cast in the unenviable position of defending the Pahlavi regime's human rights record. On these issues, he was, in the words of a Persian journalist, "the regime's artful window dressing."[48] And he performed zealously, often deflecting pointed questions about freedom and oppression in Iran either with platitudes about the lack of genuine democracy in the West or with the repetition of a favorite cliché of the shah's about the unique nature of the Iranian polity. Common standards of human rights, the shah liked to say, fade in the face of an old tradition of people's love and devotion for their monarch. Now, after years of being locked in that kind of combat with the media, of denying abuses of human rights he knew existed, Hoveyda was a victim himself. He could legitimately lament the loss of his own human rights. But Ockrent seemed bent on denying him the chance. Rather than posing questions to the prisoner, she more often railed against the corruption of the old regime, against past violations of human rights, against the despotism of the deposed shah.

A fair dose of cruelty and a hint of the transgressive are both within the professional purview of a good journalist (and a biographer). But that day Ockrent clearly crossed a line; she had not covered the news, critics said, but had become the news herself. She had been, others argued, an unwitting tool for legitimizing revolutionary terror. The Paris daily *Figaro* even accused her of having become the "executioner's accomplice."[49]

To her diatribe, Hoveyda responded with a combination of studied verbal calm and gestural defiance and disdain. He bore only partial responsibility for the mistakes of the Pahlavi regime, he said, because most of the power was not in his hands. When asked whether he knew of SAVAK's activities in Iran, of the use of torture in prisons, of the number of prisoners in the country, Hoveyda responded that SAVAK had not been under his control. Ockrent was not convinced. "Do you mean to say that the prime minister was not in charge of the secret police?" For a few seconds, Hoveyda chose silence. He finally said, "You do not understand the nature of Iranian politics," before adding more forcefully, "there were certain reserved domains over which I had no control. SAVAK was one of them."[50]

On more than one occasion during the course of the interview, Ockrent tried to incite Hoveyda to criticize the shah. But Hoveyda refused to accommodate, despite knowing full well that an attack on the shah would distance him from the old regime and endear him to his captors.

"Why do you think the shah had you arrested?" Ockrent asked.

"You should ask him," Hoveyda said curtly.

She would not relent. "Do you think you were a victim of the old regime?"

After a long pause, and after looking away from the camera and at the blank prison wall, Hoveyda finally responded: "I don't think of myself in those terms. I am not the only one in prison; this hall is full of my old colleagues."

"But it was the shah who ordered your arrest, wasn't it?" she pressed.

It was in response to this question that Hoveyda came closest to offering a criticism of the old regime. "I guess I was made into a scapegoat," he replied.

With every question that seemed to embarrass and dishearten the prisoner, Ockrent became more aggressive and abrasive. She asked Hoveyda whether, under the regime he had served, the press could ever have had similar access to political prisoners and whether prisoners had televisions in their cells. Hoveyda began to explain that he had helped convince the shah to allow Amnesty International and the Red Cross to visit prisons in Iran, but Ockrent fired off her next question before Hoveyda had a chance to finish his cautious remarks.[51] At the end, he appeared utterly distraught. He seemed to have realized that the intrigues and rivalries that had made the interview possible, the array of forces that seemed to be working against him including the ambitious zeal of a French journalist, were all now beyond his control. For a moment he was silent, and then he said, in a tone of anguish and anger, "I guess a scapegoat should just remain silent."

CHAPTER TWO

Beirut Blues

The camel labors with the heaviest load
And the wolf dies in silence.
                                    —*Byron*

Amir Abbas Hoveyda was born in Tehran, a village masquerading as a city and the capital of Iran since 1786.[1] It was "a cold day, before sun-rise," in the winter of 1919 when he was born into a family of solid middle-class comfort and faded aristocratic roots. Snow covered the ground. No official record of these facts exists; we know them only because Hoveyda's grandmother kept a record of the year and the season—but not the day—of his birth. "It was all written on the first blank page of our family's copy of the Koran," Hoveyda tells us in his "Yad-e Ayam-e Javani" (Memories of Days of Youth).[2] In those days, the practice of issuing birth certificates was still foreign to Iran. If any record of a birth was kept, it was at the initiative of the newborn's family itself and often in the back of a Koran.* People were usually known by their first names,

---

* *Current Biography Yearbook,* and other encyclopedias that have written about Hoveyda, give his date of birth as 18 February 1919. See *Current Biography Yearbook,* 1971 (New York, 1971), 200. According to a U.S. State Department profile, Hoveyda was born on 18 February 1918. Some U.S. Embassy dispatches from Tehran give still other dates. On Hoveyda's Belgian university transcript, his birthday is given as 18 February 1916. If all of that is not confusing enough, some of Hoveyda's friends give his birthday as 19 February 1921. Iraj Aryanpour, personal correspondence, 13 January 2000.

occasionally accompanied by a title. Aristocratic pedigree, profession, granted or purchased title, place of birth, even description of a bodily defect were commonly used in lieu of a surname. It would be another six years before birth certificates and surnames were required by law in Iran.[3] At that time, Hoveyda's father, Habibollah, known by the title of Ayn al-Molk (Eye of the Kingdom), chose the surname of Hoveyda. In Persian Hoveyda means the "clear and manifest" or the "visible." The ocular theme in both the family title and the name—from Ayn al-Molk (Eye of the Kingdom) to Hoveyda (visible)—becomes particularly interesting because both Amir Abbas and his father were known, among other things, for the opacity of their characters and beliefs.

The year of Hoveyda's birth coincides with a period of crisis in modern Iranian history. The Constitutional Revolution of 1905–06, the harbinger of modernity in the country, had led to a decade of civil war and social disintegration. The central government was weak, and centrifugal forces—a permanent fixture of the multiethnic nature of Iranian politics and, since 1917, encouraged and supported by the new Soviet govern-ment—had come to threaten Iran's territorial integrity.

Even nature seemed to have unleashed its wrath on both the capital and the country that year. While cholera had been regularly wreaking havoc on Tehran for some three decades, the years after the First World War also saw the spread of the infamous Spanish flu pandemic that killed twenty million people worldwide. About thirty thousand inhabitants of Tehran lost their lives to the deadly new disease.

At the same time, the British government, the perennial colonial pest of Iranian politics, fearing the spread of the Bolshevik Revolution attempted a complete domination of Iran. In 1919, English diplomats bribed three of Iran's most influential politicians to sign an infamous agreement that would have turned the country into a virtual British colony.* The British effort failed when a vast coalition of Iranian nationalists, supported by interna-tional pressure, united to fight the agreement and force its rescission.

In 1919, Iran was, at least nominally, ruled by Ahmad Shah, the last of the Qajar dynasty. He was a reluctant monarch, preferring the excitement of the European stock markets and casinos, and the comforts of the Montreux Palais Hotel in Switzerland, to ruling a fractured and factious country. Not

---

* One of the three recipients of the bribe would turn out to be the grandfather of the woman Amir Abbas Hoveyda eventually married.

long after the aborted agreement with England, talk of a republic began to spread in the country. Reza Khan, who was minister of war and was soon to become an autocratic but popular prime minister, rapidly emerged as the presumptive candidate for the post of president.[*]

Nineteen hundred and nineteen was also the year in which Reza Khan had his first son, Mohammad Reza. He would eventually become the shah of Iran and Hoveyda's fate was, to some extent, determined by the newborn's character.

Tehran was a city of a little more than two hundred thousand people in 1919. It had twelve gates, some handsomely ornate, others functionally simple; Hoveyda's grandparents owned a house just outside one of these city gates.[4] There was also a moat; it had been a folly resulting from one of Nasir al-Din Shah's extravagant trips to Europe. He ruled Iran for almost half a century and was assassinated in 1896. He traveled to Europe three times, and in one of those trips he had seen an old medieval city surrounded by fortified walls and moats.[5] The sight had impressed the "Pivot of the Universe"—as Nasir al-Din Shah was called by his subordinates—and no sooner had he returned home than he ordered the construction of a new mud wall and a moat around the capital.[6] But Tehran is a city with its back to towering mountains and surrounded on all other sides by arid deserts; and thus the moat, predictably, never saw water. By the time Amir Abbas Hoveyda was born, the anachronistic trench had become a hangout for opium addicts, musicians, pederasts, and prostitutes.[7]

As late as 1926, when Vita Sackville-West, one of the Bloomsbury set and an intimate of Virginia Woolf, visited Tehran, the city's gates were still guarded by sentries who stopped every traveler and allowed entry into the capital only after receiving a satisfactory response. Sackville-West, whose memoir of her trip to Iran is full of romantic notions about Persia, observed, nevertheless that, "Tehran itself, except for the bazaars, lacks charms; it is a squalid city of bad roads, rubbish-heaps, and pariah dogs, crazy little victorias with wretched horses; a few pretentious buildings, and mean houses on the verge of collapse."[8]

---

[*] Before declaring himself a king and the founder of a new dynasty, Reza Khan had toyed with the idea of creating a republic in Iran. Ironically, it was the clerics who, at the time, objected to that idea. Reza Khan's initial inclination toward a republic can clearly be seen in a letter in his own handwriting, dated 1923, where he orders one of his subordinate generals to bring pressure on the Parliament to change the constitution and declare Iran a republic. The letter also indicates that he feels he is clearly the likely candidate for president. For the text of the letter, see Farhad Rostami, ed. *Pahlaviha* [The Pahlavis] (Tehran, 1999), 103–4.

At sunset, with the sound of a drumbeat, a de facto curfew went into effect in the capital and lasted till sunrise. Few dared break the curfew, for that usually meant harassment by either the police or, more often, and more dangerously, the hooligans who virtually ruled the city by night.

Tehran had no universities in 1919. Dar al-Funun, created during Mirza Taqi Khan Amir Kabir's tenure as prime minister in the mid-nineteenth century, and the School of Political Science, founded at the beginning of the twentieth century, were the city's only modern institutes of higher learning.[9] The former was a polytechnic, providing courses in medicine, engineering, basic sciences, and foreign languages, while the latter was the embryo of Iran's first law school. Muslim clerics, by and large, opposed the creation of such secular institutions as threats to their own monopoly in the important fields of education and law.

By 1919, only a handful of the capital's inhabitants had ever been inside a car. Mules and horse carriages were the primary means of urban travel. In fact, 1919 was the year that Tehran's city police officially declared, for the first time, that a driving license was required to operate a car or truck. The same announcement also provided guidelines for mules, carriages, pedestrians, and cars on city streets.[10] Trains, too, were an exotic novelty. A short line, connecting the capital to a shrine about ten miles from the city, was the only existing railway in the country. It, too, was a token of one of Nasir al-Din Shah's trips to Europe.

The city's inhabitants reacted with a combination of curiosity and violence against the new contraption, which they called "the smoking machine." After a man was accidentally struck and killed by one of the trains, service was suspended. Even before the accident, throwing stones at moving trains had become a favorite pastime of the new urban children. It would take another nineteen years before Iran, in 1938, had its first transnational railway line connecting the Persian Gulf in the south to the Caspian Sea in the north.

Even bicycles were a novelty in those days. It was around 1916 that a large crowd gathered in one of Tehran's main squares to see, for the first time, a couple of English boys ride their bikes. To some of the elder members of the awed audience, the sight seemed dangerously wondrous; it meant that the end of time was near; it was a portent of the arrival of the promised messiah.[11] When, as a child, Hoveyda rode around on a tricycle in his grandparents' orchard outside one of the city's gates, he was told "that tricycles had just appeared in Tehran."[12]

✤ ✤ ✤

AMIR ABBAS HOVEYDA WAS THE FIRST CHILD of an arranged marriage. His parents had married about a year before his birth. His mother, Afsar al-Moluk, was a descendant of the Qajar family. Of her legacy, she only had the pride of pedigree. She was a poor aristocrat, a pauper princess, one in a line of tens of thousands of blue-blooded offspring of Qajar royalty.

Afsar al-Moluk was the granddaughter of Izzat al-Dowleh, who was herself Nasir al-Din Shah's only full sibling. When Izzat al-Dowleh was only thirteen years old, the shah ordered his enlightened and reformist prime minister, Amir Kabir, to divorce his wife and marry the adolescent princess.[13] Neither the young princess nor the relatively powerful fifty-year-old prime minister dared defy the despot's commandment.

Not long after this apparent token of royal favor, the king ordered the execution of his prime minister. After her husband's death, Izzat al-Dowleh went on to marry four more times. Hoveyda's mother was a grandchild of her fourth union with Yahya Khan Mushir al-Dowleh, who was for a while Iran's foreign minister. Izzat al-Dowleh came to believe that this husband, too, was murdered by the king. Whereas Amir Kabir's wrists were slit while he was taking a bath, her fourth husband Yahya Khan Mushir al-Dowleh was apparently forced to drink the infamous "Qajar Coffee," a deadly poisoned potion and one of the favorite tools of murder used by Qajar royalty.[14]

On her paternal side, Hoveyda's mother Afsar al-Moluk came from a family that owed its prominence to its own intellectual achievement. Her grandfather, Naser al-Saltaneh, was a courtier whose secular ideas had earned him the nickname of "Kofri" (the Infidel). Her father, Soleiman Khan Adib al-Saltaneh, continued the enlightened family tradition. He was a staunch advocate of modernity and an unabashed Francophile. For him, as for most enlightened Iranians of his generation, the French Revolution was the very embodiment of progress, a beacon of hope and prosperity. But even in that context, Soleiman Khan's attachment to France seemed not just exaggerated but more like the stuff of which novels are made. He encouraged his three daughters to obtain an education and learn a musical instrument. Afsar al-Moluk played the guitar, and Maleke Saba played the piano. Soleiman Khan also asked his children to sing the *Marseillaise* every night before they went to sleep.[15]

Hoveyda's maternal grandmother (Izzat al-Dowleh's daughter) reading the Koran.

In spite of this tradition of freethinking in the family, in matters of matrimony the three daughters followed in the footsteps of their grandmother, Izzat al-Dowleh. Afsar al-Moluk was fifteen when she was married off to a forty-year-old husband. As was the custom for nearly all of the women of her generation, she had only one brief and formal meeting with her future husband before the night of their marriage. She never questioned the wisdom of her family's choice. By all accounts, she grew to respect, some say even love, her husband. Her true feelings for the man will never be known. For the women of her generation, open discussion of marital problems was deemed vulgar and undignified. Though her husband died when she was thirty-six years old, and though she lived to be eighty, Afsar al-Moluk never remarried. Even in her most trying moments, and with her most intimate relatives, she only talked with respect and affection for the difficult man who had been her husband for eighteen years and who had sealed her fate for life.[*]

The husband, Ayn al-Molk, was a surly man, distant and detached, and given to brooding. He had the authoritative bearing of an ill-tempered

---

[*] Afsar al-Moluk lived the last four years of her life with Maryam Ensha. According to Ensha, Afsar al-Moluk did not once remember her husband with anything other than praise. Others who were close to her also cannot remember any disparaging comments.

Prussian bureaucrat. In most pictures of him, the stern glare of his eyes, piercing through thin metal-rimmed glasses, seem unfailingly purposeful, with little tolerance for frivolity. Amir Abbas describes him as a man reticent with words and emotions. Fereydoun, the younger son, remembers Ayn al-Molk as the archetypal patriarch of Persian mythology. When the father was around, he says, there was fear and trembling in the air; he was the authoritarian lord of the manor.[16]

When he married his young bride, Ayn al-Molk was already something of an intellectual, steeped in the cosmopolitan Levantine culture for which Beirut was the capital and the metaphor. He had been educated—like a disproportionate number of influential politicians of twentieth-century Iran—at the American University in Beirut, where he learned Arabic, English, and French. He translated into Persian an eclectic array of books that included everything from the works of the Lebanese poet Khalil Gibran to popular romance novels by third-rate nineteenth-century French authors like Michel Zevago.

Ayn al-Molk was a man of middle-class means and lineage, but he had found his way into the good graces of aristocratic families by a combination of his intellectual acumen and earnest disposition. After finishing school in Beirut, he traveled to Paris where he met Jafar-Gholi Sardar Asaad, one of the more colorful figures of the Iranian Constitutional Revolution; eventually he was chosen as tutor for Asaad's children. Asaad had grown to like the young tutor, Habibollah, and as a token of his affection had asked Ahmad Shah to grant him the title of Ayn al-Molk. Sardar Asaad was a patron of the arts; and it was at his behest that Ayn al-Molk translated some of Ponson du Terrail's popular novels, featuring the mysterious Rocambole. Serialized in late-nineteenth-century Parisian papers, the novel proved no less popular in Iran.[17]

Ayn al-Molk's trip to Paris and his meeting with Asaad was apparently the result of a rift with his father, Mirza Reza. Mirza Reza was a trusted disciple of Abbas Efendi (Abdul Baha), the eldest son of Baha'ullah, the founder of the Bahai faith in Iran.[18] Since its inception, those who have followed this religion have been persistently persecuted in Iran.[19] One result of this persecution has been a fog of mystery surrounding the history of the faith and the identity of those who joined it. The uncompromising stance of the Shiite clerics against the new religion, and their insistence that the new faith is nothing but an instrument of British, and later Zionist, conspiracies, turned the Bahais into the pariah of Iranian politics. To be called a Bahai became a grave charge—hard to substantiate, even harder to refute. For this reason, the allegation has often been used with malice, especially in the political arena.

There is no doubt that Hoveyda's paternal grandfather, Mirza Reza, was a Bahai. There is also some evidence that at least early in his life Ayn al-Molk was also a follower of Abbas Efendi. He might have been one of Efendi's scribes for a while.[20] A brief note by Abbas Efendi to his followers in Tehran is the most substantial, albeit circumstantial, evidence connecting Hoveyda's father to the Bahai faith. In the note, the exiled Efendi, living at the time in Acre, today part of Israel, enjoins his friends in Tehran to help find a suitable job for the young Ayn al-Molk. He writes, "Habibollah is the son of the esteemed Aqa Reza. Do everything in your power and that of other friends to hopefully procure for him a position, even if it is outside the capital or the country. For me this is important, because of the sentiments I have for Aqa Reza." Beyond this connection, nothing else is certain.[*]

AMIR ABBAS WAS ABOUT TWO YEARS OLD when his father, by then a member of the Iranian foreign service, was appointed Iran's consul general to Damascus. Today, a trip between Tehran and Damascus can be a two-hour flight. In 1921 it took Ayn al-Molk's family more than three months to arrive at their destination. It was, in Hoveyda's words, "a trip reminiscent of *A Thousand and One Nights*."[21]

From Tehran, they hired a horse carriage that took them and their belongings to the coastal waters of the Persian Gulf. There, they found passage on a ship bound for Bombay. In Bombay, they searched for a boat headed for a Mediterranean port. Eventually they had to settle for one going to Cairo. After a brief stay in the city, they crossed the Suez Canal, and there they hired a car to take them to Damascus.[22] The desert in those days, Hoveyda tells us, had no marked roads. T. E. Lawrence, who hap-

---

[*] When the scholar Fouad Misaghi heard that I was writing a biography of Hoveyda, he generously provided me with a copy of this very important note hitherto unpublished in any account of Hoveyda's life. The source from which the note was copied did not appear on the page he sent me. Misaghi promised to give me the information the next time we met. Unfortunately he died of leukemia before we could meet again. Until the Bahai archives are opened to public scrutiny, questions about the length of Ayn al-Molk's association with the Bahai faith cannot be answered conclusively.

pened to be traversing the same sands in the same era, called it "a pathless sea of sand."[23] At short intervals, the Arab driver, to the utter amazement of his Persian passengers, would disembark, kneel on the desert, bring his ears close to the sand, and with the help of the mysterious sounds he heard, navigate his way through the potentially treacherous terrain.

Writing about this journey, Hoveyda depended on his mother's recollections for most of the details. He writes, "My images of my childhood are opaque. Sometimes the images blur into my mother's stories about my childhood, and thus I cannot distinguish my own memories from her tales." This shared sense of memory between Hoveyda and his mother can be seen as a metaphor for the intense emotional tie, or attachment, he developed for her. In a picture taken when he is about twelve years old, we see him and his young brother standing next to Afsar al-Moluk. The young son's upright and separate stance is starkly different from Amir Abbas, who is leaning on, or more accurately hanging onto, his mother. (See page 54.)

His deep attachment to his mother—or in the parlance of psychoanalysis, the intensity of the oedipal relationship—seemed to be partly the result of Ayn al-Molk's aloof behavior and an inadvertent consequence of exile. The fact that only nineteen years separated the son from his young, exuberant, and energetic mother must have helped the intensity of this relationship. In another passage of his "Memories of Days of Youth," describing his life in Beirut and Damascus, Hoveyda laments the lack of "love-objects" in his childhood. In a tone at once tinged with melancholy and clinical in its clear articulation of a problem, he mourns the impermanence inherent in the nomadic life of a diplomat, the tormenting transience of a childhood lived in exile. Those who have spent their childhood going "from one country to another, those who have never had a corner of the world to call their home and the place of rest, those who have never had an object that could become part of their memory," he writes, "are really nothing more than orphans."[24] And he confesses that "throughout the years living abroad, I have always had the sad sense that I don't even have a chair, or a desk of my own."[25] In the Damascus apartment of his childhood, every time Amir Abbas or his brother sat down, they were admonished to "be careful, be careful, these chairs and desks do not belong to us, they belong to the government."[26]

The two Hoveyda brothers, Amir Abbas and Fereydoun, in Damascus, circa 1927.

Indeed, the trauma, and transience, of a childhood spent in exile convinced him, once he was home, never again to leave Iran. "Those who have not lived a long time abroad," he writes, "might not understand me when I say I have no desire to leave my country, even for a short sojourn."[27] He said the same thing to his brother in no uncertain terms: "I never want to become an exile again."[28] Such sentiments take on particular significance when, on the eve of the Islamic Revolution, Hoveyda is offered the chance to leave Iran for a life of exile.

Of his first years in the French elementary school of Damascus, he writes, "I did not have many friends and lived a lonely life."[29] His desolation must have been exacerbated by his stern, and mostly absent, father. Hoveyda calls him "a hard man. Though he had much affection for us, he kept it all inside himself and it would take months for us to at least see an outward sign of his affection."[30] He was by nature more "bent on anger."[31]

During those years, the Saudi Arabia that T. E. Lawrence had an inadvertent hand in creating was seething with ethnic and religious strife, and a new kind of violent politics—the "creed of the desert"—had been introduced by the fiercely fundamentalist Wahhabi branch of Islam. In their efforts to avert a confrontation with the new rulers, the Iranian government often sent Ayn al-Molk on diplomatic missions to Saudi Arabia.[32]

When he was at home, official duties consumed nearly all of his time. The consulate office was in the same building as the family residence, obliterating any distinction between home and office, work and leisure. The everyday affairs of the house and his children's education were his wife's domain. He "never asked about our progress," Hoveyda remembers, and adds, "when children most need to see their fathers, we only spent our summers with our father."[33]

Ayn al-Molk's presence was intimidating. There was more solemnity and less gaiety in the house when he was around. Even the servants behaved differently. They were normally on casual, at times even insolent, terms with Hoveyda's mother but became respectfully subservient in the father's presence. Insolence or informality he did not suffer gladly.

As for religious matters, the father's beliefs, past or present, were a taboo subject in the family—a taboo, incidentally, that lasted long after his death and was certainly maintained in the published segments of Hoveyda's memoirs. According to Fereydoun Hoveyda, the Bahai faith was never mentioned in the family. "I was fourteen years old," he says, "when I first heard the word 'Bahai' and learned what it meant from a friend."[34]

Nor did Islamic rituals or prayers figure prominently in the daily life of the Hoveyda siblings. Amir Abbas's recollections of his childhood, as well as his brother's memoirs covering those years, are in this sense remarkable for their lack of any pretensions of piety.[35]

⊹ ⊹ ⊹

IN DAMASCUS THE HOVEYDA FAMILY found a city caught in postwar convulsions and colonial intrigues. For about four hundred years prior to the First World War, Damascus had been under the domination of Ottoman Turks, like nearly all of what are now Syria, Lebanon, Israel, and Palestine. With the Turkish defeat and dismantling of the Ottoman Empire, the Levantine territory became a center of big power politics. Damascus was no exception. The newly created League of Nations, founded in the year of Hoveyda's birth, had mandated the control of Syria and Lebanon to France. Concurrent with the Syrian nationalist struggle against the French mandate, a civil war raged between Syria's various ethnic and religious minorities—particularly between the Muslim Druzes and the Christian Maronites. While Ayn al-Molk spent much of his time away on trips, Amir Abbas, his mother, his grandmother, Gohar (commonly called Khanum Bozorg), and a servant huddled inside the house, wary of walking in the war-torn streets of the city.

Amir Abbas was four years old when Fereydoun was born. The two boys turned out to be classic examples of Frank J. Sulloway's study of birth order, and its impact on political and social values and behavior. As expected, firstborn Amir Abbas did identify "more closely with parents and authority...[and was] ambitious, conscientious, and achievement oriented." Relative to his younger sibling, he was "more conforming, conventional, and defensive."[36] Fereydoun, also true to Sulloway's statistical predictions, turned out to be a bold and creative thinker, more inclined to challenge authority.

When Amir Abbas was five, Ayn al-Molk was called back to Tehran. While they had been away, much had changed in the city and the country. Reza Khan had declared himself king, and his government of "law and order" had begun to establish its authority over the capital and the whole nation.[37] He also embarked on a policy of forced modernization, much in the spirit of Otto von Bismarck in Germany, the Meiji Restoration in Japan, and Kemal Atatürk in Turkey.

For their return trip, instead of the circuitous itinerary of three years earlier, they rented two cars—both Fords, the new technological marvel of Damascus—that traversed the desert and took them directly to Iran. One car carried the household furniture; the family rode in the other.[38]

*The Hoveyda family in Beirut, circa 1929. The young woman in the white dress
is the children's nanny, Ozra.*

In describing the Tehran of his youth, Hoveyda places particular
emphasis on two incidents. One is a train ride he took with his mother to
the shrine on the outskirts of the capital. (Could it be that this act of

selective memory, this reminder of his mother's religious devotion, was politically motivated, intended to disarm those who accused him of being a Bahai?) The second is a narrative of loss. Hoveyda describes wandering the streets in the city for more than three hours, aimlessly and tearfully, unable to tell anyone the address of his grandparents' home, where he and his family had been living. When he is finally led home with the help of a policeman, the little boy vows "that henceforth I should always listen to what my elders tell me, and to never wander outside the house on my own."[39]

After eight months in Tehran, Ayn al-Molk was reappointed to Damascus. His newly expanded authority covered all of Palestine, as well as the Consular Office in Beirut.[*] This time for the journey back to Damascus, instead of a horse carriage, the family rented a truck. In the back of the truck their belongings took up half of the space, and with the help of a rug, a mattress, and some pillows, the other half became living quarters for Afsar al-Moluk, her two sons, and a nanny. Ayn al-Molk and the driver shared the cab.[40]

After a short time in Damascus, it became apparent that the work of the Beirut office was too heavy to be managed from the Syrian capital. Amir Abbas was nine years old when in 1928 his father moved the family again, this time to a two-story hillside house in the Muslim section of Beirut. The consular office was on the first floor, the family residence on the second. Amir Abbas was enrolled in the Lycée Français. An organization loosely attached to the French government and called the Mission Laique (Secular Mission) operated the school.[†]

Amir Abbas would spend eleven intellectually formative years at the school. As the mission's name clearly indicates, the school's curriculum was deeply and decidedly secular, and students were steeped in French culture and language. To ensure that his two young sons also learned Arabic, Ayn al-Molk hired a tutor for them. As for Persian, it was the only language spoken at home. Afsar al-Moluk was particularly keen on strengthening her sons' grasp of Persian culture and language. She rewarded her children with a small cash prize for every line of any Persian

---

[*] Iran's previous consul general in Beirut had been a Greek businessman who took care of diplomatic chores in his spare time. He seemed to have relished his lavish lifestyle and was known to imbibe generously, making him all too reminiscent of a character from a Graham Greene novel.

[†] As it turned out, the same mission ran the school in Tehran where, many years later, Farah Diba, a young, urbane girl from a middle-class family went, to school. She would go on to become Iran's queen.

Amir Abbas, in a sailor suit, at the consulate office in Beirut in 1928. To his left stands his younger brother, Fereydoun, and to his right sits his father, ever on the edge of his seat.

poem they could recite by heart. Persian journals and Persian music were part of daily life around the house, and Persian food was usually served for family meals.[41]

In school, Hoveyda proved to be, by his own reckoning, a mediocre student. He never failed a class, nor did he distinguish himself in any. History and literature were his favorite subjects. His teachers commented on his report cards that he did not exert himself, except in areas that were his own favorites.

Physical punishment was not altogether alien to the school. Hoveyda remembers that it was usually the Arab teachers, not the French, who resorted to corporal punishment. Exhibiting his strong Francophilia, he writes that "our school was run on the correct French model, but it was often the Arab teachers who exhibited a certain kind of violence against the students."[42] He writes of being called into the office of the Lebanese assistant principal, being paddled on the palms of his hands, and then being ordered to stand facing the wall, with one leg lifted in the air.[*]

---

[*] There is little evidence of rancor in Hoveyda's account of this incident. What makes the narrative more interesting is the rosy image it offers of the "correct French system." Contrary to Hoveyda's claim, in the 1930s, when the incident occurs, French schools were notorious for the prevalence of corporal punishment.

*A young Amir Abbas and his father in the center of a company of mourners in Damascus
awaiting the arrival of a casket carrying the remains of Mohammad Ali Shah Qajar
back from Europe, where he had died, on its way to burial in Iran.*

*Ayn al-Molk on the day he presented his credentials, as Iran's minister
plenipotentiary, to King Ibn Saud of Saudi Arabia.*

Hoveyda's father, seated on the far right, going to Mecca for haj (pilgrimage). Lounging on a deck chair, and covered in a polka-dotted chador, is the famed French spy and aristocrat Comtesse d'Andurain, who had converted to Islam to make the pilgrimage.

Above left: Amir Abbas attired in Arab dress, standing on the right, in an early "photo op" in Beirut, circa 1933. His brother, Fereydoun, stands next to him. The two children in the front row are Parvin and Farhad Sepahbodi. Above right: The Hoveyda family in Beirut, circa 1934–35. The father's frail health is already evident in his countenance.

Amir Abbas and Fereydoun standing on the balcony of the family apartment in Beirut behind their mother. Their father is seated on the left.

Members of the Hoveyda household (paternal grandmother seated in the middle) and friends in mourning at Hoveyda's maternal grandmother's funeral, in Beirut, in 1934. Amir Abbas is standing at the far right.

In 1931, after a three-year tenure in Beirut, Ayn al-Molk was dispatched to Saudi Arabia as Iran's minister plenipotentiary. His stay lasted until 1935, at which time he was forced to ask for early retirement. Amir Abbas attributes his father's request to attempts by the foreign ministry to bring younger blood into the service.[43] Fereydoun Hoveyda surmises that it had more to do with his father's fidelity to his one-time patron, Sardar Asaad, who had fallen out of grace with Reza Shah and ended up in prison. According to Fereydoun, Ayn al-Molk insisted on visiting his fallen mentor in jail, contrary to the advice of many of his own friends, and that was enough to bring about the demise of his career.[44]

Hoveyda's critics offer a more sinister scenario of the retirement. They claim that the Saudi government protested against Ayn al-Molk's proselytizing activities on behalf of the Bahai faith, and their protest brought about the old man's fall. Whatever the reason for the father's forced retirement, its psychological impact, along with the physical hardships of his last years—a prolonged period of illness, a fall from a camel while he was on duty in Saudi Arabia, and multiple unsuccessful operations—broke his spirit. He died on March 16, 1936. Amir Abbas was seventeen years old.

The elder Hoveyda's death drastically changed the family's financial fortunes. From the three-bedroom house they had been renting in the Muslim quarter of Beirut, they moved to a small two-bedroom apartment in the same area.[45] There had been three servants before; now domestic help was no longer an option. For survival, the family relied primarily on a meager pension from the Iranian government. Though many of Ayn al-Molk's friends were initially generous with promises of help, even with offers of scholarships for the two boys, none bothered to actually follow through.[46] However, Afsar al-Moluk proved resourceful under their new austere circumstances. Dipping into the family savings, she tried to shield her two sons from the immediate consequences of their more limited economic reality. Nevertheless, the sudden change of fortune, according to Amir Abbas, had a profound impact on him. "I learnt," he says, "to live life simply," and "to never become too enthusiastic about, or enamored of life."[47]

What remained unchanged in the aftermath of his father's death was the school Hoveyda attended. By then he was among the more popular students of the lycée, with a reputation for intellectual curiosity and social grace. He also occasionally dabbled in student activism. For a while, an old French leftist named Monsieur Grand-Jouan became the school's superintendent. He infused the students with more social awareness and concern for leftist causes. The Spanish Civil War, the cause célèbre of all leftists in those days, became a subject of passionate discourse at the school. The principal and one of Hoveyda's classmates, a young member of the French Communist Party and of a famous French aristocratic family, the d'Andurains—who later gained infamy for espionage—were the main instigators of these debates.[48]

Amir Abbas and his brother, Fereydoun, were not the only Iranians attending the school. In an ironic twist of fate, Shapour Bakhtiar, Iran's last prime minister under the Pahlavi regime, also attended the same French school in the 1930s. In those early days, Bakhtiar had been something of a social democrat. Indeed, Beirut was then one of the centers of activity for Iranian leftists in exile, and Hoveyda befriended some of these activists. Though Hoveyda read Marx in this period, and though some of the friendships he developed in those days created for him the lifelong reputation of a "Left Bank socialist and a boulevardier,"[49] he never embraced Marxism or even social democracy as a dogma. His voracious appetite for ideas and insatiable desire to read—not the pieties of a dogma—seemed to be the reason for his readings. In later years, aside from his reputation, all that remained of these leftist dabblings was a faded attachment to socialist ideas that echoed faintly beneath some of his pronouncements.

The same appetite led him to frequent Beirut cinemas and develop a lifelong attachment to movies.* He also delved deeply into the school's wide-ranging list of recommended books, especially of French authors. Of these, André Gide was his favorite in this period. Gide's *Les Nourritures Terrestres,* with its pagan celebration of life, its iconoclastic praise of pleasure, its defiant declaration that "I no longer believe in sin," was Hoveyda's constant companion in those days. When he boarded a ship for Europe, it was the one book he carried with him.[50]

Nietzsche, Ernest Renan, and T. E. Lawrence were also part of the school's required reading. Many an evening, Hoveyda and his friends would gather at his family's small apartment to discuss, with all the passion and certitude of youth, what they had read, and what it might mean and imply in their own lives. Sometimes their discussions turned to issues

---

* Beirut films were a favorite pastime for Amir Abbas and his brother. Fereydoun Hoveyda, interviewed by author, 11 December 1997. Fereydoun went on to become a respected film critic in France, and one of the contributing and founding editors of the prestigious French film journal, *Les Cahiers du Cinéma.*

of contemporary politics. They talked of their desire to pull Iran out of the abyss of poverty and ignorance. Infused with a modern sensibility, they dreamed of turning Iran into an enlightened society. Talk of the creation of a Jewish state in Palestine was also already in the air. Hoveyda was of that small minority in favor of the creation of such a state as a historic antidote to anti-Semitism.[51]

André Malraux was another subject of discussion at the lycée. By then he was already an almost legendary French intellectual with a storied past in Indochina. In the many hours of discussion about Malraux, Hoveyda showed a particular affinity for Baron de Clapique, a central character of Malraux's novel, *La Condition Humaine (Man's Fate)*, and considered by some critics to closely resemble Malraux himself.[*][52]

Man's Fate is an existential musing on the early phases of the Chinese Revolution, and Baron de Clapique is one of the more enigmatic, paradoxical, and complicated characters of the story. He is a lapsed aristocrat. He has an ironic disposition toward himself and the rest of the world. He knows he "shall be the court astrologer," and that he "shall die trying to pluck the moon out of a pond."[53] He is generous to a fault. He tips the waiter handsomely with the last hundred dollars he owns. To women, he is polite and deferential, yet he seems incapable of having any sustained relationship with them.

He is more a man of instincts than principles. In the momentous struggles in Shanghai that are at the core of *Man's Fate,* his sympathies are with the Communist revolutionaries, but he also has ties with the police, with the warlords, and with the different embassies that are supporting Chiang Kai-shek's imminent massacre of the Communists. He deals in antiques; some say he even dabbles in the sale of opium. Gisor, the wise voice of the novel, however, sees the baron as someone who lives in a world of his own imagination, a world full of dreams, lies, and

---

* Writing a biography is like trying to find the pattern, the gestalt, that often unbeknownst to the subject, permeates his life. It means considering the possibility of meaning and affect in every, albeit insignificant, incident. When in casual high-school banter, Hoveyda showed his preference for André Gide or Baron de Clapique, he could not have imagined that a half-century later, in the hands of a biographer, those preferences would become a map of his soul and destiny. Therein also lies the dangers of biography as a genre, for it offers the ever-present temptation to discount the incidental, to overinfuse, or overdetermine in the language of contemporary French social theory every event with meaning. Biography is a species of what Nietzsche called the "theoretical disease," the damned and damning attempt to cohere into patterns, discernible to our mind, the fleeting flow of the infinitely complex human life. Quixotic as such attempts seem, they are our only hope of capturing some sense of the utterly strange life of "another."

fabrications; in short, he suffers from "mythomania…his mythomania is a means of denying life."[54]

He is something of a nihilist. For Clapique, "nothing exists: All is dream."[55] He craves luxury yet lacks the desire, or the ability, to amass a fortune. His penchant for luxury is more Epicurean than imbued with the cult of possessive individualism. He harbors a cynical nihilism, and thus there is in him a "Thanatotic urge…a desire for self-destruction."[56] When a Polish prince of dubious connections informs him that, on pain of death, he only has until tomorrow's sunset to leave Shanghai, he spends much of his remaining precious hours, and all of his last dollars, gambling in a casino.

Clapique is, according to Gisor, a man with "a heart of gold, but hollow…At the base of Clapique there was neither affliction nor solitude, as in other men, but sensation." There is no "intense reality" at the core of his character. Instead, he "was one of the rare beings" who has no inner core.[57] Finally, disguised as a deckhand, penniless, he flees China, leaving some of his friends "in a large hall—formerly a school-yard—" waiting to "be taken out and shot."[58]

It is surely human to be fraught with paradoxes. But Clapique—like Hoveyda—was that rare human being who was defined by these paradoxes. He was at once a pauper and a spendthrift, a poor aristocrat, a cynic, and an activist full of joie de vivre. In Malraux's words, there were "two Clapiques that composed him, the one who wanted to live and the one who wanted to be destroyed."[59]

In his youth, as in his later political life, there seemed to be two Hoveydas as well. In his Beirut days, while he identified with Clapique and his cynicism, while he defended his ironic, almost diffident disposition toward life, he was at the same time also a champion of Saint-Just, "the hot-tempered, selfish and conceited"[60] enfant terrible of the French revolution who said that "to provide the king with a trial was to presuppose the possibility of his innocence," and uttered the famous line, "a king had to die so a republic could live."[61]

To some of his Persian friends, Hoveyda would also defend Leon Trotsky.[62] The infamous Moscow Trials had just taken place in the Soviet Union, and many of Hoveyda's Communist friends—indeed most of the Iranian Communists—had sided with Joseph Stalin. For them Trotsky was the devil incarnate.

*Amir Abbas seated on the far left with Fereydoun standing behind him,
and three of their Beirut friends, circa 1937.*

Clapique in his ironic mode, Saint-Just in his unfailing faith in the
purgative powers of violence, André Gide in his celebration of carnality,
and even Trotsky in his hope for a permanent revolution, were all Roman-
tics. Even Hoveyda's closest circle of French friends at the school identified with a historical phenomenon full of Romantic echoes. They

considered themselves the intellectual elite of the lycée and called themselves the "Templars,"[63] a poignant choice given that the twelfth-century
Templars were fierce knights of the Cross who fought the Muslims during
the Crusades. Ultimately, the Templars were thought to be the precursors
of the Freemasons and became the "magical humus, which fertilized
Romantic literature."[64] But the young Templars of Beirut were only partners in mischief around the school.

In friendship, Hoveyda was, even to his own detriment, steadfast. Many
of the friends he made in Beirut remained close to him for life. Some of
the Arab students at the school became part of the political elite of the
Arab world. "In one of the Lebanese cabinets," he recalls, "of the twelve
ministers, seven had been my classmates."[65]

Of his Templar friends, he had a special affinity for a beautiful young
girl named Renée Demont, with whom he performed in a school production of Racine's farcical *Les Plaideurs.* Renée played the Countess of Pim-
posh; Hoveyda was the lead, Dandin, a judge who has spent so much time
working that "he has more than one screw loose."[66] It was during their first
performance that Hoveyda exhibited the kind of extemporaneous jollity
and quick wit that would later become an essential component of his
political persona. When the audience laughed heartily at one of Dandin's
lines, Hoveyda, dressed in the official and ostentatious attire of the judge,
banged his gravel and declared, "if the audience does not keep silent, I will
have to order them out of the court."[67]

The drama teacher, apparently a firm believer in the sanctity of canoni-
cal texts, was not impressed with his student's impromptu addition to
Racine's classical play, but the audience loved it.[68]

In his future correspondence with Renée, which lasted until his arrest,
Hoveyda would reminisce about the play and, on at least one occasion,
referred to her as "La Comtesse."[69] There was, in their relationship a deli-
ciously silent recognition of unrealized mutual amorous possibilities. Early
in the summer of 1998, when I met Renée in Brussels, she was elegantly
dressed in a blue suit, subtly coifed, and exuberant in describing her much
cherished friendship with "Amir," as she called Hoveyda. She had the cosmopolitan elegance one often associates with cultured bourgeois ladies of
Europe. The stubborn coquettish beauty of her youth was still in full battle
with the inexorable work of old age, making her face a palimpsest. One
could easily see how, in her prime, she might have stolen anyone's heart.

We spoke in a random mix of French and English. Often she began a sentence in English and then, carried away by the pathos of her own narrative, would suddenly revert to the comfort of her native French.

She first met Hoveyda, she said, when they both became involved in a brief student strike at the school. The administration had expelled an Iraqi student, and Hoveyda and his comrades agitated, successfully, for his return. "Amir was kind, tolerant, and erudite," she said. In his demeanor, he was, in her recollection, "elegantly formal." About ten years after their initial meeting, in a letter written from London, Hoveyda finally relented on his use of the formal plural *vous* for "you" and instead used the more intimate *tu*. It was in that letter that the first and last hints of the silent romance can be detected.[70] Yet, in her words, "For him, as for me, friendship was more important than love. Love can never last a whole lifetime; friendships can and do."[71]

Their conversations had often revolved around literary issues. "Amir could easily quote from Molière, Baudelaire, or Apollinaire," she said wistfully. She talked of the meticulous care he took of his appearance. "There was a flair even in the way he wore the school's uniform," she said, describing the red tie, white shirt, and aqua blue pants. And then, as if by epiphany, Renée remembered a few words of a poem Hoveyda had written on the back of her book when he left Beirut for Europe. It was from a poem by Alfred de Vigny, she said, remembering vaguely the title of the poem and promising to send a copy of his handwriting, if she found it.

By the time Hoveyda left Beirut, the culture and language that resonated inside him, the ultimate source of his cultural capital, the poems that spoke to, and of, his desire and despair, the linguistic tropes that shaped his discourse were all primarily European in origin. Nearly all the books he read were in French, English, or Arabic. Only while he was at home, at the insistence of his mother, would he read some Persian poems and try to maintain his command of the Persian language. But in the choice of reading material, Beirut proved formative.

In Europe, his modern and Western sensibilities were no doubt an asset; when he went back to Iran, while the same sensibilities helped him rise rapidly to the pinnacle of power, they also became his Achilles heel. It is hard to rule a country if its language and culture have become a foreign territory to you. Hoveyda's wife put it succinctly, albeit bitterly, when she said that "he was too European for Iranians."[72]

I waited almost three months, and when Renée's letter, along with a copy of Hoveyda's handwriting, arrived, the four lines of poetry he had copied for her were chilling in their echoes of Hoveyda's own life. They were from de Vigny's most famous poem, "La Mort du Loup" (The Death of the Wolf):[*]

Gémir, pleurer, prier est également lâche.
Fais énergiquement ta longue et lourde tâche,
Dans la voie où le Sort a voulu t'appeler.
Puis après, comme moi, souffre et meurs sans parler.[73]

Wailing, weeping, praying are equally dastardly acts.
Energetically perform your long and arduous task,
On the road where Destiny has beckoned you.
And then, like me, suffer and die in silence.[74]

---

* Alfred de Vigny, it seems, was inspired by Byron's poem, "Childe Harold," two lines of which are used on page 37 as this chapter's epigram.

CHAPTER THREE

Paris Pilgrim

Dans les plis sinueux des vieilles capitales,
Où tout, même l'horreur, tourne aux enchantments.[*]
—Baudelaire

A copy of his Bible, *Les Nourritures Terrestres,* in his hands, on a hot evening in September 1938, nineteen-year-old Amir Abbas boarded a ship headed for the Europe of his imagination.

His mother had to bid him farewell at the family apartment. In those days the port in Beirut was in the seedy side of town, and ladies were generally loath to walk along the pier. She insisted on performing the normal rituals of departure for a Muslim family, and Amir Abbas acquiesced. Standing at the threshold of the door, she held high a copy of the Koran. Her son passed under the book in bowed supplication; on the last turn of the thrice repeated gesture, he, as expected, kissed the sacred book on its spine, and placed it on his eyes and forehead.[1] Tradition has it that in return for the gesture of supplication, God will guard the traveler from the intrinsic dangers of the journey.

"With tears in my eyes, and a lump in my throat," Hoveyda remembers, "I said good-bye to her. She kept her composure and advised me to be

---

[*] In the sinuous folds of old capitals / where everything, even horror, becomes enchanting.

prudent. But I knew she was at least as sad as I was."[2] His younger brother, Fereydoun, accompanied him to the bustling Beirut dockside, full of European tourists, Arab travelers and visitors, and all manner of sailors, hawkers, even louts. Two suits, a few shirts, some undergarments, and his grooming accouterment were all Amir Abbas had with him in his awkwardly shaped suitcase. "I was going to a Europe that was the source and destination of all things," he writes, "the land that had nourished my mind for the past twelve years."[3]

Even the ship that would take him to Europe was, for him, a source of awe and inspiration. "It was called *Champollion*...the name of the French scholar who for the first time succeeded in reading cuneiform.* In high school, I had read about his life and work....Was it not destiny that I would be traveling to Europe, the source of all knowledge, aboard a ship whose name is linked to science and history?"[4] Only a passing dissonant note of ambivalence is evident in his enthusiastic praise for all that was European. "I thought I was going towards a Europe that I considered the cradle and the catalyst of civilization, but I was heading to a dead land, a moribund Europe, suffocating under the weight of its old animosities and differences."[5]

In terms of geography, the trip might indeed have been a long journey across seas and continents. In terms of intellectual habits of the mind, however, the sojourn could well be construed as nothing other than an excursion into an already familiar, and beguilingly similar, territory. Many observers and scholars would concur with Claude Lévi-Strauss that Muslims and the French people are at least alike in that they both "observe the same bookish attitude, the same Utopian spirit and the stubborn conviction that it is enough to solve problems on paper to be immediately rid of them...[W]e build similar pictures of the world and society in which all difficulties can be solved by a cunning application of logic..."[6] Beirut was, maybe more than any other city in modern times, the enchanted metaphor for the marriage of East and West, of France and the Islamic world. Thus, Hoveyda, a child of Beirut cosmopolitanism, was going to a

---

* Here, in his diaries, Hoveyda commits a minor historical error. Champollion (1790–1832) was in fact the French Egyptologist who discovered the key to Egyptian hieroglyphs while deciphering the Rosetta stone. Cuneiform, on the other hand, was a system of writing developed by the Sumerians some six thousand years ago. Decoding of cuneiform is generally attributed to scholars like H. C. Rawlinson (1810–95) and G. F. Grotefend (1775–1853) whose major accomplishment was decoding Persian cuneiform.

France that, according to Lévi-Strauss, could only enhance and solidify his bookish habits of Utopian eclecticism, his tendency to believe—particularly accentuated late in his life—that an imagined, theoretical resolution of a problem is equal to its solution in the real world.[7]

So strong was his desire to see France that by the second day of the trip, all the anxieties of departure had already dissipated. Instead, there was now an anxious air of waiting, discovery, and intellectual consummation. With the aroma of "bifteck frites" hanging in the ship's cabins and decks, he felt as though he had already arrived in France.[8]

At the same time, Hoveyda's uncannily honest words about European and French cultures—words that take on more import when we remember that he published them at the time he was Iran's prime minister—are not just signposts of his own intellectual landscape but of the temptations of a whole generation of Iranian and Middle Eastern writers, poets, and politicians.[9] For many of them, particularly in the years before World War II, France was the very embodiment of modernity and change, the only effective antidote to the debilitating narcotic of an imagined glorious history, a past moored to an unbending religious tradition.[10] Hoveyda's maternal grandfather was the epitome of this Francophilia. And as Hoveyda's diaries make amply clear, he, too, shared his grandfather's longing for *Farang*.* Thus when he boarded the *Champollion*, the joy of finally visiting the Europe he had so avidly read about was all that occupied his mind.

On board, Hoveyda shared a tiny windowless cabin, in a Third-class compartment, with seven other young men. "It was a small room," he writes, "where it was natural to feel claustrophobic. It had two beds, each with four bunks."[11] In what appears as either the sediments of his early elective affinities with leftist ideas or the political posturing of his older years, he waxes poetic about the virtues of poverty. "Why should we want to become dependent on worldly goods?" he asks rhetorically. He confesses that "hitherto in my life, I had only known Third-class compartments. It was a world closer to my heart. I had gotten used to it. I understood its language. This is the language of the heart, and it has always been familiar to me."[12]

---

* Arabs used *Faranj* to refer to the Crusaders. There was a hint of denigration in the word. Gradually, *Faranj* transmigrated into the Persian vernacular as *Farang*, encompassing all that is Western European. The hint of disparagement was, by the nineteenth century, changed into one of both awe and resentment. An aura of modernity now surrounds the word.

There is, in Hoveyda's diaries, an interesting contrast between his last image of the East and his first image of the West: one is tinged with a harsh dose of realism; the other is characteristically fantastical in its source. His parting image of the Orient is of Alexandria,* of its poor children who flock to the boat and dive into the sea in search of the few small coins "that first class passengers tossed in the water by way of entertainment." It was, he writes, "reminiscent of a scene from a zoo, where the attendant would throw food into the tank, and the fish would jump up and down in its pursuit." Such poverty, he adds, tramples all vestiges of human dignity: "sometimes death is better than some forms of living."[13]

And then, on the sixth day, as dawn nears, Hoveyda writes of his first impressions of the West, and the contrast with the dire Alexandrian images could not be more startling. He goes on deck to "breathe the new fresh air." He writes that "gradually the coastline of France became visible, and one could see the island of If.† There is much talk of this island in *The Count of Monte Cristo*…how much I liked this novel in my youth."[14] While a one-sided realism shaped his images of the East, a bookish Romanticism hued his vision of the West.

After the seven-day trip, Hoveyda was excited about "touching for the first time the soil of Europe." He was joined by a group of Lebanese, Sudanese, and Egyptian young men, and two of his Persian friends from the lycée, who were all, like him, "out to try their luck in partaking of Europe's treasures of knowledge."[15]

Hoveyda's gateway to this cherished "Promised Land" was Marseilles, France's oldest city, originally built by the Phoenicians in 600 B.C. After a night in a cheap hotel, and after his first bowl of bouillabaisse, which was a novel delight to his palate, he left the crowded and dingy Marseilles for the glories of Paris, a city he had come to love even before he had seen it. He admits that he had heard and thought so much about Paris that in his mind, the myth and reality of the city had become part of the same continuum of desire.[16]

And Paris did not disappoint him. Long before his train reached its final destination at the Gare de Lyon, the lighted houses of the city, the

---

* Hoveyda's image of Alexandria becomes more interesting when it is compared, for example, with Lawrence Durrell's *Alexandria Quartet,* four sumptuously sensual novels in which Durrell immortalizes the rich and exotic life of the old mysterious city.

† Hoveyda seems to be referring to Chateau d'If, where the Count is imprisoned.

throng of automobiles, the bustle of the streets, and the glamour of its grand stores had already impressed Hoveyda. The train station was even more magnificent than he had imagined. "Here I was from Beirut," he writes, "a city that compared to Paris is no more than a little village…no wonder then that Gare de Lyon looked like a mammoth."[17]

Ever since the seventeenth century, when Iranian travelers began to trickle into Europe, many have written diaries and memoirs about these trips. These narratives provide invaluable knowledge about not just the contours of Iran's relations with the West but also the evolving Iranian sense of the national "self" and its relation to the Western "other." The kind of self-assured, even arrogant, tone of the first diaries, particularly evident in the writings of emissaries of the Safavid era, gradually gives way to one of inspired, even intimidated, awe in late Qajar narratives. Eventually there emerges the writings of often comical figures—called, with bitter sarcasm, the *fokolis*—who, at a mere whiff of the European air, had come to denigrate all that was Persian.[18] In the classic disposition of colonized souls so brilliantly depicted by authors like Frantz Fanon, and Aimé Césaire, and the novelist Patrick Chamoiseau, *fokolis* insisted that Iran's only chance of salvation was to forfeit its own culture, and language, and become entirely European.

In this historical context, Hoveyda's accounts of his European travels are in many ways unique. Contrary to the *fokolis* and their superficial love of the West, Hoveyda was deeply immersed in and informed about European culture. However, he did harbor some illusions about the historic significance and the practical applicability of the European experience in Iran—at times reminiscent of the *fokolis'* shallow exuberance for all that was European. At the same time, contrary to the *fokolis*, Hoveyda never denigrates Iran and its culture in his diaries, or in any of his later pronouncements. Indeed, in later years, the truculent nationalism he espoused in public, his often repeated celebration of what he considered the unique characteristics of the Iranian culture, all seemed to have seamlessly meshed with his continued private awe and yearning for the Europe that was etched on his mind at the Beirut lycée.

But in September 1938, the excitement of Paris so overwhelmed Hoveyda that he lost his train ticket. He would have been fined by the police had not his two Persian friends found the ticket and arrived just in time. The three young men then hired a cab and headed for the Quartier Latin, a mecca for Francophile intellectuals. Hoveyda and his friends rented a small room in one of the Quartier's side streets, and barely settled in his room, he set out to discover Paris and its grandeur. "Every neighborhood," he writes, "was a different Paris, and each had its own history."[19] But in an important sense, he was no stranger to the city and its neighborhoods. "In high school, and during elementary school," he confesses, "they had filled our mind not just with Paris but with all of France."[20]

The joys of Paris proved ephemeral. After only two days, he was forced to leave his beloved city and head for London. In explaining the reason for his speedy departure, Hoveyda is less than forthcoming. "It would be about a year before I could enter the university," he writes, adding, "I wanted to spend the time completing my study of the English language."[21] However, the real reasons for his aborted Paris sojourn were more complicated, having more to do with his restless craving for Europe. Entrance into the French university system in those days required the completion of a two-tiered diploma, or baccalaureate. Anxious to leave Beirut, and worried that the onset of war might imperil his chance of travel to France, Hoveyda insisted on leaving Lebanon before completing his second tier. In reality, then, his departure for London was both to complete the missing high-school requirements necessary for entry into any French university and to polish his English.[22]

Amir Abbas boarded a train to the French coast. He crossed the English Channel and then took another train for London. He found a room in a bed-and-breakfast and enrolled in the Institut Français du Royaume-Uni (The French Institute of the United Kingdom) in London's South Kensington district. He spent the next nine months there and seemed far from happy. Except for the experience of mastering English, and meeting René Maheu, a favorite teacher who would later become his close friend and the director general of UNESCO, nothing about London seemed to have appealed to Hoveyda. As in Beirut, he was something of a dandy. In pictures from the period, he is always sharply dressed, sometimes in a bow tie, occasionally with a dapper chapeau on his head. All his adult life, he had something of an obsession with white shirts. Even as prime minister, every time he traveled to Europe, he brought back a dozen Lanvin white shirts.[23] In London, the soot and haze of the city were a nuisance. "You wear a white shirt, in the morning," he writes, "and a few hours later it is darkened."[24]

Amir Abbas (wearing a hat) in London, circa 1938.

On April 28, 1939, he sent a note to his friend Renée Demont. He laments that "in England the weather is always foul…and in London, it is always cold; I envy you the Lebanese sun."[25] In the same letter, in the course of some gossip about mutual high-school friends—all his life, Hoveyda was never averse to gossip—he engages in some light banter about the role women play in the lives of men. "Napoleon said, 'always look for the woman.' As for me, I say watch out for the young girls. Ultimately, as I have always said, the young girls are tyrants."[26] The tone of the letter and the texture of his relationship with Renée can in retrospect be viewed as a pattern that repeated itself throughout Hoveyda's life. With women, he was more adept at friendship than at love: many of them considered him a close friend; few ever counted him amongst their lovers.

As soon as Hoveyda finished the requisite work for entrance into the French universities, he left London for Paris. His long-cherished dream of living in Paris was about to become reality when a diplomatic crisis erupted between Iran and France. A French newspaper concocted a comic pun by replacing, in a common expression of the vernacular, the word "shah" with the French word for cat: *chat.* Reza Shah, the ruling monarch of Iran at the time, was not amused and in protest recalled Iran's ambassador from France. Though the silly row did not last long, one of its collateral results was that Hoveyda could not get a student visa to stay and study in Paris. He had to scurry to Brussels and settle for the city's Université Libre de Bruxelles (Free University of Brussels). Late in June 1939, as he took the train for Belgium, he consoled himself with the promise that he would return to Paris as soon as diplomatic conditions allowed it.[27]

But at the Belgian border, while going through a normal customs check, Amir Abbas realized he had lost his passport. In spite of Vladimir Nabokov's just admonition against the common temptation of biographers to become "psychoplagiarists,"[28] it is nevertheless hard not to see Hoveyda's passport loss as the exact kind of "slip"—a case of the "psychopathology of everyday life"—Freud so famously wrote about.[29] Whatever the unconscious motives, Hoveyda was forced to disembark at the border town, go to Paris on the next available train, and search for his passport. With the Iranian Embassy closed due to the break in diplomatic relations, he imagined he could be stranded for many months. His only solace, he writes, was an Agatha Christie novel he had bought at the station.[30]

Back in Paris, to his great relief, he found his passport at the lost and found office of the train station and immediately set out again for Brussels. On July 6, 1939, he registered at the University's École des Sciences Politiques et Sociales (School of Political and Social Science). He also found a room at one of the student dormitories. Along with political science, he wanted to major in economics and finance. In letters to his friends at the time, he further declared that he planned to take some courses in journalism.[31] He soon must have given up on this last idea, for there is no indication in his school records that he took any courses in journalism.

In spite of the ease with which he settled into the life of a student, he found Brussels a dim and depressing city. "Compared to Paris, it is like a village," he laments. Indeed, he seems to have become so deeply immersed in French culture that occasionally he appears to mimic the disparaging and derogatory tone the French took when talking about Belgian culture and society.[32] For Hoveyda, not only was Brussels a mere village, but the people seemed to him "sad. They are more Northern. They speak with a peculiar accent...They are nouveaux riches and even their wealth has not brought any joy to their stern faces."[33]

At university, as in high school in Beirut, Hoveyda was, by his own admission, and as the records clearly indicate, only a mediocre student. He stayed at the Université Libre for three years. During the first year, he attempted to major in both political science and economics. In the second year, he gave up his economics major and just concentrated on political science. He finished his first-year classes with "Satisfaction," a passing grade that would be equivalent to a C or C- in the American grading system. He did better in his second year, earning the mark of "Distinction," roughly the same as a B. In his last and final year, he went back to the "Satisfaction" level again.[34] (At the height of his political glory, Hoveyda came back to his alma mater to receive recognition and gratitude for the financial assistance provided to the university by the government of Iran. He listened to the praise the president heaped on him as a favorite son of the school, and then with an affable and cynical sarcasm, that had by then become part of his style, he spoke of his student days when he had to chase the professors across the campus just to receive a passing grade.)[35]

In his university days, literature and history were his forte. Most of the courses he took were in modern, medieval, and ancient history and law. He also took several courses in Sciences Coloniales (Colonial Sciences), dealing with the Belgian rule of the Congo.

During this period, he made many new friends, and eventually left the dormitory for room and board in a house owned by a kind, old, and stingy Belgian woman. His life was awash in books and films. All manifestations of intelligence and creativity delighted him. Hoveyda was adept at the art of making, and keeping, friends. He invested much energy and his formidable intellectual insights into identifying the flower, the compliment, or the gift that would most please, or appease his friends. There was always in his large circle of friends a coterie of artists and intellectuals. With their help, he had a stimulating life that combined academic pursuits and intellectual banter. Caught in the cross currents of events, he was bent on creating for himself the life of a happy exile.

On May 10, 1940, the German army invaded Belgium and on May 17 occupied Brussels. The university was closed, the city was all but completely evacuated; even Hoveyda's landlady fled the country and left him with the luxury of the whole house to himself. Normal mail delivery was suspended; his contact with his family came to a halt; worse still, the disruption of the mail system meant that the monthly allowance his mother sent him would not be forthcoming. In the midst of this turmoil, he was nearly penniless, yet Paris still beckoned.[36] He tried to contact the Iranian Embassy and solicit their help in securing both a French visa and some short-term financial aid. The embassy was far from accommodating, and Hoveyda soon gave up "all hope of receiving any help from them."[37] Instead he resorted to an uncharacteristically adventurous solution.

On May 13, 1940, a Persian friend, intent on driving to France with his fiancée, offered to take Hoveyda along. "I accepted the offer," he writes, "and we set out around two in the afternoon. I took a few of my favorite belongings, and left everything else behind. I took one last melancholy look at my beloved books and took along only one. It was Gide's *Notebooks*."[38]

The chaos and frenzy of war had made the roads hazardous. They passed bombed villages, army convoys, and caravans of cars fleeing the rapidly advancing German army. In one village, as they stopped to see why people had congregated around a car, they saw the charred body of a young man. "This was my first face-to-face encounter with death," Hoveyda writes, "and I was nauseous and trembling…and I remembered the majestic words of Baudelaire about the decaying corpse of humanity."[39]

On Tuesday, May 14, after spending a restless night at a friend's house in Mons, close to the French border, they decided to go out for a walk. By then, Mons was filled with English, French, and Belgian soldiers. Officers of the city police found the group suspicious and took them in for questioning. At the station, Hoveyda tried to not only show the investigating officer his documents but also show off his newly acquired knowledge of international law, constitutional rights, habeas corpus, even the origins of the French Revolution. He had, after all, taken courses on Droit des Gens (human rights), Droit Public (public law), and Droit Civil (civil law). The officer was not impressed. "We have to investigate some more," he said, ordering Hoveyda and his friends to jail.[40] This would be Hoveyda's first, albeit short, experience with prison. In less than twenty-four hours, when it was established that their documents were all authentic, he and his friends were released.

The jail experience deterred Hoveyda's friend from continuing the planned journey to France. Hoveyda, however, would not be dissuaded. He convinced another Persian friend to join him and together they set out for their destination. The border was a good seventy kilometers from the city. For parts of the road, they had no choice but to walk. "The road to the border crossing," he recalls, "was so full of pedestrians that it had come to resemble a city street."[41] Sporadically, German bombers appeared on the horizon. At their sight, Hoveyda and the throng of frightened and fleeing Belgians hid in the green shrubbery off the road.

Once they reached the border, their wait was dishearteningly short. The French border guard took one look at Hoveyda's passport and, observing that he had received no entry visa, ordered him to return to Brussels. Hoveyda's explanations for why he could not get a visa in Brussels were curtly dismissed. He even tried to soften the officer's heart. "I owe all my education and my training to France," Hoveyda told him, "and the French government has always been kind to Iranians."[42] But the officer would not budge. Their only choice, he told them, was to return to Brussels and try to get a visa there.

Back in Mons that very night, Hoveyda had his first experience with a sustained bombing raid. "I was shaking," he writes, "and a cold sweat covered my body."[43] The next day, he returned to Brussels, intent on securing a French visa as soon as possible. By seven in the evening on Thursday, May 16, he had moved back to the still-vacant house he had left a few days before. Desperately short of money—in his words, "a twenty-two-year-old young man, in a strange city and only four and a half francs in his pocket"—he went back to the university looking for help. On May 17, Brussels was occupied by German forces and all classes were suspended by their order.[44] The campus was turned into the headquarters of the Belgian Red Cross, who hired Hoveyda as an ambulance driver on May 19.

No sooner had he solved his immediate financial crisis than another serious problem loomed on the horizon. He learned that he was about to lose his comfortable, and free, house. German troops had begun confiscating any house whose proprietor had fled to France. Again he sought the assistance of the Iranian Embassy, and this time, for a change, they could help. He was provided with an official paper, written in both German and French, indicating that the house he lived in was part of the Iranian Embassy, making it immune to Nazi confiscation.[45]

When classes began again at the university under the watchful eyes of the Gestapo, Hoveyda's life took on an air of normalcy. He resumed his classes and continued to work at the Red Cross. By then his job had changed; he now worked in the office responsible for relocating war refugees. He also moved back to the dorms, ate at the school cafeteria, and spent most of his time with his large circle of friends.

But then the unthinkable happened. On June 14, 1940, Paris fell to the Nazis. On June 20, France surrendered, and Hoveyda was heartbroken. "No, this I cannot, I dare not, believe," he writes. "France! The land of freedom, the sanctuary of the exiles, you have surrendered? You have given up the fight? That night, along with French friends, I wept for your misery, France; because I have always loved you. My beloved France, my thoughts yearn for you; you have surrendered but in my mind, your name is still synonymous with the most beautiful vistas, and the most beautiful cities."[46]

In the same diary, Hoveyda also writes about hearing the news of Iran's occupation by the Allied Forces. (On August 25, 1941, British and Soviet troops ignored Iran's declared neutrality, and attacked the country.) "Iran, oh, dear Iran," Hoveyda writes, "all my thoughts are now with you."[47] While the narratives about Iran and France are both effusive in their show of emotion, they are different in the kind of affect they each show. When referring to France, Hoveyda is clearly overwrought that this bastion of freedom and cradle of culture has been defeated. To the defeated nation that was his intellectual dreamland, he promises eternal fidelity. Writing about Iran, however, his point of departure is that a poor, neutral country has been drawn into a European war. He emphasizes his concern for the well-being of his family, particularly his mother. His dual affinities—one intellectual and grief-stricken, the other primarily emotional and tinged with pity—are clearly evident in the language he uses to articulate his response to the calamity that befell both France and Iran.

In the summer of 1941, after repeated efforts, Hoveyda finally succeeded in obtaining a visa to visit Paris. German authorities were as a rule reluctant to allow much travel within the occupied territories; yet, according to Hoveyda, the only exception were students like him who were of "Aryan" stock.[48] He writes of how Brussels had simply become intolerable for him; how everything, including the joy of dancing, was rationed; how all letters were opened and read by German authorities. "I sought refuge in Paris," he writes. Aside from all these factors, and aside from the yearning he had

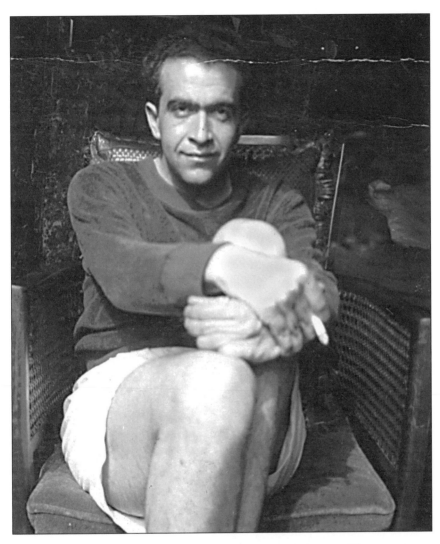

Amir Abbas in Brussels shortly after the German occupation in 1941. His pose suggests the aura of a character from one of the existentialist novels of his youth. He would soon return to Iran after an absence of almost two decades.

developed for Paris over the years, there was now an added reason for him to visit the city of his dreams. In writing about his eventful journey to Paris—a narrative that reads more like a eulogy for the occupied city than a travelogue—Hoveyda fails to mention an important component of that trip. His act of omission was probably the result of his desire to avoid opening what he imagined to be a Pandora's box. The oblique reference to the "Aryan" stock is the closest he comes to explaining why Paris had now become even more attractive.

When France was occupied by the German army, foreign embassies of countries like Iran that had severed diplomatic ties with Nazi Germany closed their offices in Paris. Iran was no exception. The embassy compound was left in the care of Hoveyda's uncle, Abol-Hossein Sardari, his mother's youngest brother.* Sardari was a man of controversy and myriad talents. A congenial man with cosmopolitan polish, he was a career diplomat. Before the invasion he had been in charge of consular affairs at the embassy. He was a shrewd operator, a bon vivant, and adept at the art of making and keeping friends. He befriended some of the more influential Germans in Paris, inviting them to lavish parties at the embassy where he provided caviar, champagne, and even beautiful young girls for their entertainment. A young Parisian model called Alexandria was often used as an agent for inviting other young girls to the embassy.[49] Sardari's hospitality soon proved highly profitable for him, and lifesaving for many Jews who lived in Paris.

During the war, a large number of Iranian Jews lived in Germany and other territories occupied by the Nazis. Paris, too, had its share of Iranian Jews. As early ominous signs of the "Final Solution" began to appear, the Iranian government set out to convince the Nazis that the Iranian Jews had, as a result of 2,500 years of active assimilation into the culture and language of Iran, become altogether Persian and should not be considered part of the "Jewish people." The fact that many Iranian Jews had either not mentioned their religion on their passports or opted to call themselves a Mussavi—Persian for a follower of Moses—rather than a Jew helped the government make its case.[50] Eventually, the Nazis were indeed convinced that the Iranian Jews, or the "Juguden," as they were called, were "members of a Muslim sect... Iranian in origin and not Semitic."[51] This declaration helped save the lives of nearly all the Iranian Jews in Europe.

---

* It is a sign of the almost incestuous nature of power in Pahlavi Iran that not only was Sardari Hoveyda's uncle, but the ambassador to France at the time was also a relative. His name was Anoushirvan Sepahbodi; he was married to Hoveyda's aunt. Contrary to the common lore of Iranian politics about the "one thousand families" that rule the country, according to a CIA report in 1977, there have been in fact no more than "40 national families and 150 to 200 provincial families who over the course of a century or more have maintained influential positions" in Iran. See CIA, "Iran in the 1980s," NSA, no. 1210.

While this question was being pondered by "race experts" in Berlin, Sardari used his intimate ties with Germans to protect the Iranian Jewish families that lived in Paris. He, too, tried to convince the German authorities that anyone holding an Iranian passport, regardless of religious affiliation, must be afforded all the protection granted to Iranian citizens. He wrote to Otto Abetz, the German military commander of Paris, that Jews had been full-fledged citizens of Iran for over 2,500 years; he boasted of Iran's shared Aryan heritage with Germany. Abetz wrote back promising that Iranian Jews of Paris would "not be subjected to the special Nazi measures."[52]

Sardari also discovered some fifteen hundred blank Persian passports that had been left behind in the embassy. When the roundup of Parisian Jews began in 1942, Sardari decided to issue the passports in the name of some non-Iranian Jews. There seems little doubt that Sardari saved the lives of some fifteen hundred innocent Jews; there is also evidence to suggest that he enriched himself in the process. Several years later newspapers in Tehran learned of these developments and asked why Sardari had not been recalled, in spite of his obvious corruption and his role in selling passports to Jews. Iranian Jews, however, had their own views of Sardari's acts. "I was in Paris in 1948," writes Fereydoun Hoveyda, "when the Iranian Jewish community (with its newly added 'citizens') visited my uncle and offered him a silver plate signed by their leaders, as a token of their appreciation and thanks."[*53]

Hoveyda, who often visited Paris and lived with Sardari at the time of these passport transactions, never mentions the events in his lengthy wartime diaries. Instead, he writes about the lively theater life in Paris, the important role the Communist Party played in organizing anti-Nazi resistance, and the fact that he "roamed, often alone, the streets and avenues of this city, and in each corner, there was something poetic to discover."[54]

Aside from spending his summer holidays in Paris, Amir Abbas used every opportunity during the year to visit the city. Along with the intellectual and emotional ties that connected him to the city, there was now a more mundane reason for Hoveyda's repeated trips to Paris. The austere life of a

---

* Paris was apparently not the only city where the Iranian diplomats used blank Iranian passports in a manner similar to Sardari. Ahmad Tavakoli, a career diplomat, tells of about 1,500 Syrian and Lebanese Jews who had similarly purchased their way to safety by buying Persian passports. Most of them somehow ended up in Milan, where Tavakoli served in the early 1950s. Ahmad Tavakoli, interviewed by author, Tampa, Florida, 15 August 1999. The story of the Iranian government's attempt to save Iranian Jews, and the help provided by diplomats like Sardari in saving other Jews, deserves more scrutiny.

*Hoveyda in Beirut, not long after graduating from university
and shortly before his return to Iran in 1942.*

student in occupied Brussels was in Paris replaced with a resplendent life
of affluence and gourmet delights. After each trip, the gaunt look on his
face would give way to the rotund cheeks that had by then become one of
his defining physical features.[55]

Hoveyda finished his studies at the end of 1941 and received a *licence*
(bachelor's degree) in political science from the Université Libre de Bruxelles. For his senior thesis, he wrote a long essay on the works of Panait
Istrati (1884–1935), a Romanian author who, in political disposition and in
the contours of his life, shared much with Hoveyda.[56] Istrati, too, was a
Francophile who had traveled widely in the Middle East and the Balkans,
had flirted with Marxism, had traveled to the Soviet Union, and like André
Gide, Hoveyda's other intellectual mentor of those days, had upon his
return written a scathing critique of life and politics in the new Utopia.[57] In
his youth Hoveyda had also read Marxist tracts and befriended Iranian,

Arab, and French Marxists. This was enough to mark him as an incorrigible leftist in the eyes of many Iranian royalists. As for leftist intellectuals— imbued as they were with the Russian notion of the intelligentsia— Hoveyda's eclectic readings that ranged from Malraux and Istrati to Nietzsche and Gide, his taste for bourgeois comforts, his distaste for revolutions, and his willingness to compromise made him an intellectual imposter.

With his studies finished, Hoveyda made one last trip to Paris in early 1942. From there, after bidding farewell, in his own words, "to the city of light," and "with a heavy heart, with Paris on one side, and Iran on the other," he found his way back to Beirut where he stayed with his mother and younger brother for the summer.[58] In September 1942, Hoveyda returned to Tehran, leaving behind his uncle's escapades in Paris. For the next five years Paris would, however, remain a constant source of diplomatic controversy and journalistic sensationalism. If in 1942 Hoveyda could ignore the rumors about Sardari, the next time he traveled to Paris, he would find himself at the center of a new, far more serious, crisis that would haunt him for the rest of his life.

CHAPTER FOUR

The Land of Oz

What country, friends, is this?
—Shakespeare, *Twelfth Night*

Tehran was an occupied city when, after an absence of about twenty-one years, Hoveyda returned in 1942. Just as Hoveyda bore little resemblance to the two-year-old who had left Tehran on a horse-drawn carriage, so, too, the city was quite different from the overgrown village it had been in 1921. The only similarity was that at both times the city and the country were profoundly changing.

Approximately a year earlier, on August 25, 1941, about 35,000 British soldiers, including many Indian and Gurkha troops, attacked Iran from the south. Another 120,000 members of the Soviet Red Army invaded the country from the north. As expected, the outmanned and outgunned Iranian army collapsed within forty-eight hours of the invasion, offering little serious resistance.

The idea for invading Iran had been initially proposed by the British cabinet during the first week of July. Ostensibly, Iran was to be occupied, and her repeated declarations of neutrality ignored, as a precaution against the potential actions of the large number of German nationals working in Iran at the time. The actual number was no more than a thousand, and the

Iranian police had been keeping them under close surveillance. The real motives for the Allied attack were more complicated. On the one hand, Britain wanted to guarantee her continued control over the vital Iranian oil supplies. Furthermore, with the German invasion of the Soviet Union, it had become urgent to secure a supply line to help Stalin's beleaguered Red Army. And last but not least, as a result of the occupation, if not as one of its implicit goals, Iran's ruling monarch, Reza Shah, could be forced to abdicate.[1] Over the years, the British government had grown to dislike and distrust the monarch. His brand of nationalism was anathema to their designs for Iran and the rest of the Persian Gulf region. They had been looking for an excuse to dislodge him, and the war had provided the perfect occasion.

Britain used every opportunity at its disposal to humiliate the once proud, fiercely authoritarian, and modernizing king. There was even talk that the Pahlavi era had seen its last days. However, the young Mohammad Reza was allowed to ascend his father's throne, though in practice the Allies more or less acted as if he did not exist. The famous Tehran Conference was convened without even notifying the young shah, and all his life, he could neither forget nor forgive this humiliation.[2] Adding insult to injury, once Franklin Roosevelt, Winston Churchill, and Joseph Stalin arrived in Tehran, only Stalin eventually came to pay the monarch the requisite courtesy visit. Power was in the hands of the Allies, and the shah was but a scarecrow.

During the foreign occupation Iran experienced a period of intense political and artistic debate and innovation. It was a time when the country saw an unexpected, fleeting period of budding democracy and flourishing cultural activity. Years of censorship, and politics of fear and authoritarianism based on Reza Shah's autocracy, had led to muffled intellectual energies and stifled the growing desire for political participation on the part of the rising urban population. With the fall of Reza Shah, the center could no longer hold, and a flurry of activity—intellectual, political, and cultural—sprang into the open.[3]

The war enhanced America's influence in Iran as well. Whereas in the first two decades of the century Britain had succeeded in keeping American oil companies out of Iran, in the early 1940s, the new realities arising from America's growing power in the world, and in Iran, made Churchill apprehensive of England's future prospects in the country.[4] Echoes of this fear can be heard in Churchill's correspondence with Franklin Roosevelt. In a language that reeks of colonial haughtiness, Roosevelt responds to Churchill's anxious queries by declaring that, "I am having the oil question [in Iran] studied by the Department of State and my oil experts, but please do accept my assurance that we are not making sheep's eyes at your oil fields in Iraq and Iran." Churchill's retort is no less chilling in its arrogant undertone. "Thank you very much for your assurances about no sheep's eyes at our oil fields in Iran and Iraq," he writes. "Let me reciprocate by giving you the fullest assurance that we have no thought of trying to horn in upon your interests or property in Saudi Arabia."[5]

While Churchill and Roosevelt were busy divvying up the oil fields of the Persian Gulf, Stalin had hegemonic ideas of his own. As was its practice, the Soviet government used the occupation of Northern Iran to help create a communist party that would become a pliant tool of Soviet policy. Lest it raise the ire of the religious and conservative communities, the party eschewed an overt communist label and opted for the more innocuous name of the Tudeh Party (mass party). The Tudeh Party's rapid expansion, its strong sense of discipline, and the help it received from "Big Brother" allowed it to play a crucial role in the politics of the next decade in Iran. Some of Hoveyda's friends from his Beirut days, particularly Jalal Miri, would become active members, or fellow travelers, of the new party.

Jalal Miri, a communist with links to the famous "Group of 53," who were arrested by Reza Shah. Miri fled to Beirut to escape arrest in the 1930s and befriended Amir Abbas.

In later years, some party leaders would even claim, with no supporting evidence, that Hoveyda, too, was a fellow traveler of the Tudeh Party.[6] Marxist ideas began to spread and soon came to dominate intellectual discourse in Iran.

Segments of the Islamic clergy, as well as a number of Muslim intellectuals, had also begun agitating for a new, modern interpretation of Islam. They wanted to shed the more irrational, and anachronistic, elements of Shiite dogma. The cult of weeping and flagellation, and the preoccupation with miracles, were high on their list of undesirable practices. Some of their ideas had much in common with those advocated by the fiercely secular intellectual, Ahmad Kasravi.[7] A relatively obscure mullah named Ruhollah Khomeini took up the modernists' challenge. In his first book written in Persian, he set out to defend the traditional values and beliefs of Shiism. In the process, he also articulated for the first time the rudiments of what later would become his theory of the Islamic state, or Shiite theocracy. He warned against the dangerous ideas of modernist clergy, and some thirty-seven years before Islamic tribunals put Hoveyda and thousands of others like him on trial for "spreading corruption on earth," he invited the "Muslim government to stop the spread of such illegal and heretical ideas and execute in public and in the presence of all true believers all such provocateurs who spread corruption on earth."[8]

Mohammad Reza Shah's temperament was also, at times inadvertently, a catalyst for change. The young monarch was shy and timid, ill-fitted to fill the shoes of his domineering parent. There is a picture that captures the problematic father and son relationship. Taken in 1926, "the father is forty-eight and the son seven. The contrast between them is striking in every respect: The huge, powerful Shah-father stands sulkily, peremptorily, hands on his hips, and beside him the small pale boy, frail, nervous, obediently standing at attention, barely reaches his father's waist."[9] On that day, the son wore a uniform that was, down to every minute detail, the exact replica of the royal regalia worn by the father. Now, barely sixteen years after the picture was taken, the son was forced to abruptly assume the father's duties, and he was not ready.

Reza Shah seemed all too aware of his son's inadequacies. When Mohammad Reza, as crown prince, asked his father what he "considered the goal of his reign," the king answered that it was to "create a governmental organization to carry on the state" after he left power. The son took the response as a slap, as it seemed to imply a lack of faith in his ability to carry on the affairs of state. "It hurt my feelings dreadfully," the son confessed.[10]

The young monarch craved to be taken seriously not just by the Allied governments but even by Iranian politicians. The shah was so isolated and politically marginalized in those days—particularly by powerful prime ministers like Ahmad Qavam—that in his attempt to solicit support, he would utter words that seem in retrospect ominously prophetic. In 1946, while talking to a delegation of Shiite clerics, the shah said:

> Iran has had two kinds of kings: good kings and bad kings. And the latter kind were themselves of two sorts: those who succeeded in doing harm, and those who failed. In my opinion, the responsibility of those kings who did harm lies with the people who permitted the rulers to misbehave. People must not remain silent, or neutral, about the actions of their rulers. They must rise up if governments trample their rights or break the laws. It is indeed one of the major responsibilities of the clergy to awaken people and make them aware of their legal rights, and thus not allow rulers and governments to engage in reckless and lawless behavior.[11]

These words certainly came back to haunt Mohammad Reza Shah. Furthermore, the shah's ingrained sense of inferiority, the despair he felt about his father's distrust in his abilities, the humiliation he felt at the hands of both Western powers and powerful Persian prime ministers in the first fifteen years of his rule proved formative in the kind of prime ministers he sought in the last two decades of his rule, and the kind of relations he established with Hoveyda.

If all these factors were not sufficient to create a fertile intellectual and political atmosphere in Iran, there was also Nilla Cram Cook.[12] The Allies had made this American woman of strong will and views the de facto cultural vizier and "official censor of public morality in Tehran."[13] Since her arrival in Tehran, she had become an avid fan of Persian letters, particularly Sufi texts. She had a large coterie of friends particularly amongst Iranian intellectuals.[14] Under her watch, Iranian newspapers and magazines not only grew rapidly in number but also began to enjoy an unusual period of freedom. Some two hundred newspapers were published in Tehran in those days. It was under these changing and dynamic conditions that Amir Abbas

Hoveyda returned home. By then he was attempting to forge an identity in the crosscurrents of conflicting cultural affinities.

Before going back to Tehran, Hoveyda had traveled to Beirut, to visit his mother and his brother. From there he traveled to Basra, in Iraq, where he hired a small boat to carry him across the river and into Iranian territory. He asked his guide to show him the border signs; he wanted to know the precise point where he was entering Iranian territory. Echoing the Romantic hyperbole of some of his favorite French authors, he writes that "[I] wanted to offer tears of joy and sorrow upon entering [my land]—joy at the sight of my own country, a country I had come to love from the pages of Ferdowsi's *Shahnameh,* whose poetry I had read in the bosom of my mother...And I wanted to shed my tears of sorrow at the thought that foreign forces are now stationed on my country's borders...and they are walking upon the silent sands of its deserts."[15] But there were no border signs, he was told. Hoveyda blamed the British, who in his words "acted like masters in Iraq and the southern part of my country" and thus had obliterated all "signs of our sovereignty."[16]

His description of the first Iranian city he encountered is no less disheartening and speaks eloquently about the depth and nature of his disillusionment. As he entered Ahvaz, he realized that this was "no city, but a benighted ruin on the banks of an arid river...its congested and infested alleys filled with indigents."[17]

Maybe nothing captures the essence of his bewildered state, and the depth of his estrangement from his homeland, more than his inability to find his way around Tehran, the city of his birth. Twenty years earlier, when as a child he had returned home from Damascus, he had lost his way in the city and needed the help of a policeman to find his grandparents' home. This time, with the help of kind strangers, and riding in a carriage drawn by a skeletal horse, he found his way to a hotel. The sense of loss in both moments of return to Tehran is in sharp contrast to the enchanted intellectual familiarity he had with Paris, even before he arrived there.

In Tehran, the next day, he contacted some of his relatives. Eventually he moved into the house of his uncle, Naser-Gholi Sardari, the brother of Abol-Hossein Sardari, the uncle he had stayed with in Paris. He would spend the next two years as Naser-Gholi Sardari's guest. His long stay with his uncle appears, in retrospect, to be part of a pattern. Strange as it may seem, after returning home in 1942, Hoveyda would rarely live in a home he could call his own. Though in the last years of his life he did purchase a small apartment in one of Tehran's fashionable, new high-rises and though he owned a small bungalow near the Caspian coast, he would still spend most of his time at the house he had shared for many years with his mother.

After a week of rest, Hoveyda registered to begin his military service. All Iranian adult males were, by law, required to serve two years as conscripts. But on January 12, 1943, before he was drafted, he also applied for a job at the foreign ministry. In this way, he hoped, his two years of military service would count toward establishing his seniority in the civil service. In his application, he wrote, "My name is Amir Abbas Hoveyda. I hold identity card number 3542, and I am the son of Habibollah (Ayn al-Molk), previously Iran's minister plenipotentiary to Saudi Arabia. After finishing high school in Beirut where I mastered the French and Arabic languages, and became familiar with English, I set out for London where I finished my studies of the English language. From London I went to Brussels and after three years, I received a bachelor's degree in political science. During this time, I also learned Italian and German. Thus, in light of my father's long years of service, and considering the fact that I have finished my advanced studies in diplomacy, I hereby humbly request that you give this obedient servant the honor of employment in your ministry."[18]

Clearly, Hoveyda saw his abilities as something of a polyglot to be the most marketable quality he possessed. Henceforth, language would be one of the ways he ingratiated himself to those in power. Furthermore, Hoveyda's attempts to capitalize on his father's long years of service seem to undermine the claim of those critics who suggest the father was forced to resign because of his proselytizing activities for the Bahai faith. Since no one has ever claimed that the acting foreign minister at the time, Mohammad Sa'ed, was also an accomplice of the Bahais in Iran, Hoveyda's confident reference to his father suggests that Habibollah retired without an obvious blemish on his record.

The letter is also the first clear evidence of some academic fudging by Hoveyda, an issue that at the height of his political power would become a subject of more controversy. His claim of "advanced studies in diplomacy" is based on a handful of courses he had taken as an undergraduate. Aside from a couple of semesters of international law and international politics, he had also taken courses on colonial history, and the economy and government of the Belgian Congo.

More crucially, in spite of later claims in various sources—from Iran's *Who's Who* to *Current Biography* to the U.S. State Department—that he had finished a doctorate degree at the Sorbonne in Paris, Hoveyda leaves no doubt in his employment application that a bachelor's degree from Brussels is all that he ever received.[19] (Later, honorary doctorates were given to him during Iran's affluent years.) Indeed, the 1965 edition of Iran's *Who's Who* indicates that Hoveyda earned a Master of Arts degree "in political science and economics in Brussels and a Ph.D. in history from Paris University."*[20] Jahangir Behrouz, the editor of the *Who's Who*, could not remember how they came to write their entry about Hoveyda.[21] As for Hoveyda's own role in this academic fudging, as prime minister, he informed Saideh Pakravan, one of his secretaries, that he had written "his doctoral dissertation on Panait Istrati."[22]

Finally, Hoveyda's foreign ministry application tells us about his understanding of the ways of Persian bureaucracy. He was apparently unaware that in Iran, civil service jobs, particularly those in the coveted diplomatic corps, required patronage. But he was nothing if not a quick study. Without a patron, he soon realized, there would be little chance of success. It would take him another three years before he found, in the person of Abdollah Entezam, a patron who was to be crucial in his rapid rise to power. For the more immediate task of facilitating his employment at the foreign ministry, he resorted to Anoushirvan Sepahbodi, a high-ranking career diplomat married to Hoveyda's aunt, who wrote a letter of recommendation on his behalf.[23] He also sought the help of his father's friend, Abolhassan Behnam, who was an important official at the ministry. With Behnam's helpful intervention, Hoveyda was hired to work as an intern in the office of the minister and thus began his long career as a diplomat.[24]

Even though it took eight months (from the day Hoveyda applied for a job) before he finally received an official letter confirming his employment

---

* Midway through his tenure as prime minister, Hoveyda issued a decree banning the use of "doctor" as a title except for physicians and dentists. While it is true that in those days many who had purchased an advanced degree in European or American diploma mills abused the title, some of Hoveyda's critics at the time suggested that he had issued the decree out of envy. Having no doctorate himself, his critics said, Hoveyda wanted to stop everyone else from using the title. The decree, of course, was widely ignored. Ahmad Ghoreishi, interviewed by author, 19 October 1997. Hoveyda was not alone in opposing the use of the doctor title. Others in the government, such as Alinaghi Alikhani, were also against such usage. Alinaghi Alikhani, interviewed by author, 12 January 2000.

at the ministry, some of his critics have found it strange that he was hired so quickly. Some even refer to a "mysterious hand" that intervened on his behalf.[25] Perhaps the more serious question would be to ask why a man of his credentials and education should, in 1942, when foreign graduates were still a rare breed in Iran, have to resort to "connections" in order to get a temporary entry-level job at the ministry. In any case, his appointment was made permanent after he had successfully passed the requisite examination administered by the foreign ministry.

Hoveyda also took the necessary steps to commence his military service. In those days, as in subsequent years, sons of the Iranian elite usually spared no effort to find a loophole and escape the drudgeries of conscription. Hoveyda wrote that while his friends were all trying to avoid the draft, he was bent on serving.[26] He succeeded in his goal and became that rarest of all breeds: an Iranian prime minister who had served a two-year term as a conscript. His strategy also paid off: he began his job at the ministry—a tedious position that required him to read the outgoing letters, prepare summaries, and enter them into the official log—before he was enlisted, and thus his two years of enlisted service counted toward establishing his seniority in the civil service.[27]

As a university graduate, Hoveyda was spared the soldier's boot camp and was instead assigned to the Officer's Academy. His facility with languages—this time English—again turned out to be his tool for advancement. He was chosen to be the translator for a group of American officers stationed in Iran at the time.

In these first months after his return home, Hoveyda was also busy catching up with old friends and making new ones. Of his Beirut friends, he would spend the most time with Hamid Rahnema, who edited a newspaper called *Iran*.[28] Hoveyda published his earliest writings in Persian in the pages of this journal. Aside from at least one book review, he also published a short story there. I have not been able to locate the relevant issues of *Iran* but Ebrahim Golestan, himself an acclaimed novelist and film-maker, says Hoveyda's story was "somewhat kitsch…it was perfectly mediocre, but it was written without any obvious mistakes. The prose was fine too."[29] The Rahnemas, Hamid, his brother Madjid, and their father, would play a significant role in Hoveyda's future.

At the foreign ministry, Hoveyda met Jamshid Meftah through whom he befriended Natel Khanlari, the celebrated editor of *Sokhan* and a man

Hoveyda as a conscripted officer in the Iranian army, circa 1943.

Hoveyda, on the far right, with a group of American officers in Iran, circa 1943. Hoveyda was assigned to be their liaison officer.

of impressive erudition and sterling academic reputation. *Sokhan* was at the center of Iran's literary life, and its luminous coterie of regular contributors included some of the most important poets, critics, writers, and philosophers of the time. As a result of his acquaintance with Khanlari, Hoveyda met the cream of Iran's intelligentsia.

Hoveyda's fluency in French, his knowledge of some of the more recent masterpieces of European literature, and finally his passion for books gained him access to the coveted literary circle around Sadeq Hedayat, perhaps the most important modern fiction writer in Iran. Hedayat was something of a recluse. The public persona he fashioned for himself often bears a striking similarity to the life and character of Franz Kafka, whose *Metamorphosis* he translated into Persian. Hedayat was highly selective in choosing those he allowed into his inner circle. He did not like to associate with fools, sycophants, or those who wished a purchase on fame by proximity to the famous. As was the practice of literary circles in those days, Hedayat and his friends would meet every afternoon in a café (usually Café Ferdows); they would eat and drink, talk of gossip, metaphysics, high art, and low life. In later years, as Hoveyda and Hedayat traveled outside Iran at different times, they kept up something of a correspondence. Hoveyda would often send Hedayat books from abroad. They included novels and works of Freudian psychoanalysis that were the intellectual fad in postwar France.[30] Kafka's *Amerika* as well as books by Jean Paul Sartre and Henry Miller were among the novels Hoveyda sent.[31] In 1959, he tried unsuccessfully to recruit Anjavi Shirazi, another of Hedayat's friends, to edit Hedayat's letters.[32] Somehow, the project was never started and the letters have since been lost.

Of these literary friendships, the one that lasted for the rest of Hoveyda's life was the tie developed with Sadeq Chubak. A member of the Hedayat circle, and himself a towering figure in the history of modern Iranian fiction, Chubak happened to be doing his military service at the Officer's Academy at the same time as Hoveyda. Most afternoons, after finishing their day at the academy, the two men would walk home together. They had no car, had even less money, and both liked to drink. They would stop at their favorite café for a half bottle of cheap vodka, which was all they could afford. Food is usually a mandatory companion to drinking in Iran, but a small bowl of pistachios, or a dish of cucumbers and tomatoes, was all they would order in those days. Throughout his adult life, Hoveyda always liked to drink. In later years, when he could afford it, he chose scotch over vodka. He also developed a palate for fine French wines. He was never a heavy drinker; indeed, he could not hold much liquor. A couple of shots of vodka or whiskey brought out a giddy or, if his critics are to be believed, silly side of him.[33]

In those carefree days of youth, Hoveyda was, by all reports, convivial to a fault, conveying an affectionate curiosity in everything his interlocutor said. In conversation, he was masterful in eliciting the confidence of strangers. He took great pains not to be easily offended. There was a quality of informality, of light gaiety about him that could, to an unforgiving eye, seem frivolous, even clownish. While in the early 1940s these qualities endeared him to the likes of Chubak, two decades later, when Hoveyda became a powerful political figure, these habits became the subject of some controversy. To his detractors, they were all part of a calculated veneer of populism to hide his subservience to every whim of a despotic ruler. To his friends, however, they were signs of his natural sweetness, of the humility that was only second nature to him.

He was, as Chubak often remembered, always a good listener. Gossip and frivolous talk, abstract debate and mundane details of everyday life all seemed of interest to him. A favorite topic of those vodka-tinged afternoons was religion. Hoveyda had been educated by French secularists; he was an avid reader of Voltaire and a genuine advocate of the Enlightenment. It was Voltaire who said, *Écrasez l'infame* (crush infamy), when referring to organized religion. Hoveyda was as likely to quote Voltaire as Nietzsche when discussing religion in private. "He was a militant atheist," Chubak often said. To the many private inquiries from his family and friends about his spiritual stance, Hoveyda would usually confess to a decided disdain for all organized religion.[34] In a culture deeply imbued with religious affinities, he was less than enthusiastic about religion. Whereas in later years, after his rise to power, he took on the persona of a figure who at least publicly, albeit unconvincingly, professed to be a Muslim and heeded the strictures of the Shiite faith, in his younger days, when he was a junior conscript officer, he espoused the ideas of Voltaire. Organized religion, in any guise, Hoveyda believed, had in the long run exercised a negative impact on the course of human history; superstition, intolerance, and ignorance had been its chief gifts to humanity. In his private attacks on religion, Bahais and Shiites, Christians and Jews were all treated with the same tone of disapproval.

The ritual of a social drink with Chubak continued throughout Hoveyda's tenure as prime minister. On each Wednesday, before going to his mother's house for dinner, Hoveyda would stop and visit Chubak and his wife, Qodsi. He would sip at a glass of scotch, take a bite or two of the Danish cheese that had been particularly bought for him, and then engage in literary gossip and chatter. It was an unwritten rule of their ritual that politics would not be broached.[35]

Hoveyda's choice of friends in this period, particularly his attraction to Chubak and Hedayat, is fascinating in many ways. The 1940s, especially the years between 1942 and 1945, are some of the most politically dynamic years in modern Iranian history. Few secular intellectuals could forgo the temptation of entering politics. But precisely during this time, when political activism was a dominant temptation, Hoveyda seemed more drawn to questions of literature and culture. There is no evidence that during this period he ever entertained the idea of political activism. Furthermore, Chubak and Hedayat were two of the most militantly atheistic and anti-Islamic modern Iranian writers; both were also uncompromising opponents of despotism. Clearly, an essential component of the self Hoveyda imagined for himself was his identity as an intellectual. In later years, he would even play a minor role in helping publish one of Hedayat's most daring antireligious works in Paris. The play, *Afsaneh-ye Afarinesh* (Creation Myth), offers a subversively satirical look at God's role in creating the world.[36] Hoveyda's choice of friends speaks eloquently of the values he upheld at least in his youth.

In later years, as Hoveyda began his rapid rise in Iranian politics his motives in choosing his friends were deemed sinister by intellectuals like Jalal Al-e Ahmad. In befriending intellectuals, Al-e Ahmad said, Hoveyda was only preparing the ground for his own advancement. The intellectual amities, he declared, were all part of his design to "co-opt" the intellectuals into the Pahlavi system.[37] But if we are to believe Al-e Ahmad, we have to afford Hoveyda an unimaginable single-mindedness. Furthermore, we would also have to discount the intelligence, and the power of discernment, of people like Chubak and Hedayat, both famous for avoiding opportunists and sycophants. Most important of all, Hoveyda never tried to pressure Chubak into changing his political views or joining one of the parties with which Hoveyda was throughout these years associated.[38]

Busy as he was during his military service, occupied as he seemed to be finding his way around the unknown territory that was his country, Hoveyda was also beginning his first serious affair with a Persian woman. Her name was Parvin (we only know her first name). Not much is known about their relationship. Those were still the days when in Tehran affairs between unmarried men and women were best kept discreet, if not secret. Though no picture of her has been found, Hoveyda did introduce her to Chubak. Hoveyda also talked about her with his brother, Fereydoun, when he returned to Tehran in 1944. In Chubak's words, she was "decidedly independent and noticeably beautiful. She dressed meticulously and was a cosmopolitan woman with a flair in her demeanor." The relationship lasted for almost two years and seems to have come to an amicable end when in August 1944, Hoveyda received his first assignment from the foreign ministry.

Hoveyda graduating from the Officer's Academy in 1943. This was his first meeting with the shah, who had himself only recently ascended the throne.

The first serious indication that Hoveyda was afforded some undue advantage on account of his vast network of friends and influential family was his appointment to the post of the second secretary of the Iranian Embassy in Paris. Though he was only a junior member of the diplomatic corps, and though nearly all the time he had been at the ministry was spent in the army, his first diplomatic appointment was to the much coveted post in the Paris Mission. Ironically, this assignment might well have been an offer he should have refused.

CHAPTER FIVE

Paris Redux

Good name in man and woman...
Is the immediate jewel of their soul.
—Shakespeare, *Othello*

I
n August 1944, Zein al-Abedin Rahnema was designated Iran's minister plenipotentiary to Paris.[1] During the Nazi occupation of France, Iran closed its embassy in Paris. When World War II ended, the embassy was reopened and Rahnema was named chief of legation. A colorful though controversial figure, Rahnema was the ambitious patriarch of a family of intellectuals. He was a writer of some repute who, later in life, translated the Koran and wrote a biography of the prophet Mohammad. He was also a renowned muck-raking journalist. Hoveyda had met the Rahnema clan in Beirut: he was a close friend of the two sons, and when the father was appointed to the Paris post, Hoveyda was asked to accompany him.[2]

In impoverished post-war Paris, Amir Abbas lived a life of relative luxury. While transportation was a nuisance for most Parisians, the embassy had two cars at its disposal: a big American Buick and a Renault.[3] At least one of the cars would become part of the evidence in a controversy that would eventually enmesh Hoveyda. The work load at the embassy was particularly heavy; the Paris office was not only responsible for all of Iran's diplomatic affairs in France, but it also had to oversee relations

Hoveyda, circa 1945, shortly before his departure for Paris on a diplomatic assignment.

with occupied Germany. Aside from outstanding economic issues between Iran and the Nazi regime, a number of Iranian citizens had been placed in German concentration camps. Furthermore, the embassy was concerned with the flow of Iranian refugees from Germany or German occupied Europe, streaming across the Continent. Diplomats from the Paris office, particularly Hoveyda and Rahnema, made numerous trips to Germany to help resettle these people.[4]

Some of Hoveyda's responsibilities at the embassy also included establishing ties with the French intellectual community. Through Rahnema's connections, he met some of his favorite French writers, including André Malraux, Paul Valéry, and François Mauriac.[5] In the poverty of postwar Paris, the embassy's ability to give lavish parties made it a favorite hangout for some of France's most reputable intellectuals.[6] Ever a man in search of interesting or useful friends, Amir Abbas also cemented some of the most crucial and enduring friendships of his life in this period.

Not long after Hoveyda's appointment to the Paris post, Hassan-Ali Mansur, another recent addition to the foreign ministry roster, arrived in Paris. Scion of an elite political family—one of the renowned "thousand families"—Mansur was at once arrogant and studiously humble. He was handsome and soon developed a reputation as a womanizer.[7] He was also a man of boundless energy, considerable charisma, and high ambition. He read little but had an avid curiosity to learn, impressive powers of oratory, and a deep respect for technocratic expertise. He had a knack for organization, an unfailing touch for public relations, and an innate talent for listening to diverse views and arguments and finding their common threads. For many of the older generation of politicians, he had only contempt. "They are shallow and ignorant," he would often lament in private.[8] In public, he treated them with the due deference they thought they deserved. His own father was one of the more famous members of that older generation. He had been a controversial prime minister, and ministerial appointments were seen almost as a Mansur family heirloom.[9] Amir Abbas had briefly met the young Mansur in Tehran, where they both worked at the foreign ministry. What had begun there as a purely formal and collegial acquaintance would in Paris turn into an intense and intimate lifelong friendship. The catalyst for this change was Fereydoun Hoveyda.

In November 1944, Fereydoun graduated from the French University in Beirut—an affiliate of the University of Lyon in France—with degrees in law and economics. He returned to Iran forthwith and, after passing the requisite entrance exam, joined the foreign ministry. He was assigned the job of managing the ministry's small library.[10] Like his older brother Amir Abbas, he soon developed a reputation for his mastery of foreign languages. Consequently, Fereydoun, though only a novice recruit at the ministry, was entrusted, for a while, with the sensitive task of drafting all the French correspondence of the prime minister, Ahmad Qavam.

Late in March 1945, Hassan-Ali, who was a student intern at the time—such internships were the chosen path for the children of the elite class to enter the diplomatic corps—came to the foreign ministry library, where Fereydoun had been working since December 1944.

Fereydoun and Mansur became close friends in Tehran. It was with Fereydoun's help that Hassan-Ali finished his senior thesis at Tehran University's Faculty of Law and Political Science.[11] By August 1946, both men ended up in Paris: Fereydoun as the secretary of Iran's delegation to the Peace Conference, and Mansur awaiting his first official diplomatic posting. Fereydoun's praise of Mansur roused the interest and curiosity of Amir Abbas. Before long, strong bonds of friendship developed between

Hoveyda leading a group of friends
(Majid Rahnema on his left and Houshang Sharifi on his far left) in Beirut, circa 1945.

the two men. Those who knew Hoveyda well concur that of all his friends, and he certainly had many, Mansur clearly enjoyed the pride of place. With every passing year, the intimacy of their friendship only increased. Within a little more than a decade, their political fates were inseparably entangled, and their emotional lives had turned into a web of enmeshed attractions, projections, and introjections. Fatemeh Soudavar Farmanfarmaian, who knew both men, spoke of "something unique and special about the way Hoveyda responded to Mansur." She tells of a night in 1970, some five years after Mansur's death, when Hoveyda came to a party at her house. "I had invited Hayedeh, his favorite Persian singer," she remembered. "As she began to perform, Hoveyda, who, leaning on a pillow, sat near the performer, asked her to sing 'Sourat Gar-e Naghash Chin' (The Chinese Portrait Artist). No sooner had she begun singing than he turned, damp-eyed, to me and said in a flat and mirthless voice, 'This was Ali's favorite song.'"[12]

A few weeks before meeting Mansur in Paris, Hoveyda had met another man who would also play an important role in his life. His name was Edouard Sablier, a Middle East correspondent for *Le Monde*. Not long after arriving in Paris, Hoveyda—as part of his media relations assignment—had invited Sablier to lunch. In those days, the fate of Azerbaijan had led to something of an international crisis; in retrospect, it has come to be considered one of the first major confrontations in the Cold War.* Hoveyda suggested that Sablier travel to Iran, meet the prime minister, and even visit the rebels in Azerbaijan. He further suggested that the Iranian government would be willing to underwrite all the expenses for the trip and provide "a private plane, a beautiful young translator and access to all parts of the country."[13] Sablier was obviously enthusiastic about the idea, but he informed Hoveyda of *Le Monde*'s policy prohibiting its correspondents from accepting free junkets from foreign governments. The policy, Sablier added, was mercilessly enforced by the journal's stern editor, Hubert Beuve-Méry. "Leave the editor to me," Hoveyda responded.

The next day Amir Abbas somehow convinced Beuve-Méry to make an exception in this case, and Sablier was soon on his way to Iran. In the process of preparing and planning for the trip, Sablier and Hoveyda became "inseparable friends."[14] Throughout the years, the two men would meet regularly: sometimes they vacationed together, and Hoveyda's trips to Paris invariably included a visit with Sablier. The two men shared a passion for music, French culture and literature, and, of course, the world of politics. The last letter Hoveyda ever wrote was addressed to Sablier.

The friendship was also of mutual professional benefit. From his first diplomatic assignment, Hoveyda clearly understood the significant role of the media in modern politics. (If anything, however, he would grow to overestimate its role. Fix the image, he seemed to believe late in his tenure as prime minister, and the problem is fixed.) Beginning with Sablier, Hoveyda was learning the art and craft of media relations. Contrary to most Persian politicians of his generation who knew only the bludgeon

* At the end of World War II, British and American forces left Iran, as stipulated by previous agreements concluded with the Iranian government; the Soviets, however, refused to leave. Furthermore, they helped create a puppet government in Iran's Azerbaijan province.

and the bribe as tools of media control, Hoveyda had a more complicated, modern sense of the media. He learned how to keep the media happy. Evidence of his savvy approach, and early hints of a utilitarian bent even in his intimate friendships, can be seen in his dealings with Sablier. On more than one occasion, Hoveyda would provide Sablier with detailed briefs about problems and prospective policies in Iran. "Some of my articles," Sablier confessed, "were in reality all Hoveyda's ideas shaped by me into an essay."[15] Thus, Hoveyda not only rewarded Sablier for his friendship but also through him used the power of the media to implement his own goals and fight some of his political battles.

Sablier's biggest scoop as a journalist began with a tip from Hoveyda. In September 1957, when Hoveyda was working at the Iranian Embassy in Turkey, he learned of a KGB operation in which a Turkish mail boat had been sunk in order to steal the highly confidential American diplomatic dispatches on board. Prior to Sablier's interview with the Turkish prime minister, Hoveyda enigmatically suggested that Sablier ask about the sunken mail boat. Hoveyda's hint was all that Sablier needed to doggedly pursue, and eventually break, the story that came to be known as the "Henderson Affair."[16]

But in Paris, long before this affair and a few months after their initial meeting, as Hoveyda and Sablier sat on the steps of Sacré Coeur Amir Abbas talked of his plans for the future and offered a promise: "I shall one day become Iran's prime minister, and on that day, I will invite you to come for a visit."[17]

IN MID-1945, HOVEYDA'S DREAMS OF A GLORIOUS political future suddenly turned into a nightmare from which he never entirely awoke. Zein al-Abedin Rahnema, Iran's minister plenipotentiary to France, and some of his staff at the embassy were embroiled in a major scandal. Financial greed was at the heart of the matter. The havoc of war had led to the loss of many a fortune in Paris. A number of the more prudent Frenchmen, however, had succeeded in surreptitiously transferring their fortunes to the safety of Swiss banks. Once the war ended, some of these people attempted to bring back their stashed fortunes without paying the often exorbitant taxes and duties at the border. Easy money could be made by anyone who could cross the border without inspection. Diplomats, protected by immunities, including the right to cross borders without a search of their personal belongings, thus became perfect candidates for the lucrative job of couriers of contraband currency and gold. A number of diplomats, from a variety of countries, seem to have succumbed to the temptation but it was Hoveyda who suffered the consequences for their lapse of judgment. The "Paris Story," which began with an anonymous letter, became something of a permanent blemish on Hoveyda's reputation and haunted him for the rest of his life. In 1979, when he was fighting for his life in a Revolutionary Tribunal in the new Islamic Republic of Iran, charges stemming from the "Paris Story" figured prominently in the indictment against him.*

On June 4, 1945, the French foreign ministry received an unsigned, four-page, single-spaced letter marred by typographical and syntactical errors, and a halting style that betrayed its author's lack of facility with the French language. It described, with authoritative detail, the work of a ring of smugglers who used the cover of the Iranian embassies in Paris and Bern to engage in the illegal traffic of gold and foreign currencies. The smugglers used the "diplomatique pouch" and cars that had diplomatic license plates—and were thus immune to searches at the border—to transfer millions of francs, gold, and other foreign currency between France and

---

* I knew that the only way I could navigate my way around the malignant rumors and malicious lies that had become the "Paris Story," the only way I could seriously examine the unsubstantiated allegations of the indictment, was to consult the archives at the French foreign ministry. But when on March 12, 1999, I visited the archives at Quai d'Orsay, I realized much to my chagrin that the most important documents were in a "file closed for sixty years, to be opened in 2007."

I sought the help of Isabelle Nathan, the archivist in charge of the file, and explained to her the nature of my project and the reasons for my singular need to consult the "dossier reservé." She kindly offered to try and read the documents in the file and let me know whether Hoveyda's name appeared in them. I told her that the serious nature of the charges against him, their prominent place in the indictment, and finally the conspiratorial proclivity so commonly found in discussions about Iran would render any judgment based on her words less than entirely reliable. Any conclusive verdict, I told her, would have to rely on a direct and thorough examination of all the pertinent documents. She suggested that I write a letter to the foreign ministry and ask that an exception—or in her words a "dérogation"—be made in this case. So, I submitted such a request, and on June 15, 1999, I received a note from Louis Amigues, the director of the archives, informing me that "by dispensation of the law of archive 3 Janvier 1979" I will be permitted to consult "Volume no. 4 de la Serie Asie 1944-1955-Iran"; in other words, I had access to the file where the most important documents about the scandal could be found. But I was also informed that I could not obtain photocopies of the documents. The narrative that follows is entirely based on the official records found in the French foreign ministry archives. In almost every important element of the story, the truth turns out to be in sharp contrast to what till now has been the accepted wisdom, and the common lore, about Hoveyda's "mysterious life in Paris." Even some of those who believed that Hoveyda, by the sheer nature of his honest, cautious, and calculating character, could not have engaged in illegal traffic of any sort nevertheless harbored a lingering sense that "something happened in Paris."

Switzerland. A number of alleged accomplices were mentioned in the letter. Rahnema was directly implicated as a key figure in the operation. The anonymous writer suggested that the foreign ministry should try to find out how Rahnema could afford his lavish lifestyle in Paris. His meager salary, the letter suggested, could not support the millions of francs he spent every month.[18] Though the list of names of alleged traffickers in the letter is long, Hoveyda is nowhere mentioned. The identity of the letter writer is also never divulged in the entire file.

The French foreign ministry had by then already received police reports about the possibility of illegal activities by Rahnema and a number of other Iranian diplomats. Based on these reports and the anonymous letter, on July 30, 1945, the French foreign minister George Bidault informed his government's ambassador in Tehran that "I will confirm that in reality, Mr. Rahnema, because of activities that he seemed to have pursued for personal gain, is no longer a persona grata…for the French government."[19] On a more practical level, on August 2, 1945, the French foreign ministry asked the police to begin a formal investigation into the alleged illegal activities of the Iranian Embassy. In a letter to the Paris police chief, the foreign minister emphasized the fact that the "comings and goings…between France and Switzerland" of some of Iran's diplomats had raised the suspicion of the police even before the receipt of the anonymous letter.[20]

In the meantime, something of a small crisis was developing between Iran and France.[*] France wanted to get rid of Rahnema, while Iran, for reasons not entirely clear to the French officials, insisted on keeping him in his post. The two sides agreed on one point: they both wanted to keep the story confidential, hoping to minimize its political damage.

On August 20, 1945, the French ambassador informed his government that he had reached an agreement with Iran on two important pending matters. Both sides, he wrote, agreed to change the level of diplomatic ties

---

[*] Even before the French government's attempt to have Rahnema dismissed from his post, another minor diplomatic row had developed between Iran and France. On July 19, 1945, a French magazine, *Nuit et Jour,* published an article claiming that every year, twelve million dollars was diverted from the Iranian government's oil revenues into the private accounts of the shah and his family. The Iranian government and its embassy objected to the article. On August 8, 1945, the Iranian legation in Paris sent a note to George Bidault, the French foreign minister, asking that he "take any measure necessary" to stop such attacks. The note bears Rahnema's signature. In light of Hoveyda's assignment at the embassy, it is more than likely that the letter was actually written by him. See Télégramme Personnelle, French Foreign Ministry, Archive Diplomatique, Serie Asie, 1944-1955, no. 781.

between the two countries from the current less powerful position of minister plenipotentiary to the higher level of ambassador. Furthermore, Iran promised that "Mr. Rahnema will not be kept in Paris. There are several other candidates. It seems that Mr. Sepahbodi [then Iran's acting foreign minister] has saved the position for himself."[21]

While these negotiations were proceeding, on September 4, 1945, the chief of the Paris police sent the result of his department's investigation back to the French foreign minister. The police declared that the charges made in the anonymous letter were by and large accurate. The embassy car, "license number 6200RN6," had been used on numerous occasions for transferring illegal currencies and gold across the border. Hard evidence for the crime had been impossible to find, the police declared, because "we cannot search their diplomatique valises...nor can we search their cars." The report goes on to add that every time such searches had been attempted, the culprits have brandished their diplomatic passports and successfully aborted the search.[22] A number of people in the Paris and Bern embassies were, according to the police, involved in the trafficking of gold and foreign currency. Furthermore, the police declared that based on "reliable sources," there was no doubt that the minister plenipotentiary, Rahnema, "knew of these activities and benefited from them."[23]

The four-page police report detailed the activities of the main culprits. Aside from those already named in the anonymous letter, the police also implicated a number of other Iranian citizens and officials.[24] Again, Amir Abbas Hoveyda is not mentioned, directly or indirectly. Instead, the report does point out a shady figure named Amir-Houshang Davalou, who later crossed paths with Hoveyda often and on at least one occasion caused him considerable trouble. During the war years, the report indicates, Davalou had been a protégé of General Jesser, a member of the German high command in France. Though Davalou had procured young and beautiful girls for the Nazi general, he was nevertheless arrested by the German police for illegal trafficking in gold and for writing bad checks. He was also one of the main culprits in the new Paris-Bern ring.[25]

Almost a quarter of a century later, in 1971, when Hoveyda was the prime minister, the same Davalou, by then notoriously rich and corrupt, and rumored to be in charge of procuring young girls for the shah, was arrested in Switzerland for possession of opium. Rather than have Davalou stand trial in a Swiss court, as the law required, the shah whisked him out of the country in his official jet. The result was, as expected, a major diplomatic and public-relations fiasco. When Hoveyda heard of the incident, he had the temerity to suggest to the shah that maybe he should have allowed Davalou to stay and stand trial in Geneva. To the shah, the mere suggestion was insolent; as punishment, he denied Hoveyda an audience for about two weeks.[26] Davalou escaped punishment only after vast sums of Iran's new-found wealth were spent on legal and extra-legal expenses—such as free vacations for Swiss officials to Iran—in his defense.[27] In 1945, though he was, according to the police report, one of the main culprits in the smuggling ring, he was somehow spared in the media frenzy that soon developed about the "Paris Story."

Newspapers and weekly magazines in Tehran had a field day covering the events in Paris. For Persian journalists of the time, freedom of the press was a new experience. Of the 464 periodicals that were published in 1947, only forty-one had been in circulation at the time of the Allied invasion of Iran in 1942. Furthermore, "the majority of the papers became mouthpieces for the various political forces present in Iran, to be used for publicizing their program or, more often, to attack opponents and their organization."[28] The ethos of responsible journalism had not yet taken root in the country. Libel laws were weak and practically unenforceable. The boundaries between investigative journalism and partisan scandal-mongering were neither clearly understood nor heeded. Some of the less scrupulous journalists even used the power of the print media as an overt tool for *chantage* (blackmail). Refusal to pay would unleash the journal's damaging, albeit libelous, wrath against a public figure, while the right financial recompense could just as easily purchase their silence. Indeed, "the most violent, critical, and vituperative scandal sheets received the most attention."[29]

The "Paris Story" was the perfect grist to the mill of these "scandal sheets." Even some of the leading Persian newspapers began their scathing editorials about events in the Paris scandal with rhetorical questions like, "What is going on in our embassy in Paris?" Others asked whether it was true that at French airports, Iranian travelers were subjected to special searches and French authorities no longer honored the validity of Persian diplomatic passports.[30] As the coverage, often mixing rumors and facts, continued to grow, the Iranian government, in a desperate attempt at damage control, officially demanded that the French authorities "declare that no member of [Iran's] embassy has ever been arrested."[31] Such an announcement would have certainly been true to the letter of the law but deceptive in its spirit. No Iranian diplomat had been arrested only because no diplomat *could* be arrested on account of the immunity they enjoyed. Precisely at the time that the Iranian government asked for such an announcement, some members of its embassy in Paris were under police watch, and the head of the legation himself had been declared a persona non grata and sent back to Tehran. In the meantime, Hoveyda, unaware that the scandal's collateral damage would soon hurt his future prospects, continued his work at the embassy, and spent most of his spare time with his brother Fereydoun, Mansur and Entezam. He also kept something of a regular correspondence with Sadeq Hedayat, sending him some of the newest books published in France. He was hoping that the whole "Paris Story" would soon die down, particularly with Rahnema's return to Iran.[32]

But Rahnema's recall to Tehran did not end the scandal. In a mysterious turn of events, after the French had reached an agreement with the Iranian government about replacing Rahnema, and after Rahnema had returned to Iran ostensibly for that very purpose, in July 1946, he again returned to Paris with great fanfare aboard the first Tehran-Paris flight. He bore a gift and a letter from Prime Minister Qavam for the French prime minister. In the letter, Qavam asked his French counterpart to accept Rahnema as Iran's ambassador.[33] As a token of appreciation, he sent along a fine Persian rug. The French officials were flabbergasted. The only conclusion they could draw was that officials in Iran had been bribed by Rahnema. In a note prepared for the French cabinet, dated July 24, 1946, foreign ministry sources suggested that both Prime Minister Qavam and the shah himself had received some payment from Rahnema. The shah, they claimed on two different occasions, was promised a private plane by Rahnema, and Qavam had, according to the reports, received a number of gifts.[34] Both suggestions seem rather improbable.

In spite of the rug and the letter, the French government refused to change its mind and insisted that Iran name another ambassador. Ultimately Qavam submitted to the French demand but still insisted that the matter be kept confidential.[35] Rahnema, too, was rather keen on keeping a lid on the story. But as he waited for the arrival of the new designated ambassador, he made numerous trips across the French-Swiss border, further angering the French officials.[36] With the agreement to keep his dismissal a secret,

Rahnema escaped unscathed from the crisis that was to no small extent his own doing. Hoveyda's fortune was altogether different.

In the whole voluminous French foreign ministry file on what one official called the "Rahnema saga"—312 pages in the section of the files closed till 2007 and a little more than 300 pages in the other files—there is not a single mention of any role played by Amir Abbas Hoveyda. His name only comes up in the Persian articles that were at the time translated by the French Embassy in Tehran. The name of his brother, Fereydoun, only appears once, and then only in conjunction with a request by Iran to allow him access to the archives of the French foreign ministry so that he could prepare a history of relations between Iran and France. If, indeed, Hoveyda had played any role in the affair, if he had been a member of the infamous ring, his status as a diplomat would have ensured his mention in both the French foreign ministry files and the Paris police reports. Nevertheless, in an enigmatic turn of events, once Persian newspapers began to write about the scandal, while no mention of Rahnema was ever made, Hoveyda's name began to appear in association with the alleged illegal activities of the embassy in Paris. The suspicious silence about Rahnema might well have been because, as the French Embassy in Tehran implied, he and his supporters had a hand in creating the whole press campaign.[37] Furthermore, an unwritten journalistic pact to protect their own peers might have inhibited Iranian journalists from sullying the reputation of Rahnema, who was considered one of Iran's senior journalists. What is less clear is why Hoveyda's name came to occupy such a prominent place in the narrative of the scandal.

The first time Hoveyda's name is mentioned in conjunction with the Paris saga is in the February 3, 1947, issue of *Mardom*, the official organ of the Tudeh Party.* It claims that some fifty Iranians were arrested in Paris on charges of smuggling. The list includes Hoveyda and "Hassan Ali Mansur, the son of the governor general of Azerbaijan." The article goes on to add that French officials asked the Iranian government to find out where Amir Abbas Hoveyda found the money to purchase his summer home in the suburbs of Paris. This part of the article is similar to certain unusual segments of the June 4, 1945, anonymous letter that in a sense

---

* Ebrahim Golestan was at the time the editor of *Mardom*. He says he has no recollection of how the story originally made its way onto the pages of the newspaper. Ebrahim Golestan, personal correspondence, 24 January 2000.

triggered the whole scandal. There the author suggested that the foreign ministry should try to find out how Rahnema supported his lavish lifestyle in Paris. Here *Mardom* claims that the French foreign ministry inquired into the sources of Hoveyda's assets and properties. The similarity between the anonymous letter and the *Mardom* article raises several intriguing questions. How did the Tudeh Party know of the contents of a highly confidential anonymous letter to the French foreign ministry? Did the party have a role in writing the letter? And finally, why did *Mardom* choose to omit the letter's clear reference to Rahnema and instead replace it with Hoveyda's name?* We do not know the answers to these crucial questions. What is less ambiguous is that by February 1947, when *Mardom* published its story about Hoveyda, it had already developed a reputation as a Stalinist newspaper, and its claims were usually taken with a large grain of salt.

The article, however, was reproduced in a popular weekly magazine called *Khandaniha*, Iran's answer to the *Reader's Digest*. In later years, as the sibilant whisper of "Hoveyda's mysterious past" turned into a recurrent refrain, the source invariably quoted was the more respected *Khandaniha*; somehow, any reference to *Mardom*, as the more dubious original source of the story, was erased from the collective memory.

One can only guess why the Tudeh Party chose to pick on Hoveyda and Mansur. It is certainly reasonable to suggest that he was used as a scapegoat. One possible key to the riddle can be the overall alignment of forces in Iran at the time. Qavam and his foreign minister, Sepahbodi, were by 1947 clearly at the top of the Tudeh Party's enemy list. The party's short-lived attempt to join a coalition cabinet with Qavam had ended in acrimony. Furthermore, Qavam's role in pushing the Soviets out of Iran had certainly not endeared him to the Soviet government, and to the Tudeh Party as its always obedient tool. Hoveyda's family relations with Sepahbodi were matters of public knowledge. Some deputies in the parliament had accused Sepahbodi of nepotism with regard to the Hoveyda brothers. Could it then be that the media attack on Hoveyda and Mansur, whose father was a member of the Qavam administration, was at least partially an attempt to damage Qavam

---

* The French Embassy in Tehran kept a close watch of the media coverage of the scandal and translated some of the most crucial articles into French for the consideration of the foreign ministry officials in Paris. They sent back translations of articles in *Mardom* (3 February 1947), *Mihan* (4 January 1947), *Aras* (20 January, 21 January, and 30 January 1947), *Akhbar-e Iran* (29 January 1947), *Setareh* (24 January, 1 February, and 5 January 1947), *Mard-e Emrouz* (5 February 1947), and *Kayhan* (4 February 1947).

and Sepahbodi? Unless the Tudeh Party archives are opened to public scrutiny, we cannot know the answer to this question.

Sadeq Hedayat, who had been following the scandal from Tehran, had a different answer to the riddle. In a letter to his friend, Hassan Shahid-Nourai, he writes: "It is strange that the newspaper *Mardom* has reported the arrest of a few people, including Hoveyda. Clearly the person who had written the story had a particular grudge against Hoveyda. Maybe he wants to replace him. The stupid explanation he had provided can only come from the mind of a genuine Shiite.* In today's edition, they have published a note retracting the [Hoveyda] story. *(Voir ci Joint)*."[38] In another letter, Hedayat, who was actively courted by the Tudeh Party, writes of his anger and dismay at the party for its role in the affair. In a language uniquely his own, combining vulgar Persian slang with refined French expressions, he declares that the organs of the party "have lost their timbre and have created a brouhaha. I hate these kinds of things. It is as if our lives are like a barrel of shit, and we have to eat it spoon by spoon and praise what we eat every time."[39]

From Hedayat's letters, we also learn how the Tudeh Party soon came to retract its story about Hoveyda. Once Shahid-Nourai received Hedayat's notes about the scandal, he immediately sent back a telegram completely exonerating Hoveyda. In a letter dated February 13, 1947, Hedayat acknowledges the receipt of the telegram and offers a ringing endorsement of Hoveyda by writing, "I know that Hoveyda lives in a rented apartment in Paris, and most important of all, I know his character, and I know he is not a smuggling Shiite type...After I received your telegram, I had no doubt that all the rumors about him were false. I went to the offices of *Mardom* and blasted them...Today, *Mardom* again retracted the story. I also showed the telegram to [Jahangir] Tafazoli, and he too published a retraction of the rumors [of Hoveyda's arrest] in the newspaper *Aras*."[40]

In 1966, when Hoveyda chose to publish portions of his Paris diaries, he made no allusions, direct or indirect, to the "Paris Story." Apparently, he hoped to bank on the cleansing power of time; silence, he hoped, would be

---

* Hedayat is referring to the false claim that the French government had asked how Hoveyda could afford to buy a villa. In another letter to Shahid-Nourai, Hedayat notes that the French foreign ministry would, under no circumstance, pry into the wealth of a foreign diplomat. See Sadeq Hedayat, *Nameha* [Letters], comp. by Mohammad Baharlou (Tehran, 1999), 391. Shiite was a derogatory term Hedayat used to refer to Persians.

his best response to the cascade of rumors and innuendoes. Instead, he offered praise for Rahnema as a man of high culture and erudition. He wrote of Rahnema's facility with the poetry of Hafez, of his ability to entertain, and to attract, "like a butterfly," the beautiful ladies of Paris.[41]

Yet, his strategy of silence ultimately failed. Indeed, in spite of a terse announcement by the Iranian foreign ministry in 1947 that there was no truth to the allegations against Hoveyda, in spite of retractions by *Mardom* and *Atash*—a Tehran weekly journal—which wrote from Paris that "neither of the two Hoveyda brothers had been arrested," and in spite of the unusual efforts by Sadeq Hedayat, a shadow of the scandal continued to follow Hoveyda throughout the remainder of his long political life.[42] If in 1946, the web of rumors and allegations were only a minor irritation to him, in 1979, the same retracted rumor of illegal trade in contraband currency was somehow transmogrified into article fifteen of the Islamic Tribunal's indictment against Hoveyda.[43] The tribunal accused him of "direct participation along with Hassan-Ali Mansur in smuggling heroin into France."* The Islamic court's reliance on these unsubstantiated charges was both a token of its reckless disregard for due process of law and a testimony to the fact that in the world of politics, image and perception, as well as rumor and gossip, are often as important as facts and reality.

---

* The indictment is fully discussed in chapters 15 &16.

CHAPTER SIX

The Wandering Years

Woe unto him who has no country.
—Nietzsche

H oveyda's eventful life in Paris came to an end in early 1947, when he was assigned to Iran's new consular office in Stuttgart. From Paris, he had often traveled to Germany on behalf of the Iranian government to negotiate the release of some factory equipment Iran had purchased during the Nazi era. Reza Shah had wanted to build a steel mill in Iran, and Nazi Germany, in its attempt to find a foothold in the Persian Gulf and the Middle East, turned out to be the only industrialized nation willing to sell Iran the requisite technology. The advent of World War II had meant that in spite of the deal Iran never received the equipment. Hoveyda's assignment was to retrieve the machinery for which Iran had already paid.

During these trips, Hoveyda's innate curiosity led to an interest in Nazi Germany's program to develop the atomic bomb. After some cursory research, and many casual interviews, he wrote an unsolicited report for the Iranian Foreign Ministry, outlining the history of Germany's unsuccessful search for the new superweapon. When the report reached Tehran, it created something of a stir and helped consolidate Hoveyda's reputation as a learned and ambitious diplomat.[1]

Mansur, Entezam, and Hoveyda in Paris, shortly before the three were sent on assignment to Germany in 1947.

After the Allied victory in Europe, the Iranian government decided to establish a consular office in occupied Germany. Hitherto, all matters pertaining to Germany had been handled from the Paris Legation. Abdollah Entezam, a seasoned diplomat, was appointed as the chief of the new office. He asked that his protégé, Hoveyda, accompany him.[2] When he heard of his new assignment, Hoveyda was, in his own words, shocked that he would have to leave Paris. "I was so distressed," he writes, "that I spent a sleepless night." But at the same time, he was looking forward to working for Entezam.[3]

Entezam was a man of formidable intellect, with a variety of interests. He and his brother, Nasrollah, were both career diplomats with sterling reputations. Abdollah had known Hoveyda's father as a colleague.[4] By 1945, he had already served in some of the most important posts in the foreign ministry, including a term, in the late 1920s, as first secretary of the Iranian Mission in the United States. In his cultural tastes and affinities, Entezam was, like Hoveyda, a Francophile. They were both omnivorous readers. Entezam's reading habits were even more eclectic than Hoveyda's—everything from esoteric books on Persian Sufism to the French translation of the *Reader's Digest*. Like Hoveyda he also enjoyed classical music. Beethoven was a favorite of theirs in the Stuttgart days.[5] At the same time, unlike Hoveyda, he was very much at home in the realm of Persian letters. Entezam also had a reputation of being a *Darvish*, a Sufi who advocates simple nobility in personal behavior and a disdain for worldly riches. By all accounts, he remained a *Darvish* to the end of his life.

Entezam's political persuasions were even more complicated than his intellectual interests. He had a reputation as a man of impeccable integrity; he was fiercely independent and unusually frank. In the mid-1950s, when the shah began to demand absolute obedience from all those around him and as a token of this submission expected everyone to kiss the royal hand at each audience, Entezam was one of very few people in government who refused to comply.[6] He was also a Freemason, and in 1960, apparently at his behest, Hoveyda joined the Foroughi Lodge, newly created in 1960, with Entezam as its grand master.[7] For more than a century now, Freemasonry has played a much contested role in the Iranian political landscape. In the lay Iranian's perception, Freemasons were the bane of Iranian politics and a dangerous clandestine brotherhood committed to serving the interests of foreign powers, especially the British. For many politicians, however, to become a Freemason was deemed a fast track to power and privilege.[8]

It is not clear why—other than the desire to get ahead in politics or follow in his mentor's footsteps—Hoveyda chose to join the Masonic lodge. He must have known that in the world of Iranian politics, where sons are often held responsible for the sins of their fathers, his own Masonic ties coupled with rumors of his father's close British connections could compromise any chance he had of cultivating the image of an independent man, bent on advocating modernity in Iran.

In spite of some evidence that once Hoveyda became prime minister he no longer attended the regular meetings of the lodge, the decision to join the Freemasons eventually cost him dearly.[9] Indeed in 1968, some of Hoveyda's enemies—specifically Court Minister Asadollah Alam, and his ally, General Nasiri, the head of SAVAK—worked behind the scenes to arrange for the publication of a controversial book about the history of Freemasonry in Iran. Written by Ismail Ra'in, the book included a long list of alleged Iranian Masons. SAVAK, at the suggestion of Ra'in, had monitored the mail and the phone lines of an important official of the Masonic lodges, gathering a great deal of information.[10] Alam had been an early champion of the book's publication. It would, as he hoped, tarnish the image of all his foes. He had apparently even suggested that the book be used as a text in the history department at Tehran University.[11] Hoveyda is mentioned in the book as a Freemason, while Entezam is listed as a grand master.[12] Hoveyda's friends at SAVAK, particularly Parviz Sabeti, had been against the book's publication. Nevertheless, neither Sabeti nor anyone else gave Hoveyda any advance warning about the book's existence and imminent release—a fact that caused him much dismay. Furthermore, SAVAK apparently used an affiliated printer to ensure that the Freemasons did not get advance notice of the book's impending publication and did not use their formidable power to stop its distribution.[13] The book's eventual publication caused something of a bombshell in Tehran. Everyone was listed by first and last name, except for Hoveyda, whose last name only was given. Of course, no one was fooled. Indeed the glaring absence of a first name only attracted attention to the unusual entry on the list.

The book further claimed that Hassan-Ali Mansur had also tried to join the Freemasons, only to have his application to the Homayoun Lodge rejected. The rejection, it was suggested, accounted for Mansur's subsequent harsh words about Masons.[14] If the Rahnema episode introduced Hoveyda to the "Byzantine world" of Iranian politics, his decision to join the Foroughi Lodge entangled him in one of the more bizarre episodes of the internecine wars that often plagued politics in Pahlavi Iran.

In his *Diaries*, Alam writes, with obvious glee, about how upon the book's publication everyone at court, including the king and queen, was talking about its contents; they wondered how almost the entire upper echelon of the Iranian government seemed to have been Masons. For the shah, whose "suspicion of the British" was, according to Alam, "quite incredible," Ra'in's book only confirmed his worst fears.[15] Alam further claims that the shah ordered him to investigate whether it was true that Hoveyda had arranged for the arrest of Ra'in. Even the American Embassy became interested and reported on the controversy, confirming the suspicions of Alam's role in the book's publication.[16] The embassy further reports that "in apparent retort" to the publication of the book, "a counter-list of so-called CIA agents in Iran was put out."[17]

But in postwar Paris, long before the embarrassing Masonic controversy, Entezam's home was a kind of cultural club for many of the Persians who lived in the French capital. He was clearly the elder statesman to a group of young Iranians that included Hoveyda. Entezam would often hold forth on a wide variety of topics to an audience awed by the versatility of his mind. He would talk of everything from a cure for the common cold to the intricate labyrinth of meaning in Sufi texts. Amir Abbas was clearly impressed with Entezam's erudition and experience, while Entezam found in Hoveyda a man full of promise and energy. Entezam was at the time almost fifty years old, and he seems to have adopted Amir Abbas as something of a surrogate son.[18] Hoveyda thus had found the patron he had sought. The close bond of friendship that had begun to develop between the two men in Paris, turned into lifelong mentorship in Stuttgart. For the rest of Hoveyda's life, even during the days when he was prime minister and Entezam a man fallen from the shah's grace and forced into retirement, Hoveyda still called him either *patron*, or *arbab*, the French and Persian for "boss." Throughout his tenure as prime minister, Hoveyda invited Entezam to a variety of high-level boards and committees. Entezam, however, was never interested in amassing a fortune, even at the height of Iran's economic boom. Nor was his lifestyle expensive to maintain. He "lived in a two-room flat on a modest government pension" and died there in 1985. In his obituary, the *Times* of London wrote that Entezam was known for his "quirkiness, brilliance, and absolute integrity."[19]

The simplicity of his taste was even evident in occupied Germany, where he lived an almost ascetic life, while Hoveyda and Mansur—who at Hoveyda's behest had also been assigned to the new Stuttgart office—lived like a pair of bon vivants.[20] Much of Stuttgart had been ravaged by the war. Housing was hard to find. Allied Forces had control over all empty or confiscated buildings in Germany. Furthermore, before the consular office could be opened there, not only did the Allied governments have to agree, but they also had to allocate the necessary office and residential space. France and Britain informed Iran that no space could be found in the territories under their occupation. The Americans, however, agreed to find a suitable location and soon offered the Iranian government two spacious houses in occupied Stuttgart. A large three-floor house was set aside as both the consular office and Entezam's residence. Another house, with four bedrooms, was to be used as the staff residence. Both buildings came fully, and beautifully, furnished in antiques; both had once been residences of high-ranking Nazi government officials; both had been confiscated by the Allied Forces at the end of World War II.[21]

Mansur and Hoveyda thus became housemates. A German woman was hired to cook and take care of household chores. Hoveyda soon bought a dark blue American Chevrolet. To the amusement of the more reclusive Entezam, Hoveyda cavorted around town in his fancy, new automobile. The cook, the car, and most important of all their ability to shop at the American Military Commissary gave their life a semblance of luxury. Furthermore, a large part of the adult male German population had been killed or maimed by the war, or was languishing in POW camps. The able-bodied survivors left behind were thoroughly demoralized by the German defeat. Thus the two easy-living young Iranian men found themselves in a rather privileged position.

Though, in later years in Tehran, Hoveyda would be described by one of his assistants as neither "a pansy…[nor particularly] oversexed," and it was Mansur's affairs of the heart, particularly before he was married, which were both legend and legion, their roles in the Stuttgart days were reversed.[22] While Hoveyda parlayed his life of luxury into a series of brief affairs with several German women, Mansur was, for the whole duration of his stay, involved with one young Fräulein. None of Hoveyda's affairs seem to have lasted long, however. A picture of one plump and young German woman was the only record of these affairs. It was included in Mansur's album of pictures, and when he got married, he left it with Hoveyda, lest his wife, Farideh, find the pictures and grow jealous of her husband's past peccadilloes. Talk of the German woman's picture, and reference to her rotund physiognomy became a subject of light banter between Hoveyda and his wife, Laila.[23] *Koon gondeh* (fat ass) was what they had called this Stuttgart indiscretion of Hoveyda's. Like Baron de Clapique, the literary idol of his youth, Hoveyda had always been polite and deferential to women but seemed, at the same time, to have been incapable of having serious, long-term relations with them—except of course as friends.

The Stuttgart days appear, in retrospect, the most sexually active period in Hoveyda's life. As his power grew, his sexual appetites seem to have
accordingly diminished. *Tofiq*, Iran's preeminent satirical journal, had an
inkling of this early in Hoveyda's tenure as prime minister. On the front
page of an issue coinciding with the fourth year of Hoveyda's appointment as premier, there is a cartoon of him, noticeably overweight, a pipe
in his drooling mouth, a cane instead of a sword dangling from the side of
his protruding belly; he is clutching a young, coquettish, big-bosomed,
thin-waisted, miniskirted, fishnet-stockinged, high-booted, fully coifed
girl called "Miss Premier." Hoveyda, fully attired in the embroidered ministerial jacket worn on official ceremonies in Iran, is beseeching an equally
drooling cleric to read the marriage vows so he can join "Miss Premier" in
eternal matrimony.

The "Miss Premier" cartoon from Tofiq.

In Stuttgart, Mansur was considered the junior and worked under Hoveyda's supervision. Yet in spite of this bureaucratic hierarchy, at this early stage of their relationship, the two men treated each other as equals. Somehow, over the next ten years, the dynamics of the relationship began to change. Hoveyda would become, at least in the public perception, not an equal but a subordinate. Many of Hoveyda's friends, and a few of the foreign diplomats who knew both men, thought Mansur the clear inferior to Hoveyda in intellectual caliber and political savvy. Stuart Rockwell, who in the early 1960s held the rank of minister at the American Embassy in Tehran and is blamed by Alam for having been instrumental in bringing Mansur to power, now says:* "I did not have a high opinion of Mansur. He was not my idea of a great intellect. He was not particularly profound or remarkable. He knew a lot of people but was not an expert in any field." On the other hand, Rockwell believes that Hoveyda stood out as "an affable, well-rounded man. There was always a twinkle in his eyes."[24]

It is in light of this kind of assessment that many of Hoveyda's friends have been puzzled by the dynamics of his relationship with Mansur and how, and why, Mansur emerged as the more dominant.[25] A key to this riddle might be that, in Stuttgart, Mansur had met John McCloy. McCloy was a powerful man in the American foreign policy establishment. He was assistant secretary of war during World War II and was later named military governor and high commissioner for Germany. Upon his return to the U.S. he took over the reins of Chase Manhattan Bank. After meeting McCloy, Mansur often boasted to both Amir Abbas and Fereydoun Hoveyda of his "contacts" with the Americans. As the years went by, he would confide in the Hoveyda brothers about his "connections," about his attempts to "keep the Americans informed of what is going on."[26] Even when he was only a junior member of Iran's diplomatic corps, his ambitions often seemed dreamily grandiose. Nothing short of a prime minister's job would satisfy him.[27]

---

* In his *Diaries*, Alam claims that on the night of parliamentary elections in 1963, Mansur called him from Rockwell's house "and begged me to order that" he be declared the representative elected with the highest number of votes. "He was really the lackey of the Americans," Alam writes of Mansur. Alam didn't much like Rockwell either. On occasion he would call him "that son of a dog." See Asadollah Alam, *Yadashtha-ye Alam* [Alam's Diaries], ed. by Alinaghi Alikhani, vol. 2 (Bethesda, 1993), 127. Rockwell indicates that Alam's claim about Mansur's call from his house is "absolutely not true." Stuart Rockwell, interviewed by author, 23 May 1999. He further indicates that he finds Alam to have been "rather duplicitous, since all through the times I knew him, he pretended to have very good and friendly relations with me."

Aside from the work at the legation in Stuttgart, Hoveyda and Mansur often traveled to Paris for leisure. By then, Fereydoun Hoveyda had joined the staff of the Iranian Embassy in Paris. He had also become emotionally involved with Mansur's younger sister, Touri. In 1949, the two married in a simple ceremony; Mansur and Amir Abbas were both present.[28] Family ties were now added to the strong bonds of friendship between the two men. And the whirligig of time would only further enmesh the two men in their love lives and political trajectories.

While Entezam's patronage had clearly helped Hoveyda rise rapidly up the ladder of Iran's diplomatic corps, beginning in 1948, events in Tehran and Paris did not augur well for the young protégé. In 1948, Sepahbodi was dismissed from his post as Iran's ambassador to France. In 1950, with his term in Stuttgart finished, Hoveyda went back to Iran. Once again the country he was returning to was experiencing a profound period of change and crisis. For a few weeks, Rajab-Ali Mansur, Hassan-Ali's father, was named prime minister. However, Mohammad Mosaddeq was unambiguously the man of the hour; he had reshaped the political landscape with his single-minded determination to defy Britain and nationalize Iranian oil. In his disdain for organized political parties, in his penchant for populism, Mosaddeq became the rallying point for a loosely structured organization of parties and personalities that called itself the National Front. It would remain an important presence in Iranian politics for the next four decades, even though the Mosaddeq legacy was its only political dowry. The National Front would play a marginal role in many of the important phases in Hoveyda's life.

Along with Mosaddeq, a politically astute and experienced cleric named Ayatollah Abolqassem Kashani had also emerged as a key figure in the tumultuous politics of the period. He had begun as Mosaddeq's ally, but after a while, tensions had developed between the two men. At the same time, Kashani was the spiritual guide to an Islamic terrorist group that called itself the *Fada'iyan-e Islam* (Devotees of Islam). In the late 1940s, the group began a campaign of terror against secular intellectuals and politicians. The remnants of the same group would, fifteen years later, assassinate Hassan-Ali Mansur. By then they had chosen Ayatollah Khomeini as their spiritual leader. Sadegh Khalkhali, who many years later came to be known as the "Hanging Judge," was one of the group's more notorious sympathizers.

In 1950, the Tudeh Party was also at the height of its power. It had attracted a large number of intellectuals to its ranks. Early in the 1940s, it had participated in elections and won eight seats in the parliament. But a few years later, when an attempt was made on the shah's life, the party was banned due to its alleged role in the assassination plot. The ban was hardly enforced; it only provided the party with the cachet of being an underground, persecuted group. Communist power in the labor unions and in a number of front organizations was on the rise. The party had even begun to create a covert and powerful network of army officers sympathetic to its cause.

It was to these highly dynamic and changing circumstances that Hoveyda returned home in 1950. His first assignment at the Foreign Ministry was to be the assistant director of the public relations office. It was a tedious job, with little intellectual or political challenge. His star seemed on the rise again, however, in early 1951, when his patron, Entezam, was appointed minister of foreign affairs. He named Hoveyda as his chief of staff, or more exactly his executive secretary, since at the time the minister's office had no other staff to speak of. Entezam's tenure lasted less than a month. The cabinet he served proved no match for the rising tide of nationalism. Mosaddeq had come to embody the ideals of this movement, and in April 1951, the shah reluctantly appointed him the prime minister.

But no sooner was the appointment made than a dark cloud of crisis loomed over the country's political horizon. Mosaddeq was an intransigent man and the shah was blatantly incapable of taking decisive action. While the moderate forces behind Mosaddeq suffered from a pusillanimous inability to unite, their fractured state stood in sharp contrast to the growing militancy of the Tudeh Party. Furthermore, with the British government doggedly determined not to lose its lucrative monopoly control of Iranian oil, and with Harry Truman hesitant to join forces with Britain against Iran, there seemed little chance for a peaceful resolution of the crisis. With early signs of the storm, Hoveyda's fortunes also began to take a turn for the worse. His prospects at the Foreign Ministry seemed bleak at best. Once again Europe beckoned.

Several factors seem to have contributed to Hoveyda's decision to leave Iran after only a two-year stay. Entezam had been replaced at the Foreign Ministry by Bagher Kazemi, who was no friend of Hoveyda's.[29] Furthermore, Hossein Fatemi was one of the rising stars of the new Mosaddeq administration. While a student in postwar Paris, Fatemi had written some of the most vitriolic articles about the embassy scandal; he, too, was no friend of Hoveyda's.

Besides these career obstacles, there was also Afsar al-Moluk's health problems to consider. She had been diagnosed with hardening of the arteries. Hoveyda was informed that Iranian hospitals lacked the requisite technology to cure her ailment. Moreover, in retaliation against Mosaddeq's nationalization of Iranian oil, the British had organized an economic embargo against Iran, and medicine was in short supply. In those days even filling a simple prescription was a problem in Tehran. All these factors convinced Hoveyda that the time for leaving Iran had come once more. He decided to look for a job with the United Nations, and with the help of some of the connections he had made over the years, he was offered a position in Geneva with the United Nations High Commissioner for Refugees. He left Iran in mid-1952, while the country was in the throes of one of its most serious political crises.

His departure was, at least in one sense, a blessing in disguise: it meant that he did not have to take sides in the battle that was brewing in Iran. From the start of his appointment as prime minister, Mosaddeq was heading toward a major confrontation with the shah. Eventually, the shah jumped the ship of state and fled Iran; only a coup, masterminded by the British and American intelligence agencies, brought him back to power on August 19, 1953. In the heat of the struggle, when it was still not clear who would emerge victorious, nearly all Iranian politicians were forced to take sides. Those who sided with Mosaddeq ended up paying a high price when the shah, unforgiving of frailty in his supporters, returned to the throne. On the other hand, those who remained loyal to the shah in his darkest hour were handsomely rewarded when the crisis was resolved in his favor. The privileged status of these faithful royalists—from the embassy official in Italy who had shown the exiled shah due deference, to the members of the parliament who, at great peril to their lives, had defended the shah even when the odds seemed stacked against him—was a story known by most Iranian politicians of the time.

If Hoveyda's departure from the crisis afforded him a chance to avoid paying a political price for a choice rashly made, his demeanor in Geneva, his knack for avoiding confrontations, his many friendships amongst intellectuals of the opposition, as well as the stalwarts of the regime, would all mean that an often incongruous mix of people would show up at his house—a house he shared with his mother after her eight-month stay in hospital. At one dinner party, for example, the guests included Dr. Gholam-Hossein Mosaddeq, the son of the prime minister, and Ardeshir Zahedi, the son of the general who had led the coup in favor of the shah and had thus become the bête noire of the opposition.[30] Of course, Hassan-Ali Mansur and Fereydoun Hoveyda were also regular visitors at the house.

In Geneva, Amir Abbas worked as a liaison officer at the United Nations High Commissioner for Refugees. His job required him to travel a great deal. He visited many countries in Asia, Africa, and the Americas as a representative of the Commission. While he befriended some of the leaders of these countries, he was awed and impressed by others. The knowledge and ties he developed in this period led him to join, upon his return home, the Iranian Committee of Afro-Asian Solidarity, committed to expanding and improving Iran's ties with countries in Asia and Africa. The high commissioner at the UN repeatedly praised Hoveyda's work. In a letter dated December 17, 1953, for example, he praises Hoveyda's singular value as a member of the Commission's staff.[31] Hoveyda's critics, as usual, see a sinister shadow in his work at the Commission. They claim that the letter was signed by a Freemason; it was but a ruse, they say, to hide the fact that Hoveyda had sometime in the early 1950s joined a Zionist organization called AZC,[*] and that much of his five years at the Commission was spent "making the creation of the Zionist state" a possibility.[32] They offer not a shred of evidence for any of these claims.

In the meantime, Mansur continued to work at the Foreign Ministry. By 1955, he was named consul to Iran's embassy at the Vatican. Hoveyda used every opportunity to visit his friend in Rome. The visits took on a more urgent purpose when Mansur's marriage to Noushi, Abdol-Hossein Teymourtash's daughter, ended after only a few weeks.[†] Hassan-Ali was devastated by the failure of his marriage and relied on his friends for consolation. It was during these visits that Mansur kept insisting that Amir Abbas give up his job at the United Nations and go back to work at the Foreign Ministry. He would often assure Hoveyda that his "connections"

---

[*] I could not find the existence of any organization called AZC.

[†] During the first half of Reza Shah's rule, Abdol-Hossein Teymourtash was one of his most trusted and influential advisors. When Teymourtash fell from the shah's graces, he was murdered in prison; many have thought that it was by order of the king.

amongst the Americans had convinced him that "our turn will come soon."[33] Eventually, Hoveyda was convinced. When, in 1957, Mansur's father was named ambassador to Turkey, Hoveyda asked and received permission from the Iranian Foreign Ministry to end his leave of absence and return to work. With the apparent intervention of the elder Mansur, Hoveyda was appointed counselor of the Iranian Embassy in Turkey.

Rajab-Ali Mansur's tenure in Turkey did not last long. General Arfa, a stern military man, was named the new ambassador. He was a hard man to work for, bent on running the embassy like a military barracks. He required his staff "to report to him every day as a group standing in order of their height."[34] It was even rumored, in those days, that during the daily lineup, he also inspected every diplomat's attire and paid special attention to the cleanliness of their fingernails. The only member of the staff to revolt was Amir Abbas.*

By then, Entezam had been appointed the managing director of the National Iranian Oil Company (NIOC). Hoveyda beseeched Entezam to have him relieved from General Arfa's strict regime.† Entezam was only too happy to oblige. Hoveyda was called back to Iran and named first as special assistant to Entezam, and soon thereafter as director of administration for the NIOC. His sudden rise to the pinnacle of power in a company that jealously guarded its own turf, a company deeply steeped in the English tradition of stubbornly heeding rules of seniority, initially met with resentment from many of the employees. His reception on his first day of work was decidedly unwelcoming.[35] Hoveyda's response was characteristically calm. As he would do so often during his years as prime minister, here, too, he used a personal touch to circumvent bureaucratic obstacles and resistance. For him, a personal connection was the panacea of politics. Instead of complaining to his patron Entezam, he used a combination of personal charm and patience to overcome the resentment of some of the unhappy employees of the oil company.[36]

---

* In his book on Hoveyda, Eskandar Doldom claims that Hoveyda was ejected from Turkey because he had proselytized on behalf of the Bahai faith. Doldom offers no evidence for his claim. His book, in its disregard for scholarly circumspection, is a case study of the animosity Hoveyda's foes felt toward him and of what sometimes passes for biography in Iran. See Eskandar Doldom, *Zendegi Va Khaterat-e Amir Abbas Hoveyda* [The Life and Memoirs of Amir Abbas Hoveyda] (Tehran, 1998), 90–91.

† Some sources have claimed that it was in fact another NIOC official, Fouad Rouhani, who upon his return from a mission to Turkey, advised Entezam to bring Hoveyda to the oil company. Alinaghi Alikhani, interviewed by author, 12 January 2000.

One of the people who was of particular help to Hoveyda in his early days at the NIOC was Sadeq Chubak. Soon after arriving at the oil company, Hoveyda offered Chubak a new position. "I want you to be my special secretary in charge of confidential correspondence."[37] Though Hoveyda had complete trust in Chubak, the real reason for his selection, as he admitted himself, was to make sure that no error of syntax or style crept into his official or private correspondence.[38] Here was the ultimate irony of Hoveyda's political life. Hitherto his linguistic versatility, his command of French, English, Arabic, and German, his "smattering of Turkish,"[39] had enabled him to get ahead in the world of politics, to rise rapidly where others had only climbed slowly. But now, his native tongue, Persian, was to become his handicap. Hoveyda was shrewd enough to recognize this shortcoming and move to control its damage. The older generation of Iranian politicians, men like Entezam, usually had an impressive command of Persian letters and language. Before the Constitutional Revolution of 1905, in the old courts of Persia, writing pithy prose and recollecting an apt poem for any occasion were, as a rule, one of the indispensable qualities required for political advancement. Hoveyda was the harbinger of a new generation of politicians for whom technobabble had a better chance of becoming their lingua franca than did the language of the poet Hafez. While some of Hoveyda's generation flaunted their foreign accents, and their ignorance of Persian letters, Hoveyda was perfectly aware of the necessity of polishing his Persian.

With the help of Chubak, Hoveyda also chose Vajieh Ma'refat as his private secretary.* For the next twenty-two years, she would remain his most trusted assistant. Ma'refat was a feisty and fiercely independent woman, whose husband, a member of the Tudeh Party, had fled to the Soviet Union. For a more cautious man than Hoveyda, such ties, closely watched by SAVAK, could have been a deterrent. Hoveyda, however, was willing to take a chance.[40]

Two other men, Parviz Radji and Yadollah Shahbazi, also joined his office. Both were handsome men and capable administrators who eventually parlayed their close association with Hoveyda into different kinds

---

* Soon, there was no actual work left for Chubak to do, and Hoveyda suggested that he use the time in his office to work on his novels. In Chubak's own words, some of his work in this period was in a sense subsidized by the oil company. His job, with nothing expected of him, was a de facto grant. Sadeq Chubak, interviewed by author, 22 November 1997.

of personal success. Radji was to become intimate with Princess Ashraf and, with her help, was later named Iran's ambassador to Britain—aside from Washington, the most important and coveted post in the Iranian Foreign Ministry. The appointment was particularly noticeable because Radji had little previous diplomatic experience. His appointment, some have suggested, was part of the shah's attempt in those days to brow beat the British.[41] Radji's intelligence, however, proved to be the only asset he needed to become an impressively articulate ambassador. Shahbazi, on the other hand, was to turn his friendship with Hoveyda into gold, creating Iran's first chain store and eventually founding a very successful shipping company. Lingering questions about his wealth made him into something of a liability for Hoveyda. Some of Hoveyda's advisors suggested that he distance himself from his troublesome friend. He refused to heed their advice.[42] A fickle friend he was not.

At the National Iranian Oil Company, it did not take long for Hoveyda to develop a reputation as a capable manager, congenial and open to ideas and suggestions. He had a new style of management, more Western than Iranian, one that relied less on a regimented hierarchy and more on the help of advisors, pollsters, and open forums. He shocked the stodgy old brass at the company by convening an open meeting of all the staff. He appeared on a stage and invited all the employees to vent their anger, articulate their complaints, and make any suggestion they wished. He began eating at the employee cafeteria, forgoing the luxuries available to directors in their exclusive private dining room. The first day he entered the cafeteria and picked up a tray to join the food line, a hushed silence crept over the restaurant. Soon, however, his presence took on an air of normalcy.[43]

During this time, Hoveyda solicited the help of Ehsan Naraghi, whom he had first met in Switzerland. Naraghi was a trained sociologist, who had dabbled in radical politics in his youth. After returning to Iran, he had become an indefatigable advocate of reconciliation between the opposition and the shah's regime. He was often used as a conduit between members of the opposition and SAVAK. On more than one occasion, he resorted to those in power—including Hoveyda, when he was the prime minister—either to free imprisoned opponents of the regime or at least learn about their fate. In an assessment of the Iranian intellectual community by the American Embassy in Tehran in 1963, Naraghi is described as someone who "in spite of his connection to the regime, is also privately critical of it." The report goes on to describe his role in facilitating something of an "interconnection" between the regime and its opponents.[44]

Through tireless efforts, Naraghi went on to create the Institute of Social Studies and Research, which was loosely affiliated with the faculty of letters at Tehran University. It was at this center where, in the words of an American Embassy report, "some of the most exciting ideas are being developed and current work projects are on such subjects as the Iranians' middle class, and analysis of the bazaar, certain aspects of the current land reform…and a study for SAVAK on the causes of the June Riots."[*45]

The creation of such a center was the result of some earlier work Naraghi had done for the oil company. In 1957, Naraghi was entrusted with the task of studying the company's labor force, sagging morale, and economic efficiency. The Iranian oil company was under pressure—from the consortium of Western companies that held the rights to nearly all of Iran's oil—to lay off thousands of workers deemed redundant. The Naraghi project was intended to promote the idea that the workers were, actually, necessary. After conducting an extensive survey of oil company employees, Naraghi found a strong level of ennui and alienation. He suggested that Hoveyda help sponsor a series of cultural programs for the workers. Some of Iran's foremost intellectuals, including Jalal Al-e Ahmad, were invited to travel to southern cities, where the bulk of the NIOC employees lived and worked, to give lectures on different aspects of culture and literature. At Naraghi's prompting, the NIOC also created special camps for the children of the employees.[46]

For the creation and management of the camps, Hoveyda again took an unorthodox path. He recruited Manouchehr Pirouz for the job. Pirouz had been an employee of the NIOC for many years; in 1953, he was arrested on charges of membership in the Tudeh Party. He was freed after about two years in prison but unofficially became persona non grata at the NIOC. With a little help from Entezam, Hoveyda succeeded in overcoming SAVAK's objections and entrusted Pirouz with starting the camps. Pirouz

---

* A complicated set of circumstances that included a worsening economic crisis, the shah's increasingly despotic hold on power, growing resentment of secular intellectuals against the Pahlavi regime, increasing frustration of the recently disenfranchised absentee landlords, and finally the machinations of the deposed General Bakhtiar, the first head of SAVAK, created a fertile social ground for the riots triggered by Ayatollah Khomeini's arrest. After the events of August 1953, the June uprising of 1963 was the most serious challenge to the shah's hold on power.

created a new camp in Mahmoudabad, in northern Iran, which turned out to be very successful. During the first summer, it housed some 4,500 children. For many of the guests, born and raised in sweltering Khuzestan province, the snow-capped mountains of northern Iran were one of the great marvels of the trip.[47]

Despite the initial success, Pirouz's tenure in charge of the camps was short-lived. It ended when SAVAK reported that no pictures of the shah were ever displayed anywhere in the camps' facilities. By the late 1950s, the shah's cult of personality had already begun taking root. He demanded absolute obedience and was intolerant of saucy minions, and his words and pictures began to become disturbingly pervasive in every corner of the country. The Bureau of Intelligence and Research, in the U.S. State Department, described this trend in a 1966 report. They wrote, "[The] imagery of the shah is everywhere. Movie theaters begin their show with clips of the Shah in various regal poses accompanied by the strains of the National Anthem. The birthdays of the Shah, the Queen, and the Crown Prince are occasions for fireworks and parades. The monarchy's influence also extends to all phases of social activity."[48]

Traces of the creeping cult of the king can even be seen in the evolution of a magazine Hoveyda created and edited for the NIOC. The first issue of *Kavosh* (Exploration) was published in August 1960. It bore Hoveyda's name as its editor-in-chief. It had been started with the help of a number of Hoveyda's friends at the oil company, including Hamid Rahnema and Sadeq Chubak. By the end of the first year, the magazine could count some of Iran's most reputable intellectuals and writers in its roster of contributors.* It was also a way for Hoveyda and Entezam to discreetly funnel financial help to banned, and financially strapped, intellectuals. The magazine paid handsomely for every article, and for each issue, it would commission far more articles than it could publish. The first issue opened with a letter by Entezam that spelled out the magazine's mandate. He writes of Iran's vast and still untapped natural resources, and he laments the fact that the country's human capital, too, has remained largely untapped. While the use of modern technologies can help "find and harness" natural resources, the task of finding and training a labor force is the more enigmatic, and the "exploration" for this rich reservoir

---

* The contributors included Nader Naderpour, Mohammad Ghazi, Massoud Farzad, Mahmoud Sanai, Farokh Ghafari, Sa'id Nafici, Ebrahim Pour-Davoud, and Sadeq Chubak.

of human resource will be the magazine's primary task. He ends his essay with his own brand of a prayer, at once modern and deeply religious. "Man has created the machine," he writes, "and God has created man and the world. We beg him to make our experimental first steps on this road the foundation of our future success."[49]

The brief introduction Hoveyda writes in the same issue is rather strange. It contains a relatively long, and somber anecdote about a gloomy day, when he first heard the news that he had been ordered to leave his beloved Paris and go to war-ravaged Germany. By way of consolation, a friend took him to the famous Père Lachaise cemetery in Paris. "Look at those people lying there," the friend told Amir Abbas, "each of them in their own time thought they, too, were more important and irreplaceable for the work at hand. After them, the world has continued to move, maybe a little faster or slower, but it has moved...None of us are necessary and irreplaceable in any position we occupy."[50] Along with offering this anecdote, Hoveyda promises to "turn the magazine into a pulpit in which the young generation of our country can use today's knowledge to open closed doors."[51]

Neither in Hoveyda's introduction nor in the inaugural note by Entezam is there any mention of the shah. Indeed, the magazine was obviously trying to keep away from the kind of panegyrics to the king that was being increasingly forced on the media by SAVAK and the minister of court. But by the second year, *Kavosh,* too, had caved in, and in almost every issue, some way was found to make a laudatory reference to the shah.

Oil company management, vacation camps for workers, and the trials and tribulations of publishing a journal were not all that occupied Hoveyda's mind in 1960. Of all that we know about Hoveyda, there is one thing about which everyone who knew him agrees: Laila Emami was the love of his life. With her he was besotted. There was also something of a consensus that she was an "unusual" woman; for some, the adjective "unusual" is a mere camouflage, a thinly disguised criticism, for a woman deemed defiantly, even disturbingly, independent. Others seem genuinely impressed by the character and reputation she had fashioned for herself.*

---

* By the time I met Laila Emami, a long and storied reputation preceded her. She openly stood up to the royal family, I was told; she had a bad temper, was easy to excite, and hard to calm. She verbally abused Hoveyda. She was an arrogant aristocrat, distant and detached. She disdained official ceremonies and refused to attend them, and on the rare occasions when she did, she drank too much and often embarrassed her husband. In a culture that values circumspection in men and demands docile silence of women, she was said to be

Laila Emami was born on March 2, 1933, in the city of Abadan, in Iran's oil-rich province of Khuzestan. Her mother was Malek-Khanoum Vosough, the daughter of one of Iran's most controversial prime ministers and one of the chief advocates of the infamous and aborted 1919 agreement with Britain that would have turned Iran into a virtual colony of Britain. Her great-uncle was Ahmad Qavam, another pivotal prime minister.[*] Her father, Nezameddin Emami, from a powerful and controversial family, was a civil servant who often served in highly sensitive posts. At the onset of Iran's battle with the British government over the control of

---

notoriously frank and opinionated. She was, in turn, described as difficult, fragile, brooding, angry, and vitriolic. She minced no words, I was warned; beware of a wrong question and the vengeance of her wrath. There seemed to be, in short, as many rumors about her as about her once powerful husband. Even arranging a meeting with her proved hard and elusive. After many entreaties on my behalf from many of her friends and family, finally one day I was informed that Laila had agreed to a meeting. On June 5, 1998, I drove from Paris to an apartment in the fashionable section of Geneva, where we were supposed to meet. I arrived there at ten o'clock in the morning and was met by Jamshid Daftary. Dressed in a dapper blue suit and a handsome red tie, he invited me in, offered me some coffee, and then began telling me fascinating anecdotes about Alam and his machinations. He told me of multimillion Deutschemark commissions paid by a German company and of their unsuccessful attempts to retrieve the money after the revolution. He showed me documents and transcripts from an arbitration tribunal at The Hague, detailing the tainted deal. He read for me his own testimony where he had offered evidence indicating that Hoveyda had in fact done all he could to abort the deal.

After about an hour of such chatter, I finally mustered the courage to tell Daftary that, interesting as his revelations and the supporting documents were, I was here to talk to Laila Emami. I told him I was pressed for time and rather anxious to talk to her. "I am sorry," he said nonchalantly, "she is not feeling well and cannot meet you." And then apparently oblivious to my angry and desolate mood, he continued with his stories. This time, he began to tell me about his relative, Dr. Mosaddeq. I had noticed the large autographed picture of Mosaddeq as soon as I entered the house; it loomed in the corner of the large sitting room. Clumsily, I stopped him in the middle of his story and left the house convinced that maybe those who had tried to dissuade me from meeting Laila Emami had been right all along. I began to think that talking to her would prove impossible, and I was painfully aware that the absence of her point of view would be a glaring lacuna in my narrative.

After recovering from the distress of the aborted Geneva encounter, I resumed my attempts to organize a meeting. After a year of entreaties, Laila Emami finally agreed to talk. By then she had left Geneva and was living in Paris with her aunt. I was to travel to Paris for the visit, and on the morning of my arrival, I called and arranged a meeting for that very afternoon. Any delay, I feared, might cause her to change her mind.

She arrived promptly at half past three. We sat in a quiet corner of a smoke-filled, Parisian brasserie. She wore an elegant black leather jacket, dark fashionable pants, black loafers, and a handsome turtleneck sweater. A pair of large brown-rimmed glasses covered her penetrating, melancholic eyes. She exuded an air of elegant self-assurance. Of the much wonted fragility, or volatility, there seemed to be no sign. She ordered a cup of coffee and began to talk.

[*] In fact, by the time we met, she could count seven of modern Iran's most important prime ministers as relatives. Aside from her maternal grandfather, and her great-uncle, Hassan-Ali Mansur was her brother-in-law; Rajab-Ali Mansur was her brother-in-law's father; Ali Amini was her aunt's husband; Ahmad Matine Daftary, also once a prime minister, was also a relative; and Amir Abbas Hoveyda was her husband. It can easily be argued that at nearly every crucial moment of twentieth-century Iranian history, one of her relatives was a prime minister, and that for nearly a quarter of the twentieth century one of these relatives was the prime minister.

Farideh and Laila Emami (right) in 1938, two future brides for two prime ministers.

Iranian oil, he was Iran's representative at the oil company headquarters in London. "He was by temperament," she said, " a timid man, averse to confrontation." The wealth of the family, particularly in the last half of the father's life, was clearly in the hands of Laila's mother, who had, after her father's death, inherited a substantial real estate fortune. Laila's paternal grandfather was a reputable and enlightened cleric, who insisted that his daughters and granddaughters receive a modern education. Laila was the oldest of a family of four brothers and sisters. Her younger sister, Farideh, was a child of unusual beauty. In contrast to Laila, who from early on had ambitions to go to college, Farideh had set her eyes on the more conventional goal of finding a suitable man and forming a family.[52]

Laila was twelve when she left Iran. Her father was assigned to a post in Bombay and took his family with him. After two years, they returned to Tehran, only to leave again in seven months. This time London was their destination. Laila was enrolled in one of England's elite boarding schools in Surrey. After completing high school in England, she returned to Iran and worked for a while as a secretary for "Point 4," the agency in charge of implementing and supervising American technical aid to Iran.[53] She was twenty-two years old when, thanks to her mother's newly inherited wealth, the family was finally able to provide for Laila's college education abroad. She left Iran in 1955 and enrolled in the University of California at Berkeley. After a year, she transferred to UCLA and began taking courses there in the summer of 1956. Responding to an ad by an American woman named Jean Boumett, she moved into her small studio in West-wood, near the campus.

Laila was on a tight budget. "I received a hundred and sixty dollars a month," she remembered. Jean, who now lives in Napa, California, with her husband Lyle Becker, a retired colonel in the U.S. airforce, remembers Laila as "always talking about how much her education was costing her parents and why she needed to graduate as fast as possible."[54] Laila was a very serious student, with little time for most of the leisurely frivolities of college life. She took courses in art and architecture, and also dabbled in sociology. When I visited Jean's lavish house, two paintings by Laila adorned the walls. A still-life, suffused in a yellow light, hung on a dining room wall. On a bathroom wall, adjoining the master bedroom, hung a nude portrait of a woman, fierce in its lines, passionately red in its color.

Soon after moving in with Jean, Laila, to the consternation of her roommate, fell in love with a young man who lived across the hall. "I guess he was the one romantic love of her life," Jean remembered, adding as an afterthought, "not that she did not come to dearly love that poor man, Amir. But it was a different kind of love."[55]

In January 1959, Laila graduated from UCLA with a degree in art and immediately returned to Iran. She was still in love with the young man from Los Angeles and imagined that the relationship would somehow continue. In the meantime, her younger sister, Farideh, had fallen in love with Hassan-Ali Mansur. Mansur had been living in Iran since the end of his assignment in the Vatican in 1957. After a couple of stormy affairs—one with a refined Iranian actress, the other with the storied Czechoslova-kian wife of a dentist who lived in Iran at the time—he was finally ready to settle down. And it was on the night of his wedding to Farideh that Hoveyda first took serious interest in Laila.* Hoveyda spent much of the evening with her. "He was a charming man, full of fascinating stories to tell," she remembered wistfully.[56] Hoveyda had just returned from a trip to

---

* The night of the wedding is also notable since three of the men present were to become future prime ministers of Iran and Pakistan—Mansur, Hoveyda, and Zulfikar Ali Bhutto. All three were young, all three were known to enjoy the support of the U.S. government, all three were reformists and unabashedly secular, and the violent end of all three was brought about by Islamic forces. Hoveyda's second trial and Bhutto's execution were in the same week of the same year.

the United States where he had taken some lessons in yoga. "He was very excited about his lessons and talked about the virtues of different kinds of yoga dietary regimens."[57] In those days, Laila was intent on making interior design her profession, and Hoveyda gave her the first job of her new career: decorating the Iranian pavilion at the trade fair in the Turkish city of Izmir.

After a few weeks of visits that always included Mansur and Farideh, Hoveyda invited Laila to his office at the National Iranian Oil Company. "I thought he had another job for me," Laila said. Till then she had kept him at arm's length. "I insisted on calling him Mr. Hoveyda," she remembered. She soon realized that his intentions had nothing to do with employment. Instead he talked of his love for her and of his desire to make her his wife. "I am not ready to form a family yet," Laila responded, "I cannot imagine having babies at this time." Babies, Hoveyda assured her, would not be a problem. He added, rather nonchalantly, that in the past he had taken a battery of tests and was told he could never be a father. Laila eventually would have to resort to the ultimate confession. "I am not ready to marry, and if I were, I love another man who lives in America," she told him.[58] In spite of her rejection, Hoveyda continued not only to see her on social occasions, but persisted in his pursuit. Politics, however, occupied most of his time. Iran was poised for some serious changes, and Hoveyda intended to play an important role in them.

CHAPTER SEVEN

The White Revolution

Enigma and evasion grows;
And shall we never find thee out?
—Herman Melville

ontrary to common perception, American pressure on the shah to implement a series of economical and political reforms did not begin with John F. Kennedy. Indeed, since the mid-1950s, U.S. policy makers had become acutely concerned about the long-term stability of Iran. In at least two reports in 1958, the CIA found "Mohammed Reza Pahlavi incapable of taking necessary actions to implement" urgently needed reforms.[1] On February 27, 1958, an Iranian general—Valiollah Qarani—was arrested along with thirty-eight other men on the charge of attempting a coup against the shah.[2] The official announcement indicated that an "unnamed foreign" power had been involved, and it was widely rumored that America had been that unnamed country. The exact nature of U.S. involvement in Qarani's coup attempt is still not known. U.S. State Department documents, however, make it clear that Qarani had been in touch with the U.S. Embassy prior to his coup attempt. For example, in a February 6 meeting, Qarani suggested that Secretary of State John Foster Dulles should approach the shah and demand that "he should reign, not rule."[3]

The imperial power of the U.S. was evident in its ability to marshal a multi-pronged set of policies—some fostered by private institutions, others advocated by the U.S. government or international agencies—to bring about urgently needed economic reforms. While the IMF tried to implement an immediate short-term stabilization program, U.S. government agencies, along with Harvard University (partially funded by the Ford Foundation), began to push for a program of long-term economic development. One eventual, albeit inadvertent, consequence of these efforts was that Hoveyda became Iran's prime minister in 1965.

Lest the purgative powers of reform prove inadequate, however, U.S. intelligence agencies also aided Iran in 1957 to transform the existing army and police intelligence units into a cohesive new body known as SAVAK. Over the years SAVAK grew in power and would eventually solicit the help of other intelligence agencies—particularly MI6, and the Israeli Mossad—to sharpen the edge of its sword, a sword needed to ensure that chaos or communism would not disturb the stability of Iranian politics.[4]

In the mid-1950s, with the Cold War at its height, few countries could match Iran's geopolitical importance. There was, first and foremost, the politics of oil. On June 22, 1953, the Dulles brothers—John Foster Dulles and Allen Welsh Dulles (the head of the CIA)—led a meeting in the State Department in which final details were worked out to dispatch a CIA operative called Kermit Roosevelt to Iran. His code name was "Rainmaker," and his mission was to help topple the government of Mosaddeq and return the shah (to whom they had given the code name "Boy Scout") back to power.[5] The coup was a success, and its most important result was that a consortium of Western oil companies was given near monopoly rights over Iranian oil.* In the words of the U.S. State Department's "Survey of U.S.-Iranian Relations," with the consortium agreement, "Iran's oil flowed again, as did American aid."[6]

To his dying day, the shah believed that the pressures for reform in the late fifties and early sixties, and the Islamic Revolution itself, were the result of his attempts to wrest power from the oil companies. The shah writes in *Answer to History*, his quixotic last book:

---

* The Consortium shares were divided amongst several oil companies: 40 percent went to British Petroleum; 14 percent to Shell (British-Dutch); 6 percent to CFP (French); and 40 percent to American companies (7 percent each to Gulf, Esso, Mobil, Standard of California, and Texaco, with the other 5 percent divided among eight companies in the IRICON Group).

The development of the oil industry constitutes the most tumultuous aspect of modern Middle East history. It is an unending series of intrigues, plots, political and economic upsets, acts of terrorism, coup d'état and bloody revolutions. To understand the upheaval in Iran…one must understand the politics of oil…From the moment that Iran became master of its own underground wealth, a systematic campaign of denigration was begun concerning my government and my person in certain of the mass media. It was at this time that I became a despot, an oppressor, a tyrant. Suddenly malicious propaganda became apparent; professional agitators operating under the guise of "student" organizations appeared. This campaign, begun in 1958, reached its peak in 1961. Our White Revolution halted it temporarily. But it was begun with greater vigor in 1975 and increased until my departure.[7]

Even if one does not accept the shah's self-exonerating rendition of history, there is no denying that oil has played the central role in modern Iranian politics. Not only was Iran a major oil-producing country, but equally important was Iran's coastline on the Persian Gulf, which was essential for the safe flow of Middle Eastern oil to the West.

In mid-1958, when the swift and brutal overthrow of the monarch in Iraq "shocked and frightened the shah (and almost certainly caused him to reappraise the future of his personal position),"[8] he became gravely concerned about Iraqi aggression against Iran. By then Gamal Abdel Nasser had also emerged as a "strong-man" in Egypt and the shah deemed his brand of fiery nationalism a direct threat to the stability of the monarchy and the territorial integrity of Iran. As a May 12, 1966, CIA Intelligence Memorandum makes clear, "Iranian foreign and military policies are heavily influenced by the Shah's belief that Arab nationalism, personified by Egyptian President Nasser is striving to dominate oil-rich and vulnerable South-Western Iran and the Persian Gulf area."[9] If in the late fifties and early sixties the shah's fears of Iraqi aggression seemed paranoid, both to the shah's critics and even to some of his American supporters, in retrospect, after an eight-year war between Iran and Iraq that began in 1980, those anxieties might almost be deemed prophetic.

The new Iraqi threat notwithstanding, Iran also shared a very long border with the Soviet Union, and the shah had always been seriously concerned about Soviet designs in Iran. One of the pillars of his foreign policy was based on the belief that the Soviets—like their czarist predecessors—were only waiting for an opportune moment to topple the Iranian government and by turning Iran into a satellite state finally gain access to the warm-water ports of the Persian Gulf. In a note written by John Foster Dulles to President Dwight D. Eisenhower, in preparation for the shah's June 30, 1958, visit to the U.S., Dulles writes, "[the shah] believes that Iran should have considerably larger indigenous forces with which...to defend itself against possible Soviet aggression. In my talks with him in late January, I made an effort to convince him that the deterrent strength of the United States constituted the primary obstacle to Soviet aggression in the area."[10] With varying degrees of success and intensity over the next decade, American officials tried to convince the shah that Iran should rely on the deterrent power of the U.S. and reduce its own military expenditure. The shah refused to accept their advice and, during both the Kennedy and Lyndon Johnson administrations, this conflict was at the center of many of his disagreements with the U.S. government. It was Richard Nixon who finally sided with the shah and gave him carte blanche to purchase any conventional arms he desired.[11]

In 1958, containment was the key strategic concept driving the U.S. policy toward the Soviet Union. The U.S., with the active support of the British government, informed the shah that it "would welcome Iran's adherence to a regional defense agreement with Turkey, Pakistan, and Iraq, and that in connection with this agreement, the U.S. was prepared to assist Iran in developing its defense capabilities."[12] Encouraged by a fifty million dollar aid package from the U.S., Iran joined the agreement, initially called the Baghdad Pact and eventually named the Central Treaty Organization (CENTO). Hoveyda had been involved in the work of the Pact while he served at the Iranian Embassy in Turkey. The decision to join the Pact, thus clearly siding with the West against the Soviet Union, was a major policy shift for Iran. For about two hundred years before the Pact, Iran had at least ostensibly tried to maintain its neutrality.

In 1958, in spite of the apparent close and cordial ties between the shah and President Eisenhower, there were growing signs of unease in the U.S. about conditions in Iran. In September of that year, the National Security Council scheduled a meeting to discuss a recent "Special National Intelligence Estimate," which had reported that "the present regime in [Iran] is not likely to last very long."[13] As a result, "between September and November 1958, a formal reassessment of U.S. policy in Iran focused on how to induce needed reforms in the country. Foremost, was the problem of how to get the shah to accede to certain demands of the middle class (which the U.S. viewed as his principal opposition) without alienating his conservative supporters…Should the shah refuse, the reassessment recommended that the U.S. take steps to reduce its identification with him by developing appropriate contacts with emerging non-Communist groups."[14] By the early 1960s, these suggested steps had become the centerpiece of U.S. policy in Iran—the creation of an alliance between the Iranian middle class and the shah, and the creation of political institutions or parties that could attract and mobilize elements of a new technocratic elite and take the wind out of the opposition's sails. Mansur, helped by Hoveyda, was marketing himself as the prime candidate for creating such a party and leading such an alliance.

Faced with these changing realities, the shah proved himself a resilient politician over the next ten years—nimble in his tactics of acceding to American demands, yet unbending in his strategy of consolidating more and more power in his own hands. For example, on the one hand he accepted the idea of the creation of a Plan Organization in 1948, as a result of which, by the late 1950s, a "small nucleus of Iranian economists" worked together with a "Ford Foundation-sponsored advisory group" to implement long-term planning for the country.[15] On the other hand, within a few years, the shah had centralized nearly all major economic decision-making so that his approval was necessary for all major public and private investments. Furthermore, even those responsible for the country's economic planning had no direct access to figures relating to yearly oil revenues. The director general of the Plan Organization had to use private channels at the NIOC or the consortium to receive approximate revenue figures.[16]

As American pressure for reforms increased in the late 1950s, the shah took a more active interest in an already existing institution called the Supreme Economic Council. Its membership eventually consisted of the shah, the prime minister, the head of the Plan Organization, the head of the Central Bank, and a changing assortment of ministers. In 1958, Hassan-Ali Mansur was named the secretary general of the council. His tasks included preparing minutes of meetings, monitoring the implementation of the council's decisions, and suggesting remedies for problems. The council also became Mansur's vehicle for gaining national recognition.

Patience, however, was not one of Mansur's virtues. He soon started to create a group of his own consisting of technocrats and mid-level administrators. They studied social and economic problems, and offered solutions. He enlisted Hoveyda's help; in Iran, as in Europe, the two had been almost inseparable friends. Hoveyda not only joined Mansur enthusiastically, but he soon became the most important theorist of the emerging group. The genesis of the group was, according to a CIA report, "a *dowreh** established by Hassan-Ali Mansur in 1959. The nine men, drawn together by professional and social association, were a youngish group with an average age of thirty-seven. They were establishment reformers with a strong component of political self-interest. Eight of them were foreign-educated, four in France. Within two years Mansur's *dowreh* became formalized as the 'Progressive Circle' with the purpose of conducting research into Iran's social and economic problems. It had expanded to some two hundred people. The majority had professional or personal ties with either Mansur or Hoveyda."[17]

Hoveyda's enthusiasm for the *dowreh* had both practical and theoretical roots. Mansur's political star was surely on the rise and Hoveyda had by then clearly hitched his wagon to that star. At the same time he had a clear theoretical grasp of the future function, and immediate necessity, of a group like the one proposed by Mansur. Soon after his arrival at the oil company, Hoveyda had taken a leading role in advocating what in those days was called the "process of Iranization" of the oil industry. During many negotiations, he was adamant in underscoring the need to replace foreign managers and technicians with Iranians. Concurrently, he attempted to forge something of an alliance with the new generation of Iranian oil experts—engineers, technicians, and accountants—who were trained in the West and had returned to Iran with high hopes of changing the country. They had become impatient with the glass ceiling imposed by the consortium that hampered their advance. Hoveyda patiently courted these "Young Turks," regularly invited them to his office, listened to their laments, and invited them to come up with concrete proposals for fostering loyalty and motivation in the ranks of the company's employees.[18]

---

* *Dowreh* is Persian for a gathering held at regular intervals. Though an old Iranian concept, it was brought to the attention of Western academic circles by Marvin Zonis in his book, *The Political Elite of Iran* (New Jersey, 1971).

From early 1960, Hoveyda also used the pages of *Kavosh* not only to write about the urgent need to train and use Iranian managers and technicians but also to discuss unfolding events in the country. Central to his editorials was the idea that the technocratic class had to join the development process if there was going to be any success. In an essay titled, "Today Responsibility Must Lie with the Technocrats and There Are Not Enough Technocrats," he writes that a fundamental change had taken place in the world. There is, he notes, a "shortage of experts," and the problem exists even in the developed world. "Those who imported machinery into Iran," he suggests, "should have first thought about training people who could maintain the machines." Here he seems to be criticizing the very policy— of hurried and haphazard development, of increases in one industrial sector without adequate infrastructural planning in the others—that in later years would characterize his own tenure as prime minister. He concludes his essay by suggesting that "it is incumbent on all those who love this country to ensure that in every field, from agriculture to industry...Iranians replace foreigners. We must train enough technocrats so that when industries are founded in Iran, there would not be a manpower shortage."[19]

In another article on the same theme, Hoveyda writes of the intricate relationship between rights and responsibilities. "There are no rights without responsibilities," he suggests, before emphasizing again the indispensable role of technocrats in the much needed revolution in Iran. Hoveyda notes that the technocrats need to display their long dormant power, destroy the old structures, and "on their ruins build a new structure—a new structure made by our people, our free and responsible people. The time for excuses has passed. There are now plans; there are possibilities; all that is missing is an Iranian labor force...Foreigners cannot help us. Ever. We have once and for all to accept this reality. We must help ourselves and not expect anyone else to help."[20] He even conjures images from Herodotus's *Histories.* "Persians," he reminds his readers, "were innovative people in Darius's days; they began to construct what would 2,500 years later become the Suez Canal."[21] Glaringly absent in all these essays is a single mention of the shah. Even when the unfolding "White Revolution" is praised, no mention of the shah is made. This reticence sharply contrasts with Hoveyda's later willingness to shower the shah with tributes of all sorts.

The leadership committee of the Progressive Circle. Back row from left to right:
Zia Shadman, Fatollah Sotudeh, Mohammad-Ali Rashti, Gholamreza Nikpay. Seated
from left to right: Hadi Hedayati, Manouchehr Kalali, Hoveyda, Mansur, Taghi Sarlak,
Mohsen Khajenouri, Manouchehr Shahgholi.

The central notion that an alliance between the government and the technocratic middle class was the key to Iran's future development can also be found in Hoveyda's notes on the origins of the Progressive Circle. He writes, "We believed that in politics you have to be realistic. You have to do what is feasible at any given time. Considering the conditions in 1960, we decided that creating a group with a monolithic ideology and philosophy was neither possible nor desirable…Thus we created the Progressive Circle where members could each keep their own ideas and would only enter into a kind of contract with one another. Making economic development a possibility was the core of this agreement…People from all political and philosophical persuasions—from communists and extreme nationalists to atheists or devoutly religious people—could join."[22]

The backgrounds of some of the Progressive Circle's early members confirm Hoveyda's claims. Aside from Hoveyda and Mansur, there was Mohammad-Ali Rashti, who held a degree in political science from Columbia University, and "during his 14-year residence in the United

States…had acted for a period as a spokesman for the Mosaddeq government."[23] Another early member, Mohsen Khajenouri, was also a member of the National Front, while Zia Shadman was a devout Muslim.

By the time the group began to meet regularly at Mansur's house, the CIA station chief in Iran was the Yugoslav-American Gratian Yatsevitch. He was a jovial man, handsome and congenial; he had a smattering of Persian and had become a fixture of high society parties in Tehran. He had learned to cook Persian food, and on Fridays, the day of rest in Iran, there were often parties at his house. He was also Hassan-Ali Mansur's tenant. However, while Yatsevitch watched the goings-on in Iran and collected information, SAVAK was returning the favor and collected information on him. In one of SAVAK's reports about his activities, he is described as an "arrogant man…who has particular affinity for women, and this can easily be used as an inducement to get what we want from him."[24] The same report names Hassan-Ali Mansur as one of Yatsevitch's six closest friends. There is no mention of Hoveyda on the list. Another report indicates that after finishing his term in Tehran, Yatsevitch tried to parlay his Persian ties into private riches.* Interestingly, the SAVAK report recommends that he should be granted the contracts he seeks, since "after signing the contracts, we might be able to place some people around him and get information from him."[25]

By all accounts, Mansur flaunted his close ties with Yatsevitch. He would openly tell many of the leading Iranian technocrats of his "ties with the highest echelons of power in America," of his connection to John McCloy, of the fact that "his American friends" had assured him that they would force the shah to reform the country and that soon he would be Iran's prime minister.[26] He was a political braggart, but there is much evidence to indicate that of all his boasts, the claimed ties with Yatsevitch were the most

---

* In parlaying a diplomatic or espionage career in Iran into private gain, Yatsevitch was in good company among American government officials. Kermit Roosevelt, the chief CIA operative in Iran in 1953, Spiro Agnew, Richard Nixon's disgraced vice president, and Richard Helms, a CIA director and U.S. ambassador to Iran, were among the most famous such officials. Both Yatsevitch and Roosevelt acted as middlemen for large American corporations. Yatsevitch, for example, had cornered the wheat market. It was Helms's company, Safeer, formed after his retirement, however, which caused something of a stir in the American media. *The Nation* was particularly critical, writing: "The announcement card told it all. President Richard Helms was telling the world that the Safeer Company 'has been established to provide consulting services in international trade and business…The word 'Safeer' in the Persian tongue called Parsi [sic] means 'ambassador.' Helms is that shameless. He comes right out and announces that his experience as the President's representative to Tehran is for sale." See *Nation*, 3 December 1977, 580.

accurate. Through Mansur, Hoveyda also met Yatsevitch. In remembering his friendship with Mansur and Hoveyda, Yatsevitch recounts that "I used to see a lot of Hoveyda...He was just a competent bureaucrat. Not a very inspiring personality...Hoveyda and Mansur collaborated for quite a number of years in trying to create an acceptable alternative to the unacceptable National Front. They tried to gain the support of the same type of educated and intellectual people that the National Front had appealed to. They used to meet in the house next to mine, and I would sit in at lunch with them once in a while. So I think Hoveyda really was the intellectual force behind it, and Mansur was the front man."[27] Out of those lunchtime meetings eventually emerged the Progressive Circle.*

By 1963, a small group headed by Mansur and Hoveyda had emerged as the "founding committee" of the circle. A treasurer, Zia Shadman, was elected, and each member was required to make a twenty toman a month—about three dollars at the time—contribution. Using the money, a small one-room apartment was rented as the headquarters of the circle. Hitherto, all of the meetings had been held in the basement of Mansur's house. All new members had to be approved by the unanimous vote of the "founding committee." Even in its embryonic stages, the Progressive Circle was a quasi official arm of the government. Once a candidate was approved for membership, Mansur would submit his name to SAVAK for security clearance. Only after receiving the requisite clearance would the candidate be contacted and invited to join. Hoveyda played an active role in these meetings and asserted himself as one of the two obvious leaders of the group. As the group grew, Hoveyda would, more and more, defer to Mansur in public meetings, while in the "founding committee," he remained more assertive. As the meetings grew larger, Mansur took a

---

* I attempted to find copies of Yatsevitch's reports about his dealings with Mansur and Hoveyda. On March 9, 1999, I wrote a letter to the CIA, asking for these reports, invoking the Freedom of Information Act. I received a prompt reply on March 19, advising me that "the records you request, if any exist, would not be indexed in such a way as for us to be able to retrieve them. The FOIA provides for public access to 'reasonably described' records...This generally requires that the records must be locatable through our indexing system." Obviously unaware of the CIA's "indexing system"—the same system, incidentally, that only a few months earlier had declared that it had lost all documents relating to the CIA's role in the 1953 coup in Iran—I nevertheless wrote back to the agency's "Information and Privacy Coordinator," this time focusing my request to "any dispatches from the CIA office in Tehran" during the early 1960s. I received another prompt reply. This time, I was informed that "what we should have added in our 19 March letter, and we apologize for this oversight, was that provisions of the CIA Information Act, 50 U.S.C. § 431, exempts the operational files of the CIA from the FOIA."

A gathering of friends from the foreign ministry. Lying down in front are Fereydoun Hoveyda, Mansur, an unidentified woman, and Amir Abbas.

more aggressive role in leading the discussions and Hoveyda turned more quiet, often silently sitting in a corner and doodling on a sheet of paper.[28]

But as Hoveyda and Mansur began to lay the groundwork for their own rise to power, the situation in Iran was reaching a crisis level according to American analysts. On May 15, 1961, the National Security Council was informed that the "continuing trend toward revolution and chaos in Iran has reached the point where the U.S. must take vigorous action."[29] Since the 1953 coup, the U.S. had provided close to a billion dollars of aid to Iran. But by the time John F. Kennedy came to power, the Iranian economy was in shambles. Inflation was rampant, unemployment was high, wages were stagnant, corruption was endemic, foreign exchange was in short supply, and the U.S. was somehow held responsible for it all.[30] Workers, students, and teachers began sporadic demonstrations in Tehran and other major cities. Well aware of these developments, the U.S. Embassy began to write gloomy reports about conditions in Iran. Its biweekly detailed economic and political reports reflected the mounting concerns of embassy officials about the crisis.

The personal and policy differences between the Kennedy clan and the shah further complicated the picture. It had been rumored that the shah had provided secret funds to the Nixon camp in the 1960 presidential campaign. Asadollah Alam hints at this in his *Diaries* and says that it was repeated in the 1968 campaign.[*31] Furthermore, John and Bobby Kennedy had come to see the shah as despotic, corrupt, and incorrigible. The shah reciprocated in turn with a visceral dislike of both brothers. He is reported to have been "not displeased when he heard the news of Kennedy's assassination."[32] Indeed, shortly after the President's death, the shah wrote a letter to Johnson congratulating him on his new job. In the letter, he used rather harsh words admonishing Kennedy for his interference in the internal affairs of Iran. The tone and the timing of the letter seemed impolitic to Alam, who was then prime minister. He decided to delay sending the letter. A few days later, he informed the shah of his decision. The king grew angry and refused to talk to Alam for a week.[33]

Faced with the mounting economic crisis, the government of Sharif-Emami fell. Sharif-Emami had long been considered a staunch Anglophile, and his eccentric brother-in-law, Ahmad Aramesh, who headed the Plan Organization, had been opposed to the American sponsored "stabilization program." Sharif-Emami's inability to solve the economic crisis brought about the fall of his cabinet, and in his place the shah, under some duress, appointed Ali Amini as the new prime minister. The event that helped expedite the appointment was a teachers' strike in Tehran. When on May 4, 1961, workers promised to join the strike, the shah, "reportedly extremely upset and ready to leave the country...offered Amini the prime minister's post late that night."[34] The U.S. Embassy in Tehran knew full well that the shah had "appointed Amini reluctantly and out of some measure of fear."[35] In later years, the shah used Hoveyda to exact revenge upon Amini and called the pressure for the Amini appointment "more or less an American coup directed against him."[36] Gratian Yatsevitch essentially confirms that the shah was made an offer he could not refuse. "I think it was made clear [to the shah]," Yatsevitch indicates, "that [Amini's appointment] would be considered a very wise appointment...We always thought that Amini was our man for some reason."[37]

* In both cases, Ardeshir Zahedi is supposed to have been the conduit for the illicit cash. He denies all reports of such contributions. Ardeshir Zahedi, interviewed by author, 4 August 1999.

The American Embassy in Tehran and many in Washington noted that Amini's appointment might be Iran's "last chance to resolve its problems under the leadership of a moderate civilian government. Internal and external pressures testify that time has about run out. If the current economic crisis is not resolved and vigorous steps taken to deal with the corruption, incompetence, and social injustice, which has for so long afflicted the country, a seizure of power by the military or the National Front is unlikely to be long delayed. The latter developments would have highly serious consequences for the U.S. interests."[38] While the embassy was unsure of Amini's chances of survival, it had no doubt that "he cannot long survive without quick and substantial financial assistance from us."[39] Indeed, Amini had come to power, at least partially, on the strength of just such assistance from the U.S.

The decision to make a desperately needed thirty-three million dollar loan conditional on the Amini appointment was based on the report of an interagency committee set up by President Kennedy to review U.S. policy in Iran. Chaired by Philip Talbot, the committee struggled with an analysis of Iran's situation, and the question of the strategic options open to the U.S.[40] The committee was faced with the knowledge that the "Shah's de facto dictatorship" had inexorably moved Iran toward a "growing chance of domestic strife leading to chaos or coup by rightist or leftist cliques, or Soviet-managed subversion. The U.S. could, at considerable expense, keep the Shah in position of personal power…[It] could also roll with the punch of history and champion the cause of moderates among the Mosaddeqists…A third alternative would be to support the best of the right-wing military leaders in a pro-Western dictatorship…The advent of Prime Minister Amini offers another course of action to the U.S. The recommendation of the Task Force represents the implementation of this course."[41] In a memorandum for the president, the committee suggests that the U.S. must do "everything feasible to give the 'Amini' experiment a fighting chance, helping to protect him against pressures from both the shah and the left."[42] Published minutes of the Task Force meetings confirm serious divisions within its ranks about what to do with the shah. There were those like Robert Komer who hinted at the necessity of removing the shah, saying that "we cannot wait forever, and that our approach must be frankly experimental. In a time of crisis, one must take risks, and perhaps play by ear, never knowing exactly what the result would be."[43]

Armin Meyer, who was deputy assistant secretary in charge of Middle Eastern affairs at the time, remembers Komer suggesting that the option of the shah's removal had to be considered.[44] Others, particularly members of the committee who were from the State Department, advocated a more conciliatory approach. At the same time, there was something of a consensus that "in the past, United States officials speaking to the Shah about the need for domestic reforms have been hampered to a significant degree by the lack of a fully coordinated U.S. position."[45]

The final report of the Task Force to the president was less radical than what was implicit in Komer's words. Though in its January 18, 1962, report, the Task Force had concluded that "the Shah's character is such as to make his years in power as the ultimate repository of power almost certainly numbered," it now suggested that rather than trying to remove the shah, "the United States must actually and vigorously, albeit discreetly, press for political, economic, social and institutional reform in Iran."[46] According to Talbot, "multiple channels can be effectively directed" toward reform in Iran.[47] The report also outlines what the Task Force believed should be the goals of U.S. policy in Iran. They included, "withdrawal of the shah from an exposed position of public responsibility...Progressive delegation, by the shah to a capable prime minister, of authority formerly yielded directly by him...withdrawal of the shah's family, private estates and entourage from entanglements with private business activities...dilution of the shah's extreme distrust of independent political leaders and of his vulnerability to sycophancy...[and finally] the transformation of the urban middle class into a constructive [political] force."[48]

Other than the ever present danger of Soviet incursions into Iran, what seems to have mitigated U.S. options was the shah's rather delicate psychic mood and mold. On February 24, 1961, the National Security Council reported that the "Shah is in a troubled and confused state of mind."[49] On March 8, the State Department declared that it had received reports that "the Shah of Iran is depressed," and that he "may be considering abdication. His abdication would result in political chaos in Iran which would only benefit the Soviet Union in the long run."[50] Finally, on May 13, in a conversation with the U.S. ambassador, the "Shah said [that the] center of power in Iran had traditionally resided in crown, and it must continue to do so. He himself would rather abdicate than accept the position of the figure-head."[51]

In 1964, when the shah had been absent from Iran for about five weeks, the U.S. Embassy in Tehran reported that contrary to official declarations that the shah was "resting," his absence had a more serious medical and psychological reason. A "fairly reliable" report from a "Vienna medical source" had, according to the embassy report, "described [the shah's] condition as 'anxiety complex.'"[52] The shah's "anxiety complex," his depression, his readiness to abdicate—his willingness to jump the ship of state, his Lord Jim complex—and finally the inability of the American government to speak with one tongue and act upon a fully coordinated position would in the late 1970s figure prominently in determining not only the shah's fate but that of Amir Abbas Hoveyda as well.

When the Task Force finally made its recommendations, a combination of factors, which included everything from the fear of the Soviet Union to the fragility of the Iranian state and its opposition, seemed to have helped the shah. The U.S. eased its pressure on the shah, and in March of that year, another important report was produced by the State Department. Written by John W. Bowling, the report offered what in retrospect can been seen as "the blueprint of the shah's reform programs."[53] It consisted of fourteen suggestions for the shah that included such ideas as:

• Channel current resentment against his ministers rather than against himself.
• Dump his family, or most of it, in Europe.
• Remove gradually most U.S. advisers from the Iranian government.
• Publicly excoriate the traditional ruling class.
• Withdraw from his openly pro-Western international posture.
• Proceed loudly with at least a token land distribution program against big landlords.
• Make menacing gestures against the oil consortium and "extract" concessions from it in such a way to make it appear that the consortium was reluctantly bowing to his power.
• Make public scapegoats of scores of "corrupt" high officials, whether or not the "corruption" could be proved.
• Appoint respected moderate Mosaddeqists to positions such as those of minister of finance and head of Plan Organization.[54]

Realizing that reforms along these lines were inevitable, and at the same time wary of what he perceived as "excessive U.S. backing for Amini personally," the shah "pointedly reminded the U.S. of the need for his personal support for any government program to be effective."[55] Not long after his state visit to the United States in April 1962, where he agreed to implement the suggested reforms, the shah, after giving advance notice to the American Embassy, removed Amini from power in July 1962 and appointed his friend and confidant Asadollah Alam to the post of prime minister. In a sense the shah, as the U.S. State Department clearly understood, had decided to co-opt "much of the reform program on which the U.S. had placed such emphasis."[56] Robert Komer, of the National Security Council, used a more blunt and less friendly language to make the same point. In a memorandum for President Johnson, he wrote, "you in 1962 and then JFK in 1963 preached reform to him. Now he takes it as his own idea, and wowed his UK hosts recently by a 45 minute peroration on the subject."[57]

But the decision to "co-opt" the reforms did not apparently end the shah's troubles with the Kennedy administration. Justice William O. Douglas, a Kennedy confidant, indicated that the question of the shah's removal was again seriously considered not long before the Kennedy assassination. Douglas writes that "I talked to Jack frequently about conditions in Iran and the corruption that was rampant. Then when he entertained the shah at the White House when he was here on an official visit [in April 1962], Jack concluded that the shah was corrupt and not a person we could trust…The idea was to withdraw American support for the shah, causing his abdication, and to put his son on the throne and establish a regency around him. (That regency had already been selected.)"[58] Justice Douglas's words not only reveal the chasm between the shah and the Kennedy administration, but more importantly they also betray an unexpected arrogance of power in the famously progressive Douglas.

Alam pursued a policy that in outline had much in common with the fourteen points suggested by Bowling. Britain, in the meantime, seemed to have a rather complicated response to the new developments. On the one hand, they resented the growing influence of the United States in Iran. On the other hand they seemed supportive of certain aspects of the so-called land reform, which many observers thought was the original brainchild of Ann Lambton, the renowned British scholar intimately connected to British centers of power. The changes brought about as a result of these reforms were hailed as the "White Revolution." By implementing them, the shah had hoped he would finally find the solid middle-class support he had sought, his dreams of changing Iran to a more modern nation would become a reality, and most important of all, he would not only consolidate his grip on power but gain the love and respect of his people. But the road to the promised land was not altogether bereft of dangers. Through all this Hoveyda would assume an increasingly important role.

CHAPTER EIGHT

The Progressive Circle

If the expression of the voice of the whole people be shut to the call of sufferance, it will make itself heard through that of force, and we shall go on as other nations are doing in the endless circle of oppression, rebellion, reformation; and oppression, rebellion, reformation again; and so on forever.
　　　　　—Thomas Jefferson, letter to Samuel Kercheval, 1816

As the shah moved to tighten the noose around Ali Amini, leaving him no option but to resign, he continued to groom Mansur for more powerful positions. From early 1961, one important element of U.S. policy in Iran had been to "give all appropriate encouragement to the Shah's bringing reliable young men into his administration."[1] At the same time, when efforts to bring the National Front into the government failed, U.S. policy began to call for backing "moderately progressive" forces and governments "in an attempt to take the wind out of the National Front's sail."*[2] They wanted a party, or a movement, that could help mobilize the

---

* Fereydoun Mahdavi, who was one of the young leaders of the National Front and some years later joined Hoveyda's cabinet as minister of commerce, indicates that in 1961 he was approached by an American who claimed to represent the U.S. government and who offered the Front a deal he thought they should not refuse: accept the shah's leadership and join a coalition government. The American official predicted that if the Front did not accept the offer, its leadership would soon end up in prison. Several years later, the offer was renewed, this time by an Iranian citizen who headed a large American-owned publishing company in Iran and who again claimed to represent the U.S. government. By then many of the leaders of the National Front were in prison. A meeting of the central committee of the Front was held in jail; with a vote of twelve to eight, the committee this time decided to accept the offer. Activists outside the prison, however, refused to heed the vote of the majority and the Front did not join a coalition government. The rest is now history. Fereydoun Mahdavi, interviewed by author, 9 August 1999.

same segments of the population—urban middle classes, the technocrats, and the intellectuals—that had historically been the National Front's turf. Mansur's Progressive Circle offered itself as just such an alternative, yet the time for its ascent was yet to come.

By 1962 it had become common knowledge in Tehran that Mansur and his Progressive Circle clearly enjoyed the support of at least some of the American diplomats in Tehran. According to Stuart Rockwell, then minister at the American Embassy, "there was clearly a faction in the embassy who thought highly of Mansur and were his advocates."[3] On May 29, 1963, the shah took the unusual step of issuing a proclamation indicating that the Progressive Circle enjoyed his support.* The king's gesture was a sure sign that Mansur's and Hoveyda's rise to power was imminent, and there was a sudden surge of people who wanted to join the Progressive Circle. Nasser Yeganeh, a jurist who in later years became Hoveyda's close friend and confidant, was entrusted with preparing the bylaws.† Throughout these tumultuous times, Hoveyda continued to work at the NIOC. In 1960, he accompanied Entezam on a visit to the United States and came back impressed with the new role of technology in the management and production of oil in the developed world. "We not only have to emulate the most recent industrial management models," he writes in an editorial for *Kavosh*, "but we have to train our youth of today to become the competent managers of tomorrow." He cites a talk given by Entezam in New York where he told a group of Iranian students, "Iran is your country, come back

---

* In his declaration, the shah said, "This group of educated, trained, and intellectual people intend to engage in a deep and serious study of Iran's socio-economic conditions...They have made us content...and we thus declare that the Circle will henceforth be our Special Bureau of Economic Studies, and that its members will be the subject of our particular attention." The shah's motives for this unusual step are not hard to fathom. Here was, after all, a group of competent technocrats who seemed to enjoy the support of the American Embassy yet, contrary to Amini, had no overriding desire to act independently of the shah. They also held out the possibility of challenging, if not rending obsolete, the National Front. One key to the riddle of the Islamic Revolution in Iran is the fact that while Hoveyda and his group, as "surrogates" for the National Front, according to Yatsevitch, failed to curb the shah's authoritarian tendencies, the National Front itself, in 1978, in its greatest hour of glory, failed to stand up to Ayatollah Khomeini's incipient despotism. In both cases, the real National Front and its surrogate Progressive Circle (which eventually became the Iran Novin Party) sacrificed long-term democratic ideals for short-term political gains.

† Yeganeh eventually fled to the United States after the revolution. He was a proud man, in dire financial straits. His friends discreetly helped him survive. He lived on a small boat he had purchased with a lump sum payment he had received for some consulting work for the State Department's legal division. In the end, benighted and poor, he committed suicide. I owe much of my information about Yeganeh's last days, and his mood, to Hormoz Gharib, interviewed by author, 11 February 1998.

home, roll up your sleeves, and help carry this heavy burden."[4]

By 1963, Hoveyda was spending more and more of his time organizing the affairs of the Progressive Circle. In October 1963, Mansur informed Julius Holmes, the American ambassador, that he expected "to be called to form a government within three or four months."[5] Later in the same month, Mansur again visited the U.S. Embassy and briefed the ambassador about his future plans. In reporting the contents of the meeting, the ambassador added that "Amir Abbas Hoveyda, presently a high official of the NIOC, has been Mansur's right-hand man in the development of the Progressive Circle…[Mansur indicated that] Hoveyda would stay on with the NIOC for some time but that he would have fewer duties and responsibilities and would have time to undertake the organization and administrative direction of the new progressive party—although Mansur made no positive statement, I believe that this has been cleared with the Shah." Holmes ends his note by emphasizing that "I still remain in serious doubt that he [Mansur] has the qualities of character and intelligence to turn him into an effective political leader."*[6]

While Hoveyda and Mansur were busy recruiting technocrats to join the Progressive Circle, Iranian politics was entering a period of bloody upheaval. Land reform pursued doggedly by a charismatic minister of agriculture, Hassan Arsanjani, gave rise to the ire of the Iranian landed gentry. One can easily argue that the most consequential component of the White Revolution was the land reform. To his credit, the shah had been talking about implementing some kind of land distribution long before the American pressure for reform began to build. But when the land reform program did begin finally, Arsanjani brought to the process the flair of rural radicalism, his own knack for populism, and finally a commitment to an egalitarian ideology. The result was historic in proportion. The economic and political structure of the Iranian countryside was irrevocably revamped. Ninety-two percent of peasants who toiled on land

---

* Holmes was not alone in this assessment. If documents published in the Islamic Republic of Iran are to be believed, then SAVAK too did not have much hope in Mansur's leadership qualities. In a profile prepared in July of 1958, Mansur is described as "the son of an enormously wealthy father…He reads a lot of newspapers. He loves women and power…He is not a particularly capable man…His father has been one of the most important agents of the British…He is humble but bereft of character…he is not moved by any lofty ideals…He owes his rise to power to his father's influence…He is unintelligent, inexperienced and unduly loved." Quoted in Khosrow Moatazed, *Hoveyda, Siyasatmadar-e peep asa va orkid* [Hoveyda: The Politician of Pipe, Cane and Orchid] (Tehran, 1999), 462–3.

they did not own benefited from the land redistribution, and became landowners.[7] In other words, "Whereas in 1960…only 26 percent of the land was sown and cultivated by the proprietor, in 1972… the proportion was 78 percent."[8] As a result of this development the "virtually absolute, and often arbitrary, political power which formerly had been the monopoly of the large land-lords was assumed by the central government."[9]

Aside from changing the pattern of ownership, land reform also brought about important demographic changes in the country. While in the early sixties, about thirty percent of the population lived in cities, by 1975, the figure had risen to 45 percent.[10] The shah had turned much of the Iranian landed gentry into his foes, hoping in return to gain the support of the newly landed peasants. In the mid-1960s, judging by the shah's popularity, the gambit seemed to have worked (though most of the clergy seemed to be against it). But when the tremors of the Islamic revolution began to shake the foundations of his regime, desperately needed peasant support "failed to materialize," and that failure was an important, if not crucial, element in determining the fate of his regime.[11]

Besides land reform, changes in the condition of Iranian women was the most far-reaching element of the White Revolution. The first important changes were new laws granting women the right to vote (once again the clergy were very much against these laws). Furthermore new electoral bylaws requiring elected deputies to local councils to take the oath of office not on the Koran but on any "holy book," all worked together to create the now famous June 1963 uprising in Tehran and a few other major cities. In retrospect, the events of that June can clearly be seen as the dress rehearsal for the 1979 Islamic Revolution. If the 1963 arrest of Ayatollah Khomeini triggered the June uprising, another attack, this time in the form of a brief article in a Tehran daily, was the opening salvo of the Islamic Revolution. If the arrest and subsequent events, including his exile from Iran, catapulted him into the center of Iranian politics, the article eventually brought him back to power as the triumphant leader of a revolution.[*]

By all accounts, the man most responsible for successfully suppressing the uprising was Alam. As he makes clear in his self-serving and self-adulating *Diaries*, in anticipation of large demonstrations by the opposition, he had told the nervous shah to give him temporary control of the military. Only a

---

[*] For a discussion of the letter, its genesis and consequences, see chapter 14, Le Bouc Émissaire.

show of force, he believed, would quell an uprising. He would order the army to shoot at demonstrators. According to Alam, he convinced the shah of the wisdom of his plan. Should Alam fail in suppressing the demonstrators, he told the shah, he could have Alam arrested and make him the scapegoat.[12] Alam also suggests that the American government was probably behind the uprising.[13] There seems little doubt that Alam thought that only his stern and steady leadership saved the shah's throne on that fateful day.

But only a week later, the shah was thinking about replacing Alam. According to a report by the U.S. Embassy in Tehran, on June 23, 1963, the shah met with an official of the embassy and offered not only his analysis of the June riots but also his strategy for the next few months. For security reasons, the name of the official who met with the shah has been deleted from the published declassified memorandum, which quotes the shah as saying:

[The June uprising] could have been avoided if SAVAK had functioned effectively...The real force behind the troubles...are the reactionary landlords and clergy.

The shah proposes to do some house cleaning among the people surrounding him; for example, there is that weak old man, Court Minister Ala who is really [of] no importance. He and his friends rushed to the shah during the troubles, wringing their hands, and proclaiming the need for [an] immediate change of government, and negotiations with the mullahs and other dissidents. There is another useless group like that including people like Sharif-Emami and Entezam.

There will be no political parties at this time, although a single political party will be established after elections to become the main political force in [the] future.

The new political party will be organized, at least in the initial stage by Hassan Ali Mansur and his progressive group.[14]

Every element of this plan was carried out within the next year. Reporting this conversation, Stuart Rockwell, of the American Embassy, offered his own comments about the shah's proposals. He wrote, "we have been coming to the conclusion that the shah intended to use Mansur and his Progressive Group as a nucleus around which to organize and produce Majlis candidates among professionals and business men...If the shah actually names Hassan-Ali Mansur as head of a new political party, or Reform League, and expects serious political results from this organization, he will indeed have to promote the leadership himself. Hassan-Ali Mansur is, to put it mildly, no charismatic leader."[15] If we remember that Rockwell was considered to be, particularly by people like Alam, Mansur's chief champion and the prime force behind his rapid rise to power, his comments, which are far from a ringing endorsement, take on more importance.

On October 25, 1963, the shah once again talked to the U.S. ambassador, Julius Holmes, about Mansur and his prospects. He told Holmes that although he was not "specially enthusiastic about Ali Mansur's potential as a political leader," he felt that Mansur was "the best thing in sight at the moment."[16] Holmes, like Rockwell, also commented on the shah's proposed changes. He writes, "I do not share the Shah's opinion that Mansur is capable of forming an effective political party or of leading the government. His standing with many thoughtful Persians, including members of the Majlis and Senate, is not high."[17]

Not long after these confidential royal conversations, the Progressive Circle changed itself into a party. For its name it chose Iran Novin (New Iran), and women were now encouraged to join its ranks. The first woman to join was Farokhru Parsa. She later became the first woman in the history of Iran to be appointed a cabinet minister and also the first woman to be executed by firing squad after the revolution in 1979. For the 1963 election, Mansur and Hoveyda, with the help of a small group of early Progressive Circle members, came up with a list of candidates for each electoral district. A committee consisting of Alam, Mansur, and a SAVAK representative went over the proposed list and haggled over how many seats Mansur's group should be allocated. Even the composition of the future Majlis leadership was decided in those meetings. Eventually, a list of the future deputies was drafted and submitted to the shah for his final ratification. Once the shah had granted his approval, not surprisingly, all those on the list won their designated seats in the supposedly "free elections."[18]

For the next few months, in spite of several meetings between Mansur and Alam to work out the details of the transition, Alam and his cabinet were in a rather embarrassing lame-duck position.[19] A month before his appointment as prime minister, Mansur had already offered various people posts in his supposedly forthcoming cabinet. A report by the American

The Mansur cabinet, moments after their appointment and audience with the shah
in March 1964. Hoveyda is on the far left.

Embassy and a cartoon by the satirical magazine *Tofiq* offer vivid details of
the surreal situation. The embassy wrote, "with Hassan-Ali Mansur and his
'team' in the wings, waiting to take over the reins of government, and with
Prime Minister Alam remaining on the stage and apparently enjoying dis-
comfiture…[the] situation [is] taking on elements of [a] bad amateur play,
with awkward pauses as everyone waits for his cue. Evidence [is] coming in
that [the] government machinery [is] idling as important decisions [are]
being held up."[20] *Tofiq*'s rendition was even more pointed. In its first issue
of February 1964, it published a cartoon that "pictures Hassan-Ali Mansur
surrounded by large quantities of Kent cigarette butts, looking impatiently
at the leaves of a calendar dropping away. The legend underneath reads,
'waiting is more painful than death.'"[21]

While Hoveyda, too, waited, he was intimately involved in the process
of selecting ministers. He had suggested the foreign ministry for himself,
but the shah had overruled the idea, insisting that Abbas Aram be kept in
the post he had had in the Alam cabinet. Finally, a few days before the Persian new year in March 1964, the shah appointed Mansur to the post he
had coveted for so many years. Amir Abbas Hoveyda was named minister
of finance.

Before the new cabinet could take power, however, Alam had to take care of one important piece of business. In March 1962, the American Embassy had requested that U.S. military personnel in Iran, as well as their dependents, receive immunity from prosecution in Iranian courts. In Iran, the question of such rights, commonly known as "capitulation rights," had a tortured history; they were deemed the epitome of colonial arrogance. When on May 11, 1928, Reza Shah annulled such rights for all foreigners, the act was celebrated with much fanfare. The Alam government, aware of this history, tried to stall negotiations on this U.S. demand. The American Embassy was relentless, and finally early in 1964, Alam chose to bring the issue before his cabinet. In one of the meetings he rather nonchalantly asked the foreign minister, Aram, to report on the proposed new legislation, regarding the legal status of Americans in Iran. Mohammad Baheri, the minister of justice and one of Alam's closest confidants, claims to have strongly objected to the proposed new law, arguing that it was against the spirit and the letter of the constitution, and "it smacked of colonialism."[22] Alam cut the discussion short and suggested that maybe in the future a more detailed analysis of the problem could be undertaken.[23]

No further discussions were ever held in the Alam cabinet. But a few days before the end of his tenure as prime minister, Alam, in accordance with constitutional practice, sent a letter to the newly elected parliament, stating that a proposed new law stipulating the special status of American personnel in Iran had been approved in a cabinet meeting. He was thus, as the constitution demanded, submitting it for parliamentary approval.[24] The letter bore the signatures of Alam and the foreign minister Aram and acting minister of war Asadollah Sanii. Since the proposed legislation dealt with issues regarding jurisdiction of Iranian courts, it should have also included the signature of the minister of justice. Yet, Baheri's name is nowhere to be seen on the document.[*] Furthermore, the alleged cabinet meeting when the proposed legislation was supposedly discussed and approved had never taken place.[25] Baheri claims that his mentor, Alam, undertook such an illegal act because "he loved the shah and wanted to share in the king's disgrace. The shah wanted the deal done."[26]

Alam, however, had cleverly timed his letter to the parliament, asking for the bill's ratification to coincide with his own last days in power. By

---

[*] Mohammad Baheri was generous enough to share with me copies of many of the documents pertaining to these events.

the end of October 1964, both houses of the Iranian parliament passed the controversial new legislation. By then Mansur was prime minister and Hoveyda the most influential member of the cabinet. It would be up to the new cabinet to defend the bill in the two houses, answer any questions, or face any criticism. The senate took up the proposed new legislation around midnight, after a long fourteen-hour session. Undersecretary of the Ministry of Foreign Affairs Ahmad Mirfenderesky was present on behalf of the government to defend the bill. He began by saying, "We could ask for another meeting tomorrow, but it is a small matter, and if you permit us, we will get it over with right now." The senators agreed. Without any discussion, those present rose in approval. The votes were not even counted. The president of the senate declared, "the resolution has passed" and adjourned the meeting.[27]

In the lower house, as confidential U.S. Department of the Army dispatches make clear, "the Shah, fearful [of] criticism [that the] measure was steam-rolled through Majlis, may have authorized some opposition to the bill, which then got out of hand."[28] Further possible proof that the shah had a hand in shaping the opposition in the Majlis is that many of the most vociferous critics of the bill in the parliament were later rewarded with high positions in the government.[29] While most of those criticizing the new law were from the minority party, and thus politically close to Alam, even some in Mansur's own party voted against the bill. This "temporary breakdown [in] party discipline" was because a "secret ballot" was allowed in the case of the bill's passage.[30] Mansur was present during the discussions and reminded the opponents of the bill that Alam himself had drafted the legislation and had been its early supporter. Furthermore, to quell the rebellion of the Majlis deputies, Mansur deliberately lied to them about the nature of the bill, and whom exactly it covered. He also lied to journalists when they asked him about reports that the proposed bill covered not just U.S. military personnel—as Status of Forces Agreements the U.S. normally signs with her allies do—but also their dependents and nonmilitary advisors as well. Mansur retorted with feigned anger that all such reports were "ill-intentioned views of biased persons and foreigners through their fifth columns." He added that "dependents and non-technical personnel are not covered by immunity and that the latter applies only to acts committed while on duty."[31]

This announcement caused serious concern at the U.S. Embassy. They feared that the pronouncement indicated a change of heart in the Iranian government. When the issue was raised through official channels, Nasser Yeganeh, then a minister without portfolio, responded that "there is no doubt whatsoever in the government's mind about correct coverage. But the prime minister, for political reasons, has found it necessary in public utterances to create the impression that coverage [is] limited."[32]

On October 31, Mansur gave what was billed as a "comprehensive foreign policy speech before the senate." Again he discussed the bill and again he repeated a number of glaring untruths about its coverage. The U.S. Embassy in Tehran was rather distressed about what it called the "ineptitude of the Government of Iran," and the clumsy efforts of its "officials to engage in back-tracking maneuvers." Stuart Rockwell sought an "urgent interview" with the prime minister himself. In the course of the meeting, Mansur was asked about each of the inaccurate statements he had made. On each issue, he "backed down," indicating that the letter of the law, and not his inaccurate public pronouncements would be honored by the Iranian government. The terse tone of Rockwell's report of the meeting leaves little doubt that the Embassy had by then grown rather frustrated with Mansur's shady tactics in this regard.

Bothered by what was a clear case of orchestrated public deception, Rockwell then asked Mansur if he intended "to rectify the erroneous public impression which his remarks had created?" Mansur's response was both instantaneous and chillingly mendacious. "By no means," he said, "must there be further public discussion of this matter…Mistakes could be corrected by amending the records."[33] The U.S. government agreed, making no further effort to push Mansur into a fuller, honest disclosure of the bill's actual coverage. "It was not my job," Rockwell now declares, "to rectify Mansur's behavior. Furthermore, this kind of a tactic was typical of him."[34]

It is not clear what role, if any, Hoveyda played in all of these decisions. Given his close relationship with Mansur, it is hard to imagine that he was entirely out of the loop on such an important question.

Mansur's lying gambit worked. After some discussion, the Majlis passed the new law by a small majority of seventy-four to sixty-eight, with thirty-six abstentions.[35] The law's passage provided ammunition to the opponents of the regime, particularly Ayatollah Khomeini. On October 27, 1964, only days after the announcement of the bill's passage, Khomeini made a fiery speech in front of his residence in Qom. Using all the rhetorical tropes of his trade, he talked bravely about the bill's shortcomings. "They have reduced the Iranian people to a level lower than that of an American dog," he said.[36] As punishment for the speech, the government of Iran first arrested, and within days, exiled the ayatollah to Turkey on November 4, 1964. The British government also joined the bill's critics. When around the time of his exile, the BBC referred to Ayatollah Khomeini as "the leader of the Shia Sect (with the implication that he is not merely one of the leaders, but the leader)," the comment raised the shah's suspicions that the "British were snipping at the bill."[37] Mansur and Hoveyda both paid a heavy price for their role in the whole sordid affair. Even though Hoveyda was not directly involved in the bill's passage, the Iranian constitution stipulated the collective responsibility of ministers for any action by the cabinet. In the Islamic tribunal's indictment against Hoveyda, the SOFA figured prominently. In 1965, the American government tried to downplay the significance of the new law by claiming that it was no different from similar agreements (or SOFAs) passed by all NATO allies. The claim was, like Mansur's declaration, simply false. But in the early days of their power, Mansur and Hoveyda were little concerned with the repercussions of a law inherited from the old cabinet.

Mansur's new government was, in many ways, different from all of its predecessors. It was a younger cabinet, primarily consisting of foreign-trained technocrats. As the shah had told the American embassy, a changing of the guard was at hand. The old guard—often aristocratic, usually well-versed in the culture and language of Iran, more likely to be independent, and rarely a tool of the king—was giving place to a new technocratic elite. The elder generation had seen the shah in his most vulnerable hours, when he was weak, marginalized, or on the run. The new elite had had its political baptism when the shah was well ensconced on his throne, in the full regalia of an authoritarian, modernizing monarch.

The old guard reacted to this transition with differing degrees of bitterness and resignation. Entezam was forced to retire to a life of reading, leisurely lunches at the exclusive French Club of Tehran, and weekly gatherings of Sufis at his house, which Hoveyda would sometimes attend.[38] Others, like Seyyed Fakhraddin Shadman, responded with a scathing, albeit indirect, attack on the new elite. Indeed, as his own star waned, that of his younger brother, Zia, a founding member of the Progressive Circle, was on the rise. In an essay published in 1965, Fakhraddin writes, "O

God! To whom can we complain that in this land, the more you are alien to the culture, the more you are likely to be embraced by the powers that be?…Why have our elite become so confused, insecure, and reckless that they show no fear of what they should be afraid of, and know nothing other than how to inadequately mimic strangers?"[39]

New York Times columnist Jay Walz, on the other hand, wrote about the Mansur appointment and his early days in power with exuberance: "Tehran is stirring with new life," he reported, "and there is more to it than spring air wafted in from the high plains…In four weeks Hassan Ali Mansur…has injected confidence into a painfully deflated community…Two days after his appointment on March 7, Mr. Mansur's cabinet of intellectuals was unanimously approved by Parliament together with a 60-page program of action the intellectuals had drafted. For the first time in Iran's history, a government rising from a political party has come into office with a detailed program."[40]

In the weeks leading to his appointment as prime minister, one of Mansur's early goals had been to forge a coalition of sorts with the National Front that had been, by and large, dormant since the 1953 coup. But in the early 1960s, invigorated by a new generation of young activists, the Front had again emerged as an active force. Hoveyda took an active interest in these negotiations. He had a wide circle of friends and contacts among members of the Front. Bani Sadr, the man who came to Hoveyda's prison cell soon after the victory of the Islamic Revolution, was indeed part of this new generation of young leaders. Even Mosaddeq's son, Gholam-Hossein, was a friend of Hoveyda. Through an intermediary—an early member of the Progressive Circle, Mohsen Khajenouri—Mansur and Hoveyda had begun negotiating with leaders of the Front a few weeks before Mansur's appointment as prime minister. Shapour Bakhtiar, the shah's last prime minister, and Hoveyda's schoolmate in Beirut, also took an active role in these negotiations on behalf of the Front. Indeed, it seems he was in favor of such a coalition, while others in the leadership opposed the move.[41] Ali Amini, still very much hoping to return to power, was also negotiating with leaders of the National Front for a coalition under his leadership. The Front ultimately refused Amini's offer as well.[42] It is tempting to imagine what modern Iranian history would have been like had the National Front accepted one of these offers and joined the government. Instead, soon after the breakdown of these negotiations, a number of the leaders of the Front were arrested by SAVAK on apparently unrelated charges. With the arrests, all chances of reconciliation were lost. The shah's resentment of the Front, a residue of his disdain for Mosaddeq, only increased the growing rift between the Front and the Pahlavi regime. It would only be on the eve of the Islamic Revolution that, in desperation, the shah would change course and try to forge an alliance with the Front against the Khomeini onslaught. By then, it was too little, too late. Furthermore, with the exception of Gholam-Hossein Sadighi and Bakhtiar, the other leaders of the Front were intoxicated with dreams of participating in a new revolutionary government, and refused the offer by the shah.

Once Mansur came to power, nearly all talk of a coalition ended. In those early days, most of Hoveyda's time was spent at the notoriously corrupt and inefficient ministry of finance, which had the thankless job of collecting taxes—a key element of the stabilization program suggested by the IMF and other American advisors had been a more rigorous program of tax collection. One of Hoveyda's first efforts in this area was to computerize most of the ministry's operations. With the help of Jamshid Garachedaghi, a graduate of the University of California at Berkeley and an employee of IBM, Hoveyda set up a modern computer system for the ministry. The goal, according to Garachedaghi, was to end the "organized chaos, founded on deep layers of vested interest, that had hitherto defined the ministry."[43]

Another early economic decision was to centralize all budgetary matters into one bureau or office. Until this time, the finance ministry had had effective control over the preparation and implementation of the budget, while the Plan Organization decided budgetary priorities. All previous attempts to streamline the process had failed, primarily because the finance ministers had refused to relinquish any of their control. Hoveyda, however, to the surprise and dismay of many of his colleagues at the ministry, readily agreed to the new arrangement.[44]

Moreover, in line with the cabinet's overall policy of economic reform, Hoveyda announced an end to the government's sugar monopoly and offered laxer new laws for the import of tea. Early in his tenure, Hoveyda also talked of the need for revising the tax laws. He recruited capable men to help with the management of the ministry. Farhang Mehr, a man of sterling reputation and a Zoroastrian by faith, described in American Embassy documents as a "forceful, able man who has stood out among mediocre officials of the finance ministry,"[45] was named an undersecretary in the ministry of finance. Farokh Najmabadi, an oil expert of unblemished reputation and known both for his financial probity and technocratic expertise, was also brought on board. Hoveyda solicited the help of Abdol-Madjid Madjidi as well. Madjidi was a capable manager and an expert on budgetary matters who would end up becoming one of Hoveyda's most trusted ministers. In those days the NIOC was also, at least nominally, under the jurisdiction of the finance ministry. Thus, Hoveyda was involved in some of the negotiations with the consortium that eventually led to an increase in Iran's income from the sale of oil. To carry out his numerous responsibilities, he worked extremely long hours. A sixteen-hour day at the ministry was normal for him. Some of his friends began to worry about his health.[46]

✦ ✦ ✦

BY LATE 1964, HOVEYDA WAS LOOKING RATHER FRAGILE. A car accident in the summer had forced him to spend several days in hospital.* But his convalescence period had one positive result: the many hours he passed with Laila at the hospital began to make them more intimate. "For the first time," Laila remembered, "I began to call him Amir† instead of Mr. Hoveyda."[47] In those days, Amir Abbas and Laila spent nearly all of their leisure time together with Mansur and his wife Farideh.

The happier home life, however, did not extend to Hoveyda's work at the ministry. There, his program had irked "the old guard among the civil servants of the ministry… [The reforms were going to] endanger or destroy the numerous rackets of these officials."[48] Pamphlets attacking Hoveyda were distributed at the ministry. On August 24, 1964, Mansur went to the finance ministry and "used strong words to attack those officials…who are

---

* At that time, Hoveyda, his beloved Laila, Mansur, and Farideh had traveled to the Caspian coast for a brief vacation. One late night, after spending a day water-skiing at Princess Fatimeh's summer resort, Laila was driving the group home in her small German-made Opel. Hoveyda and a security guard sat in the front seat, while Mansur, his wife, and another friend, Victor Khajenouri, sat in the back. Driving rain made for low visibility. As the packed car approached a small, one-lane bridge, a truck suddenly appeared. Laila, in apprehension, lost control of the vehicle, crashing it head-on into the truck. Some in the car were wounded; the whole party was soon airlifted to Pars Hospital in Tehran. Laila had a collapsed lung; Hoveyda had fractured his hip, and part of his kneecap was also damaged; Mansur was unhurt while his security guard only suffered light scratches on his face. Within a few days, they were all released from the hospital.

† Laila, Mansur, and their circle of friends all called Hoveyda Amir. His mother and brother referred to him as Amir Abbas.

opposed to the reforms his government is attempting to carry out in the ministry. According to one press report, the prime minister called such officials 'saboteurs' and 'opportunists.'"[49] A week later, Hoveyda told a press conference that he had "established a unit in the ministry which would 'weed out corrupt and incompetent officials'…He said he would carry out reforms in the ministry 'no matter who dislikes it.'"[50]

Establishing such a unit was not all the government did to fight the pamphleteers. SAVAK was brought in, and in the process, Hoveyda met Parviz Sabeti who was in charge of political analysis for SAVAK at the time. He was a friend of Mansur, and at Mansur's behest he took over the investigation of the troubles at the finance ministry. Within a few years, Sabeti would head SAVAK's "Third Division," responsible for everyday matters of internal security; he would also become Hoveyda's close friend and confidant. In a television appearance in 1970, Sabeti carved for himself an indelible image in the minds of many Iranians. His mastery of facts (or at least his version of them), his methodical eloquence, his systemic approach to issues of security were all part of his image. By 1970, his power permeated all facets of Iranian life. To the opponents of the regime, he was their nemesis, the master behind the machinery of torture, censorship, and oppression. To Iranian politicians, he was one of the most powerful and feared men in the country. All important appointments—from ministerial portfolios and university professorships to elementary school teachers and most civil service positions—needed his department's security clearance.

Tall and handsome, with penetrating eyes and a dark complexion, Sabeti did not fit the common image of a SAVAK agent: polyester pants, faux leather jackets, a vulgar tongue, and an arrogant swagger. His dapper suits, elegant ties, and coifed hair gave him the appearance of a corporate executive. After the 1970 interview, as his political power increased, his face all but disappeared from the media.* He became, like a character in a Le Carré novel, a faceless name that augured fear.

Sabeti found, after his investigation, that about thirty disgruntled or expelled employees were involved in distributing the pamphlets attacking Hoveyda. But in the long run, more important for both Hoveyda and Sabeti was the bond that had developed between them. A report from the U.S. Embassy in Tehran gave a sense of this importance when it said, "In

---

* He made two other television appearances in 1971, talking about the structure and activities of two urban guerrilla groups that had newly emerged in Iran.

any discussion of Hoveyda's assets, the name Parviz Sabeti keeps coming up. Sabeti has been close to Hoveyda all his adult life."[51]

After some early missteps, the economic policies of the Mansur government seemed to have had the desired effects. Politically, the biggest mistake was an increase in the price of kerosene and gasoline some ten months after Mansur came to power. The price increases had to be quickly repealed in response to mass popular resistance. On another occasion, in October 1964, when Mansur declared that his government intended to "redistribute wealth from the rich to the poor," the remarks created "a stir in the press, which played them up as a call for socialism." Mansur was forced to "categorically deny that his government intended to pursue a socialist course and reaffirmed his support for the private sector of the economy. He explained that his remarks referred only to forthcoming proposals to reform the tax laws and tax administration so as to obtain greater revenues."[52]

As the economic crisis started to abate with the increase in oil revenue, the shah's sense of confidence and desire to steer a course more independent of the United States and the West also began to increase noticeably. A report by Armin Meyer, the U.S. ambassador to Iran beginning in 1965, captures the mood of this important transition in relations between the shah and the American government. In a telegram, called the "Shah and U.S.," Meyer not only wrote of the shah's state of mind but seemed prescient of the kinds of tensions that would develop, over the next ten years, with the shah—tensions through which Hoveyda would have to navigate. Meyer wrote, "Shah today is no longer ward of U.S. as in 1941-45, nor vacillating youth of late forties...He is becoming more and more like his father...independent-minded, impulsive and autocratic...Shah wants [an] independent stance for his country...Shah is fully aware how U.S. saved his regime in Azerbaijan crisis and in Mosaddeq days...Yet in present state of mind he conjures up all sorts of specters...By maintaining dialogue with shah re things military we can retain influence in whole spectrum of our relations. Furthermore, by picking up large portions of...business [in pending $200 million arms purchase by Iran] we could help our dollar balance, which we gather is still problem of major concern in Washington...I am convinced we no longer have ability dictating shah's policies."[53]

Two other American reports, however, sound more ominous. In May 1964, the CIA in its National Intelligence Estimate concluded that "it remains uncertain whether modernization in Iran will proceed relatively peacefully or whether violence and revolution are in store. The Shah's reform effort has already helped to stimulate and shape forces which must eventually, in one way or another, bring basic changes to Iranian society."[54]

Yet, the most chilling prediction about Iran's future can be found in a 1966 research memorandum by the director of the Bureau of Intelligence and Research in the State Department, which states,

> On the political side, the Shah has alienated the landlords and the clergy without winning the bulk of the reform-minded intellectuals and members of the middle-class...[He] has shown no inclination to accept some of the reform-minded opposition elements and thus has, in effect, lost for his cause some of the elements most capable of making the reform program effective...Eventually, the various opposition factions may be driven together by a common desire to limit the Shah's power. Should the Shah fail to follow through on the reforms he has begun, the opposition will have an immediate cause and may eventually also acquire the necessary popular support to unseat him...Long before such an impasse is reached, however, some measure of political compromise would be profitable.[55]

The herculean task of making such a compromise possible would for the next decade lie predominantly on Hoveyda's shoulders. The very future of monarchy in Iran would depend on his success in the task.

CHAPTER NINE

The Winter of Discontent

No! I am not Prince Hamlet, nor was meant to be;
Am an attendant Lord, one that will do
To swell a progress, start a scene or two
Advise the Prince; no doubt an easy tool.
Deferential, glad to be of use,
Politic, cautious, and meticulous:
Full of high sentence, but a bit obtuse;
At times, indeed, almost ridiculous—
Almost, at times, the Fool.
  —T. S. Eliot, *The Love Song of J. Alfred Prufrock*

In 1965, Tehran had an unusually cold winter. On Thursday, January 21, the streets were covered with brown slush and snow as the prime minister, Hassan-Ali Mansur, left his car and headed for the parliament building. It was about ten in the morning, and Mansur was there "to submit for ratification new oil agreements that the National Iranian Oil Company had signed with major foreign oil groups that included the Tidewater Group, the Atlantic Group, the Philips Petroleum Company, Italy's National Fuel Board, India's Oil and Natural Gas, India's Oil and Gas Commission, Royal Dutch Shell and a French group."[1] Before he could enter the building, however, he was confronted by an assassin—Mohammad Bokhara'i—waiting for him on the sidewalk. Bokhara'i was a 17-year-old high-school student, who was found to have in his possession "a copy of the Koran and a picture of Ruhollah Khomeini."[2]

The motive for the attack was hardly a mystery. Mansur had come to symbolize the "White Revolution"; more crucially it was during his term as prime minister that the Iranian government exiled Ayatollah Khomeini first to Turkey and then, eventually, to Iraq. As the arrested band of assassins

*Mansur's assassin, Mohammad Bokhara'i,
awaiting his sentence from a military tribunal.*

confessed, the attack on Mansur was retribution for the insults hurled at their beloved *marja'* (the emulated one), the exiled Ayatollah Khomeini. As a group, they were remnants of the *Fada'iyan-e Islam*. It was the same group that, from 1949 to 1953, had murdered two prime ministers, and one minister of education; they had attempted to assassinate the shah, the minister of foreign affairs, and a third prime minister as well.[3] They were also responsible for the brutal stabbing murder of Ahmad Kasravi, an eminent secular historian and a fierce foe of what he called the "obscurantism of Shiite theology."[4]

In 1979, when Ayatollah Khomeini came to power, many of those around him turned out to be members of the *Fada'iyan-e Islam*. Some, like Hashemi Rafsanjani, confessed—publicly and proudly—their complicity in Mansur's assassination. Rafsanjani, in fact, claimed to have provided the gun used in the attack.[5] On that cold January day, before Bokhara'i could be stopped, he had fired five shots at the prime minister. Within a year, the assailant and three other accomplices were executed in Tehran. Two others, armed and ready to kill Mansur should Bokhara'i fail, were given life sentences. A number of people who had, in the past, shown allegiance to the *Fada'iyan-e Islam* were also arrested.[6] Among the imprisoned was a man named Hadji Mehdi Araghi. In his trial, he was condemned to die; on appeal, and apparently as a reward for his good behavior in prison, the death sentence was commuted to life in prison. He served fourteen years, and when Christine Ockrent and the rest of the journalists entered Hoveyda's cell for that infamous March 1979 interview, Hadji Araghi was one of the two officials who accompanied them.

Despite ample evidence that religious circles were involved in Mansur's assassination, many among the secular opposition refused to believe the government's version of who had been behind his death.[7] For example, in 1965, Hedayatollah Matine-Daftary, one of the more prominent members of that opposition and Mosaddeq's grandson, in one of his social visits with members of the American Embassy in Tehran, declared that "he was convinced that the three young men involved in the assassination were not directly linked to any religious or political group, although he thought it possible that the crime would be 'pinned on' one such group or another."[8] Matine-Daftary's statement could, in retrospect, be seen as a sign of the inability of Iran's secular forces to realistically come to terms with the nature and extent of the power (real and overt as well as potential and covert) enjoyed by the religious forces. Thus, as secular advocates of democracy sowed the seeds of opposition to the shah's authoritarianism, it was the often overlooked religious forces that ultimately reaped the harvest.

On that fateful day, as his later testimony in court clearly indicates, Bokhara'i seemed utterly convinced that he was doing nothing short of God's work on earth; it mattered little that the man he was killing had been against the idea of keeping Ayatollah Khomeini in jail. The day after his appointment as prime minister, Mansur had suggested that the ayatollah be freed. "I want to heal the rift between the shah and the people," he had said.[9] But his suggestion had been overruled by SAVAK.[10] The prime minister had been told that first of all, the shah would certainly take umbrage at the suggestion that there was a rift between him and the people of Iran. Furthermore, he was reminded that in security matters he was but a novice and should thus defer to the experts.[11]

But the experts had miscalculated, and now Mansur, bleeding but conscious, was placed back in his limousine. His driver chose to hurry not to the closest emergency room but instead to Pars Hospital, Tehran's most fashionable medical institution of the time.[*][12]

---

* The driver's decision was apparently more a matter of habit than calculated design. In 1964, after the accident in which Mansur and Hoveyda had been involved, he had driven to the hospital so often that on the day of the assassination, he went back to the same place without thinking.

Mansur was immediately taken to the operating room. He was in surgery for three and a half hours. A medical bulletin said "that part of [Mansur's] small intestine had been removed and that his bladder had been operated on."[13] Continued internal bleeding soon necessitated another operation. As Mansur fought for his life, Hoveyda was ordered by the shah to temporarily chair the meetings of the cabinet. It was important that no sign of panic be shown; an air of normalcy had to be created. Hoveyda was also entrusted with the task of keeping the shah informed about any development in the wounded prime minister's critical condition. Indeed, from the day Mansur was brought to the hospital, Hoveyda remained there around the clock. A small visiting area, near the hospital's operating room, was turned into his office. The hospital had quickly become the political center of gravity in Tehran. Mansur's relatives, journalists, and Tehran's political dignitaries converged on the hallways, foyer, and visiting area of the relatively small hospital.

Of all these guests and visitors, Mansur's wife, Farideh, was the most difficult to manage. Described by American journalists as an "Iranian beauty and heiress,"[14] she was nothing short of hysterical over her husband's rapidly deteriorating condition. She demanded constant attention, fired off orders, and accused nearly everyone of either negligence or complicity in the crime itself. It was Hoveyda's job to control her, and he did not often succeed. He showed infinite patience, bore her every insult, accommodated her every wish. But she could not be consoled. If nothing else, Hoveyda's guilt was that he was still alive while her dearly beloved, forty-two-year-old husband lay on his deathbed.[15]

On two occasions, the shah himself came to visit the mostly comatose prime minister. The king was reported to have looked grim. On both occasions, the shah had put on a surgical gown, gloves, and a mask. Mansur could not talk. Of the five bullets that had entered his body, two had entered through his neck, shattering his vocal cords. The other three had ripped through his stomach. Had he survived, Mansur, known for his oratory, would have never been able to talk again. In spite of the gravity of Mansur's condition, he was conscious enough to notice the shah's presence. A smile of gratitude covered his face each time the shah entered the room.[16]

On January 26, at around ten in the evening, Mansur's blood pressure dropped, and he went into a coma again. Infection had spread throughout his body, and efforts to revive him were of no avail. He was pronounced dead at eleven fifteen in the evening. That January 26 was also the third anniversary of "The Shah and People" or "White" revolution. A prime minister who had come to symbolize the spirit of that revolution was killed by Islamic assassins, acting if not at the behest then surely on behalf of Ayatollah Khomeini. Today, twenty years after the Islamic Revolution, with the privilege of hindsight, the day Mansur died must be seen as a day when the fate of Hoveyda, the Islamic Revolution, and the Pahlavi regime seem to have become inseparably intertwined.

After Mansur was pronounced dead, the medical team walked up the stairs to where Hoveyda had been holding office. With due solemnity, Dr. Samii, who headed the team, declared that the prime minister had died a few minutes earlier, at eleven fifteen in the evening.* Though Hoveyda had been expecting the news, though he had known of Mansur's rapidly deteriorating condition, he was nevertheless shocked. Hoveyda broke down and wept. After a few minutes, he regained enough composure to deliver the dread news to the king. The medical team was still in the room when he called the shah's direct line. The conversation was brief. Five words—in English—were all Hoveyda said: "Your Majesty, he is dead."

By then Hoveyda had developed the habit of having most of his confidential, and many of his intimate conversations, in European languages. Sometimes he used English, more often French. He also used French when he spoke with some of his colleagues and his mentor, Entezam. When, in the early sixties, he wrote love letters to Laila, he wrote them in English.[17] It seems that the most important legacy of his expatriate days was a European sensibility, a comfort and ease with French and English that he would never match in Persian. Maybe that was one of the reasons the shah, no less a Francophile, grew to feel so comfortable with Hoveyda. Speaking French, or English, might have been part of their implicit camaraderie; they were both exiles in their own country, at home only in a Europe of their imagination.

Hoveyda was, perhaps, the first true cosmopolitan—equally at home in Beirut and Rome, or Tehran and Paris—to reach the pinnacles of power in Iran. The shah, too, though less intellectually inclined, had the same cosmopolitan bent in his vision. In retrospect, they were both out of sync with the deeply traditional and often religious center of gravity that defined

---

* In later years, not only Dr. Samii, but also two other physicians at the Pars hospital—Dr. Manouchehr Shahgholi and Dr. Shoja Sheikh—were named to different cabinet posts.

Iranian culture. With the bravura of self-assured social engineers, the two men, with the shah unambiguously at the helm, embarked on a radical program, changing the socioeconomic foundation on which that center of gravity stood. Their estrangement from that culture, the speed by which they attempted the transformation, and ultimately the shah's unwillingness to share power and his indecision in times of crisis resulted, in the end, in social convulsions unimaginable in their magnitude. And the foreign language the two men used when talking about matters of state was an indication of this estrangement.

Immediately after the brief conversation Hoveyda told the physicians present that he had been summoned to the palace. In those days, the shah still spent most of his time in the Marble Palace, and the Special Palace, both close to the center of the old city and near the hospital where Mansur had died. As the tempo of modernization increased, as the shah grew more authoritarian in his style of rule, as he became more distant, haughty, and self-referential in his manners, he moved farther and farther away from the traditional center of the city. In April of 1965, while he was working at the Marble Palace, "a member of the Imperial Guard shot his way into the palace with a submachine gun in an apparent attempt to reach the Shah."[18] The incident might well have made the idea of changing his residence even more appealing to him. He would eventually move to palaces perched on the foothills overlooking Tehran—Olympian perches, befitting an aloof, authoritarian king. In politics, location is rarely bereft of symbolic value.

Around midnight, when Hoveyda entered the shah's office in the Marble Palace, the monarch, clearly distraught, was pacing the length of the room. Hoveyda followed the requisite protocol for every Persian granted a royal audience—a *sharaf yabi*, in the Persian vernacular—and kissed the extended right hand of the king.* After the ritual kissing of the royal hand came the offer of condolences for the death of the prime minister. The shah continued pacing and without much ado told Hoveyda that he had chosen him to head a new cabinet. The tone, as Hoveyda would later tell his friends, was one of a command, unequivocal and non-negotiable.[19]

---

* *Sharaf* is Persian for honor, and *yabi* connotes the act of finding. It would be hard to find another concept that so deftly captures the core of the traditional Persian theory of kingship. The king is the very repository of honor. The mere sight of him affords honor to all graced with an audience. The word's usage is not limited to royal audiences. It can also be used to refer to any meeting with a much esteemed, often elder, person.

Hoveyda also recalled that even though he had been expecting the order—
or according to some of his critics, had been hoping for it—he was nevertheless nervous. He still did not know all the rules of decorum for talking
to the shah. He had asked one of his friends about such rules and was told
to never refer to himself as anything other than *Chaker,* roughly equivalent to "humble servant."[20] Later on he would master these rules; he would
learn that in the presence of the shah no one could be called by anything
other than their last name; no honorific or Mr. or Mrs. could be used. The
practice was a slight improvement over Reza Shah's habit of calling people
not by their names but by the name of the office they served.[21]

Hoveyda's demeanor during the meeting reflected the anxious deliber-
ation of a novice in courtly etiquette. As he began to talk, the shah continued pacing his office. After the customary verbal gestures of gratitude for
the chance of serving the sovereign, Hoveyda ventured to say that he felt
unqualified for the job. He insisted that others, like Entezam, were surely
more prepared for the job.[22] Only the day before the audience, he had told
Sadeq Chubak of his reservations in accepting the post of prime minister.
Chubak had urged him not to accept the job, if it was offered to him.
"There is nothing you can do with the situation the way it is," Chubak had
said.[23] Hoveyda ignored the advice and was now ready to take on the reins
of the cabinet. He told the king that he had lived most of his life abroad,
didn't know the Iranian people and they didn't know him; he even mentioned the slight accent in his spoken Persian.[24] His was a hybrid accent,
mixing faint echoes of Arabic with the sounds and syntax of French.

How genuine these words of hesitation were is hard to say. Maybe they
were said in deference to the solemnity of the moment, so proximate to
the death of his beloved friend Mansur. They could have been an example
of the age-old Persian habit of *tarof,* a linguistic labyrinth that hides
meanings and intentions behind a convoluted maze of honorific discourse
and rules of propriety. They could even be construed as signs of Hoveyda's
innate talent as a politician, his intuitive knowledge that an assertive and
overeager prime minister was precisely what the shah did not want. At the
same time, this note of self-deprecation might not have been altogether
perfunctory. Two weeks before the assassination, Hoveyda had told
Abdol-Madjid Madjidi that he had been thinking about resigning his job
as the minister of finance.[25] Some magazines in Tehran even reported that
Hoveyda would soon resign his post and be named Iran's ambassador to

France.[26] A U.S. Embassy report confirms this early professed reluctance by writing in 1965 that among Hoveyda's "assets, of course, is the fact that he did not seek the position of Prime Minister and freely tells everyone that he is not at all anxious to keep it."[27]

But in that midnight hour, as Hoveyda haltingly uttered his unconvincing words of self-deprecation and doubt, the shah, his back to his future prime minister, gazing at the ornate and impregnable palatial gardens outside, retorted curtly, "We, ourself, shall teach you."[28] The words turned out to be partly the shah's attempt at providing psychological reassurance, and partly a prescription and prophecy. In the long run, the words would become a tacit contract with far-reaching political and constitutional ramifications.

The Iranian constitution first promulgated in 1906–07, and inspired by Belgian laws, placed much of the executive power in the hands of the prime minister. In place of a tyrannical despot, it posited a monarch of limited power whose role was to reign but not rule. But by 1965, the shah was in the last stages of changing some of the letter, and most of the spirit, of the constitution. For almost a decade, he had wanted to redefine the constitutionally mandated relationship between the monarch and the prime minister. In 1965, not long after Hoveyda's midnight audience with the king, the Bureau of Intelligence and Research in the U.S. Department of State offered a chillingly accurate and eloquently informed account of this trend. With an uncanny economy of words, the report captured the spirit of the time and offered a textbook description of the authoritarian power structure in Iran. The scope of the powers the shah had amassed by then was nothing short of alarming. The report declared:

> The present Shah is not only king; he is de facto Prime Minister and is in operational command of the armed forces. He determines, or approves, all important governmental actions. No appointment to an important position in the bureaucracy is made without his approval. He personally directs the work of the internal security apparatus and controls the conduct of foreign affairs, including diplomatic assignments. No promotion in the armed forces from the rank of lieutenant up can be made without his explicit approval. Economic development proposals—whether to accept foreign credit or where to locate a particular factory—are referred to the Shah for decision. He

determines how the universities are administered, who is to be prosecuted for corruption, the selection of parliamentary deputies, the degree to which opposition will be permitted, and what bills will pass the Parliament.

[The shah] is convinced that his personal rule is the only way Iran can be governed at the present time.[29]

In Iran, tension between the ruling monarch and his vizier is almost as old as the institution of monarchy itself. Persian historians have long written about two types of viziers. Some, they have suggested, were simply pliant tools for implementing every whim and wish of the potentate, while others exercised considerable autonomy and independence, sometimes even usurping all, save the titular, powers of the monarch.[*][30] With Iran's Constitutional Revolution of 1906–07 came an attempt to infuse into Iranian politics such modern ideas as popular sovereignty, separation of powers, a limited monarch, and the rule of law. The inherent ambiguities in the relations between the vizier and the king were supposed to be replaced by demarcated rules and laws. Nevertheless, tensions between Persian kings and their prime ministers continued unabated after the Constitutional Revolution.

Up until the meeting with Hoveyda during the early hours of that cold January morning, the shah had experienced his share of such tensions. Again, the State Department's Bureau of Intelligence and Research offers an erudite account of these tensions in a tone free of frills, and surgical in its precision:

From the end of World War II to 1953, power was in the hands of strong Prime Ministers and their cabinets. Qavam al-Saltaneh,

---

* A plethora of both kinds of viziers play often pivotal roles in the archetypal tales of *A Thousand and One Nights*. Frequently, the only match for the narrative magic of Shahrzad, herself the daughter of a prudent vizier, turns out to be the cunning schemes of a powerful vizier. Though the *Shahnameh,* the great Persian epic, offers archetypes of wise and prudent ministers, the landscape of Iranian history is strewn with the bodies of powerful viziers who were murdered once the sovereigns had used them to consolidate their despotic powers. The shrewd and cunning vizier of yesterday, often a necessary tool for a young and ascendant prince, became a liability, a potential threat to the potentate of tomorrow. In all too many cases, killing a powerful vizier became the political rite of passage for a new ruler, an unmistakable sign that a new king had indeed arrived. No wonder, then, that Persian sages often advised against serving a sovereign. Sa'di's thirteenth-century *Golestan,* considered by many a window to the soul of Persian sensibilities, is replete with advice to wise men to avoid at all cost proximity to the king. The inevitable hazards of a king's grace, Sa'di wrote, far outweighed its merits.

Razmara, and Mosaddeq, in turn, had blocked the Shah's efforts to
assume a dominant role in Iranian affairs. The Shah's struggle to wrest
power from the hands of strong Prime Ministers in large part accounts
for his refusal to lend a sympathetic ear to proposals that he delegate
some of his hard won authority. The only Prime Minister since the
overthrow of Mosaddeq in 1953 who appeared to be moving toward
reasserting the prerogatives of the office was Ali Amini in 1961-62.

Since the Premiership of General Zahedi (1953-55), the Shah has
generally appointed loyal and docile Prime Ministers. The faithful
courtier, Ala, the zealous administrator, Eghbal, the facile bureaucrat-
engineer, Sharif Emami, the Shah's life-long friend, Alam, the
ambitious technocrat, Mansur, and since the assassination of Mansur
in January 1965, the capable but colorless [sic] Hoveyda, have
constituted a progression of willing instruments charged with carrying
out the Shah's commands. None of these individuals has had
significant popular support, and there is little indication that the Shah
willingly would permit a leader with a strong popular appeal to
become Prime Minister.

The Parliament, like the Prime Minister and his cabinet, is part of
the façade of constitutional government that the Shah has felt obliged
to maintain, particularly as a means to reinforce his image abroad as a
constitutional monarch. Both houses of the present Parliament were
handpicked by the Shah through the controlled elections of 1963.[31]

Thus we see that when Hoveyda agreed to be "taught" his job by the
king, he was stepping into precisely the role envisioned by the shah in his
long-cherished dream of consolidating authoritarian rule. In a sense,
accepting the offer also ensured Hoveyda's own long tenure in an office
that was fast becoming only a hollow shell of its constitutional mandate. A
Faustian bargain had been struck. An almost inverse correlation between
Hoveyda's personal success and his political legacy began to take shape.
While the first was at least partly measured in terms of his longevity in
office, the second was determined by how far he could preserve the integrity and the independence of the office with which he was entrusted. The
State Department's "secret report" makes clear that by the time Hoveyda
was named prime minister there was little power and independence left to
the office. Hoveyda did not reverse this trend, but by allowing himself to be

taught the job, he seems to have further weakened the already enfeebled office. Could Hoveyda safely claim, as he eventually did, that he shouldered little blame for the shah's illegal interventions in politics simply because, by the time he was appointed prime minister, the system was already in place? Is there no responsibility for continued participation in an already existing, but flawed and unconstitutional, system? Would his mentor, Entezam, have disagreed with placing all the blame on the system and absolving the individual of any responsibility? Entezam, after all, chose forced retirement over feeding the shah's increasing appetite for power. Hoveyda, on the other hand, decided during his meeting with the shah to become the servant of that appetite.

After the audience with the shah, Hoveyda returned to the hospital. He walked with some hesitation up the stairs and met again with the medical team, and some of his friends and associates. He had been gone for no more than an hour. "I have been ordered by the shah," he told those gathered at the hospital, "to form a cabinet. I have reluctantly accepted. I had no ambition for this job, and the fact that I have to assume these responsibilities after the death of my closest friend makes it even less appealing."[32] He talked of honoring his friend's memory and the necessity of accepting the commands of the king. He thanked the medical team for their efforts to save Mansur, knowing full well that they had already become embroiled in a controversy that would only grow with time.

Soon after Mansur had been brought to the hospital, and the urgency of his condition discovered, it was decided that consulting physicians should be flown in from the West. A hundred or so years ago a Persian king had, for the first time, retained a European physician as his own personal doctor. Since then, it had become one of the privileges of power, and a measure of class distinction and snobbery, either to go to Europe when a medical emergency arose or to bring Western physicians to Iran for consultation. Mansur's critical condition certainly qualified as just such an emergency.

Political and cultural considerations, however, complicated the process of selecting qualified physicians to help with the care of the mostly comatose prime minister. In the postwar period, Iranian physicians and intellectuals were divided into two fiercely competitive camps. Those educated in Europe, particularly France, had, as a rule, little respect for those trained in America. The American-trained doctors, on the other hand, felt superior to their European counterparts. The composition of the medical team attending the prime minister became a subject of conflict between these two camps. Consequently, while two American physicians, affiliated with Cornell University Medical School, were flown in at the invitation of Dr. Samii, the Iranian doctor heading the team, there was ample political pressure to bring in European physicians as well. A French and an English doctor were, therefore, added to the team.[33]

Aside from the intellectual squabbles between European-trained and American-trained doctors, the larger political question of Iran's relationship with the United States, Britain, and France was also at work in the selection process. A purely American team of physicians might have sent the wrong political message to the world. It would signal a serious turn in Iranian politics away from Britain and toward America.

In any case, the multinational team could not work harmoniously. The French physician soon left Iran in protest and, after the death of Mansur, published inflammatory articles in French newspapers, claiming that Mansur was assassinated twice—once on the streets of Tehran and a second time in the hospital.

The French physician's claims only fanned the flames of an already spreading controversy in Tehran. The shah, in some of his public pronouncements, implied that the British government had a hand in the assassination.[34] Furthermore, soon after Mansur's death, his wife Farideh advocated various conspiracy theories about the assassination. For a while she believed that there had been a conspiracy in the government to kill her husband. It is not hard to imagine the pain that such accusations must have caused Hoveyda. Farideh was the widow of his closest friend, and the sister of the woman he loved and hoped to marry.

Even though Mansur's assassin confessed to the act, lingering doubts about a conspiracy in high places continued. Conspiracy theories thrive most when verifiable facts are hard to find. Ironically, Hoveyda himself eventually came to doubt the veracity of the official explanation of the assassination. He developed a conspiracy theory of his own. He apparently believed that SAVAK had a hand in the assassination. One night, five years after Mansur's death, Hoveyda had drunk one too many glasses of scotch. He overheard General Nasiri, the head of SAVAK, make a passing critical comment about Hoveyda's cabinet. Giddy and red-cheeked, Hoveyda turned to Nasiri and said, "General, if ever the time for us to leave comes, just tell us; you don't have to do to us what you did to Hassan-Ali

Mansur."[35] It is not clear whether Nasiri ever reported the incident to the shah. But many years later, when again the issue of Hoveyda's suspicions about SAVAK's possible complicity in the assassination arose, it was Sabeti who convinced Hoveyda that his suspicions were unfounded.[36]

But on the night of Mansur's death, there was too much on Hoveyda's mind to think about conspiracies. He called his secretary, Vajieh Ma'refat, and asked her to go to his office at the finance ministry and transfer all his papers to the prime minister's office. Calls were also made to all ministers, asking them to come to the prime minister's office as soon as possible. After a brief meeting of the cabinet, at around two thirty in the morning, an official announcement of Mansur's death was drafted. It was read over the radio at three thirty in the morning. It declared that Mansur had been "one of the faithful guardians of the Shah and People Revolution," and had been killed on the third anniversary of that revolution by a "treacherous conspiracy and treason."[37] It also announced that the official memorial would be held at Sepahsalar Mosque, no more than a hundred yards from the spot outside the parliament where Mansur was shot, and not far from the Refah School where fourteen years later Hoveyda was imprisoned.[38]

The problem of the burial also needed Hoveyda's immediate attention. He entrusted the task of making the preparations for the funeral and the burial to his close associate, Zia Shadman, one of the original members of the Progressive Circle. Shadman became Tehran's mayor when Mansur was appointed prime minister. Most important of all, among his friends, Shadman was known as Seyyed, a title given to those who claim direct descent from the prophet. He was the son of a cleric and a deeply devout Muslim. Having Shadman take care of the funeral, Hoveyda hoped, would ensure that all Islamic rites and rituals would be heeded, and the funeral would be spared the plague of religious controversy. He was wrong.

Shortly after Mansur was declared dead, Shadman arranged for the body to be moved to the coroner's office. Security was tight. SAVAK feared another attack on other members of the cabinet or even the body of the dead prime minister. An unescorted ambulance was used to transfer the body. Shadman, along with a security guard, sat next to the driver, while a casket holding the body was in the back.

At the morgue, the only empty slot available had been the middle drawer of a three-tiered row of refrigerated metal repositories. The body on top belonged to an old man, dead for many weeks, unmourned,

unknown, and unclaimed. In the bottom drawer was the body of a prosti-
tute, stabbed to death a couple of nights earlier. When they pulled out the
empty middle drawer, it was full of files belonging to the two people in the
other drawers.[39]

On Thursday, January 28, after an official memorial at the Sepahsalar
Mosque, Mansur's body was moved for burial to the yard leading to Reza
Shah's tomb, near Tehran. The shah's special permission had been received
so that the body could be buried there. Soon after the funeral a rumor
spread in Tehran alleging that as Mansur's body, wrapped in a traditional
shroud, was lowered in the grave, Hoveyda pulled out a pocket edition of
the Koran and placed it on the body before it was covered with earth.
Every Muslim knew, critics argued, that the Koran should never be put in
a grave where it can be desecrated by dirt. It was nothing short of sacrilege, they said; it was his clumsy attempt at disinformation about his
alleged Bahai affiliation; a sign of his pretense at piety.

The rumor was only partially true. As a photograph published in the
newspapers of the time shows, Hoveyda, with tears rolling down his
cheeks, had indeed placed a Koran inside the folds of the shroud. It was,
however, neither his own idea nor necessarily a sign of his ignorance of
Islamic law. During the burial, Zia Shadman had stood next to Hoveyda.
"As they lowered the body," he recollects, "I pulled out a little Koran I carried in my pocket, passed it to Hoveyda, and told him to place it inside the
shroud." Furthermore, as Shadman vigorously points out, "there is no
Islamic law prohibiting such an act; indeed, many shrouds are covered
with Koranic verses."[40]

No sooner was the announcement of Hoveyda's appointment made
public than Tehran's political pundits began to declare his tenure as only
temporary. He was a novice, they said, a lightweight who had no social
base; the appointment was temporary; a tribute to Mansur. Once the crisis was contained, they thought he would be forced to step down.

Ali Amini considered himself a candidate to return to power and was
"plugging a so-called 'united front' as a broadly based political party."[41]
When in a March 24 speech, the shah, in a clear and unambiguous reference
to Amini, said that "unprecedented damage [was] done to the economy
three years previously," Amini "who had hoped for a comeback was dis-
heartened."[42] The weekly magazine *Khandaniha* even attempted some bitter
sarcasm when it suggested, about a year after Hoveyda's appointment, that

he, "like his master and mentor, is learning the ways of the dervish and preparing for a life of seclusion at home."[43] Another issue of the same magazine suggested that Hoveyda had no real power; important appointments were made without even prior consultation with him; he did not, the article concluded, even "have power over hiring the help in his own house."[44] It was something of a consensus that his cabinet would be but a *mohallel.* In its common usage, *mohallel* conjured a sense of derision, an air of anachronism, an implicit message of impermanence and fleeting durability. At the same time, it is a word with obtuse but precise meanings.* By the mid-1960s it had an aura of sarcasm and jocularity attached to it. In Hoveyda's case, the joke turned out to be on the jokesters. He went on to serve longer than any other prime minister in modern Iran.

The insidious metaphor of *mohallel* was not the only talk of marriage in Hoveyda's life in his early days as prime minister. In the first week of July 1966, Laila returned from a long European trip. She had traveled there in the company of her grieving sister, Farideh. After the death of her husband, Farideh had become deeply depressed, somewhat paranoid, and intolerably bitter. Her public persona of the stoic widow owed much to her admiration for, and emulation of, Jacqueline Kennedy, the preeminent political widow of the time. In private, however, she was restless, susceptible to conspiracy theories, intemperate, and often angry at those who had outlived her young husband. "Amir put up with her every whim," Laila remembered, "and quietly suffered her every affront. He rapidly passed a special cabinet resolution, later enacted by the Parliament, that so long as she lived, she would receive the full pay of the prime minister."[45]

Mansur's death had left Farideh in a volatile mood. For a while she became enamored of Che Guevara. Then Shapour Reporter, referred to by the American Embassy in Tehran as one of Iran's chief influence peddlers, became a regular visitor.[46] Reporter was also one of Britain's chief operatives in Iran—a job he had inherited from his father—and was knighted for his services.[47] He had also been one of Mansur's classmates in high school,

---

* *Mohallel* is an Arabic word that, like thousands of others, has found its way into the Persian vernacular. It is in exile from Islamic jurisprudence. According to Islamic law, a divorced couple—or to be more precise in the lexicon of Islamic law, a trice-divorced woman—can not remarry unless the woman goes through an interim, duly consummated, marriage. The man of that interim marriage is called a *mohallel.* In the old days, each town had a coterie of such reliable *mohallels,* men who, for the right recompense, would marry the still desired but divorced woman, feign consummation, and then divorce her forthwith. A few of course always reneged, asking for a more handsome reward.

which alone would have been enough to endear him to the grieving widow.

But ultimately, neither the radical chic of Che Guevara, nor the storied past of Reporter proved to be adequate consolation for Farideh. She remained tempestuous and ill-tempered. After a while, even Laila could no longer bear her sister's blue and bruising mood, and decided to return to Iran.

While in Europe, Laila had received numerous love letters from Amir Abbas. She chose to burn them all, for they were, in her words, written in an "awkward, overstylized, arcanely romantic English."[48] A few days after her return to Tehran, in early July, she went to see Hoveyda and, without much ado, said, "Let's get married." Caught off guard, Hoveyda, nonetheless, embraced the idea. Laila was adamant that they marry as soon as possible and "without any ostentatious ceremonies."[49] They decided to marry the next week at his seaside bungalow, on the Caspian. "I had sold him the land," Laila said, "and he had built a bachelor's den on it: a large room, with a fireplace, a bedroom, a bath, and a veranda."[50]

Aside from his love for Laila, there had also been political pressure for Hoveyda to get married. A few weeks after his appointment as prime minister, Senator Matine-Daftary had said in the senate that Prime Minister Hoveyda and all other bachelors in the cabinet should be required to marry so that they would have more intimate knowledge of a family's cost of living. Earlier, when Hoveyda was appointed minister of finance, the shah, too, had told him that he "should get married."[51]

A week later, on July 19, 1966, Laila and Amir Abbas were married in a simple ceremony attended by the shah, Queen Farah, Laila's father and mother, Hoveyda's mother, and his friend Dr. Manouchehr Shahgholi and his wife. Fereydoun was at the time in Europe, and other friends and family were not invited due to Laila's insistence on a small, intimate wedding. The ceremony was performed by a local cleric, a simple man, more at home with peasants than with royalty. The sight of the king and the queen so rattled him that he could only stammer the part of the ceremony where he was supposed to recite Koranic verses.

Tradition dictates that the cleric performing the ceremony read the appropriate verses and then demand of the bride at least three times whether she will take the groom to be her lawfully wedded husband. Lest she appear unduly anxious, or wanton in her desire, the bride is expected to remain silent the first two times the question is asked. Only on the third time around is she allowed a demure, barely audible, affirmative response. True to form, Laila refused to heed the demands of tradition, and the first time the stammering mullah asked the question, she answered with no hesitation, "Yes."[52] A picture of the wedding captures Laila's mood on the night of the marriage. She sits next to Hoveyda, who has his arm wrapped around her. She seems ever so gingerly to be avoiding the embrace. She is wearing a handsome sleeveless dress, and high-heeled shoes. She is holding a cigarette in one hand and a glass of wine in the other.

Though the ceremonies were supposedly private, pictures of the wedding, along with lengthy articles, nearly all praising the simplicity of the affair, appeared in Tehran's newspapers and magazines the next day. Critics, however, then as now, have offered sinister motives for the wedding. "By marrying Laila," one critic suggested at the time, "Hoveyda has married into a family that has produced five prime ministers."[53] In other words, social climbing was the motive for the marriage. Others suggested that the marriage was a ruse, intended to quell rumors of Hoveyda's homosexuality.[54]

The Hoveyda wedding party, July 19, 1966. From left to right: Laila's father, Mrs. Shahgholi, Laila, Hoveyda, Laila's mother, Hoveyda's mother, and Dr. Shahgholi.

A languorous holiday afternoon in Laila's parents' garden, circa 1967.

The prattle of the people seems to have missed the essence of the marriage. While for Hoveyda it was clearly a marriage of love, for Laila it was a marriage of gratitude: "We in the family," she said wistfully, "were all *touchés* by his gentle treatment of Farideh."[55] But as time went by, her relationship with her husband changed in a rather unconventional way. In the meantime, there was to be but a short honeymoon of a few extra days at the seaside.[56] Hoveyda was, after all, as much married to his job as to his beloved Laila. And in that job, one of his first acts had been to send a short, one-word telegram to his friend Edouard Sablier: *"Viens!"*[57]

CHAPTER TEN

Notes from a Time of War

The fox knows many things, but the hedgehog knows one big thing.
—Archilochus

On Friday, May 10, 1940, as German planes began their attack on Brussels, Hoveyda had run out of his room in a house on Avenue Louise and onto streets filled with frantic citizens, gazing into the sky. The texture of life had, suddenly and palpably, changed. The night before, Amir Abbas and a friend had gone to the cinema to see *Ninotchka,* an Ernst Lubitsch film. Later they went to dinner at the Blue Watch Café. Hoveyda ordered "bifteck frites." After dinner they sauntered to a dance hall, where they were joined by other friends. They drank and danced till the early hours of the morning. The hall was brimming with young, carefully coifed, and handsomely dressed women; their arms, bare and beautiful, caught Hoveyda's attention.[1]

We know all this because Hoveyda chose to tell us. About a year after becoming prime minister, he began to publish small segments of the private journal he had kept since his youth. Originally written in French, they were translated into Persian with the help of a friend. Who that friend was we do not know.[2] The result, nonetheless, was a Persian prose of considerable poise and sophistication.

In Hoveyda's case, the translation was made more complicated by the linguistic and cultural labyrinth that was his life. The original version of the journals has apparently not survived. Not long after the Islamic Revolution, wary of attacks by frenzied mobs, Hoveyda's friends and family burned all his papers, including his journals.[3] Moreover, all the inevitable omissions and interventions, first by Hoveyda and then by the translator, give his published journals a particularly "fictive" quality. Hoveyda was well aware of this quality, and in another segment of the journal wrote that one day he hoped to publish a more complete version of his journals and call them "À la Recherche du Temps Perdu."[4]

But now, over thirty years later, those once translated phrases, those once concocted images of the self that Hoveyda had in mind when selecting the passages to be translated, must be turned into yet a third language. Those images must be collated with another self fashioned for him out of shreds of official Persian, French, and English documents and shards of memory.

In the treacherous terrain of cross-cultural sensibilities and hybrid identities that defined Amir Abbas Hoveyda, the dangers and temptations of this double bind are only confounded. There was, to begin with, novelty in his very act of publishing such a journal. In the history of Persian letters, there has always been a dearth of biographical and autobiographical narratives.[5] Very few Iranian politicians of his generation had ever kept a daily journal; none had ever published them while in office. Even in the West, where public figures are more prone to publish their memoirs and diaries, rare are the instances where such accounts have been published while their authors were still in office.

Furthermore, Persian is a language of circumlocution and complicated rules of decorum about the public and the private *(zaher o baten)*. It is a language that has come to replicate the Shiite principle of *Taghiya,* or "dissimulation," a concept similar in its advocacy of ingenious lies to the Jesuit ideas of "equivocation."[6] Ultimately, Persian in its written form is a language where the "I" is rarely afforded a space of its own. Instead, it often appears as an appendage, hidden both spatially and metaphorically, behind the verb. The act, in short, is more important than the actor; and biography, as a genre, posits the significance of the actor—its gaze, beneath and beyond the web of circumstances, is on the individual. Hoveyda published his youthful journals in a society obsessed with enclosures and walls, with hiding the private from the public, with abiding by the intricate laws of aloof silence about one's life. His refreshing honesty about some of his youthful foibles, his refusal to feign piety, his decision to include the mundane were all something of an iconoclastic gesture. For most Iranian politicians of Hoveyda's generation, a public reticence to talk about the private self was deemed an indispensable sign of power. Hoveyda wanted to change all of that. As with most of his political habits and values, so too in his approach to journals and memoirs, he was more Western than Persian.

Of all his journal entries, why did Hoveyda choose to first publish the segment about the war in Brussels? To a society that barely knew him, this was the first close glimpse he offered, the first self-portrait he drew.* It must have been, at least in broad strokes, how he desired to be seen by Persians. But as with any writing, journals are rarely docile tools of their writers; they invariably tell us more than the authors wish to convey.

On closer examination, "Notes from a Time of War" appears as both a deft self-portrait and a political manifesto. Of all the segments of the diaries he published, it is by far the longest. Its language is at times beguilingly simple and direct, at other times metaphorical. Any careful reader can collate from it Hoveyda's political creed, as well as some of the reasons for his decision to seek a position of power in Iran.

The self he creates for himself in the diaries is made of literary cloth, hued by multiple shades of politics. There is in them a grab bag of philosophy and history, political theory and literary allusion. If hedgehogs are, according to Isaiah Berlin's brilliant taxonomy of political persuasions, those "who relate everything to a single central vision," and foxes "pursue many ends, often unrelated and even contradictory...without, consciously or unconsciously seeking to fit them into...one unchanging, all-embracing...unitary inner vision,"[7] then Hoveyda was a fox in a culture enamored of hedgehogs.

In "Notes from a Time of War," Hoveyda emerges as a character at once brooding and exuberant; carefree about everyday life and curious about its metaphysical meaning and explanation; a self eternally optimistic about individual humans and the immediate future, and deeply pessimistic about humanity in general and the future of humankind. In the leisurely quality of life the narrative describes, the literary precursor of this self is what Walter Benjamin has famously called "the Flâneur," an

---

* Before his appointment as prime minister, Hoveyda had published brief sketches of characters from the days he worked in Geneva. "Notes from a Time of War" are the first extensive parts of his daily journals he published after he became the premier.

urban detective, unattached and astute, a roaming Gypsy-like character who is "everywhere in possession of his incognito." The Flâneur is home everywhere and nowhere. "For him alone, all is open."[8] Hoveyda, like a Flâneur, writes with equal zeal about Paris and Beirut, London and Damascus, Brussels and Tehran.

The Flâneur is more than anything else a peripatetic intellectual, and the diaries make it amply clear that for Hoveyda, an essential component of the identity he envisioned for himself was one of an intellectual. Almost every page of the published journal is strewn with references to some European intellectual, from Albert Camus and André Gide, to Karl Marx and Alfred de Vigny. This intellectual identity could well be one of the reasons for the shah's long affinity for Hoveyda. The shah craved intellectual affirmation. He paid handsomely for any intellectual of the opposition that would come to his "camp." He would often rave to journalists that "his" prime minister was a voracious reader. Hoveyda also was not averse to using his ties with the intellectual community for bridging the chasm that separated the intellectuals of the opposition from the Pahlavi regime.

The most important of these early attempts as prime minister was Hoveyda's early 1966 convocation of a group of famous Iranian writers and intellectuals: Ahmad Shamloo, Reza Baraheni, Gholam-Hossein Sa'edi, Yadollah Royaee, Darvish Shariat, Cyrus Tahbaz, and Jalal Al-e Ahmad.[9] While there are at least three different accounts of the meeting's genesis, there is something of a consensus on what transpired.[*] Once the group of seven writers were assembled in Hoveyda's office, they talked for about an hour and a half. Hoveyda seemed rather nervous. On more than one occasion, in an apparent allusion to SAVAK, he referred to "the General" and the need to coordinate policies with him. Al-e Ahmad did most of the talking and at times used rather harsh language to attack the Pahlavi regime. If ever there was a man conscious of cultivating his public image, Al-e

---

[*] In one version of the meeting's genesis Gholam-Hossein Sa'edi, one of the most celebrated writers of the time, told the interviewers in the Harvard Oral History Project about Iran that one day a man named Davoud Ramzi contacted him. Ramzi suggested that if he had concerns about censorship, a meeting could be arranged with Hoveyda. Sa'edi consulted his friends, particularly Al-e Ahmad, and together they decided that a delegation of writers should meet the prime minister. A second version is provided by Reza Baraheni. In the preface to the Persian version of his celebrated *Crowned Cannibals,* he indicated that it was the writers who initiated the meeting to protest new rules of censorship. I also talked to him on two occasions about the meeting and what transpired. A third version is offered by Ehsan Naraghi, who thought both earlier narratives were "nonsense. These people lie," he told me. According to Naraghi, it was Al-e Ahmad who initiated the meeting and talked to Hoveyda while only Naraghi was present. Ehsan Naraghi, interviewed by author, 18 June 1999. For Baraheni's account, see Reza Baraheni, *Zel Allah* [Crowned Cannibals] (Tehran, 1979), 14–27.

Ahmad was that man, and the image he had carefully, and deservedly, cultivated was one of a brave, fearless, and defiant foe of despotism. He complained of censorship. Hoveyda indicated that he, too, was against censorship. Indeed, a few months after his appointment as premier, he had declared in a meeting of the Majlis that "I am against the idea of censorship of the media…I am willing to give my life for liberty so that everyone can talk freely. We should allow everyone to speak their mind."[10] But in the meeting Hoveyda claimed to have no knowledge of censorship in the country.[11] His claimed ignorance of the existence of censorship was disingenuous at best. The magazine he himself edited in the 1960s while he was still at the National Iranian Oil Company was closed down by censors for a while—or, according to Mohammad Safa, by order of the shah himself—on account of one favorable reference to Mosaddeq in a footnote.[12] The writers group had come prepared and provided some recent cases of censorship by the government. Hoveyda called in his assistant, Karim-Pasha Bahadori, and asked him to investigate the reported incidents.

In the course of the conversation, the prime minister suggested that the writers should create a committee that would be given oversight power over all published material in Iran. "We have come to object to censorship," Al-e Ahmad retorted, "and instead you want us to become censors ourselves."[13] Then Al-e Ahmad began to wax poetic about the "battle between pen and power" and seemed on his way to delivering a long speech about the battle. Hoveyda abruptly stopped him and said, rather sardonically, "Mr. Al-e Ahmad, spare us the details; I, too, have read this stuff."[14]

The irreconcilable tone of the meeting provides some clues to the dynamics of the Islamic Revolution in Iran. Advocates of modernity, from the likes of Hoveyda and the shah on the one hand to the Iranian middle class and large segments of the intellectual community on the other, were, in spite of their strategic common cause, caught in a war of attrition. This was in part the result of differing conceptions of what modernity entailed. Political differences and the after-shock of the coup of 1953 further added fuel to the fire. The shah's insistence on his authoritarian style of rule and the opposition's insistence on the necessity for political democracy and participation rendered the convergence of modernist forces impossible. For the shah modernity meant, first and foremost, a process of economic modernization. He also tolerated modernism in the arts. Some of the most daring and avant-garde theater was performed in Iran's mushrooming arts festivals in the 1970s. Political modernity, however, a genuine constitutional democracy with guaranteed individual and political freedoms, was less palatable to the monarch.

In contrast, the forces of demodernization, led and organized by Ayatollah Khomeini, were not only united but even succeeded in forging an alliance with large segments of secular Iranian intellectuals and the urban middle class. Ultimately, the intellectuals preferred a de facto alliance with the clerics whose stated goal was the creation of a religious state and who opposed ideas such as a woman's right to vote. For many of these intellectuals "fighting imperialism" was more important than defending political freedom—it was, in the parlance of the time, "the main contradiction." That Ayatollah Khomeini spouted many anti-imperialist slogans of the left made the alliance more viable. The victory of the Islamic Revolution in Iran can in no small measure be seen as the consequence of this rather strange alignment of forces. The embryo of this historic reality can be seen in the dynamics of Hoveyda's ill-fated meeting with the writers. Because of the tortured relationship between intellectuals and the Pahlavi regime, even though Al-e Ahmad had translated the bible of Hoveyda's youth—André Gide's *Nourritures Terrestres*—their shared passion did not provide any common ground for an amicable discussion between the writer and the prime minister.[15]

After about an hour of rancorous discussion, Hoveyda realized that the mood of the meeting worked against any chance of compromise. He took another tack. He told the group of his friendship with Sadeq Chubak and of his Wednesday afternoon visits to Chubak's house. "Next Wednesday," he said, "I will buy a bottle of scotch, and you gentlemen can meet me at Chubak's house, and we will see whether we can solve our differences." Al-e Ahmad's response betrayed one of the political fads of those days; for intellectuals like him poverty was a badge of honor. He said, "We only drink cheap vodka, and we drink it in cheap cafés."[16]

Ultimately, the meeting accomplished nothing. In subsequent weeks, a new mode of censorship began to take shape. To avoid the appearance of overt censorship, all publishers were asked to submit copies of their newly printed books to the National Library, where each book would be given a number. No book could be published without the number, and the number would only be given to books that complied with the censors' procrustean parameters. Some writers blamed Hoveyda for this system.[17]

Furthermore, in subsequent months, SAVAK forcefully stopped the creation of a writers' union in Iran and arrested several of the writers who had been active in that cause.

Hoveyda also met regularly with other prominent intellectuals at his brother Fereydoun's house.[18] Yet the Pahlavi regime, particularly in the years after the 1953 coup, had become, at least for a large number of intellectuals, the incarnation of darkness. Hoveyda, as a prime minister of that regime, was, at least by contagion, if not by commission, part of the dark force. On more than one occasion, Al-e Ahmad, who was the pontiff of the Iranian intellectual clerisy, had questioned the intellectual credentials of both Hoveyda and his brother. You could not be an intellectual, he had inveighed, and a politician in the Pahlavi regime at the same time.[19] If in those days Hoveyda had been less naive in his judgment of the political landscape of Iran, if his optimism had not clouded his vision, he would have probably known that meetings like the one he had with the writers' group would scarcely be fruitful.

The failure of the meeting with the writers did not deter Hoveyda from trying to find common ground with the opposition. Six months later, he asked his chief of staff, Mohammad Safa, to invite Khalil Maleki to lunch at the prime minister's office. Maleki had been an important opposition figure for over a quarter of a century. He had been one of the chief theorists of the Tudeh Party in its early days, but it was not long before his insistence on social democracy rather than Leninism had put him on a collision course with the Stalinist leadership of the party. In subsequent years, he was demonized by the communists and distrusted by the regime. Of all the opposition leaders, Maleki had been the only one to suggest that in the June 1963 uprising, nationalist and democratic forces should have aborted their alliance with Ayatollah Khomeini.[20]

Hoveyda had met Maleki once before, in the late 1950s, at the suggestion of Ehsan Naraghi.[21] That time, he had gone to Maleki's house and talked for more than an hour. This time it was Hoveyda himself who initiated the meeting. At the time of this second meeting, some of those who considered themselves Maleki followers, particularly among Iranians in Europe, had taken harsh and uncompromising positions against Hoveyda. In April 1966, for example, one such group in Paris published an article accusing Hoveyda's government not only of "stopping the land-reform process in Iran," but also of opening Iranian markets to "foreign imperialist companies." The government's "Open Door policy," the article suggested, was simply a blueprint provided by the IMF to further enslave the Iranian economy. The article ended by calling Hoveyda's government "the most reactionary" in the Middle East.[22]

In spite of the attacks, and in spite of the fact that Maleki had only been recently released from yet another prison term, Hoveyda wanted to meet him. At first Maleki refused, suggesting that if word of the meeting leaked out, Hoveyda might end up paying a heavy price. Hoveyda responded that "Iran is not Stalinist Russia. The prime minister has the right to meet whomever he wants."[23] It is not clear whether the meeting was at the shah's behest, or with his previous knowledge or approval. When a date was finally set for the meeting, Mohammad Safa, who had acted as intermediary, volunteered to drive Maleki to the prime minister's office. They came in through a back door, lest others in the office learn of the visitor's identity.

The meeting, including lunch, lasted a little more than an hour. Most of the time was used by Maleki to lay out, with full rhetorical force, what he found to be wrong with the policies of the Pahlavi regime and Hoveyda's government. Hoveyda could not get a word in, and when he tried, Maleki briskly stopped him, saying, "You have the media at your disposal all day and night; you can easily explain your policies at that time. Let me use these few moments to tell you what I think about the country's problems."[24] And the gist of the problem, according to Maleki, was the lack of democracy and the shah's insistence on personal rule.

Hoveyda next turned to Dariush Forouhar, one of the more colorful opposition figures. Like a whole generation of Iranians, he had become involved in politics in the postwar years. In his early days, he was known more for the physical prowess he brought to bear defending his ideas than the brilliance of those ideas themselves. Hoveyda invited Forouhar, who had spent most of his life in and out of prison, to his office in early May 1968. Homayoun Jaber-Ansari, one of Hoveyda's recent protégés and Forouhar's cousin, probably arranged the meeting. In February 1979, the two cousins would play a crucial role when Hoveyda chose to surrender to the newly victorious Provisional Revolutionary Government, which had named Forouhar its minister of labor.[*] In 1968, however, he was simply the

---

[*] In early 1999, Forouhar and his wife, Parvaneh Eskandari, were brutally stabbed to death at their home in Tehran. Elements of the Islamic Republic's security forces have already admitted that they had carried out the horrible crime.

leader of a very small group known as the Nation of Iran Party [Hezb-e Melat-e Iran], famous as much for its nationalism as for its opposition to Marxist ideas.

According to the U.S. Embassy's confidential report of the meeting, "Hoveyda offered Foruhar (a lawyer by profession) a job as legal advisor in any ministry, if Foruhar would renounce his opposition to the government...Hoveyda...praised Foruhar for his leadership...and stressed the futility of continued political opposition to the shah's government. Foruhar refused the offer categorically."[25] Though Hoveyda did not succeed in bringing Foruhar into the government, he was continuing a policy that he and Mansur had begun. Now, Hoveyda, a more cautious man than Mansur, seemed on his way to creating a more broad-based de facto coalition. As early as 1965, Hoveyda had laid out the strategic vision behind his many contacts with the opposition:

> For modernization, the shah needed the help of young technocrats. It appeared to us that conditions were ripe to achieve our long-cherished goal of pulling this country out of its abyss of backwardness.
>
> The work of economic and social modernization is no simple task. It requires the cooperation of thousands of people. Many of the technocrats distrusted the shah and the coterie of people (mostly consisting of old politicians and aristocrats) that surrounded him. The technocrats were faced with a dilemma.* They could either continue their opposition, or at best be apathetic, toward the shah and the ruling class, or they could realistically cooperate with implementing reforms. Included in these technocrats were: (1) Followers of Mosaddeq and the National Front; (2) Members of the Tudeh Party who advocated unconditional support for the USSR; (3) Liberals; (4) Nationalists; (5) progressive religious elements; (6) people who belong to none of these groups.[26]

The success of modernization, Hoveyda suggested, depended on this group's "limited (that is conditional) cooperation with monarchy, particularly the shah who has come to symbolize national unity."[27] It is now evident that Hoveyda failed to follow his own advice. Gradually, but inexorably, his "limited cooperation" turned into submission to the will of

---

* The word "dilemma" is the only English term to appear in the text.

the shah while he continued to search for elements from diverse political
persuasions to include in his government. In fact, by the early 1970s, the
fabric of his cabinet was woven from threads that reflected most of these
groups. By then Hoveyda had not only included several apostates of the
Tudeh Party in his cabinet—there were at one time at least seven ex-com-
munist ministers in the government—but he was also involved in negotiations to legalize the Tudeh Party and allow its exiled leaders to come back
to Iran.[28] The shah, according to an official of the Soviet Embassy in
Tehran, eventually overruled the idea.[29]

In terms of the National Front, the most important addition to
Hoveyda's cabinet was Fereydoun Mahdavi. In the early 1960s, in his many
meetings with the U.S. Embassy officials in Iran, Mahdavi, then a rising star
of the newly invigorated National Front, appeared to be an uncompromising opponent of the shah, as well as of Mansur and Hoveyda. For example,
in a meeting on November 27, 1964, after criticizing the American government for insisting on passing the Status of Forces Agreement with Iran,
Mahdavi, according to the confidential memorandum of the conversation,
became "particularly virulent in his criticism of the Mansur government in
general and its economic policies in particular…He particularly castigated
the Mansur government for its handling of the mullahs."[30] His early views
on the Hoveyda cabinet were no less critical.

In offering these views, Mahdavi was, apparently, articulating more his
own opinions than those of the National Front's. In another one of these
casual meetings between American Embassy officials and some of the leaders of the Front, Shapour Bakhtiar told them that "he thought the present
[Hoveyda] government to be an improvement over the Mansur Government, despite his conclusion that it really had not accomplished much. He
explained that Hoveyda was a more honorable man and does not make
such grandiose promises."*[31]

---

* The Islamic Republic of Iran used some of these embassy reports to tarnish the image of its opponents
implying that anyone who had ever had a conversation with an embassy official was an agent of the American
government. I, in no way, share this view. Most of these meetings seem to fall squarely within the parameters
of legitimate contact between political activists and the embassy of a powerful foreign country. For examples
of the Islamic Republic's use of these documents, see *Rabetin-e Khoob-e America* [America's Good Contacts]
(Tehran, n.d.). This was volume 17 of the multivolume collection published by the students who had occupied
the American Embassy. Many of the documents had been shredded by embassy officials in the last moments
before the takeover. Students, with the obvious blessing of the government, used Persian rug-makers to help
them piece the documents together.

The trappings of power seemed to have had a corrosive effect on Hoveyda's initial optimism, and his penchant for bridging the gap between the opposition and the regime. The longer he stayed in power, the more that optimism gave way to a passive, sometimes embittered, cynicism. More and more he tried to use cash incentives to encourage the explicit co-option of opposition members. Some were given lucrative governmental contracts; others were given sinecures. Sometimes, Hoveyda would use the secret discretionary fund available to the prime minister to make payments to cash-strapped members of the opposition.[32] The clergy received more than their fair share of such payments. As one of his chief conduits to the clergy, Hoveyda used Hedayat Eslaminia, a man of dubious reputation who amassed a large and illicit fortune based primarily on his connection to Hoveyda.[33] On the eve of the Islamic Revolution, Eslaminia, too, would play an important role as a secret messenger between the government and some of the clerics, particularly Ayatollah Mohammad-Kazem Shariat-madari.[34] After the revolution, fearing for his life, he escaped to America. A different danger awaited him there.[*]

The office in charge of religious endowments, Edareh-ye Oqaf, was also occasionally used as a financial conduit to clerics. Contrary to the common perception, however, the office was never the main channel for giving money to the clergy.[35] According to Nassir Assar, who headed the Oqaf for many years during Hoveyda's tenure, his office was perpetually short of money and thus could hardly pay off disgruntled clerics. Furthermore, he suggests that any money that was paid to the clerics never reached Ayatollah Khomeini's stalwart supporters. "They would never deign," he said, "to accept money from the government. Most of the clerics who got the money had little political influence."[36] On those occasions where large sums had to be dispensed through his office, special funds had to be allocated by the government. For example, in the late 1960s after the Kurdish uprisings in Iraq, the Iranian government decided to take preventive action by setting aside about a million tomans a year—about one hundred and fifty thousand dollars at the time—to be paid only to clerics in the Kurdish parts of Iran.[37]

---

[*] One of Eslaminia's sons was part of the infamous "Billionaire Boys Club." With the son's help, the elder Eslaminia was kidnapped and asked to give information about his secret numbered accounts in Switzerland. While he was being transported in the trunk of a car, however, he died of an apparent heart attack. His son is still serving time for his role in the murder. The family, of course, believes the son to be innocent; it is all the work of "secret intelligence agencies," they suggest.

Hoveyda meeting with a group of clergy, long before they came to rule Iran.

It is hard to say when and where Hoveyda's genuine attempts to help members of the opposition—as was his wont in the late 1950s—ended and his new cynicism began. One of his colleagues suggested that by the early 1970s, Hoveyda had come to believe that "everyone could be bought, if the price was right."[38] By the mid-1970s, he had developed a habit of attacking members of the opposition as "little cry-baby communists trained at the London School of Economics."[39] Even some of his close friends who were known to have contacts, or sympathies, with the opposition occasionally became subjects of Hoveyda's derision.[40] He had soon developed a politician's persona. More and more frequently, a cynical smile, something of a smirk, began to appear on his face. The smile, they say, is one of those rare facial gestures understandable to all humans across different cultures. Politicians, however, seem to have mastered a smile language of their own, and by the early 1970s Hoveyda was a full-fledged politician. His repertoire of smiles included the smile of etiquette, reluctant submission, protocol, condescension, irony, joy, and cynicism. And yet, both the optimism of his early days and the embryos of his later cynical disposition can be seen in his "Notes from a Time of War."

Hoveyda had been reading André Gide when he wrote these journal segments in 1942. By then he had also been an avid reader of existential writers for a good decade. A quality of existential angst, a strain of romantic disdain for the desolate emotional landscape of modern life, a sense of abomination at the perfidy of modern man, can be found in the narrative. In a passage whose pessimism, and imagery, is reminiscent of Jean-Paul Sartre's *Nausea*, he wrote, "And I was thinking about the treachery and misery of the human race, and a sense of nausea casts its shadow over me, and I was reminded of Baudelaire, who with magisterial words, all his own, wrote of the 'rotting corpse of humanity.'"[41]

Watching the plight of war refugees and the greed of black marketers in Brussels, Hoveyda's prose, usually free from the bombast of an ideologue, turns into an impassioned indictment against the excesses of capitalism. He wrote about "the merchants who suck the blood of their fellow citizens." He chastised "the capitalists who descend to the depth of depravity and still consider themselves the noblest creatures." In a tone of Romantic irony, he wrote about money as the elixir of the twentieth century. "Everywhere you look," he declaimed, "you see money as the effervescent source of all beauty and poetry."[42] It is hard to miss the faint echoes of his early education in Beirut and his readings of Marx and Marxism, in such passages.

Along with these radical echoes, there is in Hoveyda's writing an ardent advocacy of political prudence, an Aristotelian faith in the redemptive power of politics and statesmen. It is, he wrote, the "sacred duty" of statesmen to steer the world away from the tormenting hell it can become if the darker side of humanity is given a free reign. Prudent politicians are humankind's "only hope for salvation."[43] But such people can deliver hope only if they are willing to enter the fray of politics. Here Hoveyda came closest to articulating the calculus of his desire for power. In a culture that had grown to disdain and distrust politics as a vocation, he tried to articulate, and eventually live out, an alternative model, a vision of politics at once pragmatic and prudent.

Throughout much of "Notes from a Time of War," Hoveyda seems locked in a debate with two absent, and diametrically opposed, interlocutors. The first argues for the futility of working within the existing system to bring about change; it is the voice of a peculiar political nihilism that had come to dominate intellectual discourse in Iran. Ironically, the genealogy of this form of nihilism had its roots in both Shiite theology and the secular revolutionary theories of the late nineteenth century.* For close to a millennium, most Shiite theologians had declared that secular power is, by definition, a usurpation of power. All power must reside in the hands of the imam, or his viceroys; partaking in any power other than that legitimized by holy writ, they declared, was sinful. Ayatollah Khomeini was only the latest successful advocate of this view.

Twentieth-century secular Iranian revolutionary ideas had much in common with this aspect of Shiite theology. Iranian radicals, inspired by the Russian nihilism so brilliantly depicted in nineteenth-century Russian novels like Turgenev's *Fathers and Sons,* and Dostoyevsky's *The Devils,* saw any attempt at reforming a capitalist economy, or an authoritarian polity, as not only futile but counterproductive. As a result, a dangerous infatuation with verbal debunking of all that exists—and a deep distrust of any state, or state-inspired, reform—had come to dominate much of the Persian political landscape. Hoveyda, who got a taste of this distrust in his many unsuccessful meetings with members of the opposition, seemed to be alluding to this tendency when he wrote, "We Persians live with words...we constantly bicker about what should be done...All our reforms, however, remain in the realm of words. As soon as the possibility of actually doing something arises, we all say, 'Oh! forget it. Things can never be changed.'"[44]

Hoveyda's second absent interlocutor represented a voice and a force no less pernicious. It was articulated by the paladins of traditional Iranian politics, who, in Hoveyda's words, had a quixotic faith in their own wisdom. With vehement language, he riled against "despairing circles of Persian politicians," who in their "apathy and their stupid self-righteousness" would destroy and kill all the patriotic optimism of the youth.[45]

Published in his third year as prime minister, the words are an apparent reference to the peculiar structure of Persian politics at the time. There were multiple constellations, each revolving in their own orbits, all, at the same time, circling around the shah. There was, for example, the group around the queen, the one around Princess Ashraf, the group connected to SAVAK. Hoveyda's most formidable foe throughout his tenure, however, was

---

* In a brilliant study of the origins of Russian Communism, Nikolai Berdiaev has shown the structural similarities between the ethos of Bolshevism and elements of Russian Orthodox Christianity. I suspect if ever a similarly serious study of Shiite principles and the ethos of Iranian Marxism is undertaken, many points of convergence will also be found. For Berdiaev's views, see Nikolai Berdiaev, *The Origin of Russian Communism* (Ann Arbor, 1960).

Asadollah Alam, whose posthumously published memoirs are replete with surprisingly vicious and vindictive barbs against Hoveyda. He calls him among other things, "our pathetic Prime Minister,"[46] a "lick spittle of the Americans," a "traitor," and that "creepy old Quasimodo."[47] Throughout Hoveyda's tenure as prime minister, he and Alam fought a constant war of attrition, behind a façade of amity and protocol.

Contrary to the perspectives of the two imaginary interlocutors in "Notes from a Time of War," Hoveyda's vision of politics was based on the supreme value of action—not revolutionary action fired by utopian dreams of a perfect society and doomed to failure, but action that is deliberate, pragmatic, and incremental. He was tenaciously single-minded in his rejection of radical doctrines. Hoveyda detested those who recoiled from action in fear of failure or in celebration of the sanctity of utopian ideals. He felt that prudent and patient action, guided by technocratic knowledge, was the solution to Iran's problem. Hoveyda, at least in his early years, and before the onset of his own despairing cynicism, saw himself as representing a force that could deliver democracy and civility to Iranian polity. "It is the great statesmen," he wrote, "who have hitherto provided the greatest service to humankind. Such men must wait till they rise to power and only then can they put into practice their ideas, and ideals, and work for the welfare of their countrymen."[48]

At the same time, in "Notes from a Time of War" Hoveyda suggested that it was not just political forces but strong cultural ones as well that worked against his kind of reformist activism. In a confessional tone, he wrote that "deep in my soul, I am a Persian and thus a fatalist" and with a hint of criticism lamented that "in this country, everybody wants to be the chief." Hoveyda then asked, rhetorically, "Is it not better to first change ourselves, our family, our social relations before we try to change the very structure of our society?"[49]

Though here he seemed cognizant of the inescapable role culture plays in the quest for modernity, in practice, as the prime minister, he followed the shah's lead in privileging economic growth over political development. As a special secret memorandum of the CIA in 1968 makes clear, "the shah's design for Iran is based on economic rather than political development…[He] sees rapid industrialization as essential not only to increase prosperity and national well-being, but also to provide an outlet for the energies of educated Iranians who might otherwise prove troublesome for the regime."[50] The report ominously concludes, "Over the long term, this will probably not provide a satisfactory substitute for greater participation, but for some time to come the unrest of earlier days seems under control."[51]

In Hoveyda's case, the acceptance of this form of "economism" had several roots. Hoveyda was an intellectual child of the 1930s when Marxism, particularly in its Stalinist guise, was deeply imbued with a statist and economist vision: fix the economic base, the argument went, and the superstructure of culture and ideas will automatically follow. Furthermore, most of Hoveyda's economic advisors and nearly all those who shaped Iranian planning policies in its early inception were trained in America. Called the "Harvard Mafia,"* they believed that building the infrastructure was the key to the riddle of modernization. Finally, once in power, Hoveyda soon became a political chameleon, reflecting the shah's political wishes and idiosyncrasies, and the shah was convinced that rapid industrial growth was the panacea for all social ills.

Dogma, however, would be the ultimate nemesis of the gradual reformism Hoveyda advocated. In "Notes from a Time of War," Hoveyda mounted an assault—both direct and through tantalizing hints—on precisely the kind of dogmatism that could hamper his program. Is it accidental, for example, that in the first few lines of the narrative we find a reference to the film *Ninotchka*? On one level, *Ninotchka* is a subtle political satire: it is the story of a group of dogmatic Bolsheviks, from "Russia's Board of Trade," who arrive in Paris on official business. An exiled Russian grand duchess—parasitic and frivolous to a fault, but no less strident in her dogmatic insistence on decorum—plays the comic foil of the story. Greta Garbo plays the "envoy extraordinaire," a cold, steely beauty. She is sent by comrades in Moscow to expedite the trade mission and ensure its ideological purity. When she arrives in Paris, her every demeanor, all her ideas and opinions, are nothing but distilled dogma. Soon, however, she—like the other three members of the team—is softened by the seductions of a bourgeois, decadent life. Temptations of love, as well as the comforts and complexities of the day-to-day capitalist lifestyle, easily erode her dogmatic fervor.

But *Ninotchka* is also notable from an altogether different, and no less important, perspective. One of Sadeq Hedayat's brilliant satirical novellas

---

* They were called the Harvard Mafia not because they were graduates or officials of the university but because the chief advisor to the group had been the Director of the Institute for International Development at Harvard University.

is called *The Islamic Pilgrimage to the Land of the Franks*. It describes, in a narrative line very similar to *Ninotchka*'s, the story of a group of zealot Shiite clerics who travel to Paris in the fervent hope of converting Christian infidels to Islam. Instead, they are themselves gradually infatuated by the seductions of places like the "Folies Bergères." Eventually, they shed both their zeal and clerical attire, and like the Bolshevik commissars, become smugly satisfied aspirants of bourgeois decadence. Knowing, as we do, that Hoveyda was a friend of Hedayat's, and remembering that Hedayat was inspired by *Ninotchka* in writing his satire, it is not far-fetched to assume that Hoveyda's reference to the film was not simply an innocent allusion.[52]

Another allusion, no less clever, but this time apparently aimed at the regime he served as prime minister, can be found in the narrative of "Notes from a Time of War." In describing the Nazi occupation of Brussels, Hoveyda describes how Belgian university students began to read, and conspicuously carry under their arms, works of Marx and Marxism. It was, he declares, a gesture of defiance, an act of rebellion against the brutish forces of occupation. Ironically, at the very time when Hoveyda published these lines, reading, owning, or carrying any work of Marx or Marxism was a serious crime in Iran, doggedly pursued and punished by SAVAK. Again, it is hard not to see this allusion as either Hoveyda's passive objection to this oppressive policy or his attempt, albeit discreet and symbolic, to distance himself from it.

While "Notes from a Time of War" tells us much about the exterior preoccupations of Hoveyda's life, it tells us less than we want to know about the interior emotional landscape of his mind. He tells us, with a hint of bravura, that he failed to understand the pangs of love suffered by his friends in his Belgium days since he had "hitherto, never fallen in love."[53] But by the time he published these segments, he had not only fallen in love but also felt his share of its pangs.

Hoveyda was, deep in his soul, a private man. "You could never know what he was thinking about," his wife remembered. He was secretive, reticent with words that would betray his inner anxieties.[54] Yet, he had chosen a life that had thrust him under constant, and often cruel, scrutiny. If in the West, the prurient curiosities of the masses turn them into predators of gossip about the private lives of public men, in Iran, political realities further add venom to this already destructive process. In despotic societies, gossip and rumor not only take on the authority of facts, but they also become tools of

Amir Abbas and Laila, July 1967.

subversion, weapons in cultural and political trench warfare. Long before he was to stand trial for his life in front of the Revolutionary Tribunal, Hoveyda's character had been assassinated by the erosive power of gossip. He had become, in a Jungian sense, the collective "shadow" of Iranian politics. Every feared idea, every deplorable political tendency, and every secret desire was attributed to him.

Hoveyda's sexual life was no less the subject of lurid tales. In a society where machismo is a form of social capital, he was rumored to be impotent, a homosexual, even a pederast.[55] The Islamic Republic even published what appeared to be a facsimile of a SAVAK report, indicating that on an official trip to the Caspian coast, Hoveyda was discovered by his wife *in flagrante delicto* with a young boy.[56] It was clear that in my conversations with Laila Emami, the matter of this report specifically and her sexual life with Hoveyda generally had to be raised. She generously spared me the agony, however, by saying almost peremptorily, "Our sex life was fine; it was not great, but it was also not a major problem in our relationship."[57] Emboldened by her candor, I asked about the SAVAK report. With bitter laughter, she categorically denied the veracity of the story. "They just didn't know Amir," she said. The mystery of the report was only solved for me later after much more research. I eventually learned that so great was the power of rumor in Iran that SAVAK had created special committees called "Echo," whose job was to report every rumor in their areas of jurisdiction. Sometimes the committees recommended that measures be taken to contain the damage from a rumor. For example, when it was widely reported that the shah had married a new young girl, at SAVAK's behest, a full report of the girl's marriage to another man was published in popular Iranian magazines.[*58] A closer reading of the SAVAK report on Hoveyda reveals that the reference to his dalliance with a boy was no more than the report of a rumor.

Though "Notes from a Time of War" reads, in many parts, like an antidote calculated to fight the venom of rumors that had begun to haunt Hoveyda, the main focus of his passion was for France. It is in describing French culture, and the city of Paris, that Hoveyda waxes most poetic and most romantic. The tone of the narrative, hitherto characterized by its emotional reserve, suddenly changes. A mood of epic glorification and grief sets in. "France, you have shown the oppressed world how to be free. Your writers and your revolutionaries opened the path of freedom for other countries in the world. Rousseau, Voltaire, Robespierre, Saint-Just, Hugo, Gambetta, weep for...France, you are wounded, you are wounded, and I...and I am your supporter and will never lose hope in you."[†59]

On the other hand, his eloquent and effusive praise of France contrasts sharply with his silence on such important issues as religion. As a normative system, shaping his daily life, as a creation mythology, or even as a foundation for his life's philosophical disposition, religion seemed never to have had an influence on Hoveyda's life. To his closest friends, he would talk of his Nietzschean disdain for all organized religion. "Notes from a Time of War" is perhaps the most public display of Hoveyda's deeply secular persuasion. As a politician, he would pay normal tribute to religious rites and rituals. Yet, contrary to most Iranian political figures of his generation who went out of their way to establish their affinity with God and Islam, there was no religious gloss in "Notes from a Time of War." Indeed, his confessions about drinking, dancing, and enjoying the sight of young and beautiful girls—three acts that are all strictly taboo in Islam—seem, in

---

* In his *Diaries*, Alam provides revealing trivia about this affair, showing the surprising degree to which he distrusted Hoveyda and his motives. When rumors about the affair began to spread, Alam discussed them with the shah, who declared that he "had seen her here and there." He then orders Alam to summon the girl to his office and warn her that if her rumor-mongering continues, she will be arrested. (Alam, *Diaries*, Vol. III, 87). After a while, the shah begins to think that the rumors are in fact the "work of the Russians." Alam, on the other hand, believed that the ultimate source of the rumor could well be "the [Hoveyda] government itself." A few days later, Alam gives the shah "the good news" that an account of the girl's purported marriage had been published. "The shah said, give it to the queen to read." (Alam, *Diaries*, 143-145).

† The ellipses here are in the original.

retrospect, boldly defiant of the tradition of often feigned piety amongst Iranian politicians. The shah's *Mission for My Country,* published in 1965, was a prime example of this tradition. Aside from his many unequivocal professions of faith, the shah also wrote of his divinely inspired dreams, and of a saintly character, named Abbas, who miraculously saved him when he was only a child and was about to fall off a horse. In later years he would go even further and profess to be in communion with God.[60]

Finally, "Notes from a Time of War" is important for an entirely different reason. By the time of publication, Hoveyda had already begun assuming a public persona, often at odds with his private views. As the shah grew more and more intolerant of saucy minions, as he became more adamant in his derision for democracy—"Freedom of thought! Freedom of thought! Democracy! Democracy!...It is all yours, you can keep it; don't you see? Your wonderful democracy. You'll see in a few years what your democracy leads to,"[61] the shah said in 1974—Hoveyda, too, in his public pronouncements would mimic the royal decrees and disquisitions. He would not only become the most eloquent defender of the Pahlavi regime in the court of public opinion, particularly in the West, he would not only repeatedly deny the existence of corruption, oppression, and censorship in Iran, but he would also echo the shah's disdain for Western models of democracy. In September 1975, late in his tenure as prime minister, he told a conference organized by the august Aspen Institute of Humanistic Studies that "we have witnessed the emergence of great bureaucratic empires...We have also studied societies that, beginning with a democratic consensus, are facing the danger of modern tribalization—societies that subsidize sloth and indolence and are divided against themselves."[62] Laced with fancy intellectual jargon, his speech is no more than a polished rendition of the shah's rants against democracy. In private, however, as many of his friends recollect, and as the journals discreetly testify, Hoveyda knew better. But now, he was, on the one hand, the avowed defender of the regime in public; while on the other hand, he was a critic of many of its policies in private. For Hoveyda, as with a whole generation of Iranian politicians, a stark dualism, a dissonance between public acts and private views, had become the accepted mode of operation.

CHAPTER ELEVEN

Politics in Petro-Pompeii

Our courtiers say all's savage but at court…
Th' imperious seas breeds monsters.
—Shakespeare, *Cymbeline*

oveyda was an early riser. His days as prime minister usually began at five thirty in the morning. After a cup of coffee, he would commence an almost two-hour odyssey of personal hygiene. "He was clean to the point of near obsessiveness," Laila Emami remembered. After their marriage, before they moved into the high-ceilinged old house Laila's mother had given them as a wedding gift, two additions had to be made to the building: a private bathroom for Hoveyda and a room for his books. "It was hard to imagine him being able to share those private spaces with anyone," Laila said. Then, alluding to the Ockrent interview, she added in a tone of embittered grief, "when I saw that awful woman's interview with Amir, one of the first things that crossed my mind was the filth in the jail. How will he survive it? I thought." She added that "he was also meticulous with his shaving and obsessive about the cleanliness of his white shirts, which he bought by the dozen in different sizes. He gained and lost weight easily." In fact, for much of his adult life, weight had been a problem for Hoveyda.[1] Laila convinced him to change his high-fat, high-cholesterol diet, and since he was keen on French cuisine, the chef at the official prime minister's residence was sent to Paris for a crash course in vegetarian and diet French cooking.[2]

After his long morning ablution, Hoveyda spent the next hour reading Iranian and Western newspapers and magazines. Frequently, even before arriving at his office, he had already conversed with editors, cabinet ministers, or even the shah about aspects of the news that he felt had been errors in judgment or fact. He also set up a system by which he ordered the books he read about.[3] On the margins of the magazines, he would place a small mark next to the names of the books he desired. His office staff would then order the books and pay for them through a special foreign account Hoveyda had set up. He insisted that Iranian diplomats abroad not be allowed to pay for the books he wanted to order.[4] In these kinds of financial matters, his probity was, like his cleanliness, almost obsessive. He ordered his chief of staff, Mohammad Safa, to estimate the rental value of one of the small rooms in the official prime minister's residence. "That room," Hoveyda said, "is where I conduct my private business, and the government should not have to pay for it."[5] Every month, eight hundred and fifty tomans, about a hundred and thirty dollars at the time, was paid to the government for the room that was full of Hoveyda's books and where he kept his private journal. All such financial transactions were handled by his secretary, Vajieh Ma'refat, who managed Hoveyda's private checking accounts. From this same account, a monthly stipend of two thousand tomans was also paid to his mother.[6]

Hoveyda also picked up new ideas from his early morning readings. In January 1966, for example, as a U.S. Embassy report notes, he had read about "a recent twenty-year economic projection" prepared by the French Futurists and decided that a similar projection "should be prepared for Iran…[He named] a committee of Iran's leading economists, under the chairmanship of Abdollah Entezam…to prepare a twenty-year projection of Iran's economy."[7]

Hoveyda always set out for work wearing an orchid in the lapel of his suit. The orchid was Laila's contribution to his attire. Before her day, he usually wore a carnation. Indeed, she had introduced the cultivation of orchids to Iran and went on to create the first Iranian horticultural society. Orchids are not native to Iran; they are known as a "cosmopolitan" flower.

The affected aura, the almost effeminate air that the orchid gave Hoveyda, was not the only controversy surrounding this part of his accouterment. In 1978, there was a much talked about media story suggesting that Hoveyda had a microphone installed behind the orchid. As reported to the American Embassy, the story even claimed that the gadget was used by the prime minister to tape "his conversations with the Shah and others"; the tapes, according to the same report, were then sent for safekeeping to Fereydoun Hoveyda, at the United Nations.[8] Unfortunately, no such recordings were ever made or sent to the United Nations, but the charge might well have had its source in one of the more enigmatic stories of Hoveyda's life.[9]

Not long after his appointment as prime minister, Hoveyda began compiling a highly confidential file that contained evidence of financial corruption in high places. He also made copies of orders that contravened the constitution. These documents were kept in a large manila envelope sealed with wax in a special safe in Hoveyda's office. Every time he left on a trip, he entrusted the sealed envelope to Vajieh Ma'refat, instructing her to open it only if anything should happen to him.[10] Aside from his trusted secretary, at least one other close associate and a few members of Hoveyda's family knew of the file's existence. His brother, Fereydoun, once saw part of the documents on Hoveyda's desk. When asked about their content, Hoveyda refused to talk about them, mentioning only that they involved the royal family's business transactions. In September 1978, when Tehran was rife with untrue rumors of Hoveyda's arrest, his brother Fereydoun told a concerned friend that Amir Abbas "is not worried about his own skin and has enough documents stashed away to clear him of any accusation."[11]

The first indirect evidence of the file's existence can be found in a letter written by Hoveyda himself. Dated August 19, 1969, and written in both French and Persian, the note gives directions to his brother Fereydoun, as well as his mother, about what to do with "two cases, full of my private papers."*

Hoveyda's file soon came to interest SAVAK. It first reported, in early 1977, that Hoveyda had moved some of the "most secret documents that he used to keep in a safe in his office" to "either his own house or to another secure location."[12] In November of 1978, only days before his arrest, as media attacks on Hoveyda increased, SAVAK again reported that "Hoveyda has told a visitor…that he had anticipated the attacks and thus had prepared a 300-

---

* I was given a copy of the handwritten note, by Fereydoun Hoveyda.

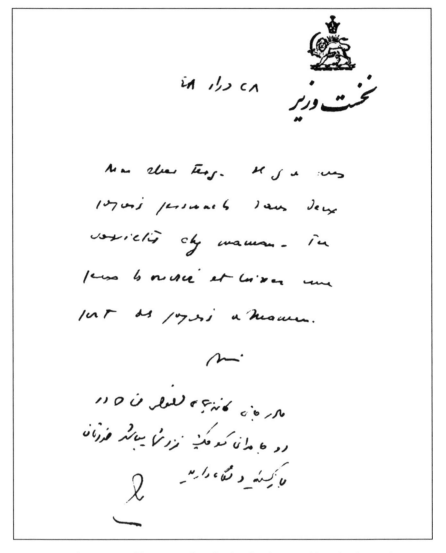

A note from Amir Abbas Hoveyda to his brother (in French) and to his mother
(in Persian), dated 19 August 1969 and written on the prime minister's letterhead,
mentioning the existence of two cases of personal papers at his mother's house.

page file covering everything he had seen personally and had sent it to a relative outside the country, so that if one day he was put on trial, or if articles
were written against him, he would then publish the material in foreign
journals."[13] If Hoveyda's conversation with the visitor was meant as a discreet threat to the shah and SAVAK, it certainly did not work.

Those in his family who knew of the file now unanimously agree that most of its contents were burnt during the terror-filled early days of the revolution. At his trial Hoveyda was asked about the file and whether he was willing to share it with the Islamic government. He politely demurred.*

HOVEYDA'S YEARS AS PRIME MINISTER can be divided into two phases. In the first phase of his tenure, he was full of optimism and energy; he went about his work with the zeal of a man on a mission. At the same time, he was bent on mending fences between the government and various strata of society. The fact that newspapers and magazines were reporting his imminent demise almost daily seemed to have had no effect on his boundless energy. Hoveyda met regularly with members of the media, helped journalists organize into a semiofficial union, and provided free land for the construction of affordable housing to members of the union. His nemesis, *Khandaniha,* reported that Hoveyda had become the most popular prime minister in recent memory and was forced to admit that "the prime minister's patience and good will and good behavior" has won the praise of even his critics.[14]

Hoveyda's second phase is characterized more by cynicism and an almost despondent air of resignation to what he had come to believe were the immutable realities of the status quo. Instead of fighting abuses of the constitution, he was now resigned to chronicling such incidents, and then only to cover his own flanks. While Hoveyda made occasional sallies into the realm of fighting, or limiting, corruption, he now told family and friends who complained about such practices that "these are the requisite by-products of development; don't worry, in the grand scheme of things, they amount to very little."[15]

Parviz Radji, who was Hoveyda's chief of staff for a while and later named Iran's ambassador to Great Britain, revealed that Hoveyda, toward the end of his tenure, would "sometimes admit in private, [that] his approach to issues lacked innovation, his public promises carried little conviction, his political utterances were bereft of credibility...He was

---

* I have been able to obtain copies of a few of the surviving pages. They are handwritten notes, listing the number of shares held in major Iranian banks by members of the royal family. I was provided with copies of these pages only on condition that I would not publish their specific content. I consented to the condition; it was more important for me to verify the existence of the file than to disclose its content.

exceedingly tired, increasingly irritable, and prone to impatience and ill-temper."[16] By then, even his most stalwart supporters admit that, he had grown addicted to the perks of power.[17] He would tolerate every indignity and every affront to keep the mantle of power. In a moment of searing self-analysis, he reportedly told Ahmad Ghoreishi, "some people are addicted to drugs; others crave a fortune; and then there are those whose affliction is power."[18]

It is hard to pinpoint the precise moment when Hoveyda's liberal exuberance and stoic detachment from his post ended and when the dangerous cynicism and clinging attachment to his post began. To friends, who at different stages of his tenure suggested that he should resign, he gave varieties of the same answer: "My presence," he would say, "is at least an obstacle to the more corrupt and despotic elements that lurk in the corridors of power in Iran." He told his brother, on one of the many occasions when he urged him to resign, "In Iran, no one resigns. You only wait till the King of Kings, the Light of the Aryans, commands you to go home."[19] Aside from Hoveyda's own financial probity, perhaps the only thing that remained the same in both periods was his attempt to appear a "modest, unassuming person...indifferent to protocol and the displays of authority."[20]

As a rule, Hoveyda drove himself to work. He rarely used the official prime minister's limousine. He drove around in his Peykan, with the head of his security detail in the backseat, while the other guards in his security detachment followed in another car.*[21] Hoveyda clearly relished power. At the same time, he went out of his way to exhibit a folksy humility that was indeed rare amongst past prime ministers, and his refusal to use the official limousine was part of this pattern.

On these drives, he would occasionally, to the consternation of his security guards, pick up a man or a woman waiting in a bus line and drive them to their destination. His chats with these unsuspecting riders were part of an informal process of both gathering information and affording access to power to those who would usually have no such access. This was one of countless antennae that kept him aware of the oscillations of the outside world. To his critics, foremost among them Alam, the fact that Hoveyda drove his own car was nothing but demagoguery. Alam claims to

---

* The Peykan was an economy sedan assembled in Iran under a licensing agreement with British car manufacturers. In the mid-1960s, the Peykan plant and a steel mill, built with the help of the Soviet government, became symbols of Iran's new drive to industrialization.

have repeatedly chastised the prime minister about the affected vacuity of such a gesture. He also recounts briefing the shah about these derisive conversations with Hoveyda. The shah reportedly laughed heartily when Alam told him of these chastisements and of what Alam called Hoveyda's "prevarication."[22]

The shah's laughter must not be seen as an isolated act of complicity in Alam's sometimes childish but unrelenting war against Hoveyda. Divide and conquer had always been a crucial part of the shah's style. Indeed, his authoritarian style, as indicated in a U.S. Embassy report, required that "managers at all levels be in a state, not only of normal bureaucratic competition, but also of intense personal rivalry. Energy and thought which should go to matters of substance are instead dissipated in chronic intrigue."[23] Alam's bitter feud with Hoveyda, tolerated if not actually encouraged by the shah, was only one example of this system.

Nonetheless, to the horror of Iran's patrician political class, Hoveyda would not only continue to drive his own car but would sometimes joke and banter in the vulgar tongue of the street, or dance suggestively at parties. During official visits he would often veer off the beaten path and mingle with surprised citizens. He provided the court with a touch of controlled eccentricity. By the standards of the Pahlavi court, he was also something of a bohemian. Early in Hoveyda's tenure, the shah had come to visit the house Hoveyda shared with his mother. After seeing its simplicity, the shah is reported to have said, "How can you live in this chicken coop?"[24]

At the office, Hoveyda's day began with a staff report of his schedule. He had assembled a highly competent and reliable team. Nearly all those who worked in his office were known for their financial probity and were measured by the rather high standards he had set for himself. But in spite of his usual gentle manners, he was also prone to bouts of anger against those who worked for him; his soft and supple tone would suddenly turn into controlled ferocity. Usually, after only a moment, he would console the hapless subject of his wrath. "I have no family," he once told his office staff. "You are the closest thing to my family. My shouts and tantrums are the stuff of family quarrels."[25]

Hoveyda, however, was also an actor who could easily feign anger, mirth, or melancholy; most of all, though, he was a consummate diplomat. He knew how to pull strings behind the scene to achieve his desired end. He used obsequious flattery as well as implicit and explicit threats with equal deftness. He was attentive to the moods and needs of his staff and friends; rarely would their birthdays, or marriages go by without some gift or token of his attention. Even with his sworn enemies and serious rivals, he used the disarming power of a simple act of kindness. Nearly all those who knew him have stories similar to Alinaghi Alikhani's. Early in Hoveyda's tenure, Alikhani, who enjoyed the support of Hoveyda's nemesis, Alam, was considered by many as Hoveyda's rival and potential successor. After Alikhani was named president of Tehran University, tensions between him and the prime minister only increased. By 1970, following a quarrel, the two men all but stopped talking to one another. But then Alikhani's father-in-law died in Paris, and Hoveyda not only immediately sent a letter of condolence to Suzanne Alikhani, but he also made sure that when the Alikhanis were sitting in a plane, about to take off for Paris, they were met by one of his vice-premiers with an envelope of foreign currency "to cover the unexpected expenses of the sudden trip."[26]

During his first months in power, ending the economic crisis that had plagued the Mansur government was Hoveyda's most important priority. Actually, after Mansur's assassination, Hoveyda promised to continue the economic stabilization and development plans, prepare the budget, revise the tax laws and the Civil Service Code. In practice, continuing Mansur's programs proved easier said than done. Faced with mounting popular opposition, the government was forced to announce, "on direct orders of the Shah, reductions in the price of gasoline, sugar and electricity."[27] The decision gained the government some instant popular support, but it brought about a larger deficit, forcing the government to prune the budgets of various agencies—except, of course, those set aside for the armed forces and SAVAK, which were always set by the shah and considered sacrosanct.

Combining finesse and firmness, Hoveyda managed to make the necessary cuts. At least according to the U.S. Embassy in Tehran, "Prime Minister Hoveyda and the Budget Bureau have come through the budget debate with flying colors."[28] The American sponsored program for economic development seemed to have worked. Even the gossip at Tehran's parties changed as a result of the program's success. According to one report, "the people now talk less about politics than about business, sex and creature comforts...There is some confidence in the future, and less criticism of the regime."[29]

After a while a different kind of economic crisis loomed on the horizon. As a result of inflationary pressures, prices went up and the government scampered for a solution. Here, Hoveyda's affinity for the French school of public policy, hand in hand with his youthful affinity for Marxist ideas and a state interventionist tendency that accompanied those ideas, all played an important role in shaping the anti-inflationary policy implemented by the government. Most importantly, the shah, too, had a particular sensitivity to price increases and always advocated the use of governmental powers— instead of market mechanisms—to check inflationary pressures. As a result, rather than using the fiscal and monetary powers of the state to curb inflation, Hoveyda chose to hire a French consultant on price control. At the consultant's behest, the government took up a policy of forced price reduction. Businesses were pressured to reduce prices or face punishment by the government. In addition, the government opened several price-reduced stores. Though the move was popular with consumers, it clearly irritated the shopkeepers and tradesmen.[30]

In the mid-1960s, this form of forced price reduction was, at least in the short term, a success. In 1974, when inflationary pressures began to build again, Hoveyda's cabinet chose to implement a more radical version of the 1967 policy. During the new crisis, Fereydoun Mahdavi, a National Front leader, and fierce critic of both Hoveyda and Mansur in the early 1960s, was brought into the cabinet as minister of commerce.[*31]

The shah gave Mahdavi one month to reduce prices, otherwise he threatened to use the army for the purpose. Indeed, the army's top brass had begun to plan for such an eventuality. Mahdavi, a German-trained economist, said, "I was well familiar with the Nazi Germany's policies of price control implemented in 1936; they simply ordered the prices frozen at a certain level. I followed the same policy."[32] A "price police," composed of university students and afforded the power of arrest, was unleashed on the already disgruntled shopkeepers. Prices stabilized after three weeks; the army was not called in, but the cure proved more dangerous than the disease. The policy helped push the shopkeepers further into the rising tide of opposition to the shah.

Back in 1965, during the first months of his tenure, Hoveyda also found passage of the new Civil Service Code to be a process fraught with

---

* In 1971, the shah still had not forgotten Mosaddeq; he continued to be puzzled and pained by his popularity. When the shah signed the new agreement with the oil companies, it was obviously important for him to have a known figure of the National Front defend the agreement in public.

political dangers. Those with vested interests in the inept and bloated bureaucracy were bent on preventing the new code from ever taking root. As a politician, Hoveyda had the gift of patience; he always knew that there would be another day to fight the battle that could not be won today. He rarely chose a battle he could not win, and when the cost of winning the Civil Service Code war seemed too great, he deferred it to a later date. On January 31, 1965, the government announced that no funds were available to make the civil code changes in the current fiscal year. The U.S. Embassy believed that the real reason for the delay was that the Iranian government "wanted to minimize opposition among important groups of civil servants."[33] As for the new tax law, it was "being drafted in the Ministry of Finance with the assistance of an adviser provided by the International Monetary Fund."[34]

Hoveyda also began to develop his own rather unique mode of operation. Every day, he would set aside lunch for informal meetings with a different group of people. One day it was the journalists, the next it was members of the parliament. Inclusion and the encouragement of political participation, albeit within the confines of the existing system, were the axioms of nearly all his actions in those days. When on March 5, 1967, Mohammad Mosaddeq—former prime minister and a symbol of Iran's nationalism—died of cancer at the age of 87, the public announcement of his death was limited to a terse press release. Hoveyda, on the other hand, had "suggested to the Shah that permission be granted for a modest funeral, in keeping with Mosaddeq's status as a former prime minister. The Shah reportedly was adamantly opposed to any such move, saying that he wished to erase every trace of Mosaddeq in the land."[35] Needless to say, no funeral was allowed for Mosaddeq. On the day Mosaddeq died, Persian flags flew half-mast all around Tehran, but not for the death of a man whom U.S. Ambassador Meyer had called "one of the great personalities of Persian history"; instead, the gesture of respect was for the "recent passing of the governor general of Canada, Georges Vanier."[36]

Early in Hoveyda's tenure there had been several attempts, according to the American Embassy in Tehran, "to arrange some kind of deal that might permit [Khomeini's] return against a guarantee of tranquillity."[37] Mehdi Pirasteh, Iran's ambassador to Iraq in 1965, confirms these reports, adding that soon after his arrival in Iraq, "a member of Khomeini's entourage came to the embassy hoping to work out a deal for his master's return. I refused to intervene, because I did not trust Khomeini. I had told the shah not to exile him; we should have kept him under house arrest in Iran."[38] Ayatollah Khomeini's emissary, according to Pirasteh, then approached Colonel Pejman, SAVAK's representative at the embassy. The colonel contacted Tehran and was told that no deal should be made.[39] It is not clear if Hoveyda had any role in these failed negotiations. Moreover, although he made a pilgrimage to Mashad and "sent his mother to Mecca," there was still widespread hostility against him from the mullahs because he was "believed to be a member of the Bahai sect, which is deeply disliked by many Iranian Muslims."[40] On the whole, however, compared to Mansur's days, there was less open friction between the Hoveyda government and the mullahs.[41]

While mullahs in Tehran might have changed their attitude because they had begun to enjoy the fruits of Hoveyda's largess, no such change— though no charge of a Bahai affiliation either—is evident in the one and only letter Hoveyda received from Ayatollah Khomeini. Written in 1967, the tone of the letter is more akin to advice of a disgruntled master to his prodigal student than that of an exiled ayatollah to the prime minister. The ayatollah wrote, "Mr. Hoveyda. It is necessary for me to offer you some advice, and remind you of certain things that need to be said, whether you are free to accept them or not." He went on to talk about "Your police state...your hypocrisies," and what he called "the domination of the country's economy by Israel, and even according to some reports, Israel's interference in our educational system." He ended by asking "how can your conscience permit you to fawn so much before the foreigners for the sake of this fleeting power, to surrender the resources of the nation to them for nothing or for a small price?...The granting of legal immunity to foreigners is a great proof of backwardness, a lack of self-respect...You know full well what treason to Islam and this country you committed by approving the bill....You are nothing more than the official charged with executing...orders [by foreign powers]....Do not extort so much from the impoverished tradesmen. Fear the wrath of god! Fear the wrath of the people...There are so many things to be said: I have said only a few in the hope that you will come to your senses."[42]

Aside from its tone, the letter is interesting in that the ayatollah reprimands Hoveyda for the same alleged breaches that, almost twelve years later, figure prominently in the indictment of the Revolutionary Tribunal against him. But in 1967, no one could imagine that within twelve years the author of this letter would become the leader of a frenzied revolution and would hold Hoveyda prisoner.

In his early days as prime minister, Hoveyda also traveled widely in Iran. Decentralizing the government was a policy on which he personally invested much energy and political capital. He would often insist on holding cabinet meetings in cities in far out corners of the country. Other times, he would go on inspection tours. Before setting out on these often unannounced trips, he would have his trusted advisers investigate the local scene and brief him on the nature of its problems. Hoveyda's trip to Tabriz, with his wife Laila, on August 24, 1967, was an example of his attempt to "crack the whip." From a report by the U.S. Consulate Office in Tabriz, we learn that there was little advance publicity for the prime minister's trip, which is described below:

> [Hoveyda] devoted minimum time to ceremonies...Instead he followed a rigorous schedule of working meetings and visits to the various institutions and projects...He viewed everything with a meticulously critical eye, issuing on-the-spot orders which sent local officials scurrying in all directions...Hoveyda's eagle eye even spotted a few holes in the ceiling of the new railroad station, which resulted in the railroad director being called on the carpet for failure to take appropriate action. And so it went for the better part of three days, with almost every department official coming in for some sort of prod or rebuke. But Hoveyda was clearly saving his big guns for the University of Tabriz.
>
> Upon arriving at the University campus, the scene of protracted student demonstrations and protests three months earlier—the prime minister laid down his cane, shed his coat, and proceeded to tell the mixed audience of teachers and students, jammed into the auditorium and spilling over outside, that beginning immediately everything would be changed: Professors, courses, living accommodations, scholarships, academic standards—everything. He then methodically, bluntly, and sometimes by name, obliterated the older order of entrenched...faculty and administration officials with one broadside after another: they had totally neglected the interests of the students...they had neglected the classroom to line their own pockets...They had, in sum, done a

disservice to the King and the country by keeping the university in the
Middle Ages…All deans would be immediately replaced…The students
(joined by a number of young faculty members) reportedly cheered the
Prime Minister for a full five minutes.[43]

Besides these occasional trips Hoveyda's schedule was dominated by
cabinet meetings, renowned lunches with various strata of society, audiences with the king, and, of course, weekly visits to his mother. He met the
shah regularly, at least once a week; he would also be granted an audience
as the situation required. To ensure that politicians like Hoveyda had as
little to do with the military as possible, even the rooms where the two
groups waited for their audience with the shah were usually separated.[44] In
addition to his audiences, Hoveyda and the shah talked frequently during
the day. Usually, the shah called on the private, secure line that connected
his office to the prime minister's desk. Sometimes they talked in French or
English. If they used the two foreign languages to ensure further privacy,
the ploy seems naive at best. If, on the other hand, they were both more
comfortable in French or English than in Persian, then, the revolution can
in some measure be seen as a linguistic backlash, a nativist resurgence
against the rule of cosmopolitanism.

Ironically, in spite of their precautions, the shah and Hoveyda might
not have been the only two people privy to these private conversations.
Hoveyda had come to believe that his phones and his office were wired by
SAVAK. Even his mother's house—where he sometimes lived and often visited—was, by his reckoning, bugged. On more than one occasion, while
visiting his mother, Hoveyda had silenced a friend or a member of the
family who was about to broach a politically sensitive topic. With a gesture of his index finger over curled lips, and a movement of the brow, he
would invite the interlocutor to silence. Only outside, in the small yard,
amid the trees, did he feel free to engage in these kinds of discussions.[45]

Indeed, ever since his return to Iran, Hoveyda had an uneasy relationship with SAVAK. While his critics, in an apparent attempt to besmirch him
with every conceivable fault, have claimed that he joined the secret police
as soon as he came back, most of the evidence actually points to a complicated, often troubled relationship, mostly based on a combination of fear
and mistrust.[46] Though, nominally, the head of SAVAK was a vice-premier,
it was the shah who took a direct role in running the secret police. Not

only did the head of SAVAK, General Nasiri, report directly to the shah, but in sensitive cases, where a high-profile opponent was arrested, the king would receive daily reports about the ongoing interrogations.[47] Yet in his *Answer to History,* in an all too transparent attempt to shift the blame, the shah flies in the face of evidence to the contrary and claims "our prime minister was directly responsible for day-to-day operations of SAVAK. As head of state, I could only intervene at the request of the Minister of Justice to exercise the right of pardon."[48]

Aside from the shah's decision to keep SAVAK a domain reserved for himself, General Nasiri's notorious financial corruption and close ties to Alam seriously strained Hoveyda's relationship with the general. But Hoveyda was a cunning and astute politician. He knew that power in Iran was, in no small measure, in the hands of SAVAK. Despite the structural obstacles the shah had placed on Hoveyda's access to the secret police, Amir Abbas, as was his wont, found a personal and indirect way to circumvent these obstacles. And here the friendship he had developed with Parviz Sabeti played a crucial role.

By the late sixties day-to-day affairs of internal security were in the hands of Parviz Sabeti, head of SAVAK's "Third Division." While every Monday and Thursday morning, the shah gave an audience to Nasiri and heard his reports on security matters, every Wednesday afternoon, not long after most of the staff at the prime minister's office had gone home, Sabeti would visit Hoveyda in his office. In addition, the two men would have lunch from time to time. Sabeti was also an occasional guest at Hoveyda's dinner parties. During their conclaves, the two would discuss a wide range of topics, with the exception of the security forces' operations.[49]

Under Sabeti's direction, the Third Division not only fought to eliminate or constrain all opposition to the regime, but it also took a keen interest in government corruption. For Sabeti, corruption had become a political issue and a security concern; it threatened the very stability of the system. His office monitored the activities of the Iranian political, economic, and military elite for any indication of graft, paybacks, dummy partnerships, overbilling, and other forms of corruption. Even members of the royal family were not spared the scrutiny of his office. Some of his reports about their illicit activities angered the shah. Though the shah never removed Sabeti from office—except in the waning days of the Pahlavi regime—he also never granted him an audience.* Even during the high tide of revolution, when some of the shah's advisers, including the queen, urged him to meet with Sabeti, he refused. Sabeti probably knew more about the system's strengths and weaknesses than anyone else; and yet the shah, for reasons we may never know, would not deign to meet him.[50]

Hoveyda, on the other hand, met Sabeti every week. During these informal meetings, not only would the two discuss a whole range of political issues, but Sabeti would also brief Hoveyda on the financial activities of the Iranian elite.[51]

When, during his controversial interview with Ockrent, Hoveyda declared that SAVAK was a domain reserved for the shah; when he later told the Islamic court that he had nothing to do with running SAVAK; when he claimed that he had never ordered the execution, or torture, of anyone, he was certainly, in a literal sense, telling the truth. But the question of his moral responsibility is more complicated. On the one hand, his close and intimate relationship with Sabeti would render his claim of clear disentanglement from the secret police less than entirely accurate. Knowledge always translates into power, and the kind of information Sabeti provided Hoveyda was certainly an important element in Hoveyda's consolidating and prolonging his hold on power.

Furthermore, Hoveyda could not claim to have had no knowledge of SAVAK's activities during those years. The foreign press he diligently read often reported on these activities. In addition, during almost every foreign trip he made, the media asked him about the question of torture and censorship in Iran. The only viable moral argument Hoveyda could have made would have been something along the lines eloquently suggested by one of his cabinet ministers, Farokh Najmabadi. In discussing the question of ends and means, rights and responsibilities, economic development and political oppression, Najmabadi said, "In those years, we knew there was torture going on somewhere in Iran, and we chose silence, and for that we are guilty; but we chose silence because we thought what we were doing for the country as a whole was worth our silence. In spite of that potentially guilty silence, my colleagues and I have a record we can be, on the whole, proud of."[52] While as prime minister Hoveyda went out of his way to publicly deny the existence of all breaches of human rights

---

* When Sabeti was given the, mostly titular, post of "Special Adjutant to the Shah," the two men met briefly, though no more than a few words were exchanged between them.

in Iran, during his trial, he came close to offering a defense much along
the line of that offered by Najmabadi.

Besides his regular meetings with Sabeti, Hoveyda had other liaisons
with the secret police. In 1965, Daryoush Homayoun, a young, bright
nationalist journalist, traveled to the United States on a Harvard fellow-
ship. While in America, he wrote an essay on political development in
Iran, arguing for the urgency of reforming the Iranian system from within. The essay created something of a stir in Tehran, and when Homayoun
returned home, Hoveyda invited him to a meeting at the prime minister's
office. Homayoun was, by then, a recognized personality among Iranian
journalists; he was known for his extreme nationalism, his unwavering
anticommunism, and the pristine quality of his prose. In response to the
prime minister's query about what should be done to ferment the kind of
political development he had been writing about, Homayoun suggested
that a new, independent, liberal yet loyal paper should be created; such a
paper, he said, could be an instrument for "elevating political discourse in
Iran."[53]

About two years after that initial meeting, and after many other lengthy
discussions involving numerous government agencies, in mid-1967 in a
meeting at the prime minister's office, Hoveyda, General Nasiri of SAVAK,
and Daryoush Homayoun approved final plans for the creation of just such
a newspaper. A corporation was created in which the government held a
fifty-one percent majority share. The remaining forty-nine percent came
from Homayoun and a small group of his journalist friends. The new newspaper was called *Ayandegan*. As the government's representative on the
newspaper's board of directors, Hoveyda, at the behest of SAVAK, chose
Manouchehr Azmoun, a seasoned operative of the secret police who had
been a communist in his youth and would later go on to become a cabinet
minister.

Although *Ayandegan* often took unseasonably liberal positions, and
occasionally offered scathing criticism of aspects of government policy,
the paper's genealogy continued to cast a sobering shadow on its image.
When *Ayandegan* took unusually strong positions defending the American war in Vietnam, and when word of the government's role in creating
the journal leaked out, the paper acquired a tarnished reputation as a
SAVAK or American creation. Ironically, the paper did eventually contribute
to enriching political discussions but only after the Islamic Revolution,

when under a new editorial board, it truly emerged as the most militantly liberal, antigovernment voice of the time. Its closure at the hands of the Islamic government is often thought to have been one of the early turning points of the revolution. But the newspaper had also had problems with the Pahlavi regime.

Even though the majority of the newspaper was state-owned, even though SAVAK had—in the person of Azmoun—a constant presence at the newspaper, even though Homayoun was a journalist with a long record of anticommunist struggles, *Ayandegan* was soon in trouble with the shah. Both of its founding contributing editors—Homayoun and Jahangir Behrouz, another old hand in Iranian journalism—were at one time or another ordered by the shah to leave the journal, or cease writing for it. Behrouz was expelled in 1971 for writing an article about freedom of the press in Iran. For the insolence he had shown, he was ordered to leave the corporation altogether. His shares, totaling about one hundred thousand tomans, or a little less than fifteen thousand dollars, were bought out by the government.[54] Mansur's brother, Javad, who had been one of the earliest members of the Progressive Circle and became minister of information not long after his brother's assassination, was also "fired from his post late in the evening of April 14 by the prime minister Hoveyda on instructions from the shah. Mansur's downfall apparently was also triggered by an article in *Ayandegan*."[55] Though Hoveyda seems to have made an unsuccessful attempt to temper the shah's anger against Mansur, he made no effort to save Behrouz, who, according to the U.S. Embassy in Tehran, was "known to be close to Hoveyda."[*56]

In an unrelated incident, Homayoun, too, was subjected to the royal wrath. His sins were twofold: in one article, he suggested that what had come to be known in Iran as the "White Revolution" was, in reality, more a process of reform. In another article, he took indirect aim at the cult of personality that was developing around the shah. For this walk on the wild side, the shah ordered Homayoun expelled from the newspaper. "For five weeks, I was not allowed to even enter the building," he recounted.[57] This time, however, Hoveyda did intervene. After waiting for the shah's wrath to subside, Hoveyda convinced him to allow Homayoun to return to the

---

* According to Fereydoun Hoveyda, who happened to be in Iran at the time, Amir Abbas tried to get the shah's permission to give Javad Mansur another job. The shah apparently rejected his plea. Fereydoun Hoveyda, interviewed by author, 12 October 1999.

newspaper he had founded. In July 1977, Homayoun became the minister of information. The job gave him privileged insight into the workings of the censorship process in Iran. "In my experience," he said, "it was always the shah who read the Iranian newspapers and then wanted to reprimand the journalists." Hoveyda's policy, he added, "was more to co-opt the journalists. He believed that they all could be bought; it was only a question of finding the price."[58]

Though much evidence indicates that, early in his tenure, Hoveyda made a concentrated effort to befriend editors and journalists, there are also reliable accounts that, in the second half of his tenure, he tried to install editors friendly to the government in major magazines and newspapers. His greatest success in this area was the appointment of Amir Taheri as the editor of Tehran's most important daily, *Kayhan*. Described by the American Embassy as "a Hoveyda man," Taheri soon established himself as one of the most important voices in Iranian journalism.[59] According to Mostafa Mesbahzadeh, *Kayhan*'s owner and publisher, "Midway through his tenure, Mr. Hoveyda decided to increase his own influence in the media. Up to that time, he had tried to turn a number of journalists into his personal friends. His main advisor in these attempts was Farhad Nikoukhah...One day, Nikoukhah told me that the prime minister wants you to appoint Amir Taheri as *Kayhan*'s editor. I told him the current editor had been in that post for almost twenty years and that I was perfectly satisfied with his performance. I added that he was my relative...A few days later, the prime minister himself called and indicated that he wanted to see me. When I arrived, he brought up Taheri's editorship, and indicated that he really wanted this thing done. I repeated what I had said earlier. Hoveyda thought for a minute and then changed the topic...A few days passed and then he called again and invited me to lunch. During lunch, he asked me what happened to the question of the editor. As I began to make my excuses, he raised his head, pointed to the picture of the Shah, and said, 'this is not my request, the boss wants it done.' I said 'if it is by order of His Majesty I will oblige.' I was put in a tough situation so I decided to consult Alam...I asked him to figure out what was really going on and let me know. He told me not to hurry, and said he would tell me the outcome of his inquiry. Two weeks later he [Alam] asked me to breakfast at which time he told me that '[The Taheri appointment] is indeed the wish of the boss and you have no choice...' And thus it was that Amir Taheri became the editor of *Kayhan*."[60]

Alam's *Diaries* not only confirm Mesbahzadeh's story but add truly Byzantine twists to it.[*] In Alam's rendition, the idea of Taheri's editorship had in fact come from Hoveyda, who then not only enlisted the shah's support for the proposition, but succeeded in convincing him that the idea had been the king's to begin with.[61]

Alam's comments are also interesting from an entirely different perspective. There are some knowledgeable observers of the Iranian political scene who believe that, contrary to the common perception of Hoveyda as a mere tool of royal decrees, he was more often the one who manipulated the shah into doing his bidding, all the while having the shah think he himself was in command.[62] In either case, with the Taheri appointment, Hoveyda was one step closer to consolidating his hold on the media.

In 1968, Hoveyda's influence in the media allowed him to orchestrate a media attack on former Prime Minister Ali Amini, at the shah's behest. In February of that year, the shah, "before leaving for Europe instructed Hoveyda to take action against Amini." The shah believed Amini to be the "fair haired boy of the oil Consortium," and in attacking him, the king was "moving to batten down his political hatches."[63] Articles in the media attacked Amini as a stooge of foreign powers. Hoveyda also took part in the offensive, declaring in a fiery speech that the days when foreigners could dictate policy, or choose prime ministers in Iran, had come to an end. To further pressure and embarrass Amini, an old case about his wife's supposed financial corruption was reopened at the Ministry of Justice. The case alleged that during her husband's days as premier, she had sold a piece of property to the city of Tehran at an inflated price. Amini, too, was declared to be under investigation for the putative misuse of government funds when he was Iran's ambassador to the United States.[64] On February 26, 1968, a special tribunal, designed to adjudicate possible crimes of prime ministers, "found that a prima facie legal case existed for prosecuting Amini."[65]

None of these allegations ever resulted in a conviction and no one doubted their political nature. More than anything else, the allegations showed the shah's growing inability to tolerate even a modicum of resistance to his rule. Furthermore, they illuminate an ironic twist in Hoveyda's politics. He and his Progressive Circle had come to power as an alternative

---

[*] In Hoveyda's trial, the question of his role in appointing editors for different newspapers and magazines was discussed. Hoveyda categorically denied any role in any of these appointments. See Chapter 15, page 320.

to the National Front. Their stated purpose had been to create a viable atmosphere for the political participation of Iran's middle classes and moderate political forces. Now, Hoveyda had become the shah's instrument for exacting revenge on a moderate figure like Amini. Both he and the shah would live to rue the day when all viable moderate forces in the country—from Amini to the National Front—had either been destroyed, isolated, or politically tainted by often false and fabricated charges. When, beginning in 1977, the combination of an economic crunch and a new policy of liberalization created a political crisis that began to shake the foundation of the Pahlavi regime and lay the groundwork for the Islamic Republic, the political landscape had been so thoroughly scorched that no legitimate moderate force capable of steering through the turmoil existed. The arrogance of power in 1968 led to the fragility of the regime's structure in 1978. When, after more than a decade of constant jibes at all moderate, secular forces, the beleaguered shah once again tried to solicit their help and advice, it was too little too late. In the end, radical Islam emerged as the only alternative.

IN THE SAME YEAR THAT THE SHAH ORCHESTRATED the attacks on Amini, he also gave Hoveyda permission to make an important trip to the United States. The prime minister's trips abroad, and indeed, those of every minister, ambassador, general, and head of a university, as well as those of all retired prime ministers such as Amini, required royal permission.[66] In December 1967, the U.S. Embassy in Tehran sent a cable to the State Department strongly recommending that "Amir Abbas Hoveyda be invited for an official visit to the United States." The embassy wrote, "The nature of U.S.-Iranian relations are undergoing a significant change as Iran is becoming increasingly independent…Hoveyda himself is very anxious to visit the United States and like most Iranians will attach particular importance to this personal attention…Although he has exhibited some tendencies toward assertive nationalism and some sympathy for an Afro-Asian orientation, he is anti-Communist in his convictions and Western in his training and in his natural tendencies…Hoveyda is likely to be a significant figure on the Iranian political scene in the foreseeable future and his visit would stand us in good stead for some time to come."[67]

*Amir Abbas Hoveyda and Lyndon Johnson walking up to the White House
in December 1968.*

The White House and the State Department ultimately agreed with
the embassy's suggestion but seemed to have had altogether different reasons for their decision. As far as the White House was concerned, the
"secret purpose for inviting [Hoveyda] was, frankly, to give a little expo-
sure to Iranian leaders other than the Shah on the grounds that (a) they
rate it and (b) it's probably wise to help emphasize that Iran isn't just a
one-man show."[68] In preparation for Hoveyda's visit, President Lyndon
Johnson was advised by the State Department that, in his discussions
with the prime minister, "praise for Iran's recent progress should largely
be directed toward the Shah, and the Empress Farah too should be credited with good works…To do otherwise could be interpreted by Iranians
as clear American 'support' of particular individuals or policies." The
State Department even engaged in a bit of cultural anthropology and
suggested that "Iranians will be quick to resent any implication that
Americans lump Iran with other Moslem countries or with other 'emerging' countries. They particularly do not like to be thought of in the same
terms as Arabs or Turks. They will be embarrassed by talk about religion
because the educated Iranian is likely to be contemptuous of pious Islam
but cannot admit it to a foreigner." Finally, the president was also offered
some political advice. "Queries about party politics in Iran," he was told,

"should be avoided because the Iranian Parliament is a one-party body, hand-picked by the Shah in an effort at 'guided democracy.' Freedom of the press is similarly a touchy subject."[69]

Hoveyda was also described by Johnson's advisors as someone who is "simple, informal and direct...He is fully capable of talking military and foreign affairs, but he regards those as the Shah's preserves and concentrates on domestic programs."[70] Johnson, when being coached for his talks with the prime minister, was asked to show interest "in hearing about the latest domestic developments in Iran. In this context, it would be worthwhile to discuss how the Shah and the Prime Minister plan to expand the political and economic institutions necessary to continue absorbing Iran's young people into active participation in the exercise of power. This is a delicate subject, but an important one."[71]

In addition, the president was provided with often astute and informed biographical sketches of everyone in Hoveyda's party. For example, Hoveyda's wife, Laila Emami, was described as "one of Iran's new generation of completely emancipated, Westernized women. She is bright, argumentative, energetic, unconventional and strong-willed. She is very alert to what is going on in the world and is quick to generate strong ideas, even to the point of appearing opinionated. Mrs. Hoveyda sometimes gives the impression of being exceptionally high-strung, tense and impatient with slow-moving events and the requirements of protocol."[72] They further noted that she smoked Winston cigarettes and drank scotch whisky.

Hoveyda's preparations, in comparison, seemed haphazard. Most of his information about American politicians he would meet came from Cyrus Ghani, who had emerged as his key adviser on American affairs. The son of a famously erudite physician, Ghani was described in the State Department profile as "a remarkable young Iranian lawyer of far-ranging interests...[He] has been described as an Iranian constitutionalist...His greatest complaint against the current regime has been the Shah's autocratic system of government...He is extremely well read in Persian, English and American classics...and is also a student of cinematic art. His research [in the spring of 1968] into the current American political scene may have induced the prime minister to include him in his party for his trip to the U.S."[73] As Ghani sardonically remembers, his research was no more than a careful reading of the American media. Based on this reading, he made an early prediction that Spiro Agnew would be chosen as

The Johnsons and the Hoveydas exchanging gifts, December 1968.

Nixon's running mate. To Hoveyda and many others in his administration, the prediction was a sure sign that Ghani was well-connected and uncommonly knowledgeable about American politics.[74]

Hoveyda decided to break with the past and, instead of the Persian rug or miniature commonly given as gifts by Persian politicians, give modern Persian paintings to his American hosts. After some consultations with friends and advisors, Hoveyda purchased fifteen paintings by Sohrab Sepehri, one of Iran's most gifted contemporary poets and painters.[75]

In turn, the American officials, in appreciation of Hoveyda's "lively mind," had decided to give him a large, engraved pipe stand and desk box in vermeil, three or four pipes, and a selection of books on politics, history, and government.[*76]

In spite of the detailed preparations, by the time Hoveyda and his official party arrived in America, Johnson was a lame-duck president. Little more than a month was left in his term of office. As the minutes of the Oval Office meeting between Hoveyda and the president make clear, there were very few specific policies discussed. Instead, the tenor of the talk was

---

* For Laila Emami, the gift suggestions included a "centerpiece by Gorham, shaped as an orchid and done in vermeil or engraved tea set in vermeil, books on American gardens and a gardening encyclopedia." LBJ Library, "Gift Suggestions" in "Visit of PM Amir Abbas Hoveyda."

the horizon of international affairs. While Hoveyda indicated that "he hoped more U.S. firms would come and work in Iran," the president, expectedly, responded that this "is a very enlightened viewpoint...He said he did not know any country—and he has been in dozens—where the leadership has been wiser or more effective."[77]

Some of the most interesting discussions in the meeting revolved around the question of military expenditure and the future security of the Persian Gulf region. Johnson gingerly alluded to what had been, for more than a decade, the sore point in Iran-American relations by saying that he "had always been concerned that Iran's military expenses not become so great as to undercut economic development. The Prime Minister said, 'There I can assure you that they are balanced.'"[78] The tone of Johnson's discourse here—cautious, politic, almost deferential—stood in sharp contrast to the declamations of the Kennedy administration. In 1961, Kennedy and his team not only did not eschew discussion of "sensitive topics" like democracy and political participation in Iran but insisted, in the shah's own words, "to dictate in minutest detail what [Iran's] military establishment may or may not have."[79]

Much of Hoveyda's tenure, specifically the decade that began in 1965, coincided with the era when Iran and the shah enjoyed the greatest degree of independence. In 1966, a CIA special memorandum, entitled "The Shah of Iran's Current Outlook," claims that "After twenty-five years on the throne of Iran, the Shah is for the first time acting like an independent monarch. He is fashioning his own image as a modern-minded, progressive ruler."[80] In anther report the CIA warned that the shah's "increasing feeling of independence will make for occasional friction" between the U.S. and Iran, adding that in achieving his accomplishments, the shah had in recent years "often acted against U.S. advice. As a result, he attributes his considerable success to the correctness of his policies and to his own skill in political maneuver. This belief has transformed the Shah from a timorous, titular monarch into a self-confident potentate."[81] Iran's decision to purchase a steel mill from the Soviet Union and pay for it with natural gas was only one of the signs of this new-found independence. Iran's active and often leading role in OPEC, and the shah's willingness to stand up to the West, and even to Nixon, when it came to the question of increasing the price of oil was another key element of this independence.

Tragically, events in the next decade showed the fragile quality of the king's self-confidence. As the first cracks began to appear in the armor of imperial grandeur, the vaunted self-confidence gave way to erratic policies, indecision, and timid submission to the will and whim of Western powers. In their search for a key to this riddle, Persian monarchists blame the medications that the shah had been taking in those days to fight the onset of lymphoma—the cancer that ultimately killed him. While it is hard to deny the debilitating effects of these drugs, augmented by the heavy dose of anti-depressants he took, there is also a long history that indicates the real cause to be more internal. In 1941, for example, the shah had been anxious to leave the country with his father when Reza Shah was forced to abdicate; he fled Iran in 1953; he was ready to abdicate and leave again in 1962 and 1963; and in 1979, when the high tide of opposition to his authoritarianism came, he could not wait to leave the country. But in 1968, his glory days were still ahead of him and the trend toward his new sense of independence had only just begun.

Hoveyda was surely not the cause of this newfound sense of independence, but his own cosmopolitan flair and his coterie of technocrats, who were far from intimidated by the West, worked hand in hand to help further cultivate this new attitude. At the same time, even some of his most staunch supporters admitted that Hoveyda's "shrewdness enabled him to recognize in the Shah a weakness for flattery, particularly his wish to be compared to de Gaulle."[82] But just as surely, Hoveyda did his part to create a veritable cult of personality around the shah. The increase in oil revenues was, of course, also instrumental in providing the requisite economic muscle for the king's new political bravura and a self-confidence that bordered on megalomania. In the first year of Hoveyda's premiership, the Iranian Central Bank was desperately in need of a five million dollar short-term loan to carry on the day-to-day affairs of the government. Mehdi Samii, the head of the Iranian Central Bank, relied on his friendship with executives of Bank of America to procure the funds. In 1974, however, the shah was able to go on a "lending binge," agreeing that Iran should give, in loans and grants, close to two billion dollars to seventeen foreign countries, including France and Britain. Early omens of these changes can be detected in the tone of Johnson's talk with Hoveyda in December 1968.

In that conversation, Hoveyda went on to add two points that would, in later years, become centerpieces of Iran's foreign policy. Referring to

Britain's announcement that by 1971 British forces would leave the Persian Gulf, Hoveyda declared, "It is up to the people of the Persian Gulf" to provide for the security of the region. Hoveyda went on to mention a "disturbing report that the Iraqis are trying to develop the capacity to wage germ warfare. The Soviets had refused to help, but the Iraqis are approaching Bulgaria now. The thought of germ warfare in the hands of such an unstable government made him shudder."[83] Shudder indeed, for no more than twelve years later, the same "unstable government" of Iraq used germ warfare in its long and bloody war with Iran.

Hoveyda's comments about the security of the Persian Gulf after Britain's departure are also interesting in several other respects. On the one hand, they can be seen as the backdrop to what would later be called the "Nixon Doctrine." Rather than try to police the whole world, the U.S., according to this doctrine, would help arm and strengthen a number of different countries, each selected to safeguard one region of the globe. First enunciated during a speech in Guam in 1969, the doctrine, as it applied to Iran, was founded on the notion that "the U.S. would continue to 'cooperate with Iran in strengthening its defenses' as the best hope for regional stability and security...The U.S. agreed that...decisions on the acquisition of military equipment should be left largely to Iran."[*84] In other words, in order for Iran to police the Persian Gulf region, the shah was finally given a carte blanche to buy all the arms he wanted without any curbs imposed by the U.S. It is tempting to imagine what modern Iran would have become had Nixon continued the Eisenhower, Kennedy, and Johnson administrations' policy of limiting the shah's military expenditures. For no one in the upper echelons of power in Iran, and certainly not Hoveyda, ever dared challenge the shah's insatiable appetite for arms. As Hoveyda often lamented, more than seventy percent of the budget was always set aside for programs over which the cabinet had absolutely no say.[85]

---

* Armin Meyer, the U.S. ambassador to Iran from 1965 to 1969, offers an interesting hypothesis that certainly deserves closer scrutiny by students of American foreign policy. He suggests that the shah, during a 1967 Nixon visit to Tehran, played a crucial role in shaping the Nixon Doctrine. In recently declassified documents from the U.S. Embassy in Tehran, and from the Department of State, there is much evidence to indicate that the shah had in fact begun to think along these lines even before the Nixon visit. In November of 1966, for example, he told Averell Harriman, who was visiting Tehran at the behest of President Johnson, that it is not wise for a country like Iran to consider dependence on even as good a friend as the U.S. Great power intervention "anywhere these days is more difficult...It is therefore imperative for Iran to develop capabilities of taking care of itself in deterring or coping with regional threats." See U.S. Embassy, Tehran, Iran, "Telegram from the Embassy in Iran," in *Foreign Relations of the United States, 1964-68*, Vol. XXII (Washington, D.C., 1999), 327–330.

Spurred by the sudden increase in the price of oil, and in line with the new Nixon Doctrine, the shah commenced a major build-up and modernization of the Iranian armed forces. The use of Iranian Special Troops to put down a Marxist rebellion in the Dhofar region of Oman in the early 1970s turned out to be one of the success stories of the Nixon Doctrine. The decision to send these troops to fight in that war was never discussed in the cabinet. By all accounts, Hoveyda only learned of it when news of the engagement reached the press. Questions of foreign policy, national security, oil, gas, atomic energy, and of course the army were never discussed in the cabinet. When extra funds were needed for these projects, the draft resolution of the law was offered for the cabinet's approval. It was clearly understood by all the cabinet ministers that no discussions of such bills would be tolerated by the shah. Hoveyda, according to his trusted plan and budget minister Madjidi, would quell any attempt at serious discussion of military appropriation bills in the cabinet. Madjidi remembers that "when military appropriations came before the cabinet, some [ministers] had doubts about it, but Hoveyda would not allow any discussion; although he knew that according to the law such bills must be approved by the cabinet, and such passage requires a discussion, nevertheless on these matters Hoveyda would not allow a discussion to take place."[86] Madjidi, of course, does not explain why these ministers never voiced their objections in the Majlis or why none ever resigned.

Iran's attempt to become the dominant force in the Persian Gulf, however, as well as the shah's insistence on sharply increasing the price of oil, put him on a collision course with the British government. Numerous cables from the U.S. embassies in Tehran and London, and the State Department, all testify to this "deterioration of Iranian-British relations." Walter Annenberg, the U.S. ambassador to London at the time, wrote that "we detect a certain reluctance here to accord to Iran a role in Gulf affairs as great or as determining as Iran itself appears to anticipate...Britain's political interests are weighed toward the Arab side of the Gulf, at least until withdrawal is completed. This special commitment, while it endures, enhances the continuing possibility of friction between the U.K. and Iran."[87] In July 1970, Iran objected to the fact that "recently in the Queen's speeches from the throne and elsewhere, Her Majesty's Government referred to 'Gulf' rather than 'Persian Gulf.'"[88] Not long after this incident, the U.S. Embassy in Tehran warned of a "possible Iran-British crisis brewing," observing that there were a "number of tell-tale signs in recent days that seem to indicate very strong anti-British sentiment rapidly building up here in the government of Iran."[89] By January 1973, not only had relations further deteriorated, but the ongoing oil negotiations only added to the tensions. At that time, the British ambassador in Iran delivered a message from Foreign Secretary Sir Alec Douglas-Home, "which he was instructed to deliver to the Shah personally. [The message was written in a way] as to amount to not so veiled threats."[90]

Oil also figured prominently in Hoveyda's discussions with Johnson. Hoveyda "mentioned that South Africa was stock-piling oil in its old empty coal mines" and raised the possibility that the U.S. government might buy more oil from Iran for the same purpose.[91] Johnson had been warned that "Hoveyda may raise…[the issue of] Iran's desire to sell additional oil to the United States" and was ready with the scripted answer. Johnson said the U.S. would certainly consider the purchase of Iranian products "whenever their prices are competitive."[92] He, of course, deferred all serious discussions to the newly elected Nixon administration. Indeed, before Hoveyda left the Oval Office, Johnson "invited Walt Rostow and Henry Kissinger to meet the prime minister, predicting that under the new administration, close relations would continue to exist between the U.S. and Iran."[93]

Johnson made another prediction, this time unwittingly, in the course of a state dinner given in Hoveyda's honor at the White House. The president quoted Shakespeare's *King Lear,* and his borrowed words turned out to be an uncannily accurate foreshadowing of Hoveyda's fate. For, though the shah and many of those around him left Iran, Hoveyda remained to face the storm. Johnson said:

That sir which serves and seeks for gain
And follows but for form,
Will pack and leave when it begins to rain,
And leave thee in the storm…[94]

While in the United States, Hoveyda also made the customary visits to the National Press Club, and the Council on Foreign Relations, both requisite parts of every foreign dignitary's visit to Washington. In New York, he met Nelson and David Rockefeller; he also had conversations "with

Hoveyda and Johnson having a discussion, December 1968.

executives of the American member companies of the Oil Consortium. He stressed to them Iran's desire that the Consortium increase its capacity to 5 million barrels per day, saying that the existence of such a large capacity…would have a restraining effect on any possible Arab moves in the future to deny the export of oil to the West."[95] The comment was prescient in terms of the Arab oil embargo in conjunction with the Arab-Israeli war of October 1973—an embargo which Iran, to the great relief of Israel and its Western allies, did not join.

Though Hoveyda's attempt to sell more oil was by and large unsuccessful, on the night of his Oval Office meeting, Johnson surprised everyone, including Hoveyda, by showing up at the party given at the Iranian Embassy. In terms of presidential protocol, the visit implied that Hoveyda was afforded the status of the head of state. Those in the prime minister's party were elated at the honor thus afforded Hoveyda. But Hoveyda knew better, and his response was emblematic of his whole approach to handling the shah. While for the White House the "secret purpose of inviting [Hoveyda] was to emphasize that Iran isn't just a one-man show," Hoveyda's tenure in office was at least partially predicated on his willingness to accept, indeed to advocate, the fact that Iran was nothing but a one-man show. On more than one occasion, he had said that Iran had only one leader, one commander, one guide. He was but His Majesty's chief of staff, he would often declare. Early in his tenure, it had become evident to him that his liberalism was in sharp, maybe even irreconcilable conflict with the shah's authoritarian bent, yet like a whole generation of technocrats, he seemed to have made a wager that economic growth, and the rise of the middle class, would eventually mitigate, if not entirely obviate, the shah's desire to continue his one-man rule.[96] In Hoveyda's trip to Washington, the price for that wager was that he forbade the Iranian journalist in his party to file a report about the special treatment he was afforded. Instead, a more sedate story, bereft of any praise for Hoveyda, was filed.[97]

Hoveyda's discussion of military and oil policies might also have been a calculated ruse intended to hide the actual extent of the shah's power and the political impotence to which the prime minister's office had been reduced. On other foreign trips, Hoveyda had not only discussed foreign relations but also talked with some authority about Iran's nuclear program. He would feign intimate knowledge of the program. The truth of his relationship with the atomic energy program was more complicated.

According to Akbar Etemad, the first president of the Atomic Energy Organization of Iran, in early 1974, Reza Qotbi,[*] a cousin and close confidant of the queen, called Etemad and informed him that the shah wanted Iran to have an atomic energy program and Etemad had been picked to head the effort. After only a month of study, Etemad prepared a fifteen-page report. Hoveyda was present when Etemad submitted his report to the shah. The shah carefully read the entire report three times, and then turned to the prime minister and said, "This is the country's atomic plan, not one word more, not one word less. This is it. I accept it all."[98] Thus it was that one of the most important new projects undertaken by the

---

[*] From the early 1970s Reza Qotbi, who headed Iranian Radio and Television, had begun to play a more important role in the politics of the country. By many accounts he would become one of the key decision-makers in the last days of the Pahlavi dynasty and as such end up entangled in the decision to arrest Hoveyda. I attempted to interview Qotbi; at first he agreed to speak with me, engaged in one brief conversation, and then decided that he did not want to be interviewed. Shortly before going to print, I once again contacted him, highlighting every statement made about him and asking him to comment. Once again, he gave me a few comments and then abruptly changed his mind. My experience with him was an exact repetition of the queen's behavior—first agreeing to an interview and then refusing to talk after seeing the questions I had submitted.

Hoveyda government, one that required two billion dollars in yearly capital investment, was approved without a word from the prime minister, without any prior consultation with his cabinet, without any prior input from the parliament.[99] Instead of objecting to this strange process, Hoveyda suggested on the spot that Etemad be appointed a vice-premier. Henceforth, Hoveyda would show no further interest in the work of the organization. He understood that atomic energy was the king's pet project and decided to steer clear of it. Hoveyda never asked Etemad what he was up to and never inquired whether the atomic program could also have military applications. In fact it was Etemad who asked Hoveyda whether he knew of any "secret plans [for the military use of atomic energy]." Hoveyda apparently responded with a question of his own. "Why do you want to know?" he inquired, and when Etemad said because it would make a difference in what they should do, Hoveyda answered, "I really don't know the answer."[100] In his unwillingness to inquire seriously into this sensitive question, Hoveyda was joined by Etemad himself, who claims rather enigmatically that early on he had "easily understood what they had in mind, but I pretended not to know...I could see that pieces of a large mosaic were thus coming together."[101]

The only person who knew what the mosaic would look like was the shah himself, and to make sure that the situation remained that way, he wanted the Atomic Energy Organization to directly report to him. Such a structure directly contravened the Iranian Constitution. When one of the senators had the temerity to raise the issue, the help of the powerful Senate president, Sharif-Emami, was solicited to "solve the problem."[102] Hoveyda's pragmatic decision to disengage himself from the Atomic Energy Organization, did not preclude him from, often publicly, talking about the project and defending its peaceful intent.

In 1976, when Hoveyda traveled to France on a state visit, after announcing that "Iran had signed contracts for two French-built nuclear plants," he went on to declare that Iran had "no intention of using nuclear plants to be built in Iran by France to develop nuclear weapons."[103] Indeed, during his 1968 trip to Washington, long before the creation of the Atomic Energy Organization, Hoveyda had raised the issue of Iran's hopes for developing atomic energy. The joint statement issued on the last day of Hoveyda's official visit to the U.S. declared that the president and the prime minister had reviewed "cooperation for the civil uses of atomic energy."[104]

Hoveyda at the height of his glory in the early 1970s. He often signed copies of this photo and gave them to friends and relations.

Hoveyda's American trip was, however, not entirely without friction. He had indicated a desire to visit President-elect Nixon in California, whom he considered a "personal friend." The State Department, "after consulting with the President-elect's staff…informed the Iranians that Mr. Nixon would not receive the Prime Minister because he would receive no foreign dignitaries prior to January 20. After Mr. Hoveyda's departure from California, Mr. Nixon received Israeli Minister of Defense Dayan and the Ruler of Kuwait." The Iranians were understandably upset, as Hoveyda was "put in an embarrassing situation."[105] No official explanation was ever offered for the snub. When Hoveyda left California, he went for a private vacation with Laila to Hawaii. But trouble was waiting for him at home.

CHAPTER TWELVE

The Ghost Valley

*A disposition to preserve and an ability to
improve, taken together, would be my standard
of a statesman. Everything else is vulgar in the
conception, perilous in execution.*
                                        —Edmund Burke

By late 1968, public prognostications of Hoveyda's imminent demise
had vanished. Seeds of discord, however, had been growing within
his own cabinet, where there were always ministers thought to be
Hoveyda's potential rivals. Foremost among these was Jamshid
Amouzegar; in a few years, Houshang Ansary would also emerge as a likely candidate. The first was a dour but consummate technocrat, who had
taken over oil negotiations since mid-1965 and reported directly to the
shah. The second was a flamboyant businessman turned politician, who
had amassed an enormous fortune and joined the cabinet in 1969 and
served in a variety of capacities in the cabinet, from minister of economy
to minister of finance.[1] He would eventually become the head of the
National Iranian Oil Company.

But these two "super ministers" were not alone in having direct access
to the shah. Other ministers also began to first report to the shah and then
come to cabinet meetings having already received royal consent for their
projects. Hoveyda would often lament that the ministers would all go
directly to the shah when there was good news to report and come to

Hoveyda when there were problems. Alam essentially confirms this pattern by writing that "every minister reports directly to the shah who then issues orders. The poor incompetent prime minister is altogether ignorant of what goes on. Maybe that is the key to his survival."[2] Toward the end of Hoveyda's tenure, when he felt more entrenched, he tried to forbid his more junior ministers from directly contacting the shah.[3]

Hoveyda handled Amouzegar and Ansary with great aplomb; in cabinet meetings he treated them with the kind of deference they thought they deserved. Ostensibly, the relations between the three were cordial and cooperative; political pundits, however, offered often vivid tales of the vicious behind-the-scene battles between them, and of Hoveyda's genius in thwarting their ploys and ascent. Troubling as these relations were, they paled in comparison to Hoveyda's Zahedi problem.

Ardeshir Zahedi was one of the more controversial political figures of the last three decades of the Pahlavi dynasty in Iran. According to a CIA profile, he came to the shah's attention in the course of the coup to oust Mosaddeq. While his father, General Fazlollah Zahedi, was a key participant in that drama, Ardeshir "served as a liaison between groups of the Shah's supporters and his father."[4] Not long after the 1953 coup, while his father was prime minister, Ardeshir traveled to Geneva—"a confidential trip, to discuss the question of oil"—where he met Amir Abbas Hoveyda for the first time.*[5] He found Hoveyda to be a "likeable man, cordial and congenial."[6] In 1957, Zahedi married the shah's daughter and divorced her in 1964. It was a measure of Zahedi's resilience that, after the divorce, not

---

* I met Ardeshir Zahedi at the Petit Palais restaurant, part of the famous Montreux Palais Hotel that has been a favorite resort of the world's rich and powerful for more than a century. Ahmad Shah, after losing the throne in the 1920s, and Ardeshir's father, after losing the post of prime minister, had each spent some time at the hotel. In the right-hand corner of the vast dining room, with the blue lake and towering mountains in the backdrop, there is an alcove where Zahedi holds court. In deference to his continuous patronage, the hotel management has engraved a set of crystal tea cups with his name and a concocted coat of arms. An old Persian gentleman, who I soon learned had once been a diplomat, was also present. Zahedi had asked me to submit my questions in advance. As I sat down, he brought out a few sheets of paper. The one that had my questions on it was scribbled with notes all over the margins. On the other sheets, he had prepared an outline of his troubled relationship with Hoveyda. He wore a casual blue shirt, no tie, white pants. His companion was fully dressed in a black suit, white shirt, and a well-worn tie. Throughout the five-hour interview, Zahedi's guest said at best five words. Even his food was ordered by Zahedi. "Give him the salmon," the once flamboyant ambassador said, and then turned to me and asked what I wished to order. During my student days, when he was Iran's ambassador to the United States and I was part of the Iranian student movement against the shah, we had often been on opposite sides of the fence. Now, my curiosity about a man he clearly disliked had brought us together.

only did he not lose his power and position but was soon offered an even more challenging assignment. Up to that time, he had served as Iran's ambassador to both the United States and England. In early 1967, the shah ordered him to take over the post of foreign minister, and the appointment was, from its inception, a disaster waiting to happen. Before he had even taken over the job, Zahedi, after a discussion with Hoveyda, decided that he was not going to come to most of the cabinet meetings. Using his own famously slang-strewn, deeply undiplomatic style, the new foreign minister declared that much of what transpires in those meetings is bereft of substance. Indeed, throughout his tenure, Zahedi only attended a handful of cabinet meetings and the rest of the time he dispatched his deputy minister.[7]

According to the U.S. Embassy in Tehran, Zahedi "introduced a completely new style, a new spirit of activism and even flamboyance into the conduct of the foreign ministry…During the first few weeks of his tenure…[he] spent not only his days but most of his nights there…[His] metallic blue Rolls Royce is still seen parked in front of the ministry at two o'clock or even later in the morning."[8] It also didn't take long for him to pick his first public fight with Hoveyda. In the words of U.S. ambassador Armin Meyer, "In a recent showdown within the cabinet, Zahedi won hands-down by appealing to the Shah over the head of the Prime Minister. This had to do with the budget for the Foreign Ministry, which he deemed insufficient. By tendering his resignation telegraphically to the Shah…Zahedi won his point."[9]

The next confrontation was more personal. When a new German ambassador was named, he turned out to be, probably not by mere coincidence, someone Hoveyda had known in his Stuttgart days. On the day of the new ambassador's arrival, Hoveyda went to the airport to meet his old friend. According to diplomatic protocol, however, the ambassador-designate can only meet with Iranian government officials after he has offered his credentials to the king. When Zahedi heard of Hoveyda's action, he first called him to protest and then sent him an unusually nasty letter. "My written Persian is not very good," Zahedi noted with a mischievous glee in his eyes, "so I ordered someone on my staff who was known for his fine prose to write a letter to Amir; I told him that he should not mix his private and personal affairs with the business of diplomacy."[10] Hoveyda plaintively took the letter to the shah who in essence sided with

Zahedi. By measures of diplomatic protocol, the shah declared, Zahedi had been right. As to the letter's insolent tone, the shah only said, "You should try to solve your differences."[11] In other words, firing the rambunctious minister was out of the question. It is hard to imagine too many politicians who would have hung onto power after such indignity. But Hoveyda seemed to have had the patience of Job; he bided his time for the right moment to rid himself of Zahedi.

The most serious political difference between the two men took place during the "bus crisis." Early in 1970, as part of an austerity program, the government decided to increase bus fares. University students took to the streets and demonstrated against the new hike. Many of the demonstrators were arrested. There was an emergency meeting of the cabinet which Zahedi attended. Some university presidents, including Alikhani of Tehran University were also invited. Zahedi and Alikhani thought that the fare hikes had been a mistake, and before the crisis could escalate, the government should back down, rescind the price increase, and release those arrested. There was much heated argument, and no consensus. The shah was skiing at a Swiss resort at the time and since he was the one who had to make the final decision, a call was put through to him. Hoveyda gave his report—with "some prevarication," according to Alikhani—and then Zahedi offered his frank and gloomy analysis. The shah sided with Zahedi and Alikhani, who also advocated a policy of reconciliation. The students were freed, the bus fares were reduced but the acrimony between Hoveyda and his foreign minister only increased.[12]

The issue of Bahrain also further strained the two men's relationship. For over a century, Iran had claimed sovereignty over Bahrain. In 1968, the British announced their intention to withdraw from the Persian Gulf within three years. The shah, in secret negotiations that apparently involved the British and American governments, as well as officials of the United Nations, decided to give up all Iranian claims to Bahrain. He also agreed to allow a UN-sponsored referendum so that the people there could decide their fate; in return, Iran would claim dominion over the three strategically significant islands of Abu Musa and the two Tumbs.[13] While these negotiations were going on, in the foreign ministry, there had been a secret committee supposedly studying the Bahrain problem for some time. They had no knowledge of the ongoing negotiations and were as surprised as the rest of the nation to hear of the shah's unilateral decision.[14] Yet, at the time, the shah was committed to maintaining at least the facade of a constitutional monarchy, and thus the legislation formalizing these royal decisions had to be submitted to the Majlis for approval. There was, according to Alam, a bitter fight between Zahedi and Hoveyda over who should defend the controversial bill in the parliamentary sessions, which promised to be, for a change, tense and raucous. Zahedi claims that the struggle with Hoveyda was in fact not about which of the two men should take part in the meeting of the Majlis, but instead about what should be said at the meeting. "Two draft speeches," he says, "had been prepared, one at the foreign ministry, the other at the prime minister's office. His Majesty had to decide which of the two drafts would be used at the meeting."[15] A small nationalist party called the Pan Iranist—whose leader, according to U.S. Embassy reports, was connected to SAVAK and usually toed the line prescribed by the government—promised to attack the new proposal.[16] The party's parliamentary faction had already asked for a vote of no confidence against the government. In the end, both Zahedi and Hoveyda participated in the session devoted to the question of Bahrain.[*] The vote of no confidence, as expected, came to naught; Bahrain gained its independence, but Iran's prime minister and his foreign minister could not solve their problems. For almost a year, they even refused to talk to one another. In parties, Zahedi would turn his back to Hoveyda, once loudly declaring that he would not shake hands with "a piece of shit."[17]

Several other issues brought what the U.S. Embassy called the "continuing rivalry and bitter personal friction" to a breaking point. In 1970, in spite of Hoveyda's objection, Zahedi ordered nine hundred Vacheron Constantin watches to be given as gifts by the foreign ministry.[†] Alam claims to have chastised Hoveyda for allowing such extravagant expenses at a time when there was a budget crisis. As Hoveyda began to lament his

---

[*] A measure of the distrust that existed between the prime minister and his foreign minister can be seen in one particular part of Zahedi's rendition of this meeting. "I sweat easily," he said, "and they had intentionally, and in spite of my request, increased the heat in the Majlis chamber. Thus when I spoke, my face was covered with sweat. Minutes after my speech, the shah called me and said, 'it has been reported to me that you wept while delivering your speech.' I told him the report was false. There were no tears, only sweat." According to Zahedi, Hoveyda had been behind the whole sweat-inducing scheme. The story becomes less strange when we remember that in the famous 1960 television debate between Nixon and Kennedy, the Kennedy camp conspired to have the heat in the studio increased, knowing full well that Nixon sweated easily.

[†] Zahedi claims that there were in fact only one hundred such watches ordered and that he paid for them out of his own pocket. Ardeshir Zahedi, personal correspondence, 12 January 2000.

relations with the foreign minister, Alam interrupted the prime minister only to admonish him. "It is all your own fault; you show weakness," Alam declared. And then referring to a Zahedi diatribe against Hoveyda that took place in front of the shah during a state visit to Pakistan, Alam offered him advice on how he would have handled such insolence. "If he had done it to me," he said, "I would have punished him. I mean I would have had his ass beaten with a stick long enough to bring him close to death."[*18]

But in the twisted texture of Alam's relationship with Hoveyda, even this admonishment and braggadocio was not enough. The last turn of the screw would come when Alam ventured a prediction that was obviously intended to further distress Hoveyda, a prediction that turned out to be more true than Alam might have imagined at the time. "If the economy falters," said Alam, "remember that you are the one they are going to use as a scapegoat. Look at what they did with the minister of planning in Tunisia. He was in power for ten years. When his programs failed…they arrested him and sentenced him to ten years hard labor. Your turn will come."[19] According to Alam, Hoveyda was visibly shaken by the prospect of a similar fate for himself.

Aside from personal animosities, there were also new policy issues between Hoveyda and Zahedi. Zahedi had been adamantly opposed to the appointment of Princess Ashraf as the head of Iran's delegation to the meeting of the UN General Assembly. It was about this time that Hoveyda attended a lavish party in Tehran. He was reported to have said that the night reminded him of a veritable Pompeii. Now, a woman who, at least in the common perception, was more than anyone else the emblem of this Pompeii was to lead Iran's delegation to the United Nations, and Zahedi was not happy. He placed much of the blame on Hoveyda, who in his words "not only facilitated the trip but paid out more than three hundred and fifty thousand dollars to cover her personal expenses."[†20]

---

* Alam's claim that he would have "paddled" Zahedi into submission is not only strange by any common standard of civility, but also seems to have been nothing but empty political posturing. In fact, according to Zahedi, when he was the foreign minister, he received a letter from Alam deprecating some of Iran's ambassadors. Zahedi fired off another of his famously tough-tongued letters in response. Alam, Zahedi says, not only did not attempt any paddling, but instead sent back a letter of apology, claiming that the original letter had been written by a subordinate and that he, Alam, had signed it without reading the text. Ardeshir Zahedi, interviewed by author, 12 January 2000.

† Zahedi further claimed that the princess wanted to take one of her lovers with her to a UN meeting. The alleged lover was described by a State Department report as "a clever 'graduate' of Ashraf's stable of young

Another issue arose around September 6, 1970, according to the U.S. Embassy. "Hoveyda (through a secretary) returned to Zahedi [the] list of awards Zahedi wished conferred on foreign ministry personnel because [the] list had been received after [the] agreed cabinet deadline."[21] Zahedi offered a more complicated story. He claimed that his anger was roused when Alam and Hoveyda conspired to add a few of their cronies' names to the list. In either case, the outcome was another nasty Zahedi letter to the prime minister. Hoveyda again took the letter to the shah and offered his own resignation. The shah did not accept the resignation but promised to look into the matter. Zahedi was called to the court and informed by the shah's chief of staff that he must take back the harshly worded letter. It had become clear to Zahedi, however, that he must either comply with the royal command, or resign. He chose the latter and soon departed for a vacation to his villa in Montreux.[22] After a brief hiatus, Zahedi was back in favor with the shah, who again named him Iran's ambassador to the United States—where this time he gained a reputation as a "good looking, rich and powerful" host who, according to Sally Quinn, the doyen of the social scene in Washington, threw "some of the best parties in town. Ardeshir was well known for being extravagant, and one of the things he did was send tins of Iranian caviar instead of thank you notes to those who had him for dinner."[23]

The fact that the shah did not allow Hoveyda to fire his ribald foreign minister is clearly congruent with the implicit agreement the two men made when Hoveyda was appointed prime minister. For Hoveyda to fire a minister as powerful as Zahedi would certainly have augmented his power in the eyes of the cabinet and the nation. It would have also meant a degree of independence the shah could not tolerate in his prime ministers. Nevertheless, Zahedi's dismissal, even at the hands of the shah himself, did increase Hoveyda's stature with most of his ministers.

Furthermore, the shah certainly would not have allowed such power in the realm of foreign policy. In March 1973, the shah ordered Alam to "tell

---

men." (See "The Iranian Imperial Family," NSA, no. 928.) According to Zahedi, the man asked for three hundred and fifty thousand dollars to accompany her. The cabinet, over Zahedi's stern warnings, ultimately agreed to pay the sum. Ardeshir Zahedi, interviewed by author, Montreux, Switzerland, 5 June 1998.

I have found copies of a cabinet resolution from the period to which Zahedi is referring. The resolution indeed authorizes the payment of three hundred and fifty thousand dollars to Princess Ashraf to cover her expenses for the trip. It is impossible to verify whether, or how much of the said expenses were for the individual allegedly accompanying the princess.

the foreign ministry that no one other than me should interfere in the affairs of the ministry. I have even ordered that Hoveyda's brother, who is our representative in the UN, cannot report to the prime minister. He cannot even call him. I recently reprimanded his brother for sending a report to his brother."[*24]

In a sense, the strange relationship that existed between the shah and Hoveyda—less that of a modern constitutional monarch to a prime minister, and more that of a potentate and his vizier—was replicated in at least one aspect of Hoveyda's relations with the ministers in his cabinet. Though Hoveyda had come to power with the promise of modernizing the civil service, cabinet ministers were paid in a system reminiscent of old feudal bureaucracies or *divans*. Every month, a sum equal to half of each cabinet minister's salary was paid as a bonus through a secret discretionary fund available to the prime minister. It was as if the ministers were in Hoveyda's employ. The shah, too, gave the ministers a bonus once in a while to underscore that ultimately they served him.[25]

FOR HOVEYDA 1970 WAS A YEAR OVERSHADOWED by his battle with Zahedi; 1971 was, on the other hand, a year of discord in his private life. His marriage to Laila was coming to an end. As is often the case, there was no single event or cataclysmic confrontation that signaled the end of their marriage. Instead, the gradual grind of small incompatibilities, the tense tedium of official ceremonies, the often vapid ceremonious duties of a prime minister's wife, and perhaps, most important of all, her unwillingness to make the kind of compromises, big and small, by which Hoveyda survived—an empty smile here, an appreciative nod there, a silent acquiescence of corruption everywhere—all tore away at the fabric of their common happiness. Ironically, Hoveyda's main assets as a politician, namely his penchant for compromise and disdain for open confrontation, were his major failings as a husband. His unwillingness to engage in the

---

* Freydoun Hoveyda had no recollection of such an order. In fact, he noted that on numerous occasions, when the shah had entrusted him with sensitive negotiations—like in October 1967 when the shah used him to sound out the North Vietnamese authorities in Paris about the possibility of a negotiated settlement to the Vietnam War—Freydoun was ordered to send all reports only to his brother, Amir Abbas Hoveyda. Freydoun Hoveyda told me about his secret trip to Paris in our meeting on February 17, 1999, and about the alleged incident quoted in Alam's *Diaries*, on August 21, 1999.

The shah presides over a meeting with government and military leaders in a calculated topography of power sometime in the late 1960s. Around him, from left to right, are Hoveyda, Mansour Rohani, General Esmail Riahi, Zia Shadman, General Asadollah Sanii (standing), General Hassan Pakravan, and General Sajadi (standing). The conclave was held in Qazvin, on a Shiite day of mourning, in a tent-room covered with tapestries.

kind of verbal banter that shapes most marriages tormented Laila. Silence was his response to her every complaint or criticism. "He was reticent with words," she said, "an introvert who kept all his problems to himself. You never knew what he was thinking about or what was bothering him. And contrary to [Hassan] Ali [Mansur], who every night regaled his wife with all the political gossip of the day, Amir never talked about politics at home."[26]

As her unhappiness increased, so did her acerbic comments, often made in public, about her life, about the difficulties of being the prime minister's wife, and about Hoveyda. Some attributed the occasional biting edge of her comments to her drinking habits. Word of tension in the marriage even reached the shah, who in early 1970, during an official ceremony, half-jokingly asked Laila, "Why do you bother this man so much?"[27]

One of the earliest sources of tension had been Hoveyda's bodyguards. In the first year of the marriage, one of the guards accidentally shot and

The Hoveyda brothers, dressed and plumed for an audience with the shah. Amir Abbas was prime minister and Fereydoun was Iran's chief representative to the UN.

The Hoveyda brothers standing next to their mother on the veranda of the house in Tehran she shared with Amir Abbas.

killed an old gardener who had been an Emami family retainer for many years. Laila began to complain about the presence of the guards in the house. When, a few weeks later, she heard that another one of the guards had called his superiors from a phone in the house and reported an argument between Hoveyda and his bride—"The prime minister spent last night on the couch," the agent had said—Laila forbade the agents and guards to enter the house.[28]

After a few earlier, quiet separations during which Hoveyda moved into his mother's house, Laila finally decided a divorce was what she wanted. As with her desire to marry, there was to be little forewarning. One night, as Hoveyda came back from another long day at work, she told him her decision. Hoveyda was angry and heartbroken but offered no resistance; he packed a suitcase full of his clothes and left Laila's house the next morning, never to return as her husband.* A couple of days later, as he sat forlorn in his office, suddenly and silently tears rolled down his face. His chief of staff, Safa, happened to be in the room at the time. "Laila wants a divorce," Hoveyda said. No other words were exchanged between the two men caught in an awkward moment of forced and unexpected intimacy.[29]

Five days later, Laila called Hoveyda at his office and suggested that they have lunch. "I had rarely called him at work before," she said. He agreed to the meeting, and over lunch, she tried to convince him that divorce was the only way they could remain friends. "We had little in common," she said wistfully. Books, films, and classical music, they had both always enjoyed. But these shared tastes were not enough to save their strained marriage.

In talking about her divorce she added with a damp-eyed burst of emotion, "When I think back on my life with Amir, I cannot find a single bad thing he did to me. He was all goodness to me; I just couldn't bear to be his wife."[30] After twenty years of exile, of time often spent in reassessing her past, she now had a solemn sense of renewed appreciation for a man she had married, always respected, never loved, and now mourned more than ever. "His greatest failing," she said more than once, "was tolerating all my bullying."[31]

---

* Hoveyda did not own a house in Tehran at the time. The house he had shared with his mother was being used by Fereydoun and his family. Eventually, the shah ordered the government to purchase a palace that belonged to one of his sisters and use it as the prime minister's official residence.

Hoveyda, too, resigned himself to the bitter reality of their broken marriage; in March 1971, he dispatched his trusted friend, Nasser Yeganeh, to work out the details of the divorce decree that was finalized on July 26, 1971. "He wanted nothing," Laila said. "He only took his clothes and his books. Even the set of paintings he had bought, and we had used to adorn our living room, and the Limoges china set he had brought back from Europe, he left for me."[32] On April 22, 1971, in a letter to her lifelong friend Jean Becker, Laila revealed much the same sentiment in writing; "Amir and I got divorced last month. I meant to write to you sooner but didn't get a minute to myself since. What with work in the greenhouses and friends not wanting to leave me alone, I seem to be busier than a PM's wife. Amir and I are still the best of friends and I want to keep it that way and I guess that is the reason for the divorce—to remain friends."[33] And friends they remained. Henceforth, they would spend most of their vacations together; they saw each other regularly, and the orchid she provided, and he wore every day, was the very token of this continued love. Not only their marriage but also their divorce and friendship were shaped by the civilities and eccentricities that each brought to the relationship.

Indeed, once Hoveyda got over the initial pangs, he, too, seemed to have come to a clear understanding of the reasons for the divorce. In 1972, when Jean Crooker visited Iran, Hoveyda not only arranged for her to travel around the country in his "plane, then helicopter, then Jeep" but was also present when Laila gave a dinner party in Jean's honor. "Amir was there," Jean wrote at the time. "He said, 'Laila didn't divorce me, she divorced the prime minister.'"[34] Indeed, this had become his refrain about the divorce; more importantly, it seems to have captured the most salient aspect of the separation: Laila simply did not want to put up with the daily demands imposed on a prime minister's wife.

The divorce was, for a while, one of the favorite subjects of Tehran's often vicious rumor mill. It took on an almost legendary status after the announced estrangement more or less coincided with the government's controversial decision to close down a large number of magazines and newspapers, ostensibly because of low circulation.

The government used a 1963 cabinet resolution that rescinded the license of any publication whose circulation did not reach a certain level. According to Parviz Radji, a Hoveyda confidant, "most of the newspapers closed were unworthy of the name...By far the greatest majority were four-page broad-sheets with inflamed headlines predicting the imminent change of government or of a particular minister (depending on the editor's preference), with virtually no readership and maintained entirely by the ads that the editor could obtain from a friendly minister...*Tofiq*, with its huge popularity and large readership, stood in a different league. I believe the absence of any semblance of humor when the shah's power was at its apogee, doomed its fate. Hoveyda, an undoubted liberal serving an intolerant master, would have been a mere tool in implementing the shah's wishes."*35

Looking back at all the reliable evidence, remembering the shah's repeated orders to reprimand this journal or that editor, Radji's explanation seems reasonable. Madjidi, another close confidant of Hoveyda, also exonerates him by implication but does not go as far as Radji. Madjidi writes that on a couple of occasions, he had asked Hoveyda about the closure of *Tofiq* and "he refused to answer my questions, which showed that there were things he did not wish to discuss."36 According to Madjidi, Hoveyda believed that a "satirical journal was needed for the country...He was not the kind of person to stop a magazine for making a joke, even a bad one, about himself or his wife. Furthermore, Hoveyda knew the [three] Tofiq [brothers who ran the magazine], and later [after the closure of their journal] helped them a great deal. One of them worked at the Plan and Budget Organization; he received a salary but never showed up, and when we tried to expel him, Hoveyda stopped me...But why they would close the journal particularly for the issue that included an attack on Hoveyda, I don't know, but I cannot believe that he was the one who made the decision."37

In mentioning "the issue that included an attack on Hoveyda," Madjidi repeats a rumor that has come to be taken as gospel. While we don't know what role, if any, Hoveyda had in closing down *Tofiq*, we can be sure that a last issue attacking Hoveyda never existed. As Abbas Tofiq, one of the editors of the journal, now readily admits, once they received news that their magazine was about to be closed, they purposely spread the rumor that

---

* In fact, aside from *Tofiq*, a couple of other popular magazines, with high circulations, were also closed. Ali Behzadi, the editor of one of those closed, blamed Hoveyda. Until the Islamic Republic allows access to all Hoveyda-related government documents, the question of his role in the whole sordid affair cannot be convincingly answered. For Behzadi's view, see Ali Behzadi, *Shebheh-khatarat* [Pseudo-memoir] (Tehran, 1998). Behzadi's chapter on Hoveyda is ripe with criticism. He even thinks that Hoveyda was no more than an intellectual imposter who only pretended to like Woody Allen films!

the reason for its closure was a cartoon making fun of Hoveyda's rumored
sexual problems. "In the cartoon," Abbas Tofiq and his brothers told
everyone, "Hoveyda asks Laila why she wants a divorce; Laila answers, 'ask
your *dowlat*.'" The crux of the cartoon is a double entendre; *dowlat* in Persian means the "cabinet"; *doolat* is the common term for "your penis." In
reality, there never was such a cartoon. The Tofiq brothers, nonetheless,
spread the rumor because they believed Hoveyda was responsible for the
closure of their journal.[38] Other informed sources believe, however, that
the magazine was closed on the direct order of the shah; some believe he
was angered by a cartoon depicting Iran as a haunted cemetery.[39] In any
case, the populace's readiness to accept and spread the rumor speaks eloquently to the political breach that continued to exist between the people
and the regime.

FURTHER EVIDENCE OF THIS BREACH, with Hoveyda at the center of the controversy, can be seen in some of the literary work of the period, particularly the writings of Ebrahim Golestan. Golestan's personal relationship
with Hoveyda made the literary allusions in his work particularly
poignant. The two men first met in the late 1950s when Hoveyda was still
at the NIOC and Golestan was the deputy head of public relations at the
Oil Consortium headquarter in Tehran. But they shared more than a
common employment history in the oil industry. They had a number of
common friends, foremost among them Sadeq Chubak. Golestan had
also met Hoveyda's brother and mother; he had grown to like and respect
the mother and become life-long friends with the brother, and it is fair to
say that Hoveyda did not "love any woman as much as his mother, and
any man as much as his brother."[40] For much of Hoveyda's tenure in
office, Golestan was a formidable presence in the Iranian intellectual
community. Hoveyda's elective affinity for the intellectuals, his own
strong sense of identity as a man of letters and ideas, all worked to make
Golestan a particularly interesting case for Hoveyda.

The complicated web of these relationships at times facilitated
Golestan's work; at other times it had the opposite effect. For example, he
directed a short documentary commissioned by Iran's Central Bank about
the country's crown jewels. The film needed to be sent to London for final

technical work. But for reasons that are hard to fathom and had to do with bureaucratic turf wars, the ministry of culture refused to grant the permit the film needed to clear Iranian customs. When Hoveyda heard about the problem, "he got fed up and arranged for the four cans of cut copy and sound tapes to be put in a 'diplomatic pouch' and be sent to London."[41]

Another of Golestan's films did not fare as well. This time he made a documentary about land reform in Iran. It showed a "rustic entrepreneur on the rise," what Hoveyda, upon seeing the film, called an attempt to portray a "new Iranian Kulak class."[*42] As a metaphor for the increasing encroachment of the government into the countryside, Golestan showed that this new Kulak was also a functionary of Hoveyda's New Iran Party. When Hoveyda saw the film, he immediately offered to purchase it for the government, agreed on a price, and took possession of what Golestan told him was the sole copy. But Golestan was never paid the agreed purchase price. Nor did he ever receive back the film. Every time he inquired about its fate, Hoveyda told him that he had sent it to the court where it continued to languish. Faint echoes of these entangled webs, as well as manifestations of a more general disgruntlement with the Pahlavi regime and Hoveyda as one of its most visible symbols, can also be seen in some of Golestan's other writings and films, where Hoveyda often appears more directly in the narrative.

In a novella called "Tales of Old Times," Golestan uses his richly poetic and uniquely sparse narrative style to offer the readers a sense of the existential experience of Iran's transition to modernity. With finely sketched characters and carefully culled images, he recreates the world of an earlier generation of Iranians. He writes from the point of view of a man reminiscing about his youth, caught in the clutches of a taciturn and authoritarian father, who is himself benumbed by the radical changes society is experiencing. Among his father's friends, there is a man, "Whose accent was mixed, whose intelligence was fine, and whose jokes were from notes. He used a cane for no reason and hid his lust for power and position behind a claim of having no desire for power and being resigned to his fate—this was obviously visible."[43] Golestan has thus ended the description with a pun on the name "Hoveyda," which in Persian means "visible."

---

* *The American Heritage Dictionary* describes a Kulak as "a prosperous landed peasant in Czarist Russia, characterized by the Communists during the October Revolution as an exploiter."

Hoveyda with some of his advisors and ministers on a visit to a Tehran neighborhood. Zia Shadman is at the far left next to the smiling Yadollah Shahbazi.

Hoveyda smiling and waving during a ceremony to celebrate the anniversary of the White Revolution. Next to him stand Jafar Sharif-Emami, Abdollah Riazi, Jamshid Amouzegar, and Mehrdad Pahlbod.

Furthermore, in Golestan's production of a part of George Bernard Shaw's *Man and Superman,* called *Don Juan in Hell,* the devil wears an orchid in the lapel of his suit, a reference hard to miss in the context of Iranian politics.[44]

In *Mysteries of the Treasure at Ghost Valley,* made as a film some seven years before the Islamic Revolution and published as a book in the same year, Golestan offers a satirical parable that is ostensibly about the perils of sudden wealth but is actually a subversively clever account of Iran's skewed path to modernity. The story revolves around a crude and poor villager, or "the man," bereft of any culture or refinement. By accident, he discovers a treasure trove hidden in a cavern in the land he farms. Suddenly, money and riches, fantastic in proportion, and apparently infinite in supply, are at his disposal. In the village, there is also a teacher, earnest in disposition, refined in his tastes, but bombastic in his discourse, who soon becomes an "easy tool" of the new pasha. The teacher who uses a cane, and on occasion has a flower in his lapel, believes in the redemptive power of action. In words that clearly echo Hoveyda's repeated motto, "the teacher" declares "human beings should engage in action…The important thing is to be doing something…You've got to get into the fray of things instead of standing idle; laziness and naysaying are of no use. Work is the best excuse for work."[45] When "the man" throws a brash party to celebrate his second bigamous marriage—a party not unlike the shah's extravagant 2,500 years of monarchy celebration—everything, from French foie gras from Fauchon to kabobs from the village's back alleys is served while the people of the village are banned from the party, and kept at bay by barbed wires.[46] "The man" also orders the construction of a tower in his backyard—an absurd structure that reverses the traditional dome and two minarets to two small domes and a towering minaret and clearly resembles a phallus. During all these harebrained actions, "the teacher" stands with "the man." At first, he tries to convince "the man" that it is more important to "fix the inside of the house, and make room for things like a bath and a kitchen," but "the man" brushes aside all such suggestions and orders that only the façade should be fixed to fit his new station in the world. "It is the appearance that counts," the man declares, "people only see the appearance."[47] Without much resistance "the teacher" falls in line but confides to a friend, "I want to do something here; the tower is only an excuse. This guy's got some money, and he wants to give it to me to spend…but it's hard…a bunch of vultures are all around him...they steal whatever they can."[48] Ultimately, in an unmistakable metaphor for revolution, the earth around the village begins to shake from explosion during the construction of new roads to the village. Oblivious to the dangers that lurk in the air, "the man" is all the while enthralled by a painter who has been hired by the teacher to draw "the man's" portrait. And when the flimsy yet gaudy house, the treasure, and the phallic monument are all buried under the rubble, "the man" vents his anger at the teacher by beating him with his own cane.

It was a measure of the cultural illiteracy of the Iranian censors that Golestan's film, in spite of its overt allusions to both Hoveyda and the shah, was allowed to be shown in Tehran cinemas. After three weeks, as word of the film spread throughout the city, it was suddenly banned, never to be shown again in Pahlavi Iran. If the censors were too illiterate and incapable of understanding Golestan's jibes, Hoveyda understood them only too well. There are at least two versions of how the film was banned. Some sources have told Ebrahim Golestan that the film was shown at court, where Hoveyda decoded its subversive imagery to a confused royal audience.[49] On the other hand, "High Ranking Security Official" indicates that it was he who, in spite of resistance from the government, banned the film. "I wrote a fifteen-page report," he says, "explaining the film's explosive message and sent copies to the shah and to Hoveyda."[50]

The harsh tone of criticism about Hoveyda in *Mysteries of the Treasure at Ghost Valley*, as well as in Golestan's other stories, inevitably translated into more tension in the two men's personal relationship. A few months after the film was banned, Golestan, by chance, saw Hoveyda at Fereydoun's house. That night what began as jocular verbal banter soon escalated into a serious confrontation. Angered by something Hoveyda said, Golestan took off his shirt, "made it into a ball and threw it" at the prime minister, saying in a loud voice, "smell it, it has the sweet smell of conscience...not the stench of someone who has sold his soul."[51] As Hoveyda's bodyguards moved to restrain Golestan, Hoveyda waved them away with a gentle motion of his cane. Moments later, he invited the indignant writer to come and sit next to him. He asked a servant to bring "a bottle from the case the French ambassador had sent. It was a bottle of Hors d'Age cognac," and then in an anguished voice, the voice of "an unhappy man" who felt that he "had already been betrayed," he talked about the shah's increasing authoritarian bent and his hare-brained idea for a new one-party political system in Iran.[52]

A few weeks later, Hoveyda again met Golestan, this time at an official reception for Jacques Chirac, who was visiting Iran at the time. With no hint of rancor in his voice or demeanor, Hoveyda walked to where Golestan was standing, introduced him to his French guest, and said, "this is our best writer and film director and we invariably suppress his work."[53] That turned out to be the last time the two men met.

The Fall of Pompeii

The pale-faced moon looks bloody on the earth,
And lean-looked prophets whisper fearful change;
Rich men look sad, and ruffians dance and leap—
The one in fear to lose what they enjoy,
The other to enjoy by rage and war:
These signs forerun the death or fall of kings.
　　　　　　　　—Shakespeare, *King Richard II*

Two unsuccessful coups against King Hassan of Morocco, the first in July 1971 and the second just over a year later, alarmed the shah of Iran.[1] He had always had an anxious affinity for the royalty of the world and, in the early 1970s, splurged some of Iran's newfound wealth on helping many a fallen, greedy, or supplicant monarch or ex-aristocrat. More importantly, however, every time a monarch fell or was threatened by a coup, the shah became very concerned. His belief that the American government had been behind the Moroccan incident only heightened his anxiety. For his court minister, Alam, the fact that "the son of a dog, Stuart Rockwell (that supporter of Mansur)," was the U.S. ambassador to Morocco at the time of the coup clearly confirmed an American conspiracy.[*][2]

Not long after the second coup attempt, the shah called Hoveyda to a marathon nine-hour audience. Hoveyda mentioned the meeting to some

---

* According to Stuart Rockwell, the king of Morocco also suspected that the American government was behind the clumsy coup attempt. "The planes used in the attack," Rockwell said, "were all American made; the pilots used English in their communications, and the planes had taken off from an airfield managed by the American air force." The coup attempt failed, Rockwell says, because "the planes were only armed with blanks." Stuart Rockwell, interviewed by author, 24 October 1999.

of his friends and colleagues, though little is known of what transpired.[3] One evident result of the long meeting was a change of tone in Hoveyda's discussions with some of his friends and advisors. He had created a loosely organized, informal group of six people whose mandate was to keep Hoveyda abreast of the public mood, as well as to act as a liaison with the business community. The six were Cyrus Ghani, a prominent lawyer; Fereydoun Mahdavi, a respected banker and one of the leaders of the National Front; Rokneddin Tehrani, a lawyer and class-mate of Hoveyda's in Brussels; Mohammad-Reza Amin, a well-educated, honest, and innovative manager; Shahin Aghayan and Abdol-Ali Farmanfarmaian, both successful businessmen and friends of Hoveyda.[4] From its inception, however, there was discord and distrust among the group. At least three of the six were dis-inclined to talk frankly and honestly in front of the others. It was generally assumed that in every important meeting, there was at least one person reporting to the shah. A wrong word, a hint of insolence, a derisive, albeit discreet, comment, and a career could easily end.[*] The group met for lunch twice a month, usually on Tuesdays, but the gatherings soon turned into per-functory exercises, where little of substance was ever discussed.

But then, on the first Tuesday after the 1972 Moroccan coup, Hoveyda opened the group's discussion with a sense of urgency and offered his advisors a new mandate. He declared that financial corruption had become the regime's Achilles heel and the greatest danger to its survival. His almost defiant tone, sharply at odds with the circumspection that usu-ally defined his demeanor, surprised those present. He beseeched the group to provide him with any information they had about financial impropriety in the country.[5]

Since his appointment as prime minister, Hoveyda had often privately complained about corruption, particularly the growing involvement of the royal family in the financial life of the country. All those who were close to Hoveyda have a story about his lamentations on this festering sore.

---

* Most of the Iranian political elite were aware of the story of a meeting called by Minister of Court Hossein Ala in the aftermath of the June uprising in 1963. Ala had invited a number of people to his house to discuss what the government should do now that the army had fired on and killed demonstrators. Amongst those invited were Abdollah Entezam, Jafar Sharif-Emami, and General Morteza Yazdanpanah. When the latter two realized that the meeting had been called without prior permission from the shah, they informed the king who was not pleased. Soon afterward, he dismissed Ala from his post and Entezam from the directorship of the NIOC. The shah apparently believed that the meeting was masterminded by the British government and, in his meeting with an American official, talked in sharply disparaging tones about those who participated in the meeting. See Alam, *Yadashtha-ye Alam* [Alam's Diaries], vol. 2, 128.

Hoveyda's critics, however, offer a different view. They accuse him of not only tolerating but also encouraging these royal sallies into influence peddling and illicitly gained governmental contracts.[6] Houshang Nahavandi, an Alam protégé, claims that "Hoveyda tried to get Princess Ashraf, Princess Fatemeh and Princes Abdorreza, Gholam-Reza and Mahmoud-Reza some commissions; he tried to make money for them as middlemen."[7] Nahavandi offers no evidence for his claims, and needless to say, in the always-murky water of illicit financial deals, paper traces and conclusive evidence are hard to find. At the same time, others like Farokh Najmabadi indicate that in fact contrary to the claims of people like Nahavandi and Alam, Hoveyda tried to "shield" his ministers against "pressure from the royal family" and the dictates "of the Imperial Court....He told us that we can refer any demands from the royal family to his office for consideration. In most instances you would not hear anymore of the request, as it would be dropped."[8] Unless the Iranian government archives are opened, we cannot know to what extent Hoveyda condoned the alleged illegal activities of the royal family and to what extent he used the power of his office to stop them.

There is, however, no doubt that in 1972, with the apparent blessing of the shah, Hoveyda embarked on a limited program intended at least to curb the problem of corruption. He met several times with three of his Tuesday lunch group—Ghani, Mahdavi, and Farmanfarmaian—and delved more deeply into the nature and dimensions of the problem. The meetings had some short-term results but were, nonetheless, soon disbanded. For example, Princess Ashraf's eldest son, Shahram—a notorious influence peddler, who, according to a CIA report, "has followed in his mother's footsteps in some respects" and is "widely and unfavorably known in Tehran as a wheeler-dealer, with holdings in some 20 companies," and whose "most flagrant act of irresponsibility was the sale of national art treasures and antiques"[9]—who by special dispensation was allowed to use the name Pahlavinia was suddenly and without a trial or any public announcements, told by the shah to take a long vacation abroad and ordered to cease his financial activities in Iran. The ban, however, did not last long; soon, he was allowed to return and resume his work. The shah had, apparently, been convinced by members of the royal family that receiving commissions was a perfectly legitimate way for them to make their living. The shah's vacillating and ultimately complacent attitude toward the financial activities of the royal family can be seen from a CIA report that says, "the governor of one of Iran's largest banks told an embassy officer that he had brought to the Shah's attention some business ventures that put Ashraf in a bad light. The Shah merely shrugged the matter off. The bank governor commented to the embassy officer that such deals would land other people in jail for ten years."[10] Even Parviz Sabeti was threatened by the shah when he filed one particularly damaging report about the illegal financial activities of some members of the royal family.[11]

In their lucrative economic activities, the royal family was joined by a few of the shah's close friends, who were also deemed impervious to prosecution.* There was Alam who, even according to his own protégés and supporters, was involved in many shady deals. There was the infamous Amir-Houshang Davalou, known as Iran's "King of Caviar." And there was the "Duke of Dark Corners," Dr. Karim Ayadi, described in a U.S. Embassy document as "the shah's personal physician [who] is a shareholder in numerous companies, such as the Pars Oil Company, and owns 15 to 40 percent of these firms. In such cases the shares are registered under variations of his name such as Abdle-Karim, Karim or Eyadi. General Ayadi holds an exclusive right to develop shrimp fishing in the Persian Gulf."[12] In another report, this time by the CIA, Ayadi is called "the major channel through which the Shah dabbles in commercial affairs. He is said to have been a childhood friend of the shah...It is said that Ayadi accompanied the Shah on his honeymoon with his second wife, Soraya. Ayadi was reported at one time for fronting for the Shah in the Southern Iran Fishing company...Ayadi, a Bahai, is credited by one observer with being one of those who protects the sect against persecution by the more fanatical Iranian Moslems."[13]

---

* An example of Hoveyda's attempt to fight corruption can be found in his labyrinthine confrontation with a flashy and gaudy entrepreneur who happened to be a Bahai. The entrepreneur used what bankers call a "float" to purchase bank stocks. By 1975, the new governor of Iran's Central Bank, Hassanali Mehran, discovered that these unauthorized "floats" had reached the staggering figure of one billion tomans—close to 140 million dollars. Mehran decided to act and solicited Hoveyda's help. Hoveyda called the entrepreneur to his office and in harsh words warned him to stay clear of the banking industry. A couple of days later, the Central Bank received a letter from the court ministry: the shah had insisted that the man was a hard-working capitalist and that the government must not impede his growth. The day the letter was received at the bank, the victorious capitalist went to the prime minister's office—this time, uninvited—and flicked his thumb, the Persian equivalent of the middle finger, at Hoveyda's chief of staff, saying, "Tell your boss, here! I got the bank." Eventually, an agreement was reached after negotiations involving the shah himself. The entrepreneur agreed to sell his shares in all banks except for his forty percent equity in one bank. For financial details of the "float" saga, I have relied on Hassanali Mehran, interviewed by author, Washington, D.C., 16 February 1997. For details of the entrepreneur's trips to the prime minister's office, I spoke with Hoveyda's chief of staff, Mohammad Safa, interviewed by author, 21 November 1997.

By the mid-1970s, some members of the royal family along with these courtiers and a couple of Hoveyda's friends and at least a couple of his ministers had developed a badly tarnished reputation for "having their hands in the public till." A 1978 U.S. Embassy report declared, "Corruption has become a major political issue in Iran in recent weeks, with much of the criticism of the shah being couched in terms of the corrupt activities of his closest advisors and even members of his family...[The] issue is not likely to disappear without first profoundly shaking Iran's most basic political institution—the monarchy."[14]

AS IRAN'S OIL REVENUES INCREASED, the country's development took on a staggeringly fast tempo. From 1968 to 1972, the industrial sector grew at an annual rate of fourteen percent. The big leap, however, was yet to come. In December 1972, the price of oil began its sharpest rise. Within a year, the price of a barrel of oil increased from about five dollars to close to twelve. The country's economic plans had to be fundamentally revised in light of new revenue figures. It was also at about this time that the shah began to talk about his "Great Civilization." Before the end of the century, he promised, Iran would become the world's fifth industrial power; it would surpass Japan and leave behind the tormenting vicious cycle of underdevelopment and poverty. Indeed as early as 1966, he boasted to Averell Harriman that "only Japan and Iran have the possibility of attaining, within the next 20 years, the state of development reached by European countries..." adding, "Iran has more abundant natural resources than does Japan."[15]

Economists have argued that behind the idea of the Great Civilization lies the strategy commonly known as the "big push." According to this strategy, economic development in Third World countries is constrained by "vicious circles" of poverty. If an economy is to break free, the state needs to industrialize "on a wide and diversified front."[16] Advocates of this strategy know, of course, that in each country, the big push has to be commensurate with that society's "absorptive capacity."[17] The shah wanted the big push but had no patience for such murky and mundane concepts as absorptive capacity. But economic realities are stubborn facts, oblivious to royal commands. One would expect, however, that Hoveyda, given his

training in economics and his temperament—a man of moderation—
should have known better than to follow the shah's line. But one can find a
voluntarist economic thread in Hoveyda's thoughts as well. This kind of
approach can be traced to the big leap that Marxist economics was enamored of during the days of Lenin, Stalin, Trotsky, and Mao. Even in the early 1970s, long past his salad days, Hoveyda had been deeply impressed with
developments in Maoist China when he traveled there as part of the
queen's entourage.[18]

Within the Plan and Budget Organization, however, there were enough
experts who had the courage of their convictions to declare in a March
1974 report that Iran could not become "the world's fifth industrial power
in this century" and that "major infrastructure bottlenecks need to be
addressed immediately."[19] They articulated their views in July of that year,
in a meeting presided over by Hoveyda at Gajereh, a ski resort near
Tehran. The experts offered their analysis, based on econometric models
and statistical predictions, concluding that only a moderate increase in
domestic expenditures was warranted. The fragile infrastructure, they
argued, could not bear more. The surfeit of capital, they warned, could
easily become a poison pill and a sudden influx of goods and services
would certainly create bottlenecks. Alex Mazhloumian, a high-ranking
official at the Plan and Budget Organization, even went so far as to predict
that, if the government spent all the sudden revenues from oil, there could
be a revolution in Iran.[20] Initially, Hoveyda suggested that the government
could eliminate the bottlenecks by quickly building the requisite roads
and docks. He even mentioned, apparently not in jest, the names of two
contractors who were renowned for being corrupt but who were also
known for being able to finish projects on time. Hoveyda's message, that
the government was willing to accept a certain level of corruption in order
to get its projects completed expeditiously, was not lost on those attending the meeting.[21] But the planners remained steadfast in their objection
to what they deemed to be a dangerously rapid tempo in government
expenditure. Eventually, Hoveyda seems to have been convinced and concurred with the studied view of the experts.[22] Indeed, ever since assuming
power as premier, he had repeated often in private what he told the U.S.
ambassador in 1967. At that time, Hoveyda told Armin Meyer, "although
Shah tends toward wishing progress more rapid than is realistic, he
[Hoveyda] is determined to maintain a realistic 'cruising speed.'"[23] Now,
his economic advisors had also recommended such a "cruising speed."

   The recommendations of the Gajereh conference were presented to the shah for his approval at a meeting in Ramsar, an idyllic Caspian Sea resort. The conference began on August 1, 1974, and lasted for two days. The shah, with his two thumbs in the pockets of his vest and the other fingers dangling out, began the proceedings by declaring: "As to future planning, we shall of course ourself issue the appropriate directives in due time. But now, since you have done some work in this area, let us hear your discussion."[24] But after hearing only some of the reports, the shah grew visibly angry, and in a tone derisive of economists, he brushed aside all suggestions of moderate growth. He then commanded that "what we have already said" about next year's revenues should become government policy. And what he had said, namely the necessity of spending all of the new revenue, was the recipe for a potentially dangerous and volatile "hyperboom." Hoveyda offered no resistance; nor did any of the ministers. Some of the planners who had helped develop the more moderate proposal suggest that Hoveyda and his ministers should have resigned, adding further, that "it is untrue to suggest that they had not been warned."[25]

   In September 1975, during a conference organized by the Aspen Institute, Hoveyda and some of Iran's top bankers, technocrats, managers, and social scientists tried to put a theoretical varnish on the policies ordered by the shah and place the economic accomplishments of the past decade in a historic context. Hoveyda talked to the conference in the language of an optimistic social engineer. He posited that, "given a sufficient body of pertinent data, and our estimate of the vigor of the human will, the future can not only be predicted but indeed created." He talked of the rise of Iran's GNP per head, from around $100 per year in 1963 to an estimated $2,069 in 1977. He referred to the increase in the number of institutes of higher learning, from 10 in 1963 to an estimated 184 in 1976, with "over 400,000 Iranians attending universities in Europe, North America and elsewhere."[26] Others mapped out Iran's industrial development, showing that the annual rate of growth in industry increased from "5 percent per annum in 1962 to over 20 percent per annum in 1974." The automotive industry was given as an example of a successful policy of "promoting indigenous technology development."[27] There was also talk of major strides in the field of women's education. For example, whereas in 1947 Iran had only 7,840 girls in secondary schools, the figure had reached 334,757 in 1974.[28] In the shadow of the ruins of Persepolis, Iranian participants boasted, often quite legitimately, of impressive changes that the new generation of technocrats and men and women of politics had made in transforming Iran from a poor and underdeveloped economy, to one of the most thriving countries of the hemisphere. In a sense, in his own speech, Hoveyda tried to weave these different strands of argument into a cohesive narrative. He made his most important theoretical pitch by arguing, "We have witnessed the emergence of great bureaucratic empires...At a time when both the ideological man and the technological man can be seen vacillating between unrelieved gloom and Panglossian optimism, we believe we are not only entitled but duty bound to seek our own path to the future."[29] And no doubt, as Hoveyda never tired of repeating, the shah was the trailblazer of this unbeaten path.

By this time, the shah was more than ever convinced that he understood better than anyone what was in Iran's best interest. In economic and political meetings he would abort a serious discussion or a dissenting voice with a wry, implicitly menacing question: "Have you not read my books on the subject?"[30] And by the mid-1970s, in his three books—*Mission for My Country* (1961), *The White Revolution* (1967), and *Towards the Great Civilization* (1977)—he had offered strong views on almost every subject conceivable. He had taken on the air of a prophet come to bring salvation to his unruly flock. The much-displayed picture of him standing on a firmament of clouds, a stern smile on his face, his hands outstretched in a gesture of benediction, best captured this prophetic predilection.

Contrary to claims by nearly all of the shah's opponents, who kept insisting that he was but a "lackey of imperialism," there is an abundance of evidence indicating that since the mid-1960s he had pursued a far more independent oil and foreign policy than he had been given credit for. This often put him at odds with Western powers. The shah was, however, too grandiose in his goals and too timid in using the tools necessary to achieve them. In the classic typology of characters, he was an authoritarian personality: bellicose and belligerent with the weak, lambish and obedient with those he perceived as strong. In a State Department profile, he is described as a "complex person, full of contradiction and embodying an unpredictable mixture of severity and gentleness."[31] On another occasion, the U.S. Embassy in Tehran talks of his "depressed moods which have in the past resulted in excessive insecurity."[32] And, he was tone deaf when it came to the question of genuine democracy for Iran. As Iran's petrodollars increased, the shah was no longer in need of Western aid but instead could pursue an ambitious array of welfare programs as well as a major arms build-up. They included free elementary, high-school, and college education, free health care, free snacks for all students in school, and a new extended system of social security.[33] As a result the shah became more intransigent in the face of journalists' questions about democracy. In a tone that sometimes bordered on racism, he talked of how the democracy of the blue-eyed world was of no avail for the people of Iran. "It is absurd," he said, "to think that Western style democracy could be automatically transplanted to countries like Iran." He firmly believed that if ever a referendum was held in Iran, "all but the smallest fraction (mostly a few American and British trained maladjusted Iranians) would register enthusiastic support" for his style of leadership and economic reform.[34]

According to the U.S. State Department profile, the shah's formal education was "limited consisting of secondary school in Switzerland, followed by the Iranian Military academy," and "his attempts to arrive at decisions by intellectual processes are sometimes submerged by instinctive reactions."[35] By all accounts, he was uncomfortably shy; rarely did he look anyone in the eye. Invariably, his eyes wandered off to an unknown yonder. His insatiable desire to be loved begot a spirit of sycophancy in those around him. Ironically, it was Hoveyda's mentor who might have best captured the essence and the inherent dangers of this condition—apocryphal though the story may be. When Entezam was fired from his post at the National Iranian Oil Company, he is reported to have told the monarch, "To your father, no one dared lie; to you, no one dares tell the truth." In the Ramsar conference, many knew the truth, but none dared challenge the king's hubris against the stubborn economic facts and models.

Iranian politicians were not the only ones feeding the shah's increasing appetite for sycophancy. There was never a shortage of Western journalists, photographers, and writers willing to produce some panegyrics to the king, if the price was right. Even foreign governments engaged in their own peculiar form of sycophancy. The British catered to the shah's craving for praise by comparing him to General de Gaulle.[36] As early as January 1958, Secretary of State John Foster Dulles wrote to President Eisenhower, "It would be helpful if he came to Washington and talked with you and some of the top Pentagon people about the military problems which so engross him. I am sorry to have gotten you in for this, but since the visit would be entirely unofficial, it should not involve much entertainment, and it was, I think, of very great value in holding the situation stable to flatter the shah with the prospect of an exchange of views with you on modern military problems."[37] Eight years later, the U.S. Embassy in Tehran suggested that "the shah regards himself as a world statesman and will be flattered by a discussion of world affairs."[38] In the same vein, President Johnson is advised, "take the shah into your confidence on other major international problems."[39]

Even the tone of the CIA and State Department reports about Iran began to change in a strange pattern. Whereas in the early 1960s the reports often had predicted imminent chaos and revolution, in 1977, they declared that "Iran is likely to remain stable under the Shah's leadership over the next several years...The Shah, [who] has become increasingly self-confident over the past decade, will become less amenable to advice from the U.S. or from domestic counselors."[40]

Surrounded by a sea of sycophancy, the shah's grandiose sense of certitude and self-importance increased over the years. If scholars are right that one of the causes of the Islamic Revolution was the shah's attempt to modernize the society too rapidly, if they are correct that the bottlenecks brought about as a result of the country's insufficient "absorptive capacity" fanned the flames of dissent and dissatisfaction, then the Ramsar conference and the shah's rash dismissal of the advice of his economic planners should be considered a turning point in Iran's history. Of the many moments that Hoveyda should have resigned, the end of the conference certainly figures as one of the most obvious. The "development program" that had helped catapult him into power was predicated on the shah's willingness to share power with the Iranian middle class. The hyperboom the shah mandated clearly increased the economic power of the middle and technocratic classes; yet, the self-referential manner by which he arrived at the decision left little hope that the political demands of these classes would be satisfied. The shah was averse to the idea of sharing his power not just with the middle classes but even with Hoveyda, who had served him as a compliant prime minister for many years. In the words of Richard Helms, "the cabinet under Hoveyda has developed the institutional capacity to make decisions and formulate policies...if it is allowed by the Shah. Having become more closely involved with the day-to-day governmental activities since 1963, the Shah is unwilling to relax his control."[41] Hoveyda and his coterie of technocrats had wagered that increased economic prosperity would gradually convince, or coerce, the shah into sharing power; at Ramsar, it was more than evident that their wager had failed. At least part of the failure was because the luster of power and the desire to stay on top seem to have mitigated Hoveyda's own initial desire to create the requisite institutions essential for genuine political participation.

While the radical strategy of totally debunking the autocratic system, of working only to undermine it, of refusing any kind of compromise ultimately helped create a new form of autocracy in Iran, the policy of total surrender to the shah pursued by Hoveyda was no less quixotic and dangerous.

IF, ECONOMICALLY, THE RAMSAR CONFERENCE was the embodiment of this autocratic rule, then the almost whimsical royal decree for the creation of a single party in Iran was a sure sign that the political field was even more subject to the vagaries of what Helms called "an autocrat in his declining years."* Furthermore as Helms himself concluded, "the recent establishment of the one-party system removed even the façade of the existence of a loyal opposition to His Majesty's Government…[T]he portents are hardly encouraging for the eventual creation of a more democratic system of government."[42] More prophetic was what Helms wrote by way of a conclusion. "Over the next 5–10 years, the shah will either himself begin to share political responsibility with other, newer groups or be forced to. Should a succession crisis occur within the next 6–7 years, the Regency Council would probably hold the country and the monarchy together initially, but power could quickly come up for grabs if the centrifugal forces of change drove various groups to put their own interests ahead of unity and stability."[43] The fate of the Iran Novin Party (New Iran) was only one example of the shah's unwillingness to share power.

---

* In his "End of Tour Report" in 1975, Richard Helms showed a clear understanding of this problem by writing that "the conflict between rapid economic growth and modernization vis-à-vis a still autocratic rule…is the greatest uncertainty marring an otherwise optimistic prognosis for Iran…And alas, history provides discouraging precedents about the declining years of autocrats. I can recall no example of an absolute ruler willingly loosening the reins of power." U.S. Embassy, Tehran, Iran, "End of Tour Report, Richard Helms," August 4, 1975, NSA, no. 979, 9.

By 1975, the Iran Novin Party, initially created at the behest of the shah, had grown into a very powerful organization much beholden to Hoveyda. The party's primary "attraction was as a route to the top for its members, but more importantly, it also offered a vehicle for the expansion of the influence and power of its leaders, particularly Hoveyda. With its nation-wide organization tied into local power structures, its contacts with the security organizations, its patronage power, and its success in filling virtu-ally all significant government positions with party members, Iran Novin wielded genuine power."[44] Alam's *Diaries* are replete with his laments about the constraints put on the Mardom Party (People Party) in trying to play its designated role as the loyal opposition. He lays much of the blame on Hoveyda's machinations, but from his own *Diaries,* it also seems clear that the shah was himself altogether impatient with any criticism offered by members of Mardom, or, for that matter, any party in the country. The fate of one of the Mardom Party's leaders was emblematic of this impatience: he was summarily dismissed from his post by the shah because he had the temerity to suggest that elections in Iran had not been entirely free.

Hoveyda had understood that he needed a political power base if he was to survive. Though in public, he more than once declared that his was a constituency of one in the person of the king, in practice he had a more shrewd sense of how to augment his own position through the party. From its inception, the shah had wanted to ensure that the Iran Novin Party did not become a vehicle for Hoveyda's personal power. For this reason, he had, according to the American Embassy sources, insisted on placing one of his own confidants, Ataollah Khosrovani, as the party's leader.[45] But apparent-ly Khosrovani was not all that welcome in the party, and soon two factions developed. The first included the original party members, particularly those that had been members of the Progressive Circle. They considered themselves the more "intellectual" wing of the party. The second wing brought together the more recent additions, particularly those associated with the party's membership from the ranks of government-sponsored labor organizations. As the party grew, Hoveyda consolidated his power and began to develop what seemed like an independent power base. This might have been enough to bring about the demise of the party by the shah. Eventually, Hoveyda even succeeded in placing one of his own allies as the leader of the main opposition Mardom Party. As one of Hoveyda's colleagues aptly put it, "In Hoveyda there was an inherent contradiction. On one level, he was but a pliant tool of the shah; yet midway through his tenure as prime minister, his tentacles reached deep into all layers of Iranian society. He had become an institution himself."[46] Hoveyda's control over the party apparatus was a key element of this institutionalized power.

In 1975 the party held its biggest convention and invited some five thousand activists from all over Iran. Foreign delegates representing over a hundred different parties from across the world also attended the conference. Hoveyda gave a rousing speech to the party convention, extolling the accomplishment of the last ten years; at every turn he praised the wise and revolutionary stewardship of the shah. If Hoveyda's profuse praise was intended to appease the shah and nip in the bud any insecurity the monarch might have felt about the party, or the prime minister's increased authority, he certainly failed. On March 2, 1975, in a swift move, the shah eliminated the Iran Novin Party as well as the other two legal parties that had members in the Majlis, and in their place ordered the creation of a one-party system. Even by the standards of the shah's own behavior, the manner in which all political parties were dismantled and a new one was willed into existence was oddly cavalier. While the result of the single-party experiment was clearly a fiasco, its genesis is, at best, murky.

A group of technocrats, associated with the queen, had at one time drawn up a plan calling for the creation of something to be called a *Rastakhiz,* or a "Resurgence."* Gholam-Reza Afkhami, Manouchehr Ganji, Amin Alimard, and Ahmad Ghoreishi were among the group that first advocated the idea. Three of the four members in the group have quite different recollections about when the proposal was first formulated, and what it essentially contained. Afkhami puts the date of the proposal as far back as 1971.[47] Amin Alimard thinks the time of the proposal was about two years before the fated announcement by the shah. Ghoreishi, who joined the group for only the last part of its deliberations, remembers the date to have been some six months before the shah's announcement in 1975. In Ghoreishi's rendition, the shah angrily rejected the Rastakhiz proposal, asking as he was wont to do, "Have they not read our book?"

---

* In the early 1960s, Mostafa Mesbahzadeh, the publisher of *Kayhan,* had started a rapidly growing organization called Rastakhiz. It was soon reported to the shah that in the group's meetings no pictures of the monarch were displayed. The organization was ordered to display royal pictures. The "Resurgence" soon withered away on the vine of public apathy.

Ghoreishi recalls Hoveyda asking him a few days after the proposal's submission to the shah, "What have you done to make the boss so mad?"[48]
Indeed, the shah had been hitherto against the idea of a single party. In
1961, in his *Mission for My Country*, the shah had declared that one-party
systems were the scourge of communist regimes, and he had repeated his
admonishments again in 1968.[49]

In their own mind, the group had intended their suggestion as a step
toward the "democratization of the political process."[50] Cognizant of the
shah's unwillingness to tolerate a genuine opposition party, and wary that
the domination of the Iran Novin Party had begun to stifle even a modicum of serious political participation in the country, the group had hoped
to use the Rastakhiz to bring more power to the masses and "open up the
political process."[51] Since no copy of the group's proposal seems to have
survived the vicissitudes of exile and revolution, it is hard to pinpoint the
exact details of their suggestion. Nevertheless, it is difficult to imagine how
such a group of well-trained social scientists could have assumed that a single party or mass movement with the shah as its supreme leader could lead
to anything even remotely democratic. According to Alimard, the group's
original idea had "much in common with Yugoslavia's model of worker's
self-management in Yugoslavia."[52] Incontrovertible historical evidence had
by then clearly shown that single-party structures, or the plebiscitary politics of a mass movement, even the facade of worker's self-management,
invariably end up in fascist or, at best, populist power structures.

Because of the confusion about the timing of the original Rastakhiz
proposal, it is hard to establish with certainty its relationship to the shah's
single-party idea. In 1975, the shah visited Egyptian president Sadat, who
had become the monarch's close friend and ally. The Egyptian connection
is important because there is a lingering suspicion that Sadat had a hand
in convincing the shah of the virtues of a single-party structure.[53] From
Egypt, the shah went for a vacation to Switzerland. So far as we know, he
discussed his plans only with Abdol-Madjid Madjidi, who was there to
report on the new budget. In broad strokes, the shah explained his new
political vision. Madjidi was caught off guard, just as the whole country
was to be in a few days. He claims to have told the king that a single party
would not necessarily solve Iran's problems; he advocated a more genuine
multiparty system; he even ventured to suggest that the real problem in
the country was corruption. The shah's response clearly betrayed the

degree to which he was isolated from the moods and perceptions of the Iranian public. "How do you define corruption?" he asked. And when Madjidi says he offered a few examples, the shah retorted, "Other than these cases, and in fact more important than them, is the fact that people don't do their work properly, and civil servants don't perform their tasks well."[54] To the shah, that was the real corruption in the country. As a last point of conversation, the shah told Madjidi that he could inform Hoveyda of what the two had discussed that day.

Madjidi rushed to the basement of the Suvretta House Hotel in whose compound the shah owned a large villa and from a public telephone called Hoveyda in Tehran to tell him about the shah's new ideas. Hoveyda was reluctant to talk at any length on an unsecured line, but in the course of the conversation, he did learn that not only was the party he had helped build soon to be dismantled but, far more importantly, the political party structure in the country was to be fundamentally revamped. By all accounts, other than informing Madjidi, the shah had discussed the idea with no one else. Even Alam, considered easily the shah's closest confidant, had no knowledge of the idea for a new single party.[55] With the zeal and certitude of a prophet, the shah had come back from his Egyptian trip convinced that a one-party system was the political panacea for Iran. Even SAVAK was in the dark about the shah's new plans.[56] So far as we know, no one in the shah's inner circle dared tell him that a single party, by limiting freedom of association, was against the very letter of the Iranian constitution. By then no one, with perhaps the exception of the queen, dared defy a royal decree, and the queen was hardly in a position to object to an idea that originally might have come from a group of her own advisors. Hoveyda certainly chose not to fight the decision. Instead of resigning, as many of his friends and colleagues suggested, he resigned himself to the role that the shah would assign for him in the new scheme of things.[57]

On March 2, 1975, during a press conference that was surreal even by the standards of the time, the shah announced the creation of the new party, one that the whole nation was to join. Hoveyda was present during the conference. According to some of his aides, there was a look of "shocked disbelief and bewilderment" on his face when the shah made the announcement. The facial expressions made it clear to "one and all that this was the first time he was hearing of so radical a decision."[58] Knowing as we do that Hoveyda certainly knew of the single-party idea at least a week in advance of the announcement, we must rethink the meaning of his facial gestures.[*] It could be seen as Hoveyda's attempt to distance himself, at the moment of birth, from an idea that he found ignoble. At the same time, he did not hesitate to become the leader of the very same party.

Many pundits, as well as the U.S. Embassy in Tehran, saw the creation of the new party as an attempt by the shah "to curb the growing power of Prime Minister Hoveyda." Nevertheless, during the same press conference, the shah appointed Hoveyda as the first secretary general of the party.[†59] No one asked under which provision of the law the shah was naming the leader of a yet-to-be-formed party. Indeed, the shah not only chose the party's future leader, but he even had a suggestion for those who did not want to join. They could get a passport, he said in a strange tone of sardonic equanimity, and leave the country. In the words of Afkhami, "while the original idea [for the Rastakhiz] had been proposed basically for the purpose of national reconciliation...His Majesty's mood [when he decreed the party's creation] was rather combative."[60] That every citizen in Iran had as much right to live in the country as the shah was by then altogether strange to him. He saw Iran not so much as a modern nation but more as his private fiefdom, and commensurate with this vision, he saw the people as his subjects, not citizens of a modern polity.[‡]

Strangely, Hoveyda accepted the appointment to be the new party's secretary general and began to work immediately. But by then, the wear and

---

* In conversations with Ahmad Kashefi, one of Hoveyda's vice-premiers and for many years the man in charge of the prime minister's special secret fund, at least a week before the shah's press conference, Hoveyda ordered Kashefi not to renew any leases for buildings that had housed the offices of the Iran Novin Party. He gave no explanation for his order. Kashefi understood the reason only after the press conference. (Ahmad Kashefi, interviewed by author, 31 October 1997.) Even more intriguing is the idea suggested by Fereydoun Hoveyda that on a couple of earlier occasions, the shah had broached the topic of a single party for Iran and that Hoveyda had succeeded in changing the shah's views. Fereydoun Hoveyda, interviewed by author, 10 October 1999.

† Dr. Manouchehr Shahgholi, a close friend and confidant of Hoveyda's, declared to U.S. Embassy officials that the breakup of the Iran Novin Party had occurred because "the shah realized how strong the party itself was getting. Because on one occasion, all of the shah's efforts and the Pahlavi foundation money used through Sharif-Emami was unable to switch the vote of the people in Ramsar from the Iran Novin to the Mardom candidate. When they saw they could not do it, the Shah decided it was time to crush yet another organization which was getting strong." See U.S. Embassy, Tehran, Iran, "Hoveyda Loyalist Lets off Steam," 25 January 1977, NSA, 2177. The event Shahgholi is referring to was in fact a run-off election in Shahsavar, not Ramsar, and indeed, the Iran Novin candidate won the seat.

‡ In his *Diaries,* Alam recounts a revealing moment when he gave the shah the deeds to the palace on the island of Kish. "I had registered the palace in the shah's own name. He threw the deed back at me. He said, why do you want me to own a small piece of Iran, the whole country belongs to me." See Alam, *Yadashtha-ye Alam* [Alam's Diaries], vol. 2, 265.

tear of his many years in office, or maybe the weight of the many compromises he knew he had made, was beginning to show. On more than one occasion, he was seen at parties late at night, stooped over a table, dozing off. What most people did not know was that by the early 1970s Hoveyda had felt under such stress that he would often begin his day by taking ten milligrams of Valium.[61] Even in photographs, the shadows of fatigue seem permanently etched on his face. His eyes were now further sunk into the furrows of his face. His famously impassive look was turning into the tired look of a spent man.

Hoveyda's approach to the whole problem of the new party smacked of cynicism. His behavior had a "strong sense of the absurd exuding from his sophisticated and often ensnaring cosmopolitan view of the world."[62] Acquiescing to the new party might well be considered the moral nadir of his collaboration with authoritarianism. He would soon confess in private that the whole business of the new party had been "a complete failure."[63] Even before it began its full operation, it was torn by inner strife and suffered from popular resentment. Like the farcical exuberance of political rallies in Stalinist Russia or Maoist China, Iranian cities, factories, and universities vied with each other for a larger advertisement in newspapers to declare their mass registration in the party. Joining had become, at least as the whisper of the people went, mandatory. It was rumored that those who did not join would have their passports taken away. How much of this atmosphere was orchestrated by the government to intimidate people into joining and how much was simply the result of public hysteria is hard to say. Ironically, Hoveyda, and his Progressive Circle (later named the New Iran Party) had come to power with a promise of delivering more democracy, but he had now become "an attendant Lord" and an "easy tool" of a pseudo-totalitarian movement. The change had been gradual, and not overnight. The U.S. Department of State had inklings of this change as early as March 1968. In a research memorandum by the director of the Bureau of Intelligence and Research, it is said that "Despite growing prosperity and dwindling opposition activity the Shah has not permitted Iranians to involve themselves in free political activity on an organized basis. The New Iran Party, established in 1963, soon lost its pretension of representative political activity and became simply a creature of the government in power....The Shah seems to have made a conscious decision to emphasize the pursuit of higher standards of living in order to keep Iranian minds off any movement to secure participation in the political process."[64]

While this was going on, the economy was also beginning to falter: shortages of commodities were widespread and prices were, once again, rapidly on the rise. Tehran, the capital and showcase for the "Great Civilization," was beset by regular disruptions of electricity. Shantytowns began to mushroom around the city, and when the government tried to use force to stop them spreading, the poor fought back. In spite of many warnings about the coming economic crisis, the shah "refused to decelerate the rate of economic growth. In fact the government increased taxes and resorted to foreign borrowing...Iran's surplus of $2 billion in 1974 was turned into a whopping deficit of $7.3 billion...Taxes levied on salaried groups increased from $4.02 billion in 1975 to $5.86 billion in 1978."[65]

In the middle of all this, the crucial Jimmy Carter factor suddenly appeared. His candidacy, his human rights policy, his occasional acerbic comments as a candidate about the shah's undemocratic rule, and the growing Western media coverage of torture and censorship in Iran suddenly invigorated the long-dormant Iranian opposition. The arrival of William H. Sullivan, the new U.S. ambassador to Iran, in May 1976, further complicated matters for Hoveyda. By his own admission, Sullivan was a novice in matters Iranian. He spoke no Persian and had no knowledge of the country's history and culture. He had built his reputation dealing with, or taming, despots in South East Asia. Even before arriving in Tehran, he was given a taste, by Ardeshir Zahedi, of the kind of friction and backbiting that defined Iranian politics. He writes about his first meeting with Zahedi: "His tone when he spoke of the shah was one of reverence...His only deliberate indiscretion was when he spoke of the prime minister, Amir Abbas Hoveyda, whom he disliked and denigrated."[66] When Sullivan arrived in Iran, he was, in his words, less than impressed with those he met in positions of power. The only two exceptions were Hoveyda, who in Sullivan's estimation "was a delightful boulevardier with a razor-sharp mind and a politician's personality," and Hoveyda's chief rival, Amouzegar.[67]

In Tehran, Sullivan began organizing a series of meetings with a handful of select Iranians; the subject was the future of Iran's economic development programs. In audiences with the shah, he tried to lay out some general observations about Iran's future based on these discussions and his own analysis of the situation. In Sullivan's own words, "[the shah] became quite defensive. He listened very intently and then responded rather querulously...He slumped lower in his chair and seemed to act peevishly...After our conversation on the economy, there was a long gap in which the shah did not initiate any contact with me; I assumed that this was a sort of banishment...During this period, however, I began to hear reports from the embassy officers and from Iranians associated with the economic scene. It seems that the shah had called his economic ministers for a complete review of the industrialization program...At the end of that time, the shah let it be known that some changes were in order. Shortly thereafter, the cabinet resigned, and the prime minister was made minister of court. I did not know exactly what cause and effect there was between my conversations with the shah and the actions he subsequently took to revise the economic program. I frankly preferred not to find out, because the implication of it troubled me."[68]

It is indeed not clear what role Sullivan's words had in determining Hoveyda's fate. In early 1977, the political and economic situation in Iran took a turn for the worst. Aside from economic difficulties, which now included budget deficits, more and more writers and intellectuals were suddenly emboldened to brave the dangers of arrest and write open letters, many of them addressed to Hoveyda, criticizing the regime. One of the earliest acts of epistolary disobedience was by Ali-Asghar Hadj-Seyyed-Djavadi in January 1976, at the time when the shah had just announced that corruption was a major problem in Iran. Hadj-Seyyed-Djavadi accused the Hoveyda government of not only condoning corruption but actually "fighting against the real enemies of corruption."[69] Hadj-Seyyed-Djavadi went on to write several other letters, many of them also attacking Hoveyda. As he now readily admits, many of the attacks on Hoveyda were surrogates for attacking the shah himself.[70] Nevertheless, of all these letters, the one he wrote in June 1977 would figure prominently in Hoveyda's trial.

Hoveyda knew that his days in office were now numbered. He had served longer than any other prime minister in the modern history of Iran. Already, in March 1977, he was, in the words of one of his trusted secretaries, "indescribably tired, incredibly bad-tempered and quite genuinely fed-up."[71] In one of his moments of somber doubt and scrutiny, he had told a trusted cabinet minister, "Whatever we do to the Iranian people, they take it in silence."[72] As it turned out he was tragically mistaken.

CHAPTER FOURTEEN

Le Bouc Émissaire*

...So we'll live,
And pray, and sing, and tell old tales, and laugh
At gilded butterflies, and hear poor rogues
Talk of court news; and we'll talk with them too—
Who loses and who wins, who's in, who's out—
And take upon's the mystery of things,
As if we were God's spies; and we'll wear out, ?
In a walled prison, packs and sects of great ones
That ebb and flow by th' moon.
　　　　　　　　—Shakespeare, *King Lear*

n the last week of July 1977, Hoveyda took what turned out to be his last vacation as Iran's prime minister. He went to one of the Greek islands with his ex-wife, Laila, along with Foreign Minister Abbas-Ali Khalatbari and his wife. Edouard Sablier joined the company for part of the vacation.[1] Most of Hoveyda's days were spent lounging on the beach, reading *roman policiers*.

On August 4, 1977, he returned to Tehran, and the next day he went to see the shah, who was himself vacationing on the Caspian coast. As soon as the shah spoke, Hoveyda realized where the conversation was heading. Before the shah could ask for his resignation, Hoveyda himself "volunteered the view that new blood was needed."[2] As for much of his tenure, this time, too, he had read the shah's mind and acted before the shah had to take the initiative. The shah accepted Hoveyda's resignation and on the same day appointed Amouzegar as his replacement. Indeed, a week earlier, while Hoveyda was still in Greece, the shah had told Amouzegar to think about the composition of his cabinet.[3] Hoveyda's departure was not, how-

---

* Bouc émissaire is the French for scapegoat.

Hoveyda (in profile) and the shah, wearing dark glasses. A glum Alam looks on.

ever, in disgrace. During the same audience, the shah appointed him minister of court. As an August 1977 CIA report makes clear, Hoveyda's appointment to the new post put him into continuing close contact with the shah: "True to the shah's modus operandi, Hoveyda, with the contacts and influence he has built up over the years, is retained as a counterweight to Amouzegar and one can expect rivalry between them for the shah's ear."[4]

The shah's treatment of Alam revealed his methods even more. For many years, Alam was considered to be the shah's closest friend. He rode with the shah, was his confidant in matters political, diplomatic, filial, and financial; he even acted as a decoy, or go-between, for his majesty's extramarital trysts. But ultimately the shah seemed incapable of intimate friendship. To even a faithful servant like Alam, he could act with striking brutality. While Alam was in the South of France, fighting cancer, the shah called to ask for his resignation, and informed him that he was giving his job to his archenemy, Hoveyda. Writing about the phone call in his daily diary, a clearly distraught Alam calls the Hoveyda appointment a "mystery."[5] Alam died an embittered man, and his fate should have been a warning to Hoveyda.

Hoveyda found the court an unruly organization of vested interests and stolid traditions. He confided to a friend that "if the government was corrupt, the court ministry is a nest of vipers."[6] Many of the employees owed their allegiance to Alam and resented Hoveyda for taking his place. But compared to the changes that were happening in society at large, the squabbles of the court were indeed petty and insignificant.

Not long after Hoveyda's resignation as prime minister, there was a rapid rise of demonstrations and acts of defiance against the government. Amouzegar, who had replaced Hoveyda as prime minister, was an accomplished, albeit surly, technocrat, but the game of politics was not his forte. He was clearly wanting in the political savvy required to handle the unfolding crisis. Faced with mass demonstrations, Amouzegar's first guess was that Hoveyda and his ally in SAVAK, Sabeti, had organized the disturbances to destabilize his government. He asked one of his friends, Ahmad Ghoreishi, to intervene and beseech Hoveyda and Sabeti to cease their machinations. Both men vehemently denied having any hand in the disturbances. "Does he think we have lost our mind?" they asked incredulously.[7]

A few Iranians, like Amouzegar, saw the early tremors of the revolution as nothing short of dastardly acts of rival factions. Others blamed the revolution on Amouzegar's decision to cut the secret subsidies paid by the prime minister's office to the clerics. Some, like the shah, saw the revolution as nothing but a conspiracy of the oil companies. Yet others, such as the Marxists, saw the revolution as either a leap forward or backward in the inexorable march of history. Finally there were those of a religious disposition who saw the revolution as part of a divine design, a moment of history mandated by God himself. All have one important point in common: they abjure individual responsibility; they each fail to envision what alternative paths Iran could have taken in the years leading up to the revolution. At each historic moment, had a different choice been made or even had the same choice been made earlier, the revolution could have been averted. One of the most glaring examples of such a moment was the decision on January 7, 1978, to publish an apparently innocuous piece called, "Iran and Red and Black Imperialism."[*]

A few days before the now infamous article's publication, in his audience with the shah, General Nasiri, head of SAVAK, reported on a recent

---

[*] "Iran and Red and Black Imperialism" began by declaring that opposition to the "White Revolution" was masterminded by foreign imperialists. The piece then went on to claim that "Ruhollah Khomeini had been a suitable agent for this purpose…[He] was known as the 'Indian Seyyed'…Some sources believe that he had spent several years in India and was connected with the British colonial centers." A translation of the article is included in a dispatch from the U.S. Embassy in Tehran. See NA, "FYI: Political Digest," 14 September 1978.

broadsheet issued by Ayatollah Khomeini on the occasion of his own son's death. The ayatollah had said that his grief paled in comparison to the grief he felt for all the crimes committed by the Pahlavi regime in Iran. The ayatollah's defiant and belligerent tone so angered the shah that he ordered SAVAK to prepare an article lambasting the exiled leader and accusing him of being a foreign spy.[8]

Unbeknown to SAVAK, the shah had also asked Hoveyda to prepare a similar letter. Before long, Hoveyda had entrusted two of his advisors with the task of drafting the letter. Within forty-eight hours of the angry royal command, Hoveyda called Daryoush Homayoun—who by then was the minister of information—and reportedly said, "There is an article that His Royal Majesty wants published, and it is on its way by courier."[9] Only minutes later, one of Hoveyda's secretaries arrived with a sealed envelope, bearing the insignia of the royal court. Without reading the article, indeed without even opening the envelope, Homayoun sent it to the editors of *Ettela'at,* one of Tehran's two important dailies, and ordered them to publish it. Homayoun says he knew that "anytime the shah ordered something published, there was nothing to do but publish it."[10]

As soon as the article reached the editors, they called Homayoun to warn him that it was incendiary in nature and they were loath to publish it. Homayoun decided to solicit the help of Prime Minister Amouzegar. His answer was brief and emphatic. Without showing any inclination to read the controversial piece, he said that if His Royal Majesty had ordered the article published, then it had to be published. Neither the editors, nor the paper's publisher, and certainly not the prime minister and his minister of information, dared defy the royal command. And thus the article, bereft of any serious substance, was published and immediately gave rise to bloody demonstrations in several cities. Each demonstration turned out to be contagious, begetting others; eventually, they turned into the feverish pitch of a revolution.

Hoveyda's role in preparing the article was more or less known at the time. What has remained less clear are the motives behind his involvement. One obvious explanation is that Hoveyda, like Amouzegar, Homayoun, and SAVAK, had no choice but to follow the royal decree. But over the years, the whisper has been that Hoveyda probably knew of the article's potentially incendiary effects, and that he helped with its publication only to weaken or depose his archrival, Amouzegar. Joseph Kraft, of the *New Yorker* magazine, suggested as much in December 1978, by writing that "my impression is that part of the motive [for publishing the letter] was to embroil the Amouzegar government with the religious opposition."[11]

As the tempo of opposition to the regime increased, and as it became clear that corruption was high on the list of people's complaints, Hoveyda finally convinced the shah to agree to and enforce a "code of conduct for the imperial family." Ratified by the shah in July 1978, the code had twenty articles that, among other things, forbade the royal family from "conduct considered distasteful to social customs," as well as from "contacts with foreign companies…receiving commissions for any reason…direct or indirect partnership in companies that are parties to deals with the government…accepting positions on boards."[12] In conversations with family and friends, Hoveyda would often boast that the ratification of the code was his most important accomplishment as minister of court. But it was too little, too late.

While Amouzegar's response to the political crisis was to search for a conspiracy by his foes, his solution for the economic crisis was to enforce a strict program of austerity. At the same time, the shah promised new moves toward political democracy. In retrospect, the concurrent pursuit of an austerity program and political liberalization was an invitation to catastrophe. Furthermore, since Aristotle, it has been a political adage that for despots, the most dangerous hours are those when they try to relinquish power and turn into democrats.

At least two factors contributed to the strange timing of the two concurrent policies. Firstly, the shah was sick and acutely aware that time was against him; and secondly, Jimmy Carter's presidency made the liberalization process urgent. Even before embarking on the process, the shah had called General Abbas Gharabaghi to a special audience. The shah told him that as a result of "international pressure," and in the interest of a "peaceful transition of power," he had decided to change course and liberalize the political process; the army chiefs, the shah said, must rest assured that it is all under control.[13] A few days later, a meeting of army commanders was convened. Hoveyda and General Azhari, the army's chief of staff, talked to the military's top brass, assuring them that "the totality of the unfolding events" were all "calculated and measured," and there should be no cause for concern.[14]

The first signs of the move toward democratization were more freedom of the press and more freedom for members of the Majlis to offer their criticism of the government. Assuming that the next elections would be free, and members would be elected only if they had the support of the public, the traditionally docile Majlis was transformed overnight into a forum for constant, radical pronouncements. Suddenly, nothing short of a torrent hit the airwaves and the pages of newspapers. Hoveyda's tenure as prime minister became the focal point for much of the attacks. Almost every social problem—from censorship in the media to elections, from the economic development plans to the corruption of governmental officials—was blamed on Hoveyda. It is not clear how many of these attacks were spontaneous, how many were masterminded by the shah and other members of the royal family, and what influence, if any, Hoveyda's foes had in channeling the criticism toward him.

But as political pressure continued to build, and as the economy showed little sign of overall improvement, the shah asked for Amouzegar's resignation. For over a decade, Amouzegar had pined for his turn as the prime minister, but his tenure proved to be ingloriously short.* In his place, Jafar Sharif-Emami was named to head the new cabinet of "national reconciliation." It would have been hard to find a more unsuitable candidate for such a sensitive job. As the American Embassy was told at the time by Shapour Bakhtiar, one of the leaders of the National Front, Sharif-Emami's government was "hopelessly involved in the very corruption it was supposedly stamping out....Bakhtiar had first hand knowledge of the Prime Minister's corrupt past."[15] The new prime minister had a notorious reputation for corruption; his nickname was "Mr. Five Percent," given to him because he was rumored to receive a five percent commission on nearly all governmental contracts. He was also the grand master of the Freemasons' grand lodge in Iran.[16]

Pandering to moderate religious forces at the time was probably the most important factor leading to the strange choice of Sharif-Emami for prime minister. A U.S. Embassy telegram, dated August 17, 1978, offers insight into the calculations that went into the decision to appoint Sharif-Emami. The report states, "very sensitive source related to us the substance of a meeting

---

* I tried, through several channels, to talk to Jamshid Amouzegar and hear his version of events. All my efforts came to naught. Talking about the past and Amir Abbas Hoveyda, he told my intermediaries, "was like spitting upwards." Ahmad Ghoreishi, interviewed by author, 22 September 1999.

between SAVAK chief Moghadam* and Shariatmadari's† son-in-law Abbasi [on the] night of August 15. Moghadam reportedly asked what the religious community wanted and Abbasi ticked off [the] following points: A) There must be a new government…B) The next government must at a minimum call to account some of the major individuals suspected of corruption…C) The activities of Princess Ashraf are anathema to the religious community. She must be curtailed….D) People must be free to talk and worship. Shariatmadari's people greatly approved of the Shah's Constitution Day speech [in which he promised to fully implement the constitution] and Moghadam was told to tell the Shah this. Moghadam replied that he would be seeing the Shah that evening…We understand from our best religious source that religious groups at some point have discussed possible prime ministers‡…Moderate religious leadership believes [a] senior statesman is necessary…Our source thought that two names had been bandied about: Ali Amini and Senate President Sharif-Emami…According to [a] source, Sharif-Emami was thought to be the best candidate because he is a very religious man himself and has solid political backing."[17] The shah's firm belief that the British government was actively working to foment the revolution was probably another factor contributing to the choice of a Freemason for the post of forming a government of "reconciliation."

Hoveyda's choice for Amouzegar's replacement, however, had been Ali Amini. In mid-July, recognizing that a combination of economic difficulties and political paralysis "was deteriorating public confidence in [the] Amouzegar cabinet" and that "change had to be made or demonstrations would get out of hand," Hoveyda had contacted Amini and encouraged him to call for a "national unity government."[18] Hoveyda had also asked Fereydoun Mahdavi, who was vacationing in Europe, to come back to Iran

---

* After General Nasiri was dismissed from his post in June 1978 and sent away to Pakistan as an ambassador, Moghadam was named the new head of SAVAK. Eventually, as a ploy to calm the rising tide of revolution, the shah called Nasiri back from Pakistan and ordered his arrest. He would end up being one of the first people executed by the Islamic Tribunal. Moghadam was not spared, either.

† Shariatmadari was a grand ayatollah of much influence at the time. In terms of strict religious hierarchy, he was higher in the clerical pecking order than even Ayatollah Khomeini. During the days leading to the revolution, he was in contact with the court and the government, trying to abort a Khomeini takeover. For his "sin" he paid heavily. After the revolution, he was accused of being involved in a coup attempt against the government; he was put under house arrest and eventually forced to participate in a public recantation much in the spirit of the Moscow Trials of the 1930s. He died a broken man.

‡ The comment is crucial in understanding the context for the shah's strange decision to make a controversial speech a few weeks later.

right away and try to get the National Front to form a government of reconciliation. None of these efforts bore any fruit. With Mahdavi's help,
Hoveyda also organized a meeting with Mozaffar Baghai, a colorful relic
who had played an important role in the Mosaddeq era.[19] The shah
refused to meet Amini, the National Front was in no hurry to help a
beseiged shah, and Baghai was truly a relic of a bygone era.[20]

Sharif-Emami's policy of appeasement was a crucial step in the incipient revolution. From his first day in office, he made it clear that he hoped
to arrive at a rapprochement with the religious community. He decided to
abolish "the portfolio of the minister of state for women's affairs; created
a new ministry for religious endowments; shut down the few operating
casinos [all owned by the Pahlavi Foundations whose president was
Sharif-Emami himself]; closed many nightclubs; restored the Islamic calendar; granted freedom of activity for political parties; lifted censorship
of the media; allowed parliamentary debates to be televised; began an
anti-corruption campaign; gave across-the-board salary increases to government employees...and finally dissolved the Rastakhiz Party."[*21]

As Sharif-Emami engaged in his policy of offering concessions to the
religious opposition, the shah, who for many years had disdained the idea
of having advisors, began a spate of meetings with different groups, many
of whom were elder politicians who had fallen from grace for more than a
decade.[22] Hoveyda's mentor Entezam was back in royal favor, as were
Mehdi Pirasteh and the shah's old nemesis, Ali Amini. Some of these advisors advocated the continuation of the policy of reconciliation, while others suggested that any sign of weakness now would be abused by the
mullahs. "I know the mullahs. The only thing they understand is a show of
force," Pirasteh claims to have told the shah.[†] In addition, he states, "I suggested that he should dissolve the parliament, rule by special decrees, and
gradually implement the changes needed."[23] In his meeting with a member
of the U.S. Embassy in Tehran, Pirasteh, who was trying to fashion himself

---

* Until the mid-1970s, a religious event—the Prophet Mohammed's trip from the city of Mecca to Medi-
na—marked the beginning of both the solar and lunar Islamic calendars. As the shah grew more confident of
the inexorable march of his "White Revolution," he, like the radical revolutionaries in France and the Bolsheviks in Russia, decreed a change in the calendar. While the two other experiments both wanted to start the new
dates with the revolution, in Iran, the advent of monarchy, some 2,500 years ago was set as the year zero of the
new calendar.

† One of the common characteristics of the memoirs of the Pahlavi elite is that in retrospect, they all claim
to have told the shah—clearly, categorically, and fearlessly—the truth about the crisis and the way out of it.

as a viable alternative to the current government, told the embassy officials that "he had proof Hoveyda really is a Bahai despite disclaimers and criticized Hoveyda as a poor prime minister."[24] Pirasteh's dislike for Hoveyda would later figure in Hoveyda's arrest by the shah.

Pirasteh was not the only advocate of a get-tough, "law and order" policy. Hoveyda was also despondent that the government had no strategic policy to deal with the crisis. "It is all reaction, and no action,"[25] he would lament. He, too, was in favor of a show of force by the government that would allow a "cooling period," a needed respite for the regime to recompose itself and shed the siege mentality that had hampered its every move. When some of his friends objected to the government's attempt to flex its muscle by creating "Revenge and Vengeance Committees," Hoveyda responded by noting that "new situations lead to new reactions to those situations, and we must wait and see and hope that pressure on both sides will subside."[26]

The most persistent advocate of an ironfisted policy, however, was Parviz Sabeti. He consistently suggested that the government should first confront and suppress the demonstrations, and then gradually allow a loyal and serious opposition to have an open hand in criticizing the system and members of the royal family.[27] In April 1978, using Hoveyda as his emissary, Sabeti asked the shah to give his office free reign to quell the rebellion. The shah had been interested enough to ask for a specific proposal. Sabeti had helped prepare a list of fifteen hundred people whose arrest, he believed, would put a quick end to the disturbances. The list was sent to the shah, who brooded over it for a day and then ordered that only those whose names he had marked should be arrested. By the time the list came back, there were only about three hundred names on it.

In *Answer to History*, the shah alludes to his dilemma by writing, "My generals urged me often enough to use force to re-establish law and order in the streets. I know today that had I then ordered my troops to shoot, the price in blood would have been a hundred times less severe than that which my people have paid since the establishment of the so-called Islamic Republic. But even that fact does not resolve my fundamental dilemma—a sovereign may not save his throne by shedding his countrymen's blood."[28] Another crucial factor working against the shah's use of violence was that both the British and the U.S. governments were strongly in favor of a tempered response to popular demands and demonstrations. At every turn both governments, or at least strong elements in both governments, insisted that the democratization process must go on, and force must not be used. For example, in mid-December 1978, the shah told the U.S. ambassador that "he was considering three broad options:—try to form a national coalition;—'surrender' to opposition demand and leave the country;—form a military junta and apply an 'iron fisted' policy. In his frequent contacts with the Shah, the ambassador encouraged the Shah to try and form a coalition."[29]

But in early April of that year, the night Sabeti's proposed list came back, SAVAK arrested all those sanctioned by the shah. Soon, there was a temporary lull in the demonstrations. As a U.S. Embassy report indicates, "Despite occasional incidents here and there…relative quiet has replaced the recent turbulence." The report goes on to add that several hundred people were arrested and then ends with a note of cautious optimism. In spite of the reduced violence, Sullivan, the author of the report, writes, the government is still "not out of woods. Hard, dedicated efforts will still be required on the part of government leaders such as court minister Hoveyda before the trend of the past five or six months can be reversed. But a beginning has been made."[30]

But for reasons that will only become clear when all Iranian, British, and American archives are opened, the crackdown was soon aborted. Sabeti, its architect, was dismissed and eventually allowed to leave Iran. The night before his departure, he went to Hoveyda's house for a visit. "The shah, I think, has given up," Hoveyda had said that night. "Your dismissal is a sign that he does not want to fight anymore." Hoveyda also said, "The shah has decided to let you go because he knows you are outspoken. Me and Nasiri, he is sure of and will keep us here for the rainy day."[31] That rainy day was not far away, and Sabeti's dismissal should have given Hoveyda an early warning. As the government vacillated between a policy of rapprochement and suppression, all hopes of appeasement were dashed on September 8, 1978, when the army fired upon and killed a number of people at Jaleh Square. Martial law had been declared the previous night, and the demonstrators, either unaware of the declaration or in a calculated attempt to defy it, refused to leave the streets when ordered to do so by the armed forces implementing the curfew. The bloodshed gave rise to one of the most potent mobilizing mythologies of the new movement. Tehran was suddenly ripe with rumors of exaggerated numbers of people killed in what was dubbed "Black Friday." Black Friday, along with the arson of the Rex Cinema, played a crucial role in further radicalizing the protest movement.[*] While the government tried to lay the blame for the arson on radical clerics, the opposition somehow succeeded in making the government complicit in the act. Even twenty years after the revolution, the question of responsibility for the fire has not been entirely settled. Pressured by the families of those who had lost someone in the fire, the Islamic government put a group of religious vigilantes from the city of Isfahan, along with a number of SAVAK agents on trial, charging them with masterminding the arson. Important questions about the alleged role of clerics, however, were never raised in the trial and popular perception now holds the clergy responsible for the fire.[†]

The day after Black Friday, September 9, 1978, Hoveyda resigned as minister of court. He claimed later, in a letter smuggled out of prison, that his resignation was in protest at the bloodshed. At the time of the resignation, however, he told some of his friends that his departure was a direct result of Ardeshir Zahedi's intervention. By Hoveyda's reckoning, Zahedi, who was still Iran's ambassador to the United States, had finally convinced the shah that if Hoveyda was dismissed, then some kind of compromise could be reached with moderate mullahs.[32]

The Pahlavi regime had by then fallen into a spiral of confusion and chaos. Overnight, Sharif-Emami's policy of appeasement was changed to a supposedly ironfisted posture of "law and order." A military government was appointed, and many of the shah's advisors wanted General Gholam-Ali Oveissi to head it—a man already dubbed "The Butcher of Tehran" because of his role in the Black Friday massacre. Instead, the shah chose General Azhari, who immediately became the subject of public ridicule for his utter lack of gravitas.

More bizarre was the shah's decision to give a speech on the day after the Azhari appointment. Nothing captures the confusion of the shah's decisions in those crucial days better than this speech. It was meek in tone

---

[*] On August 19, 1978, the Rex Cinema in the oil town of Abadan was drenched in incendiary material and set ablaze, killing 164 people.

[†] At the time of the Rex movie theater trial, a radical underground journal, published by a group that called itself Sazeman-e Vahdat-e Komonisty (The Communist Unity Organization), published a series of scathing and detailed accounts of the trial and its inherent discrepancies, alluding at the same time to evidence indicating clerical complicity in the arson.

and pathetic in delivery. In it, the shah declared, "I, too, have heard the voice of your revolution." In the tone of a genuflecting sinner, he confessed that "the revolution of the Iranian people cannot be disapproved by me...Once again before the Iranian people I swear that I will not repeat past mistakes and I assure you that previous mistakes, lawlessness, oppression, and corruption will not happen again."*[33]

ON THAT SEPTEMBER DAY WHEN HOVEYDA RESIGNED from the court ministry, the shah offered to send him away from Iran and appoint him Iran's ambassador to Belgium. The shah refers to this in *Answer to History:* "Mr. Hoveyda, who still has my wholehearted esteem, was one of the favorite targets of the opposition. Knowing that it was I whom they hoped to reach through him, I suggested that he go abroad for awhile, and offered him the Belgian Embassy."[34] Hoveyda asked for a little time to think about it. After consulting with his family and friends, he decided to refuse the offer. Those who have tried to explain Hoveyda's decision to stay in Iran have erroneously sought to find a single cause or culprit. Several factors worked toward Hoveyda's decision. There was the question of his mother. As he told Sir Anthony Parsons, his mother was too old to leave Iran, and he did not have the heart to leave her behind. Furthermore, he was averse to a life of exile. On many occasions after his return home in 1957, he had told his family and friends that he never wanted to leave Iran again. There was also the question of his allegiance to the shah. Hoveyda was convinced that the end of the line had not come yet for the Pahlavi regime. By all accounts, he believed that there was a "scenario," a masterplan lurking behind the facade of spontaneous mass demonstrations. And not least of all was his ex-wife Laila's advice. She suggested that accepting an ambassadorial post—a "sinecure position" in her own words—was beneath his dignity.† She told him the time had finally come for him to make his long cherished

---

* The speech was not unlike the "penitential walk" that the besieged Louis XVI took on the eve of the French Revolution. Just as Louis' July 14, 1789, walk to the Assembly signaled that the "court of the Bourbons had died," so too the shah's speech marked the beginning of the end of the Pahlavi dynasty.

† She now has a more sober and critical view of the advice she gave at the time. She writes, "In hindsight, I think now how out of touch I was with reality. How could Amir run his book shop in a country that censored all books then and does even more now." Laila Emami, personal correspondence, 19 December 1999.

Hoveyda's last trip with Laila; they traveled to Kish island in the Persian Gulf.
About three months after the picture was taken in 1978,
Hoveyda was arrested by order of the shah.

dream a reality and open a bookstore. Together they had even picked a name for it. The bookstore would be called "The President."[35]

The shah's offer was not the first chance Hoveyda had to leave the country, nor would it be the last. In June 1978, Claude de Peyron, a friend of Hoveyda's and a man with many connections in the French corridors of power, went to Iran on a special mission from Jacques Chaban Delmas, the president of the French Assembly. The message was simple: "We are sure things are going to get far worse soon. We want you to leave Iran on a medical pretext; once you are in Paris, we will hospitalize you and then keep you in France."[36] Though the two men, according to de Peyron, spent the whole night discussing all the available options, Hoveyda ultimately refused to leave. He gave two reasons for his decision: as always, the first had to do with his mother; the second was more political. "Things are not going right in Iran," Hoveyda is reported to have said, "and the shah has lost the ability to make decisions. I must stay." According to de Peyron, Hoveyda had "illusions about what awaited him in Iran."[37]

Rumors of Hoveyda's imminent arrest, which had begun when Sharif-Emami became prime minister in August 1978, now spread more widely. Not long after his appointment, during a meeting of a select group of ministers and advisors with both the shah and the queen present, Sharif-Emami declared that "decisive action needed to be taken if the country was to be saved." It was soon agreed that corruption was a key grievance of the people. Several of those present, particularly Manouchehr Azmoun, Houshang Nahavandi, and Mohammad Baheri, were adamant that "all those guilty of corruption had to be severely punished."[*] Though Hoveyda's name was never mentioned, it was clear that those advocating swift action had him in mind as well. Betraying the degree of political delusion in some of the shah's most important advisors, and with sediments of his Stalinist days still evident in his designs and devices, Azmoun suggested that "people want a revolution…The shah must become the leader of the revolution." He then advocated the formation of military tribunals to "swiftly, and publicly, punish those who were guilty of corruption." No decision was made that evening. The shah ended the meeting by saying, "We will think it over."[38]

If Hoveyda is to be believed, aside from those in that meeting, other individuals, foremost among them Ardeshir Zahedi and his group, were interested in using Hoveyda as a scapegoat.[†] Others have also suggested that Zahedi played a key role in Hoveyda's arrest. For example, Shahin Aghayan, a close friend of Hoveyda's, claims that on the day he was leaving Iran, Zahedi happened to be sitting next to him on the plane and declared with obvious glee, "I finally convinced His Majesty to arrest that son of a dog Hoveyda."[39] Zahedi confirmed talking to Aghayan on the plane, but he denied talking about Hoveyda. "What I told him," Zahedi said, "was that sons of bitches like Aghayan should be lined up against the wall and shot."[40] As further proof that the Aghayan story cannot be believed, Zahedi added that "I had a lot of respect for Amir's mother. I visited her house once and would have never used profanities about her."[41] It is hard to establish which of the two versions is closer to the truth.

---

[*] Aside from Sharif-Emami, Azmoun, Nahavandi, and Baheri, those present in the meeting were General Oveissi, General Samadianpour, Manouchehr Ganji, Reza Qotbi, and General Moghadam.

[†] Hoveyda offers his views on Zahedi's role in a letter he succeeded in smuggling out of prison. For the text of the letter, see page 326 in chapter 16, "The Frozen Lake of Cocytus."

In either case, for a while, the shah thwarted efforts directed at arresting Hoveyda. On at least a couple of occasions, he is reported to have said that arresting Hoveyda was tantamount to putting the whole Pahlavi regime on trial. As late as the day before Hoveyda's arrest, the shah reassured British Ambassador Sir Anthony Parsons that "Hoveyda would not, repeat not be arrested."[42] However, the next evening, November 8, 1978, it was announced on National Iranian Radio and Television that Hoveyda had been arrested. Interestingly enough, the British ambassador had not been fooled by the shah's words of reassurance and called Hoveyda after his audience to warn him of the imminent danger of his arrest, suggesting that he try to escape. Hoveyda refused to heed his friend's advice. On the day before the arrest, the shah had also told a deeply concerned Entezam and Mehdi Samii that Hoveyda's arrest was out of the question.[43] Hoveyda was in close contact with both men and must have heard of the shah's words of assurance.

While the shah was brooding over the question of Hoveyda's arrest, Hoveyda was mistakenly confident that he had the king's unwavering support and was busy contemplating the possible creation of a centrist, monarchist party. As a U.S. Embassy report makes clear, "Hoveyda and some of his political associates are having some type of discussion…[about] the reestablishment of the Iran Novin Party. Hoveyda commands personal loyalty of a number of active lower level politicians. But [the] main question among this group is whether Hoveyda himself has not been or will not be too tarnished by his governmental role in the past. At least one local columnist has hinted that Hoveyda may get back into active politics. But stories also continue to circulate that he may be picked up on charges similar to those under which other former ministers have been detained." Sullivan, filing this report, adds what he calls a "humorous note." He writes that many of these politicians who were "thrashing around for appropriate organizational forms to contain the new wine of their political activism…also seek assurance from the shah that their activities will receive at a minimum a benign smile from the throne."[44]

But forces pining for Hoveyda's arrest were no less busy behind the scenes. On the morning of November 8, 1978, the shah called a meeting of another group of his advisors. Besides the queen, Mehdi Pirasteh, Javad Shahrestani, Houshang Nahavandi, General Hassan Pakravan, Reza Qotbi,

and Aligholi Ardalan (recently appointed minister of court) were present.[*]
After some discussion about the necessity of revamping the structure of
the Pahlavi Foundation, and offering a public scrutiny of the financial
affairs of the royal family, the shah changed the subject by indicating that
for a while, a number of his advisors, particularly many of his generals, had
been suggesting that Hoveyda should be arrested. He then asked the group
to discuss the proposition.

While they talked, the phone rang. The shah answered and after listening for a few seconds, said, "There is a group here talking about the same
thing." The identity of the caller was not known. Some of those in the
meeting have indicated that it was General Oveissi, another Hoveyda
nemesis, who had been a close ally of Alam. After a few moments of
silence, the shah smiled faintly, put his hand on the mouthpiece, and said,
"He, too, thinks [that arresting Hoveyda] is more urgent than the
evening's meal."[†45]

After a while, the shah decided to bring the meeting to a close. He
wanted those present to vote for or against the arrest. There are lingering
ambiguities about how everyone voted. Pirasteh, who still defiantly
defends his own vote in favor of the arrest, claims, "No one in the room
was against the idea or voted against it. The way the shah talked, it was
clear he had already made up his mind that Hoveyda was going to be
arrested. I even think the phone call was arranged by the shah to strength-
en the resolve of those in the room in favor of the decision."[46]

Nahavandi's rendition of the meeting confirms that no one voted
against the idea of Hoveyda's arrest. Nahavandi then claims that he was the
one who suggested to the shah that a general should be sent to arrest
Hoveyda, and that the shah should himself call Hoveyda and let him know
of his impending arrest![47] He describes, at some length, the overall tone of
the meeting. His account, in its general outline, shares much with Pirasteh's
narrative. He recounts how the shah, gingerly, broached the topic of
Hoveyda's arrest, and how everyone in the room ultimately concurred with
the suggestion.

---

* For an account of the meeting I have relied on interviews with Mehdi Pirasteh, Houshang Nahavandi's
Harvard Iranian Oral History interview, as well as his book, *Iran: Deux Rêves Brisés* (Paris, 1993). A second-
hand account of the meeting can also be found in the Harvard Iranian Oral History interview with Fatemeh
Pakravan, General Pakravan's wife. Also see Fatemeh Pakravan, *Khaterat* [Memoir] (Tehran, 1999). A fictionalized account of the meeting can be found in Saideh Pakravan, *The Arrest of Hoveyda* (Costa Mesa, 1998).

† Traditionally, the evening meal was the most important for the Iranian worker.

Once the fateful decision to arrest Hoveyda was made, the shah turned to the queen, and asked that she call and inform Hoveyda of his imminent arrest.* The queen angrily refused to make the dread call and something of a verbal scuffle broke out. The shah sent everyone except the queen out of the room and they continued their discussion in private.[48] What was said between them just before the arrest of their long-serving prime minister is not known.†

Even before the call, Hoveyda's first direct clue that the shah was now seriously contemplating his arrest was a visit by Reza Qotbi. During an evening at Fereshteh Ensha's house, some three weeks before the meeting that sealed Hoveyda's fate, Qotbi suggested to Hoveyda that one way out of the current quagmire would be "for a tribune in which top leaders

---

* Not only was the shah unwilling to call Hoveyda, he also never took any responsibility for the decision. Instead, he blamed others, writing in *Answer to History*, "General Gholam-Reza Azhari…immediately arrested twelve highly placed officials, among them Mr. Hoveyda, whom he put under house arrest." See Mohammad Reza Pahlavi, *Answer to History*, 167.

† Attempting to get information about this debate, I sent a letter on 9 April 1998 to Queen Farah, indicating the nature of my project and requesting a chance to ask her some questions. After about a week, I was informed by her chief of staff, Kambiz Atabai, that my request had been denied. "Her Majesty," he said, "finds it hard to talk about that past." Recognizing the significance of her narrative, I did not relent. I solicited the help of several friends, who I imagined might have some influence with her. After many entreaties, my efforts seemed to have borne fruit. Early in May 1998, I was informed that the queen had changed her mind. She would agree to talk to me, I was told, on two conditions: I would have to submit written questions in advance, and before publication, I would have to show her any direct quotes I intended to use. I immediately agreed and on May 16, 1998, I wrote her a letter clearly outlining my questions. Mindful of the necessity of using the requisite royal titles, I wrote, "Her Royal Majesty is the most crucial source for understanding some of the most important aspects of Mr. Hoveyda's political life." I then asked many specific questions, including, "In what areas did Mr. Hoveyda seek the help of Her Majesty in countering pressures from his opponents, including those from Mr. Alam? Is it true, as some sources have claimed, that Dr. Nahavandi [who had been head of the Queen's Private Office] worked to undermine Her Majesty's relations with Mr. Hoveyda? What was the nature of Mr. Hoveyda's relationship with Dr. Ayadi?…Did Your Majesty know of Mr. Hoveyda's government's decision to close down some of the newspapers and magazines? Some sources have claimed that the decision was the direct result of His Majesty's orders. Others claim that Mr. Hoveyda wanted to thus eliminate his political opponents. A third group claims that the decision was made in a meeting, in which officials from Her Majesty's office also participated, and the government was then ordered to carry out the decisions reached at that meeting. Which, if any, of these versions is true? Some sources, including Mr. Radji, have stated that in private Mr. Hoveyda had claimed that he could never report the true conditions of the country to the king. Did Mr. Hoveyda ever try to give a report to the king through Her Majesty? Many sources have claimed that an array of forces— from Mr. Ardeshir Zahedi to General Oveissi—advocated the arrest of Mr. Hoveyda. The same sources claim that meetings to discuss the decision were held at the Royal Palace…No doubt those advocating the arrest of Mr. Hoveyda must have had some logic in arguing for the necessity and the justice of this decision. What were those arguments?…Did Mr. Hoveyda, during his days under arrest, ever send a message to Your Highness, asking to be allowed to leave Iran?" On May 26, 1998, as we had previously agreed, I called the queen's office in New York to arrange the time and place of the meeting. Kambiz Atabai said he had bad news. "The queen has changed her mind. She will not do the interview."

would appear and answer questions about their past."[49] With his pipe in his mouth, Hoveyda hardly said a word in response, remaining instead silently nonchalant.

FINALLY, IN THE EARLY AFTERNOON OF NOVEMBER 8, 1978, the shah called Hoveyda at the house he shared with his mother. "For your own safety," the sovereign said, "we have ordered that you be taken to a safe place for a while."[50] For a few weeks now, Hoveyda had already been under something of a house arrest. His guards had been ordered not to allow him to get near the airport.[51]

Minutes after the call, Hoveyda called the Ensha residence and asked both mother and daughter to come to his house as soon as they could. "*Aqa* was pacing the room," Maryam Ensha said.* "He looked nervous. He told me the shah had called and told him about the arrest. I told him to escape right away. I said the car is ready, I can find you a place to hide. A bitter smile curled on his face, and in a sardonic tone he said, 'Since when have you become a politician.'" He then told Maryam Ensha the real purpose of his call. "I want you to take care of my mother while I am gone." Tears welled up in both of their eyes. "Don't worry," Maryam Ensha promised, "I will take care of her as if she was my own mother."[52] And it was a promise she kept at great peril to herself and to her family.

About three hours after the call, two generals came to the house in two black sedans. Laila was there, as were some of Hoveyda's friends. He had particularly asked his trusted advisor, and one-time head of Iran's Supreme Court, Nasser Yeganeh to come to the house. Hoveyda had wanted to ensure that there were witnesses to his arrest.[53]

Laila, as was her style, defiantly chastised the two hapless souls who had come to arrest Hoveyda. "You have shit all over this country, and now you want to make a scapegoat out of him," she said. With a gentle nudge of his foot, Hoveyda tried, in vain, to calm his combative ex-wife.[54] After the tense conversation, Hoveyda asked whether he might be allowed to drive his own car. The two generals said they needed to ask headquarters. They made a call and, moments later, told Hoveyda that permission had been granted. He had already packed a small suitcase, filled with some clothes,

---

* Aqa is used in Persian in roughly the same ways as *monsieur* in French.

his most urgent medications, and a bundle of books. Sitting alone in his blue car, with the two dark Mercedes sedans following him, Hoveyda left his mother's house, never to return.

That very night, he called the Ensha family again and asked that they bring his mother to see him in the morning. He was being held at a SAVAK safe house on Fereshteh Street, in the fashionable northern part of Tehran. Save for the guards, he was the only occupant. The next day his mother and Maryam Ensha visited him in his make-shift prison. A few weeks later, there was another brief and tearful visit. On both occasions, Hoveyda tried to put on a happy, reassuring face for his increasingly anxious mother. Ever since Mansur's assassination, she had worried that a violent end awaited her son.[55]

Hoveyda's family could visit him in jail as often as they wished, and though they attempted to afford him some amenities, with every passing day, he grew more and more bitter and melancholic. His lunches and dinners were brought from home: Fereshteh Ensha took care of his lunches, and Laila managed the dinners. Hoveyda had a phone at his disposal, and he used it readily to call his friends and colleagues, and even their families.

A few days after his arrival in prison, Hoveyda sent a message to the shah. Fereshteh Ensha was the conduit. Hoveyda wanted to know what "the scenario was" and who was behind his arrest. The shah never responded himself. Through an intermediary—Fereydoun Djavadi, who was a confidant of the queen—the shah sent back a message, explaining that there was no scenario, and the pressure for his arrest had come, not from one source, but from many.[*56]

Another regular visitor Hoveyda received in jail was General Moghadam, the new head of SAVAK. He had been playing a key role in negotiations between the opposition and the government. He visited Hoveyda about once a week and kept him abreast of outside developments. Perhaps, as a result of the general's briefings, Hoveyda had come to expect an imminent military coup. The memory of the 1953 coup that restored the monarchy could only have strengthened his belief in the viability of such an option. Until Ayatollah Khomeini's return to Iran, Hoveyda was confident that at any moment a monarchist coup would turn back the tide of revolution.[57]

---

* Fereydoun Djavadi, like the queen, refused to talk with me.

Hoveyda's other known visitor was Uri Lubrani, Israel's de facto ambassador to Iran. Although Israel did not officially have an embassy in Tehran, its mission was "in every substantial respect treated by the government of Iran like any other embassy."[58] Since the early 1970s, the head of the legation had been Uri Lubrani, and he had developed a particularly close relationship with Hoveyda. He had been a frequent guest at Hoveyda's dinner parties and met with Hoveyda regularly at the prime minister's office. While Hoveyda was in office Lubrani was the only exception to Hoveyda's rule that one of his secretaries take notes at all his meetings with foreign ambassadors.[59] Lubrani says he was not "aware of any special treatment," though he did feel a special affinity and friendship existed with Hoveyda. "That is why," he said, "I used all my power to arrange a farewell visit with him in prison before I left Iran."[60]

While Hoveyda was still a prisoner of the Pahlavi regime, a few weeks before Ayatollah Khomeini's return to Iran, French officials used a reliable go-between and contacted Fereshteh Ensha and asked her to get Hoveyda's approval for a commando operation to free him from jail. The first step of the plan called for the handful of guards to be drugged to sleep. Then, American mercenaries would descend on the jail, snatch Hoveyda, and fly him to a plane waiting at Tehran's airport. Ideally, before the Iranian government even knew what had happened, the prisoner would be out of the country. Hoveyda listened to the plan and then said impishly, "They have been watching too many James Bond movies."[61]

The day Hoveyda heard that the shah and queen planned to leave Iran, his mood changed perceptibly. Palpable darkness was now on the horizon. Hitherto, he had resisted any attempt by his family to solicit the royal family's help in his release. But when he heard, from General Moghadam, a week in advance, about the royal departure, he grew more concerned. This time, when Fereshteh Ensha suggested that she should contact the royal family and ask them to take Hoveyda along when they leave the country, he agreed for her to proceed with her plan but warned, "They will not respond to you."[62]

His prediction was correct. In spite of several attempts, using Fereydoun Djavadi as an intermediary, she never succeeded in arranging an audience with the queen. Other emissaries were also of no avail. When Hoveyda heard of these developments, a look of dejection appeared on his face. "If they ever ask you what I felt like in these hours," he volunteered, "tell them, *il était écœuré* (he was disgusted)."[63]

The shah's tearful departure from Iran on January 16, 1979, brought out a deluge of demonstrations and celebrations in the streets of the capital. The end of the Pahlavi dynasty was now a foregone conclusion. In August 1977, Sullivan had predicted that the "fabric of this society, under the stress of a genuine democratic opportunity, may disintegrate…That sort of thing has happened before and the U.S. assisted in the re-establishment of 'internal security.' If we consider it in our interest to see the shah persevere…we should consider what we can do to help."[64] As it turned out, the U.S. offered no help; instead it often spoke with multiple voices to a distraught shah. From George Ball and Zbigniew Brzezinski to Cyrus Vance and Jimmy Carter, each offered a different bit of advice. While some in the administration advocated a "get-tough" policy, others like Sullivan told the shah in December 1978 that, of the three options he was considering—"Try to form a national coalition; surrender to opposition demands and leave the country; form a military junta and apply an 'iron fist' policy"—he should "try to form a coalition."[65] Furthermore, the same ambassador had by early January 1979 decided that the U.S. "must put the shah behind us and look to our own national interests."[66] Indeed, by late December, "Ambassador Sullivan reported his belief that the Shah's options had 'narrowed' to his departing in a manner that would preserve the substance of the constitution and maintain the integrity of the armed forces."[67]

The shah's departure came the day after a new cabinet was sworn in on January 15. This time it was Shapour Bakhtiar, of the National Front, who took on the now pallid mantle of premiership. From the start Bakhtiar had no chance of success: the secular forces failed to rally to his support; his own National Front expelled him from its ranks; and the army had little trust in him. Furthermore, by February 1979, the U.S. Embassy had again changed its mind, coming to a new conclusion about the future of Iran. It now declared that "our best estimate to date is that the Shia Islamic movement dominated by Ayatollah Khomeini is far better organized, enlightened and able to resist communism than its detractors lead us to believe. It is rooted in the Iranian people more than any Western ideology, including communism…It is possible the process of governing might produce accommodations with anti-clerical intellectual strains which exist in the opposition to produce something more closely approaching Westernized democratic processes than might at first be apparent."[68]

In practical terms, after Bakhtiar's dissolution of SAVAK in the first weeks of his tenure, what truly signaled the end of the Pahlavi era was the Iranian armed forces' "declaration of neutrality." On February 11, 1979, after "Chief of Staff General Gharabaghi agreed in a meeting with PM Bakhtiar and new PM Designate Bazargan to withdraw [the] army from the city of Tehran, leaving the city in the control of [the] revolutionary movement,"[69] the Imperial armed forces declared their neutrality and their desire to return to their barracks. All along, Hoveyda had been waiting for a coup; as it turns out, his wait had not been altogether quixotic. The day after the army's declaration of neutrality, and hours after many of its commanders had been arrested or killed by the new regime, the U.S. Embassy in Tehran received a call from the White House, giving the go-ahead for a coup by the Iranian army.[70] Previously, General Robert Huyser had been secretly dispatched to Iran to make it amply clear to the Iranian army's top brass that the U.S. would not abide such a military coup.[71] As with the shah's policies, so too with the U.S. decision to thwart a revolutionary takeover, it was too little, too late.

With the army's declaration of neutrality, Hoveyda's guards, all members of SAVAK, decided to escape themselves. They left behind the key to a car and a pistol, and urged Hoveyda to flee as well.*[72] Hoveyda demurred. Instead, he called Fereshteh Ensha, and asked her to arrange for his surrender to the new authorities. He also made one other call that morning. About a week before, Laila had left Iran to finish the dental work she had started late that summer in Paris, and her last meeting with Hoveyda had ended in acrimony. She had objected to what she considered his meek and passive disposition toward the shah. Now, with the phone at his disposal, he called her in Paris. He inquired about her health. "Forget about me, how are you?" she responded. He indicated that he was fine but that he was worried about what was happening to the country. She, too, recommended that he escape. "No," he said, "I have nothing to fear; I have decided to turn myself in; tell my French friends."[73] That turned out to be Hoveyda's last telephone conversation.

Fereshteh Ensha eventually contacted Dariush Forouhar, who had been named the new minister of labor in the Provisional Revolutionary Government of Iran. Through his intervention, a posse consisting of a mullah, a revolutionary guard, a representative of the minister of justice,

---

* Two of these people now live in Iran. In deference to their safety, I have chosen to omit their names.

Fereshteh Ensha, and her brother-in-law drove to the SAVAK villa in Shian, on the outskirts of Tehran, where Hoveyda had been held for the past few weeks. They traveled in two black sedans, navigating their way through often blockaded streets. The chaos of revolution was palpable and the anxious energy of random revolutionary terror permeated the city. Youths giddy with the joy of victory roamed the streets with their newly "liberated" pistols, machine guns, and rifles. Radical groups had even driven off with a few tanks, which they now paraded in the streets. In a universal ritual set by the French Revolution, prisons were attacked. By then, all political opponents of the Pahlavi regime had already been set free, so only those unlucky members of the old regime, who had been jailed by that same regime and had failed to escape, were now arrested by the mob, sometimes badly beaten, and then taken to the Refah School, the unofficial headquarters of the unfolding revolution.

The road to Hoveyda's jail was hard to navigate, but the mullah's presence helped them traverse the treacherous terrain. At every checkpoint the mullah's statement, "We are on a mission for Imam Khomeini," opened the barricades for the two sedans.

An angry crowd of villagers, skittish with the joys of revolution, had already gathered outside the villa that held Hoveyda. Oblivious to who was inside, they were angry simply because they knew of the villa's SAVAK connection. Again with the mullah's help, the two cars threaded their way through the crowd and entered the iron-gated compound. As they drove up the gravel road, they saw Hoveyda waiting for them on the veranda, alone and unguarded. He was wearing a gray turtleneck and dark slacks. He was clean-shaven and cordial to his new captors. He offered them some tea he had prepared. The group was more interested in trying to get safely out of the dangerously restless village as soon as possible. Fearing the frenzy of the crowd, they needed to find a way to safely transport the revolution's trophy prisoner to a new location. Hoveyda was less concerned with these logistics and more interested in emphasizing the fact that he had chosen to turn himself in.[74] In any court of law, he had hoped, such a gesture of goodwill would mitigate his alleged guilt.

On the way to the house, the posse had noticed an ambulance parked in a nearby street. With the help of their machine-gun-carrying revolutionary guard, they commandeered the ambulance, drove it to the villa, and asked Hoveyda to get in. As they began to enter the vehicle, the mullah

suggested that it might be safest if Hoveyda lay on the floor of the ambulance, lest the mob recognize his familiar face and engage in some violent
act. Hoveyda refused; instead he donned a dark Nelson cap, pulled it down
over his brow and sat on the far corner of the bench. Fereshteh Ensha sat
next to him, and next to her sat the representative from the justice department. Others sat on the opposite side, with the bed in the middle of the
ambulance separating the two groups. The mullah chose to sit in front
with the driver; his presence, they hoped, would guarantee their safe passage. Slumped deep in his seat, Hoveyda sat in the shadow of Fereshteh,
making him invisible to the angry, intrusive eyes of the mob who at every
stop pressed their faces up against the back door glass, searching for clues
of the passengers' identities.

The posse's hopes of a safe journey back to town were quickly dashed.
When the ambulance failed to stop fast enough at one of the checkpoints,
though the siren was running and the mullah was riding shotgun, the
guards opened fire, slightly wounding the driver. Eventually, they reached
the headquarters of the victorious National Front. The long-cherished
American policy of bringing a National Front government to power in
Iran had finally materialized: nearly everyone in the new Provisional Revolutionary Government had had some affiliation with the Front in the
past. Ironically, their rise was under a mullah, and not the shah.

At the crowded National Front headquarters, the ambulance drove to
the lower-level garage; Hoveyda was quickly whisked away to an isolated
part of the sprawling building. The prisoner was met by Dariush
Forouhar, who treated him cordially, ordered tea and soft drinks, and
chatted with him for a few minutes. Hoveyda spent the next hour in the
building; the place was bustling with new and old members of the Front,
only a handful of whom knew that Hoveyda was there as a prisoner. All
the while, Forouhar and a couple of his associates were trying to decide
what to do with the prisoner. Eventually it was decided that Hoveyda
should be taken to the Refah School, which had fast become the heart and
soul of all revolutionary committees. By contacting Forouhar, Hoveyda
had thought he was surrendering to the new Provisional Government.
Forouhar's decision to send Hoveyda to the Refah School was in a sense
an abrogation of the power and authority of that government. Such abrogation was a harbinger of the dynamics of post-revolutionary politics in
Iran. With every passing day, the committees, usually led by a cleric,

gained power, and the Provisional government of religious and secular intellectuals and technocrats was more and more weakened. Hoveyda's fate would eventually be decided by the outcome of this dynamic. For now, however, the problem was how to transfer the prisoner to his new jail. It was cold outside when the posse was on the move again. Snow covered the ground.

A vast crowd had overflowed from the sidewalks onto all the streets leading to the school. The ambulance had to needle its way through the throng. After an agonizingly long and slow progression, the door to the Refah School was opened to allow the ambulance inside the compound. Fereshteh Ensha, a guard, and the mullah accompanied Hoveyda to the second floor of the school. They climbed some stairs and reached a long, dim-lit hall; they were met by an armed guard, bearded and shabby, with a pair of plastic slippers on his feet. Behind his gray metal desk, not far from where he was sitting, a pile of shoes languished in front of the closed door of a room that had been, not so long ago, one of the school's classrooms. Hoveyda was led to a small room across the hall. The windows were covered with the previous day's newspapers. In bold headline type, one of Tehran's dailies had reproduced a line from a classical Persian poem: "When the Devil Departs the Angel Shall Then Return." Hoveyda now lived in the same compound as the man many thought was the promised angel, the expected messiah, of the poem. By the time a tired and despondent Fereshteh Ensha left the Refah School, into the dark night, she could hear the hum of the crowd: "They just brought in Hoveyda."[75]

CHAPTER FIFTEEN

The Hanging Judge

My unsoiled name, th' austereness of my life,
My vouch against you, and my place i' th' state,
Will so your accusation overweigh,
That you shall stifle in your own report...
Say what you can; my false o'erweighs your true.
　　　　　—Shakespeare, *Measure for Measure*

angerous are those who purchase fame even at the price of infamy. Yet, Hoveyda's fate was now in the hands of such a man—Sadegh Khalkhali, who cherished his reputation as the "Hanging Judge."[1] Accidents of history, and the exigencies of revolution, had hurled him into a position of inordinate importance.

Of peasant stock and little education, Khalkhali had come to Qom to train as a cleric. His round face, fleshy cheekbones, low brow overhanging small, shifty eyes, thin beard jutting from his jaws, and oversized turban all created an eerie image of the marauding Mongol horseman who haunts so many Persian miniatures. Abstract theological debates were alien to Khalkhali's mind. A fearless honesty, however, had made him one of Ayatollah Khomeini's minions—more an enforcer than a scribe—used for tasks requiring bravado rather than brain. In 1963, when SAVAK agents came to Qom to disrupt a lecture by Ayatollah Khomeini, he chose Khalkhali to deliver a stern ultimatum. Khomeini, through Khalkhali, warned that if his talk was disrupted, he would lead a demonstration out of the lecture hall all the way to the shrine—the economic and spiritual epicenter of Qom.[2] Not long after that confrontation, the Ayatollah was forced into exile, first to Turkey and then to Iraq. Khalkhali was also arrested and sent to live in a remote village, away from the political bustle of the city.

In Khalkhali's memoirs of his internal exile, there is a chilling mix of anticolonialist political cant and personal gossip, delivered in a self-righteous style. He even sallied into historical scholarship with a fifty-eight-page monograph on the ancient Persian king, Cyrus the Great. Khalkhali claims that he had finished the manuscript ten years before the revolution, but SAVAK prohibited its publication. Cyrus the Great—who is praised in the Bible as the great liberator and entrusted by the Lord "to build him a house at Jerusalem"—is here chastised as a bloodthirsty common criminal and a sodomite. But then again, Khalkhali also calls the Bible a book of "nonsense and shameful lies," and Jews a criminal race.[3]

With Ayatollah Khomeini's return to Iran, Khalkhali became the chief judge of Tehran's Revolutionary Tribunal. He was an ardent advocate of the omelet theory of revolution, glamorizing the cruelties of terror and execution as the necessary ingredients of a successful social transformation. His emotional scars, personal need for vengeance, and rhetoric of revolutionary justice created in him a frightening anger. In less than three months, he boasted to a journalist that he had ordered the execution of at least four hundred people. From then on, he was dubbed the "Hanging Judge." Khalkhali's international notoriety reached new heights after he appeared on television, accompanied by his ten-year-old son, poking a wooden stick into a bag containing the charred remains of a slain American soldier.[*]

He was, in short, the embodiment of the revolution's brutality and its seedy side. And as if fate had worked its marvels to best capture the contrast between the victors and the vanquished, Khalkhali was entrusted with presiding over the trial of the most polished cosmopolitan of the old regime.

Hoveyda's first interrogation had been an ominous harbinger of the kind of justice the Islamic Republic would embrace. We know about the conditions of this interrogation from a note he succeeded in smuggling out of prison. On March 1, 1979, during a visit from Fereshteh Ensha, Hoveyda used a moment of confusion to pass her the note. She briskly stuffed the crumpled paper into her brassiere. "I was sweating, and my heart was

---

[*] This was after the ill-fated attempt in 1980 by American Special Forces to free the U.S. Embassy hostages.

thumping," she remembered. After a couple of minutes, she picked up her doctor's bag and, with as much calm as she could muster, walked into the yard.* The gate seemed dangerously far away. Passing an armed guard, she suddenly heard a voice behind her, "Where are you going?" She turned to find an old man; he was holding a machine gun. With as much authority as she could muster, she said, "I am a doctor; I was here visiting patients." The old man apologized and she continued to walk toward the gate. "My knees were about to buckle under me," she said.[4]

Once outside the Refah School, she was too nervous to drive. She took a taxi home, preferring to come back the next day to pick up her car. At home, she took out the note. It was written in French on a small piece of paper. Hoveyda had written that he had had his first interrogation that day and that he was sure he would be tried in an Islamic court: "There will be no attorney; they hate us and think we destroyed all that was dear to them; they will kill us all; conditions are worse than you can imagine. Death will be a blessing."[†] Khalkhali's court was the embodiment of this hatred.

IT WAS WELL PAST MIDNIGHT ON MARCH 15, 1979, when Hoveyda was first brought before Khalkhali's tribunal. Norouz, the Persian New Year, was only a few days away, and the February 11 revolution was only a month old. Tehran, a city with four distinct seasons, was experiencing the last freezing nights of the receding winter. The prisoner was awakened and ordered to dress. He looked weak and wan.[5] He put on his new pair of glasses. In the chaos of the first hours when he had surrendered to the Islamic authorities, he had lost his reading glasses. Fereshteh Ensha had brought him a new pair; she recognized them in photographs of Hoveyda.[6] A two-day stubble darkened his pallid face. He had lost fifty pounds over the last few weeks, giving him a gaunt, almost desolate appearance. Before leaving his makeshift cell, the guard insisted on placing a scapular-like sign around Hoveyda's neck. It was reminiscent of the common cruelties of China's

---

* All of Dr. Fereshteh Ensha's visits were granted because she had been Hoveyda's doctor for many years.

† The note is in the possession of Fereshteh Ensha. Parts of it she deemed too private to publish. We agreed that we would read the entire letter together, but I would quote only the parts she agreed to. We read the note in March 1998, during my visit to her mother's house in Paris. Tears rolled down the mother's face as she heard her daughter read the letter.

Cultural Revolution, where deposed leaders, cardboard hats on their heads and crude signs on their chests, were forced to run the gauntlet of the self-appointed commissars of revolutionary purity. Hoveyda's emblem of penitence was a piece of cardboard dangling round his neck from a piece of twine woven through two clumsily made holes.[7] His name was awkwardly handwritten on it. Its perfunctory appearance and the unusual time of the trial were all a ruse to disguise the premeditated purpose of humiliating the prisoner and breaking his resolve.

The ploy worked. There was an air of discomposure about Hoveyda when he entered the big room. He was sweating profusely. Journalists reported that when he first walked into the room, he had no idea why he was there. Khalkhali's stern face was the only clue he needed. Hoveyda's every gesture, the rapid movement of his eyes, the agitated expression on his face were clear indications of his anxious state.[8] Some three hundred people were in the room.[9] These were not the accused's family or crime aficionados; this moment of history was intended for the revolution's privileged. As Hoveyda looked around the room, he only recognized a few faces: a couple of the journalists he had known in the past and the prosecutor he had met the day before.

He was led to the only empty chair in the hall. He slumped down, his head deep in his shoulders, his hands tight together over his groin. By the time he sat down, however, he had regained some of his composure. All his life, he had the reputation of a survivor, a consummate master of the art of compromise. Could his talents save him yet again? He appeared, ironically, relieved to learn the purpose of the gathering. Before the proceedings began, he took his first step to take some control of the room. Ever a gentleman, he apologized for the way he was dressed. "What I wear is all I have," he said. He went on to add, in a tone of jocund irony, that "everyone here knows both my face and my name," and then asked permission to remove the humiliating sign around his neck.[10] Khalkhali gave his consent.

One of the journalists took advantage of a brief lull in the proceedings to ask Hoveyda whether he knew who had been the ghostwriter of the shah's last book, *Toward the Great Civilization.** Fighting for his life in

---

* Hoveyda knew the book *Toward the Great Civilization* well. It had been written in 1976 and hailed as His Majesty's brilliant blueprint for the future of Iran. Hoveyda's brother Fereydoun, Iran's ambassador to the

front of the Islamic Tribunal, Hoveyda cautiously whispered, "Don't quote me, but it was written with the help of Shojaedin Shafa."[11] The journalist, of course, did quote him the next day. Hardly had the conversation ended, when a mullah began reciting Koranic verses, which were fast becoming the new compulsory ritual for commencing every meeting in Islamic Iran. "In the name of God the merciful," the mullah recited in Arabic, which according to Islam is the language of God. Like Latin in medieval Europe, Arabic is the only sanctioned language of prayer and recitation of the Koran. But God works in mysterious ways sometimes. That early morning, Hoveyda was on trial as "An Enemy of God" and a "Corrupter of the Earth," yet few in that room could probably match his mastery of Arabic.

After the perfunctory Koranic verses, it was Khalkhali's turn to speak. He said, "In the name of God the merciful" and then declared the court in session. A normal court requires a clearly delineated topography, meaningful boundaries, and rigidly respected and ritualized solemnities. At one end, perched on a lofty bench, sits the judge—ideally, at least, impartial and impervious to prejudice and pressure. Equidistant from the bench stand the two identical tables behind which the accused and the accuser sit, while the audience is kept a safe distance from the proceedings. In Khalkhali's court, however, the prosecutor was an accomplice of the judge and sat next to him, along with a panel of advisors. The seating arrangement left no doubt that the judge, the prosecutor, and the advisors were all part of the same team. Meanwhile, Hoveyda was placed in a chair, in the midst of the audience, rubbing elbows with those sitting next to him. Behind the apparent informality of the proceeding, behind the absence of ritualized solemnities, there lurked the cruelty of a lynch mob that masqueraded as Islamic revolutionary justice. Furthermore, the indictment was treated more as a verdict, vindicated by God and history, than a set of accusations in need of scrutiny and judgment. To underscore the verdict's foregone conclusion, there wasn't even a table for Hoveyda to take notes. He listened impatiently as the indictment was read.

United Nations, and a seasoned intellectual of high culture and refined taste, was chosen to translate the book into French. The shah had been in a particular hurry to have the book published in Europe. On several occasions, Fereydoun had talked to his brother about some moments of embarrassing grandiosity in the shah's narrative. "Don't you think I know?" Amir Abbas had said with some indignation, insisting that the book's many merits still outweighed its shortcomings. In spite of his many reservations, Fereydoun continued to translate the book. "Refusal was not an option," he said. Fereydoun Hoveyda, interviewed by author, 6 December 1997.

It was a much-anticipated document. Hoveyda was, after all, the highest official of the *ancien régime* to fall into the hands of Islamic authorities. He had been at the center of power for the past fifteen years, and his name had become synonymous with the glories and the failings of the fallen monarchy. The revolution had won power on the strength of slogans, which were wide in appeal and short in detail. Dislodging the monarchy had been offered as a panacea for all social ills. Now the revolution had a chance to make a reasoned argument for its legitimacy. Furthermore, breaches of human rights, military tribunals, and show trials had figured prominently in the roster of complaints against the old regime. The revolution could show, by example, the kind of justice it hoped to deliver. It could put the past on trial and set the record clear. In the end, however, passion for a quick revenge won. Of high drama, memorable rhetoric, historical revelations, judicial acumen, there was little in Hoveyda's trial. Instead, the Islamic Revolution had chosen flagrantly to disregard even the rudiments of a fair trial.

The indictment read:

> Amir Abbas Hoveyda, son of Habibollah, birth certificate number 3542, issued in Tehran, born in 1295 [1917], previously minister of the deposed royal court, and the shah's ex-prime minister, a citizen of Iran, is accused of:
>
> 1. Spreading corruption on earth.
>
> 2. Fighting God, God's creatures and the Viceroy of Imam Zaman, may praise be upon him.*
>
> 3. Acts of sedition detrimental to national security and independence, through forming cabinets that were puppets of the United States and England and defending the interests of colonialists.
>
> 4. Plotting against national sovereignty by interference in elections to Majlis, appointing and dismissing ministers at the behest of foreign embassies.
>
> 5. Turning over underground resources: oil, copper and uranium, to foreigners.
>
> 6. Expansion of the influence of American Imperialism, and its European allies, in Iran by destroying internal resources and turning Iran into a market for foreign commodities.

---

* Imam Zaman is the anticipated twelfth Imam of the Shiites. The reference to his viceroy is an allusion to Ayatollah Khomeini.

7. Paying national revenues from oil to shah and Farah and to countries dependent on the West and then borrowing money at high interest, and enslaving conditions from America and Western countries.

8. Ruining agriculture and destroying forests.

9. Direct participation in acts of espionage for the West and Zionism.

10. Complicity with conspirators from CENTO and NATO for the oppression of the peoples of Palestine, Vietnam and Iran.

11. Active member of Freemasonry in the Foroughi Lodge according to existing documents and the confessions of the accused.

12. Participation in terrorizing and frightening the justice seeking people including their death and injury and limiting their freedom by closing down newspapers and exercising censorship on the print media and books.

13. Founder and first secretary of the despotic "Rastakhiz of the Iranian People" party.*

14. Spreading cultural and ethical corruption and direct participation in consolidating the pillars of colonialism and granting capitulatory rights to Americans.

15. Direct participation in smuggling heroin in France along with Hassan-Ali Mansur.

16. False reporting through the publication of puppet papers and appointing puppet editors to head the media.

17. According to minutes of cabinet meetings and of the Supreme Economic Council, and the claims of private plaintiffs, including Dr. Ali-Asghar Hadj-Seyyed-Djavadi, and taking into account documents found in SAVAK and the office of the prime minister, and the confessions of Dr. Manouchehr Azmoun,† Mahmoud Jafarian,‡ Parviz Nick-khah,§ and the confessions of the accused, since the commission

---

* The Rastakhiz of the Iranian People Party was the single resurgence party.

† Manouchehr Azmoun was a communist in his youth, then joined SAVAK, and eventually became a cabinet minister. The Islamic Republic executed him.

‡ Mahmoud Jafarian, a high-ranking official in Iranian radio and television, was also rumored to have been a member of SAVAK. The Islamic Republic executed him.

§ Parviz Nick-khah was a member of the opposition and spent four years in prison until he decided that the "White Revolution" had indeed helped move Iran toward a more modern and equitable society. Bravely defiant at his trial, the Islamic Republic executed him.

of the crimes is certain, the prosecutor of the Islamic Revolutionary Court asks the court to issue the judgment of the death penalty and the confiscation of all your property.[12]

The form of the indictment, long on its catalogue of general accusations, was revealing in its commissions and omissions. Contrary to persistent rumors that had haunted Hoveyda ever since he had taken office as prime minister, he was not accused of being a Bahai. On the eve of the revolution, many documents, including registries, belonging to Bahai circles fell into the hands of the new regime. Had there been any credible evidence connecting Hoveyda to the Bahais, it would have certainly figured prominently in the indictment. Equally important was the indictment's silence about personal graft and corruption. Hoveyda had always taken pride in his own financial probity; for what it was worth, the indictment was a vindication of this pride.

Nonetheless, like the revolution, the indictment trafficked in slogans. It offered an eclectic mix of old leftist catch phrases and new Islamic radicalism.

Aside from the alleged confessions, the indictment gave as evidence of Hoveyda's guilt "the claims of private plaintiffs, including Dr. Ali-Asghar Hadj-Seyyed-Djavadi." Ironically, there is far more judicial acumen, and a much more detailed discussion of the question of Hoveyda's constitutional and political responsibility in that private complaint than in all of the court's indictment. Written in June 1977, the complaint was in fact an essay, mimeographed and distributed in limited numbers in Tehran. It was one of the first political salvos in the unfolding movement toward a more democratic Iran. A dissident of long standing, Hadj-Seyyed-Djavadi had, in his own words, "wanted to attack the shah. But in 1977 a direct assault on the shah was still deemed recklessly dangerous."[13] Hoveyda was thus attacked primarily as a ruse for attacking the monarch.

The essay accused "Mr. Hoveyda and all of his ministers" of breaking at least fifty-six principles of the Iranian constitution, including those mandating freedom of press and association, as well as the independence of the judiciary. It talked of torture and censorship during Hoveyda's tenure and his tenacious denial of their existence.[14] It referred to different articles of the Amendments to the Constitution that stipulated clearly that the shah must reign and not rule. It pointed out that the constitution warned that ministers were not responsible to the shah but to the parliament, and that no written or oral command of the king could absolve any minister, or prime minister, from legal responsibility. It talked about the collective responsibility of the cabinet and thus declared that Hoveyda and all of his ministers were responsible and accountable for every crime committed by SAVAK.

The last section of the essay referred to articles of the Iranian constitution and the Declaration of Human Rights positing freedom of association as an inalienable right of every man and woman. Referring to the Resurgence Party, Hadj-Seyyed-Djavadi claimed that during Hoveyda's tenure people's rights of free association were repeatedly abrogated. The essay went on to chronicle a number of other breaches of the law and challenged Hoveyda to come to a court of law, "Even under the current judicial system, so entirely under the yoke of your police."[15] Hoveyda never took up the challenge. In August 1977, he told a confidant that "the recent expression of dissent and the spate of letter-writing have their origin not in Iran."[16] Hadj-Seyyed-Djavadi was invited to participate in Khalkhali's so-called trial but refused to take part.[17]

No sooner was the dread litany read than Hoveyda began to object. On the day after the victory of the Islamic Revolution, when he was forced to participate in a news conference, there was defiant buoyancy in his tone. He even went so far as to reprimand a belligerent interviewer for acting more like a prosecutor than a journalist. "This is a news conference," he had said indignantly, "not a court of law."[18] But now, as he began to speak, the sharp edges of his wit seemed dulled by a gradually deepening sense of resignation and fear. "I have never seen, or read, this indictment before," he declared. He asked whether he should not have been given some time to prepare for his defense? He objected to the timing of the trial. He reminded the court that he had met with a prosecutor that very afternoon and that he had been given twenty questions. "I was to be given ample time to prepare my defense," he said.* He confessed that he had already

---

* Until a few months ago, Persian newspapers from the early months of the revolution, along with a handful of memoirs were my only sources about what actually transpired in the trial. The government has never published a full and reliable record of the proceedings. In a recently published Persian biography of Hoveyda, however, the last two chapters are devoted to the trial, and though no source is given in the text, the structure of the narrative, the kind of punctuation used, all make it look like an actual transcript of the trial. I have used this source only when I have been able to corroborate its material with accounts provided in Iranian newspapers of the time. See Khosrow Moatazed, *Hoveyda, Siyasatmadar-e peep asa va orkid* [Hoveyda: The Politician of Pipe, Cane and Orchid] (Tehran, 1999).

taken a sleeping pill, prescribed by the prison doctor, when he was awakened and ordered to dress for the trial. "How can I respond to such an indictment in my present condition?" he asked.[19] Without jest, Khalkhali suggested that the time of the trial was simply a matter of coincidence. "The Court of Islamic Justice," Khalkhali declared, "works around the clock. Day and night is no different. We convene the court, as soon as all the evidence is gathered."[20]

Hoveyda then began his assault on the indictment itself. In words carefully calibrated to be clear but not confrontational, he declared that he had never made the confessions the indictment alleged. He informed the court that convening the trial now was in contradiction to an agreement he had reached that very afternoon with the prosecutor. "Our conversation was taped," he said, adding that "the prosecutor asked me twenty questions, and I convinced him that I needed time, and some documents, to prepare my defense."[21] Hoveyda had indeed sought the help of his family to search for statistics and documents he felt he needed for his own defense. The great bulk of what he had asked for was evidence of Iran's impressive economic and social progress during the years of his tenure.[22]

"Since your arrest," Khalkhali said, "you've had ample opportunity to make your case to the prosecutor, and prepare your defense." Hoveyda dared to disagree. "Ever since my surrender," he responded, "I have had only two conversations with anyone in an official capacity."[23] The two interrogations had lasted no more than a few hours. The judge's response would be hard to match even in the annals of kangaroo courts. "Most of the charges against you," he said, "are general in nature and need no proof or evidence."[24]

As the proceedings continued, it became clear that rules of evidence, notions of innocence until proven guilty, and a dispassionate judge, dispensing impartial judgments based on incontrovertible evidence, were all alien to this court. Here, the judge was more vituperative than the prosecutor. There was no jury, nor was the accused allowed to have a defense attorney. Gossip had the authority of fact, as evident in article fifteen of the indictment, and unsubstantiated rumors were taken as proof of guilt. The judge would later boast in his memoirs about his forceful and unrelenting attack on Hoveyda in the court. "I had him so flustered," wrote Khalkhali, "that he could hardly talk."[25]

It did not take long for the hapless prisoner to recognize that not only was the trial unlike anything he had envisioned, but that his fate had already been decided. The proceedings were a mere formality. He began by first taking semantic issue with the indictment's most dangerous charge. How could a mere mortal, he asked, fight the infinite power of God? How could a Muslim, born to a devout Muslim mother, fight the heavens?[26]

Hoveyda conceded that granting capitulatory rights to Americans in 1964 was a mistake, but he argued that when these rights were granted, he was still only at the finance ministry and, more importantly, out of the country at the time. The argument was disingenuous at best, for Hoveyda certainly knew that according to the Iranian constitution, the cabinet bears collective responsibility for the acts of government.[*]

On the charge of smuggling heroin in Paris, in 1944, he retorted angrily that the source of the allegation was a leftist newspaper of dubious repute, and if the court was going to give credence to such sources, then he would have nothing more to say in the trial. Indeed, it was in discussing this charge that Hoveyda gallantly challenged the very legitimacy of the court. "Your honor," he said, "this indictment is weak; the court must take back this indictment."[27] He reminded the court that had he been guilty of smuggling, there was sure to be some evidence, some record, in the French foreign ministry or even in the file of Interpol. He then offered a wager: "If it is found that I have indeed committed such crimes, then I accept my guilt." The Hanging Judge curtly dismissed the bet and invited Hoveyda to continue with his defense.[28]

On the more nebulous, but serious, charges of sedition and treason, Hoveyda tried to deflect individual responsibility by placing the blame on the system. He said that he did not create the old system but only served it. He suggested that his responsibility was no more than anyone else who lived under the monarchy. He was only a cog in the great wheel of the old machine. Under his watch, along with the many mistakes that were made, much was also accomplished. In being judged, he suggested, both aspects had to be taken into consideration. Hoveyda emphasized that he had nothing to do with running the SAVAK, and all evidence clearly indicates that he was justified in his claim. He also denied any role in censorship, or in placing his cronies as editors of Tehran newspapers.[29] He reminded the

* On more than one occasion, Hoveyda had reminded his ministers of the collective responsibility of ministers in the cabinet.

court that foreign policy, and matters relating to the army and to Iran's oil policy were altogether the monopoly of the king. His voice boomed with anger when he declared that, as prime minister, he learned of the Iranian military's engagement in Oman's civil war more than a month after the invasion had taken place. Defiantly he declared that even members of the tribunal could not shirk responsibility for the old regime since they, too, had lived under that system and tolerated it.[30]

Khalkhali then asked a question that many of Hoveyda's friends had asked him before: "Why didn't you resign, when you realized that you could not perform your constitutional duties?"[31] Hoveyda skirted the question by saying that all he could be accused of was a failure to exercise all of his constitutional powers.

Despite Khalkhali's forfeiture of even a pretense to impartiality, despite the court's disregard for even a semblance of due process, the charges levied against Hoveyda posed some fundamental questions central to any historical judgment of him. Was Hoveyda a victim, or at best an accomplice, to a corrupt system of despotic rule? Did he help create and consolidate that system? Ironically, the Islamic Tribunal was not alone in denying Hoveyda's claim that he was only a victim of the system. Many in the royal family and quite a few royalists have also found Hoveyda more a culprit than a victim. In an interview with Edouard Sablier, the shah, not long after he had left Iran, angrily dismissed the idea that he should have freed Hoveyda while he still had the power to do so, saying, curtly, "he lied to us."[32] The shah's twin sister, Princess Ashraf, also placed much of the blame for the fall of the Pahlavi regime on Hoveyda's shoulders. She is reported to have said, "[He] lied to my brother for fourteen years and did nothing to arrest the thieves."[33] Princess Ashraf's claim, as well as the shah's argument are both hard to take seriously. Over the years, in fact numerous people told the shah about the deteriorating conditions, rampant corruption and the unhappiness of the people. If Alam is to be believed, hardly a week went by without him reminding the shah of the growing sense of discontent in the country. Though Alam blames nearly all of the problems on Hoveyda's incompetence, he nevertheless was constantly warning the shah of the worsening situation. In August 1977, while in France in the hope of curing his cancer, Alam wrote a long letter to the shah, outlining the serious nature of the crisis and the growing disgruntlement of the people.[34]

Alam was not the only one sending the shah letters of warning. In early 1977 another trusted advisor and the head of the NIOC, Manouchehr Eghbal, wrote a note to the shah, cautioning that "people are unhappy in the country." The shah told Eghbal that he "had lost touch and that the shah knew better."[35]

The other important question the trial raised, but did not address, was ethical in nature. It touched on the serious question of individual responsibility for collective, or systematic, acts. Is silence in the face of perfidy tantamount to committing a perfidious act? If the court that tried Hoveyda had any semblance of legitimacy, it could have raised, discussed, and even come to some judgment on these important questions.

Instead, the judge relished generalities, and when the discussion ground to an impasse, Hoveyda ended his defense by talking about his private life. "I bear no grudge against anyone," he said; "my life is like a crystal ball. My hands are clean from the taint of blood or financial corruption."[36] He reminded the court that had he been guilty, he, too, would now be promenading on the Champs Elysées, just as five other former prime ministers were doing. "I chose to stay," he said, "because I love my country and am convinced of my own innocence."[37] He then talked of his simple life; of worldly possessions, he said, he only had a house, which had already been confiscated by "Revolutionary Committees." He talked of his attachment to his aging mother. "She is eighty years old now," he said, "and I love her dearly."[38] He then implored the court to keep her away from the proceedings. "I hope she never sees me in this condition," he declared wistfully, "let her be happy with the pleasant memories of the past."*[39]

As Hoveyda began to talk about his mother, a surge of emotion overcame him. With subdued dignity, he pulled out a white handkerchief from his pocket, and slowly wiped his eyes and face. In a voice halting in its delivery but commanding in the power of the emotions it conjured, he asked the court to adjourn and allow him more time to prepare for his defense. It was close to three in the morning. The "Hanging Judge" consented. One can only surmise that an important factor in the judge's decision might

---

* Hoveyda had also left two letters, one for the shah, the other for the queen, beseeching the royal couple to help his mother. The letters had been written shortly before his arrest. They never reached their destination. Both were burned along with numerous other documents left behind by Hoveyda. Maryam Ensha, interviewed by author, Pacific Palisade, California, 15 February 1998. Fereshteh Ensha had read the letters before they were burned and told me of their content. Fereshteh Ensha, interviewed by author, Paris, France, 2 June 1998.

well have been that many in the Islamic government, particularly Prime Minister Bazargan, were working hard behind the scene to ensure that Hoveyda received a public trial. Whatever the impetus, with the adjournment, Hoveyda had won a temporary reprieve.

CHAPTER SIXTEEN

The Frozen Lake of Cocytus*

The mere breath
Of memory stirs the old fear in blood.
—Dante, *Divine Comedy*

K halkhali begins his account of Hoveyda's second trial with a reference to what he himself ate for lunch that day. The date was April 7, 1979, and by the time he arrived at Qasr Prison, the kitchen, he tells us, had already run out of food. Lunch had been rice with dill and lima beans. "I ate bread and cheese, and then started to get the court ready," he writes.[1] Though accounts of culinary delights figure prominently throughout his mangled memoirs, it is hard to miss the political significance of the "bread and cheese" allusion in the opening paragraph of his trial diary.

In the Persian vernacular, "bread and cheese" is not just a description but a metaphor. While the leg of a turkey or of a chicken conjures the food of the rich, "bread and cheese" is no less a metaphor for folksy humility and simplicity. In other words, Khalkhali's account of the trial begins with political posturing. Here is a man of the people, it implies, out to punish and pass judgment on one of the servants of the decadent and deposed oppressor.

---

* In Dante's *Divine Comedy*, the Frozen Lake of Cocytus is the ninth circle of Hell.

In an apparent attempt to truly lay bare the moral turpitude of Hoveyda and the regime he served, Khalkhali uses a rather revealing anecdote. "This Hoveyda," he opines in his own uniquely clumsy style of prose, "slept a lot in prison, but he did it stark naked, and the guards objected to this fact several times."[2] Traditional men in Iran are generally ill at ease with a naked body, even their own, and rarely, if ever, sleep without a shirt and shorts. Contrary to the West, where personal comfort is usually the only criterion for deciding the kind of clothing one will, or will not, wear to bed, Iran's traditional demands of a puritan piety usually dictate the choice. The Islamic Revolution in Iran was, certainly for the Islamic forces, partially a culture war, a clash between the Western-inspired modernizing ethos of the Pahlavi regime on one hand and traditional Islamic elements of society on the other. Consequently Khalkhali's complaint about how Hoveyda slept in his solitary cell becomes not only more meaningful but also a clue to the range of issues and differences—everything from the mundane to the fundamental direction of society—that separated Hoveyda from his captors.

Qasr Prison by then had become an "antechamber of death" for those arrested on the eve of the revolution. There was always a contingent of reporters around the compound, waiting to cover a new round of executions. Around two in the afternoon of April 7, all doors to the prison were suddenly locked from inside. No one, including reporters, was allowed to leave. Phone lines were ordered disconnected. As an extra precautionary measure, Khalkhali decided to hide all the telephones inside a refrigerator.[3]

The strange, and extreme, security precautions had little to do with any fear of a terrorist attack. Rather, they rose out of the harsh and uncompromising rivalries between different factions of the Islamic regime. Khalkhali's intention, as he makes clear himself, was only to ensure that the Provisional Revolutionary Government of Iran did not learn about the resumption of Hoveyda's trial. All along, Bazargan, the mild-mannered prime minister of that government, had been against Khalkhali's brand of justice. Some three weeks earlier, as the two men were waiting for an audience in Ayatollah Khomeini's antechamber, their verbal disagreements about the conduct of the revolutionary tribunals had escalated into a physical scuffle.[4]

Even before that confrontation, Bazargan and his allies had mounted a full campaign to end the embarrassing summary trials. They wanted to ensure that Hoveyda received a public trial commensurate with internationally recognized standards of justice and human rights. Some have suggested that arrangements had already been made for a French attorney—a jurist named Le Blanc, in one account, or Edgar Faure, once himself a prime minister, in another—to fly to Iran and act as Hoveyda's attorney. Hoveyda's brother, Fereydoun, who had wisely decided not to return to Iran after the fall of the Pahlavi regime along with many of his other friends abroad, had helped marshal international public opinion in favor of a fair trial for the imperiled ex-prime minister. From the secretary general of the United Nations to six past and present French premiers, from writers like Jerzy Kosinski in America to a large contingent of French intellectuals, all had made appeals to the new government in Iran to spare Hoveyda's life.[5]

Hoveyda was well aware of these efforts and had begun to take some action of his own in prison. In the first week of April, he succeeded in smuggling out of prison a handwritten note. The document is extraordinary not just on account of the dire and dangerous circumstances under which it was composed and carried out of prison but because it is the only written evidence we have of what Hoveyda thought about the plans that led to his arrest under the shah's regime and those most responsible for the decision. Furthermore, the note seems partly addressed to posterity. In it Hoveyda is bent on taking an active part in shaping his own legacy. On some crucial points, he wants to put on record his narrative of the events. At the same time, the note shows not only his mood, and his expectations, but also the strategy he hoped to pursue. Finally, it shows the active role he took in his own defense.

In contrast to the despairing note he had sent out earlier, there was more buoyancy, and a hint of hope, in his tone. This time, Hoveyda wrote in English and addressed the letter to Fereshteh Ensha's brother, Ali. As the convoluted syntax of some of the sentences in the following pages indicates, he obviously wrote the note in some hurry:

1. I have added a paragraph to my note (in red) requesting to receive as soon as possible a typed text on <u>MOHARREBEH</u> and <u>BOHTAN</u>* giving the necessary explanations for the court and the name of the *Koran Sourats*.† I will also appreciate to receive the list of the religious books which might be of interest for my defense. I could ask people here to buy them for me.

2. I will try to see as soon as possible the *Dadsetan Kol*‡ to talk about the future and get a copy of the prosecution *Kayfar khast*.§

3. I think you should think about a panel of lawyers adapted for this kind of defense. <u>Angel</u>** has talked to someone—it is better you contact her.

4. Ask our friend who has contact in Bazaar and religious circles if we could get also (added to other lawyers) an expert on religious matters. Does he think that <u>FALSAFI</u>†† will be ready to do something about it (in court, if this not possible, out-side court?) (TV-Press?)

5. There are few ideas I wish to explain here: Why have I been arrested on Wednesday 17 Aban. This was a plot under Zahedi (which started with Sharif-Emami and Amini) and army people to bring the Shah to accept the idea to put all the blames about everything which took place in this country during the last 15 years on me. The Shah would say he didn't know about anything, and how he got the assurance from the people. *Ruz as no, ruzi as no* [new day, new start]. This was a stupid idea and

Facing page: A copy of the first page of Hoveyda's original letter smuggled out of prison.

---

* Moharebeh (fighting god) and Bohtan (libel) were written in capital letters in the original text. All italicized words were written in Persian in the original. The underlined words, or sentences are all as they appear in the original.

† Suras (sections) of the Koran.

‡ Attorney General.

§ Persian word for indictment.

** Angel is underlined in the original letter. It is a code for Dr. Fereshteh Ensha. *Fereshteh* in Persian means "angel."

†† Falsafi was a controversial Iranian cleric who posed as an opponent of the royal regime but also kept in close contact with men of power in those times. When Hoveyda was the prime minister, Falsafi had on more than one occasion asked for, and received, favors.

(1) I have added a paragraph to my note (in red) requesting to receive as soon as possible a typed text on MOHAREBEH and BOUTAN giving the necessary explanations for the court and the name of the Koran sourats (سورتهای). I will also appreciate to receive the list of the religious books which might be of interest for my defense. I could ask people here to buy them for me

(2) I will try to see as soon as possible the فرنگیس to talk about the future and get a copy of the prosecution كیفرخواست.

(3) I think you should think about a panel of lawyers adapted for this kind of defense. Angel has talked to someone - it's better you contact her.

(4) Ask our friend who has contacts in bazar and religious circles if we could get also (added to other lawyers) an expert on religious matters. Does he think that FALSAFI will be ready to do something about it (in court; if this not possible outside court?) (TV- press?)

(5) There are few ideas I wish to explain here: why have I been arrested "Wednesday 17 ABan. There was a plot under Zahedi (which started with Sharif-Emani and Amini) and as my people to bring blames to accept the idea to put all the blames about everything which has took place in this country during the last 15 years on me. The shah would say he did'nt know about anything, and how he got the news from the people - these اطرافیان چاپلوس. This was a stupid idea and

people would not accept this as a solution. Don't forget how the press and M.P.s in Majlis started their attacks after my resignation. Zahedi and his group wanted to make a <u>Ghorbani</u> [sacrifice] out of me and the Shah did cave in. (Amouzegar helped.)

6. Why and when did I <u>presented</u> [sic] my resignation from the Court Ministry? <u>Saturday 18 Shahrivar:</u> It means the day after the <u>Black Friday</u> when so many people were killed. <u>This was not a solution. I told the Shah and I left. Few days later when I moved from my residence and he got a Court Minister.</u> I was against what they did.

7. I think these two informations [sic] could be used in public and private* speaking by our friend of the bazaar and the religious circles.

8. Too many people have been arrested—ministers, army people, officials…It will take ages before a trial is set for anyone. Really, the last regime should be purged, and this would include over two million people.

9. I think we should find when the court will get in session and what to do about the lawyers—in this connection, get in touch with Angel.

10. What was the result of foreign personalities demands? I think we can use the Shiites of Lebanon and other Moslems through former Lebanon P.M. Takieddine Solh—to get a delegation here. I think Angel knows about it and she should be contacted. <u>I don't know when she will be back.</u>

11. In your note, give me a gist of what is happening—I am really out of everything.

12. As far as it concerns the channel, please ask Angel to do what is necessary.[†]

Facing page: A copy of page two of Hoveyda's original letter smuggled out of prison.

---

* This word is illegible in the original, "private" is our best guess.

† I received a copy of this extraordinary document courtesy of Dr. Ensha.

people would not accept this as an
ocultion. Don't forget how the press
and m.p. in majlas started their attacks
after my resignation. Zahedi and his group
wanted to make a gorbani (؟؟) out of
me and the Shah did give in. (Amozegar helped)

(6) why and when did I presented my
resignation from the court ministry?
Saturday 18 shahrivar: it means the day
after the Black Friday where so many people
were killed. This was not a sinetion I told
the Shah & I left few days later when
I moved from my residence and no got
a court minister I was against what they did.
I think these no injunctions could be
used in small speciality areas of friend
of the bazaar and religious circles.

(8) Too many people have been arrested - ministers -
army people - officials..... it will take ans
before a trial is set for everyone. Really
the past regime should be judged and this
would include over two million people.

(9) I think we should find when the court
will get in session - and what to do about
the lawyers - in this connection get in
touch with Angel.

(10) What was the result of foreign
personalities demarches? I think we can
use the shiite of Lebanon and other moslem
through former Lebanon P.M. Takieddine
Solh - to get a delegation here - I think
Angel knew about it and she should be
contacted. I don't know when she will be back.

(11) In your notes give me a gist of
what is happening - I am really out of
everything.

(12) As far as it concerns the channel
please ask Angel to do what is necessary.

The "channel" was one of the guards at the prison. Acting on his own initiative, and with greed as his only apparent motive, he contacted Hoveyda's family and suggested that for the right recompense, he would be willing to carry messages back and forth between Hoveyda and his relatives. By then the family had become wary of such offers. Several other people, claiming to be prison guards, had earlier called the family with similar offers of help. They all turned out to be nothing but hoaxers and frauds, hoping to milk an anxious family. The "channel" however delivered on his promises, and his demands were not exorbitant. The most expensive payoff he ever asked for was a color television, and thus "channel" became his code name.[6]

Hoveyda did not limit his activities to sending these surreptitious messages. Early in April, he also sent a note to Asadollah Mobasheri, the minister of justice in the Provisional Revolutionary Government, asking for a private meeting.* He further indicated that should his trial be public, he would then reveal all he knew about the nature of the Pahlavi regime and its secrets. Hoveyda knew that his only hope for due process, his remote chance of survival, rested with the Provisional Government. But Mobasheri, though nominally the highest judicial authority of the land, was unable to even arrange a visit with Hoveyda. Prison authorities, apparently acting at the behest of clerics like Khalkhali, refused to allow the meeting.[7]

Frustrated in his efforts, Mobasheri solicited the help of Bani Sadr. As they both knew, in all matters of import—and Hoveyda's trial was surely such—ultimate authority was with Ayatollah Khomeini. They took a short helicopter flight from Tehran to Qom and asked for an audience with the ayatollah. They took a sack full of documents and a note from Hoveyda, scribbled on a small piece of yellow paper. "Here we have," they told the patriarch, "documents gathered by the ministry of justice that show a pattern of corruption in the old regime. Hoveyda is willing to tell all he knows, if he is allowed to have a public trial."[8] Bani Sadr insisted that such a trial would be a political bonanza and a perfect chance for the revolution to make its case in the court of public opinion. "We shall thus be vindicated," he told his mentor.[9]

The old man first demurred. "These criminals need no trial," he said. Eventually, he was apparently convinced. He told them to go back to Tehran and prepare the work for the trial. The meeting ended late in the

---

* When in his twelve point note Hoveyda wrote of his intention to see as soon as possible the "attorney general," he might have been alluding to his note to Mobasheri.

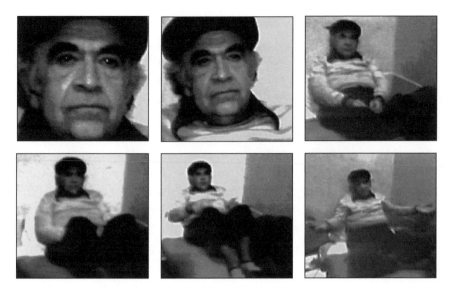

Still shots of Hoveyda in Qasr Prison just before his second trial from a videotape.

afternoon. Mobasheri decided to visit Hoveyda in prison the next day and inform him of the new arrangements.[10]

However, in spite of the ayatollah's words of assurance, a few hours after the audience, at about three in the afternoon, Hoveyda was brought before a tribunal of the "Hanging Judge." "No one other than Khomeini," Bani Sadr ventured to guess, "had the authority to order the trial."[11] Over the years, Khalkhali has confirmed this fact by repeatedly declaring, most recently to a *New York Times* reporter, that "Everything I did, I did under the holy authority of the Imam. I did only what he wanted."[12]

Caught in a web of factional intrigue, frightened by the possibility of a royalist restoration, worried that an earnest trial, long and judicious, would politically benefit the moderate forces, radical clerics—led by Ayatollah Khomeini—chose the politics of revenge. Bani Sadr believes that Khomeini ordered the secret trial out of fear: "While *he* was worried that his secret dealings with America would come to light, other clerics who helped change his mind about the trial were worried about their own future. When on the eve of the revolution we took over the SAVAK headquarters, some forty highly classified files, all relating to clerics close to Khomeini, mysteriously disappeared. The honorable gentlemen were worried that in a public trial, Hoveyda might talk about his government's dealings with, and covert payments to, these clerics. When later two of my aides compiled a hundred-page confidential report about secret dealings with America, both were summarily executed on trumped up charges."[13] Bani Sadr further claims that in the Revolutionary Council—a secret committee appointed by Ayatollah Khomeini and entrusted with the task of running the day-to-day affairs of the state in the early months of the revolution—everyone, at least ostensibly, was in favor of a public trial.[14] In other words, the only person who could have ordered Khalkhali to conduct the secret and summary trial was the patriarch himself. Whatever the motive, Hoveyda's trial would usher in a period of *paksazi* (purges), in the parlance of the day, that brought terror to the heart of every civil servant, every army officer, every member of the Jewish or Bahai faith, and every opponent of the regime in Iran. Islamic piety, feigned or real, turned out to be the only safe recourse for survival.

THERE WERE ABOUT FORTY PEOPLE IN THE ROOM when Hoveyda was brought in. He was wearing a suede jacket, a light crew-neck sweater with a dark shirt peering through its collar, and a pair of brown corduroy pants. A couple of days before the trial, someone from the prison called Maryam Ensha and asked her to bring him a new set of clothes.

To Maryam Ensha, the caller from the prison sounded like a villager. It had been the same voice that had called on earlier occasions. In Iran, as in other societies, linguistic habits and tropes are replete with markers that often betray the social origins of the interlocutor. In this case, she knew the cultural identity of the caller from the way he had addressed her. For nearly all the Persian men who live in villages, a woman's name is part of her honor; it is something sacred and private, a totem that must be kept from the eyes, or the ears, of all strangers. And thus, if such men have to address a woman, they do not refer to her by her own name; instead, they choose from a litany of other titles. The most common of such linguistic veils is calling a woman by the name of her son. In Ensha's case, she had become, on account of her son's name, "Mother of Ali." "Mother of Ali," the caller said curtly, "bring him some fresh clothes and his medication."[15]

The atmosphere in the room was stuffy and tense when Hoveyda entered. He was led to a chair, in the middle of the room, facing the table of judges and the prosecution. Two tiny tea tables stood next to Hoveyda's chair, giving him a tiny space on which he could take notes. On one of the tables he placed his heavy leather-bound notebook. Hoveyda had asked

Hoveyda at his trial, presided over by the "Hanging Judge."

for it the first time Dr. Ensha visited him in prison. "I want to keep a journal of what happens to me," he had said.[16] What eventually happened to it, nobody in the family knows. A photograph in which it can be seen, printed in a newspaper during the trial, would turn out to be the last trace of the notebook.

To Hoveyda, the faces in the audience apparently looked more hostile than those present in his first trial. Fewer journalists were allowed to witness the proceedings. A cleric named Hadi Ghafari—already infamous in Tehran for his reckless radicalism, his penchant for rhetoric, his craving for violence, young girls, and fancy houses—sat, like a predator, next to the accused victim. There was in Hoveyda no sign of the buoyancy of his early days as a prisoner of the revolution, of the defiant poise of a man bent on defending his record; all that was now left was a dignified resignation to a fate he felt to be both inevitable and imminent. "Are these all Revolutionary Guards?" he asked Khalkhali, with obvious discomfort. Rather than offering a direct response, the judge chose to attack the spirit of the question. "What difference does it make?" he said. "Brothers in the Revolutionary Guards are not like your SAVAK agents."[17]

Around three in the afternoon, the tribunal was called to order. "In the Name of God the Merciful," a mullah said, and recited some Koranic verses. Then the indictment was read again. No changes had been made in the substance, or the language, of the indictment. While the seventeen counts against Hoveyda were being read, the sound of an approaching helicopter brought a tense halt to the proceedings. The chopper flew low, descended parallel to the windows of the room where the court was in session, and lingered there for a long minute. No one had expected, or authorized, such a flight; its intentions—hostile or friendly—were unknown. Anxious anticipation gripped the room.[18]

What Khalkhali and Hoveyda probably did not know was that on the night before the resumption of the trial, Henry Precht, who was at the time in charge of the Iran Desk at the U.S. Department of State, received information that Hoveyda's trial was about to resume and that his life was in danger. Precht immediately sent a cable to the U.S. chargé d'affaires in Iran, Charles Naas, instructing him to contact Iranian officials and convey the U.S. government's concern for Hoveyda's life.[19]

Early in the afternoon of the next day, Naas met Ibrahim Yazdi, a highly visible, and relatively powerful member of the Provisional Revolutionary Government. No sooner had Naas broached the topic of Hoveyda than Yazdi pulled out a dossier and in a tone that was "neither friendly nor forthcoming" delivered a long disquisition on SAVAK's atrocities, and Hoveyda's complicity in them.[20] In the end, however, Yazdi reassured Naas that Hoveyda's life was in no immediate danger. In fact, by the time Yazdi uttered these words, Hoveyda's fate had already been determined by the tribunal. "I have never been sure," says Naas, "whether Yazdi already knew what had happened to Hoveyda when he gave me those words of assurance."[21]

The wait did not last long. Mysterious in its appearance, the helicopter was no less mysterious in its sudden departure and disappearance. The fleeting moments of that mysterious flight might well have been Hoveyda's last hiatus of hope. The reading of the indictment resumed. An air of imminent danger was added to the already tense atmosphere of the room. Once the reading ended, a prosecutor began to talk. Ultimately, however, he offered no new evidence. He simply reiterated, albeit in a more articulate rendition, all that had been said earlier.[22] Once the prosecutor's presentation ended, it was time for the harangue of the presiding judge. Again, in his memoirs, Khalkhali makes no pretense of impartiality. He boasts about talking incessantly for some forty minutes, recounting the crimes of the Pahlavi regime and Hoveyda's complicity in them. He makes no attempt to hide the fact that Hoveyda's fate had already been determined even before the trial began that Saturday afternoon. "We weren't going to be fooled," he writes in a frightening tone of earnest self-righteousness, "and I made every effort to ensure that before the end of the trial, even up to Hoveyda's execution, no one learned of his fate."[23]

Hearing the prosecutor's, as well as the judge's blistering attacks, listening to the indictment, gauging the somber mood of the court, and recognizing its unusual timing seemed to create a deep sense of grief, despair, and anger in Hoveyda. He began by again attacking the court's mode of operation. He declared that in recent discussions with representatives of the court, he was led to believe that a new indictment was going to be drawn up. "Which indictment is it going to be?" he asked, adding, "if the court wants to kill me, I am ready. I'll accept any decision you make. Otherwise, I must be given a chance to defend myself."[24] At one point, detecting a smile on Khalkhali's face, which he clung to as a last straw of hope, he said, "Your smile, sir, brings some comfort to my heart."[25]

In form, the two-hour ordeal was only memorable for its brazen disregard for any notion of due process. In substance, both the indictment and the harangues of the "Hanging Judge" covered much the same ground as the first trial. Hoveyda, too, did not change his basic defense strategy. He accepted only partial culpability, insisting, once again, that the ultimate culprit was the system. He offered an apology to all those who had suffered at the hands of SAVAK. He pointed out to the court that since the end of World War II, every Persian prime minister, with the exception of Mosaddeq, had operated within the same systemic parameters he worked in. "I did not know any better than to operate within the same age-old system," he said.[26] He added that foreign policy, the army, SAVAK, the oil company and its policy, and nearly all important areas of decision making had been the monopoly of the shah. He also denied being the "puppet" of the United States. "Your honor," he asked with some sarcasm, "if the Americans were really my masters, what would I be doing here now?"[27]

Hoveyda's line of defense seemed flawed in one important aspect. He was an astute student of politics and must have known that his strategy of blaming the "system" was at best on shaky constitutional, and ethical, grounds. Furthermore, early in his tenure, after an audience with the shah in the company of a group of politicians and advisors that were to guide the impending "Revolution in the Civil Services"—one in a rapidly rising list of principles of the "Shah and People Revolution"—Hoveyda drove back to his office with one of the participants in the meeting, Ehsan Naraghi. During the audience, Naraghi had, with the help of a pithy anecdote, suggested that civil servants must be taught to disobey illegal orders. In the car, while Hoveyda drove, as was his wont, with the guards in the backseat, he engaged Naraghi in a conversation. As with all sensitive discussions, this one, too, was in French. "If what you say is true," Hoveyda said, "then we are all guilty. Under the present circumstances, we have no choice but to obey the sometimes unjustifiable orders of our superior."[28] Indeed, Hoveyda had wagered, as he never tired of telling his friends, that such submission was the necessary price of progress in Iran. Throughout his years as a prime minister, many of his friends would remind him that his submission to every whim and will of the shah had gone beyond the pale of pragmatic politics. They had suggested that he should resign. Now, he was paying with his life for that wager. Yet, unjustified and unconstitutional as the wager might have been, Khalkhali's ignorance of the law, his insensitivity to any fine point of ethics, his habit of trafficking in inflammatory rhetoric, and his insistence that Hoveyda refrain from any discussion of specific points aborted the possibility of the trial ever becoming a serious forum for deciding guilt or innocence. Like Ockrent in her prison interview, the judge insisted that it was inconceivable that he, as prime minister, had no power over policy and no knowledge of SAVAK's work. Incredible as Hoveyda's claim seemed, there is much evidence to vindicate his claim. Yet, on one point Khalkhali was not only insistent but uncharacteristically correct. On more than one occasion, he repeated the notion—sound by the standards of the Iranian constitution under the Pahlavi regime itself—that as the prime minister, Hoveyda could not shirk responsibilities for breaches of law and sovereignty committed during his tenure. "You should have resigned," Khalkhali said, "when you realized that all you could do was enforce the orders of the king."[29]

In the course of these discussions, two new points were briefly raised. Hoveyda was asked whether it was true that he had in his possession a secret file documenting the corruption of the royal family and whether he would be willing to turn over the documents to the court. Hoveyda declined with diplomatic finesse. "If I am given some time," he said, "I will certainly write a book about the history of the last twenty-five years. Many ambiguous points will be clarified, and I certainly do have some documents."[30]

The other question was about Hoveyda's alleged role in financing, or facilitating, repairs to some of the religious sites of the Bahai faith located in Israel. Hoveyda was surprised by the question. No such allegations had been made in the indictment. This was, in fact, the one and only time that the question of the Bahai faith had been broached in the entire proceeding. Hoveyda denied any involvement with the repair efforts.[31]

The belligerent and unequivocal tone of Khalkhali's declamations seemed to have convinced Hoveyda that the proceedings were just a mere formality, that his fate was doomed. When the judge began yet another of his attacks, Hoveyda stopped him and said, "your honor, how can a judge talk against the accused."[32] In desperation he asked the judge, "What is it that you want me to do?"[33] Proclaiming his verdict even before the defendant had a chance to offer the summation of his defense, the judge intoned, "You are a corrupter of the earth, all you can do now is offer your last defense." Instead of attempting to make a summation of his defense, Hoveyda decided to engage Khalkhali in a discourse about the wisdom of accusing someone of "spreading corruption on earth." There was something sadly quixotic about Hoveyda's line of argument. Here was a judge already infamous for his brisk brutality,[34] thirsting for his blood, pronouncing a verdict even before the end of the kangaroo court, and part of Hoveyda's defense was to engage him in a discourse about the fine points of the Arabic language and Islamic doctrine.[35]

Hoveyda then went on to admit that he had made some mistakes but also stressed his many contributions to Iranian society. He asked to be judged for all he had done, not just for his errors. By then he seemed to have regained his almost defiant, and always dignified, posture. He then offered the most direct defense of his record. He declared that his vision for this country was just and progressive; the government only failed, he suggested, because it did not have enough time to fully implement its goals. Then he began to give statistics on social progress during his tenure, facts and figures he had asked his family to gather.[36] He had hardly begun reciting the figures when Khalkhali interrupted. "Don't delve into details," the judge declared. "I am trying to save my life here," Hoveyda retorted, "I have to talk about details." Khalkhali was not convinced. "Continue your argument, but no details," he commanded.[37]

In a final gesture of defiance, Hoveyda fluttered his right hand in the air to indicate that he would say no more to this court. It took Khalkhali only moments to come to a verdict. The other clerics on the panel—Azari, Janati, and Gilani[38]—were there as observers and would only interfere if they witnessed a gross miscarriage of justice. And having seen none so far, they remained silent!

"You are found to be a corrupter on the earth," Khalkhali declared. "You are to be executed; all your possessions shall be confiscated."[39] Covered with sweat and pale in countenance, Hoveyda made one more effort to save his own life.* "I know you will and want to kill me," he said; "give me a month to write the history of the last two decades." Time, he knew, would be on his side. Khalkhali, aware and afraid of the same fact, immediately rejected the plea. There will be many others, he declared, who will write that history. He then ordered that the condemned be removed and that everyone else remain in the room. He was still worried that someone might report the verdict to the government, who might then intercede on Hoveyda's behalf. Khalkhali, bent on carrying out his mentor's commands, was not about to let anyone spoil his moment.

Once outside the room, Hoveyda, in a last-ditch effort to at least stay the verdict, turned to Khalkhali and, apparently hoping to cash in one of the favors he was owed, asked whether he could be allowed to talk to Ahmad Khomeini. Khalkhali refused the request. "There is nothing he can do for you," he said. Then he went on a diatribe about the countless families who had suffered under the Pahlavi regime. "The big thing you did for Ahmad Aqa [Ayatollah Khomeini's son] is that supposedly you ordered that he, or the Imam's wife or daughters, be issued passports.† This is not something that can help, or exonerate, you."[40]

Hoveyda was then commanded to write his will. He refused. Khalkhali claims the refusal was a ruse to delay the execution. "He assumed we won't kill him unless he writes a will."[41] Other interpretations, however, are just as tenable. Shortly before his arrest, Hoveyda had in fact written a will and left it with one of his secretaries. He had told his brother, Fereydoun, about the document and instructed him to look for it, should anything happen to him.[42] Furthermore, writing a will under those circumstances would be tantamount to accepting the legitimacy of the shameful proceedings.

---

* In his account of the trial, Khalkhali claims that at this point, and on a couple of earlier moments, Hoveyda broke down and wept. Other accounts of the proceedings by journalists make no such claim. They all mention Hoveyda's melancholic mood.

† Hoveyda had enabled the family to join the exiled Khomeini.

Hoveyda was then led through a corridor, toward a yard. He probably knew what awaited him at the end of that walk. Hadi Ghafari, the cleric who peered at him throughout the trial, along with Khalkhali and a small coterie of clerics and Revolutionary Guards, walked behind him.

As he took the first step into the yard, someone from the group pulled out a pistol, aimed at Hoveyda's neck, and fired two shots. Hoveyda fell at the impact. Blood gushed out. Slow and painful death, rather than the quick finality of a firing squad, was apparently what they had in mind for the sixty-year-old prime minister. Mortally wounded, Hoveyda beseechingly turned to a man called Karimi, another member of the death posse, and begged for a quick death. "Please finish me," he implored. The man took the pistol and fired a final shot into Hoveyda's skull.[43] Dying, Hoveyda mustered enough energy to say, "It wasn't supposed to end like this."[44] Pictures of the corpse, the official autopsy report, and Dr. Ensha's firsthand observations of the body leave no doubt that Hoveyda was killed not by firing squad but in assassination style, with three bullets. "Those killed by the firing squad all have cobalt blue faces; almost like someone asphyxiated. No such symptoms were visible on Hoveyda's face," she said.[45] Khalkhali took away the pistol and kept it as a badge of honor, a token of his glory days of dispensing revolutionary justice. When V. S. Naipal visited the "Hanging Judge" at his house in Qom, Khalkhali still cherished his own role in the execution of Hoveyda. "I killed Hoveyda, you know," he said. When the interpreter interjected that "the son of a famous ayatollah'*" actually killed the condemned prisoner, Khalkhali added, "but I have the gun...[it] is in the other room."[46]

Once assured of Hoveyda's death, Khalkhali walked back into the courtroom and broke the news of the execution to those present. As he was leaving the prison, one of the officials asked Khalkhali, "What are we going to do with Hoveyda?" Even prison officials, it seems, had been kept in the dark about the trial and the execution. "Hoveyda is no more," Khalkhali responded and walked away.[47]

On the day of Hoveyda's execution, giddy with the exuberance of victory, the front pages of Tehran's evening newspapers were covered with grotesque pictures of his body. During the first days of the revolution, Tehran was a city with no government. Nonetheless, mobs in the capital

---

* V. S. Naipal makes clear that he is refering to Hadi Ghafari.

had been, on the whole, tame and free from the frenzy of blood retribution. Since the French Revolution, such frenzy has often characterized modern mass upheavals. But in Iran, while the masses had been relatively calm, it was the state, and its paramilitary forces, that went on a blood binge. If in the French Revolution the public display and ceremonious use of "the machine"—as the guillotine had come to be called—became the ultimate metaphor of the revolutionary spectacle of punishment, in Iran "the photo" seems to have served the same purpose.[48]

One photograph shows Hoveyda's sprawled body, partially covered by a blanket, tiny spots of clotted blood on his neck and forehead. A piece of cardboard languishes on his chest; on it is his name and no more. In another he is depicted entombed in the steely cold drawers of the morgue in the coroner's office; two men, looking more dazed than delighted, flaunting their guns, stand over his body. Despite the ungainliness that often comes with rigor mortis, there is a disarming dignity about the corpse. Counterpoised to these macabre images are pictures of Hoveyda during his trial, as well as old photos from his days in power.

There was calculated malice in the selection of these old pictures as well. In one, he is shown bent over like a bow, kissing the hand of the monarch. In another, he looks clownish in a big cowboy hat, a gift from Richard Helms, who was the United States ambassador to Iran in the early seventies. The implicit message of the photo was hard to miss. In Persian, "to put a hat on someone" means to fool or cheat them. Helms and America had fooled Hoveyda.

In more normal and civilized times, those bearing news of death to the immediate family of the victim often use what discretion they can muster. In revolutionary times, all too often, such civilities are replaced by petty cruelties masquerading as revolutionary justice or populist vengeance.

First there was the call. The same voice that had called before, rang Maryam Ensha's house at around seven thirty in the evening of that fateful Saturday. Ever since the day her son was arrested, Hoveyda's mother had been staying at Maryam Ensha's house. That afternoon, the living room was filled with a small group of septuagenarian ladies, invited to the house at the behest of Hoveyda's mother. She wanted to lead a special prayer and in a gesture of supplication to God, the ladies had all placed their Korans on their heads. As they murmured verses from the holy book, they wailed and rocked solemnly to the tune of their private grief. The bursting sound of the ringing phone forced them all into a moment of anxious silence.

Maryam Ensha picked up the receiver. "Is this the Mother of Ali?" the voice boomed. Once assured of the listener's identity, with a cruel brevity, the voice said, "You don't have to bring him clothes no more. He was executed a few minutes ago." Stunned, yet under the anxious scrutiny of every eye in the room, she knew she had to put on a face to meet the anxious mournful gaze of Hoveyda's mother and her praying companions. "Thank you very much," she said to the caller; then with studied calm, she placed the phone back in its cradle, and holding back tears that had welled up in her eyes, she feigned a gesture of joy and declared, "*Khanum* (ma'am), congratulations, they have exiled him to Europe." The mother made no comment, asked no questions, showed no emotion; she only resumed her prayers; a haunting emptiness filled her tearful eyes.[49] She seemed to have learned of her son's death, by some magical intuition, the moment he died.

That evening, keeping the mother relatively isolated from the outside world was not the only concern of the Ensha family. Indeed, they spent much of the night burning documents they had hidden in their house. "They were all Hoveyda's papers," said Dr. Ensha, "and among the documents burned were the two letters, one to the shah and the other to the queen. He had told us to destroy the papers should anything happen to him."[50] Well into the night, another close associate of Hoveyda's, who had worked with him for over twenty years, also burned documents that Hoveyda had entrusted to him.* The family and the friend were both afraid that not only would the documents fall into the hands of the Islamic regime, but that they too would be considered accomplices of the dead prime minister. It is not unreasonable to conjecture that the documents burned that night included the file Hoveyda had kept about the royal family's improper financial dealings. The file, he had thought, would be his insurance policy under the old regime and his trump card should he be forced to play his hand with a new regime. What he had not imagined was the rise to power of a new revolutionary clerisy that was far more bent on the politics of revenge than of preserving historical documents, more keen on retribution than affording the accused a fair trial to defend their

---

* The close associate of Hoveyda's still lives in Iran, and in deference to his safety, I have not indicated his name here.

record. Now that he was dead, the documents he had so carefully culled and preserved could only be of use to future historians. However, frantic with the fear of danger, Hoveyda's family and friend were, on that mirthless night, hardly concerned about the intellectual curiosities of posterity.

Not long after the ominous call, Tehran's daily newspapers published special editions devoted to Hoveyda's execution. "Hoveyda Was Sent to the Firing Squad by the Court of Islamic Justice," the bold headline, covering almost half of the front page, announced. Only minutes after the publication of the newspapers, someone surreptitiously crept by one of the large windows of Maryam Ensha's house and placed a copy of the afternoon's special edition on the windowpane. No one knows whether Hoveyda's mother ever saw the paper or read the headlines. Maryam Ensha removed the paper almost as soon as it was up on the window. Radio and television sets in the house were also turned off, lest the poor mother hear about her son's fate.[51]

Afsar al-Moluk Hoveyda turned out to be more than a compliant player in her family's desperate attempt to keep her in the dark about the news of her son's death. She had already turned inward; the outside world had lost all of its luster for her. The very afternoon of her son's execution, she began a regime of silence. Until her death, some four years later, she would utter few words. Instead, she would spend all of her days in prayer, never asking anyone about her son. She never asked to be taken to her own house again; she showed no emotion when the family pretended to read her letters Hoveyda was supposed to have sent from Europe. Even the gifts he was supposed to have sent—"scarves, slippers, and socks"—summoned no response.[52]

By the end of the night on which he was executed, the house Hoveyda had shared for many years with his mother, and the small apartment he had bought in one of Tehran's new high-rise buildings, not long before he resigned as prime minister, had both been ransacked. Everything of value was taken away by the mob. Pictures from the family albums were strewn all over the sidewalk. In the apartment, "they even tore down most of the walls, looking for secret caches of cash or other valuables."[53]

Tehran newspapers went out of their way to legitimize the execution. Not a single word critical of the summary trial, or of the verdict, found its way into the many pages devoted to the killing. Instead, journalists and pundits alike trafficked in revolutionary rhetoric, vicious gossip, and venomous innuendo. The orchid was a facade, one article claimed; behind it was a recording device used by Hoveyda to entrap his enemies. Another wrote of how the orchids were daily flown in from France. His intimate relationship with his wife was ridiculed, while in yet another piece, it was intimated that Hoveyda had developed a secret sign language with SAVAK. Wherever he went, he used this lethal semiotic device to point out his foes to SAVAK, who then arrested the enemy. SAVAK itself, another article claimed, "grew into a monster in Hoveyda's lap."

Around midnight, there was another call to the Ensha family, this time from the coroner's office, informing them that Hoveyda's body had been transferred there. "Someone should come to the morgue," the family was told, "and arrange for its identification and burial."[54] Once again, Fereshteh Ensha was entrusted with the unenviable task. When she arrived at the morgue, she saw a hall strewn with bodies, some covered, others naked. A small twin tag, tied to a toe, was all that remained of the identity of the many dead, of the "unburied and unwept."[55] The death in them seemed to have percolated into the air, giving the room a blanching sense of terror. Persephone, goddess of "death and dread," seemed to rule supreme in that urban Hades.[56] Remembering the visit, Dr. Ensha said, "I am a doctor; I have been around death all my adult life, but in that room there was more death than even I could bear."[57] In one corner, she saw the bulky corpse of a man. All life seemed to have been augured and pecked out of him. By his side stood a young boy of about fifteen, silently weeping. "He was a policeman," she was told, "and this is his son."[58]

Fereshteh Ensha was then led to a room, beyond the vast hall. Stainless steel drawers from floor to ceiling covered the wall. One of the drawers was pulled out; in it was the naked body of Hoveyda. On his now limp skin, over the ribs, someone had used a marker and written Amir Abbas Hoveyda. "The pallor on his face was haunting," Fereshteh Ensha remembered. The sight of Hoveyda's abandoned, naked body brought tears to her eyes. Angrily she asked, "Why have you treated him in this way?" The coroner's response was brief: "What difference does it make Madam; he is dead."[59] After the perfunctory affirmation that the body, indeed, belonged to Hoveyda, the two doctors from the coroner's office led her to a room where she was given a copy of the coroner's report and told she could take the body for burial. The report, written in the dry language of medicine, talks of a "corpse... height, one hundred sixty-seven centimeters (5 feet 7

THE PERSIAN SPHINX

inches) weight, 68 kilos [150 pounds]…upper false teeth, and with corrective work on lower teeth. Bloody in his head and his hands." It talks of three bullet wounds, and a 38 caliber revolver used in the killing, leaving no doubt that Hoveyda was killed not by firing squad, but by single pistol shots. More disturbingly, it talks of several "superficial bruises…which must have been created as a result of contact with a hard object," while Hoveyda was still alive. The report's reference to "contact with a hard object" seems to indicate that shortly before his death, Hoveyda was beaten up by someone. In its candor, and with its many coded messages to posterity, the report can be seen as a sign of the brave honesty of the coroner, Dr. Garman.

There would be other signs of his commendable decency. Dr. Garman, a burly man, taciturn and stern in demeanor, and red in countenance, suggested to Dr. Ensha that they walk to his office. There he told Ensha that if the body was taken away immediately, or within the next few days, frenzied crowds that gathered regularly around the coroner's office might desecrate it. "We can do one of two things: I can arrange for the body to be burned, or I can try to preserve and hide it for a while, and when it is safe, I will call you and ask you to come and arrange for its burial."[60] Here was a doctor, fiercely independent all his life, from a family with a long history of opposition to the shah's regime, in the twilight of a long career in the bureaucracy, risking not only his position and pension, but possibly life and limb, all to ensure that his political foe of yesterday could be buried with all the dignity that death is owed.*

The next day, officials of the regime were informed that Hoveyda's friends had used the chaos of the coroner's office to steal the prime minister's corpse. From that small piece of calculated disinformation, Khalkhali would later concoct a whole fantastic tale of high crimes and Zionist plots. "After the execution, they were supposed to first take the body to the coroner's office and then to Kahrizak [in the outskirts of Tehran] and bury it there. We did not follow the case however and we did not notice that the body had stayed at the morgue for a little more than three months. Ebrahim Yazdi, on the orders of Bazargan from one side, and the Jews, the Bahais, the [Free]Masons, the Israelis and the French on the other, put the body in a coffin and aboard an Air France flight, took it to France…From

---

* Dr. Garman died last year. Common annals of revolutions, obsessed as they often are with the grand sweep of events, are oblivious to such acts of quiet heroism that sometimes shape everyday life in tumultuous times.

there, they took the body to Israel, and by the order of Menachem Begin…they buried [Hoveyda] in a Jewish cemetery next to his father."*[61]

Of this fantastical tale, the only part that is accurate is the fact that the body did stay in the morgue for some three months. After that long wait, Dr. Garman called the family one afternoon. "Come tomorrow early in the morning," he said. "There should not be too many of you, lest you attract attention." The next day, before sunrise, a two-car caravan left the Ensha residence. One car carried the four members of the family—all women. The lone driver of the other car was Maryam Ensha's brother. He did not dare join the company of mourners and would follow their every step from a discreet distance.

At the coroner's office, the four ladies, all ebony-clad, were given the necessary "John Doe" papers for the burial. "If at the cemetery, they should ask for more papers, tell them he was a distant uncle who died in a car accident and all his papers were stolen," they were instructed.[62] A shroud, provided as a gift by one of Hoveyda's old friends, was used to wrap the chemically preserved, azure-colored corpse. "It was a religious feast day," remembers Fereshteh Ensha, "the day celebrating the advent of Mohammad's journey as the prophet. Streets were alight with signs of celebrations."[63] Apparently, Dr. Garman had chosen the day of the burial to coincide with a day of celebration, hoping to thus diminish the chance of detection. For the same precautionary reason, the family went through the burial process at the cemetery rather quickly. The only overt sign of grief came moments before the shrouded body was laid to rest in the grave. Maryam Ensha knelt at Hoveyda's feet, and then quietly whispered the words she thought he would be most anxious to hear: "I promise," she said, "to take good care of your mother."[64] The body was lowered into the ground, covered with earth, and the family moved away.

For several months, there was no gravestone. Eventually, a small headstone, etched with an oblique reference to the man who laid there, was provided.† After a sixty-year life of many upheavals, accomplishments, and failures, of loves gained and lost, of political victories and defeats, of the poverty of exile and the seductions of power, of hopes of freedom and despair over his own fate, to the visitors of the rapidly expanding Tehran

---

* Ebrahim Yazdi was Iran's foreign minister at the time.

† Lest the grave be desecrated, the family has asked me not to provide the words that appear on the gravestone.

public cemetery, he was no more than an anonymous dead man.

On the day of his execution, in spite of all the cheap rhetorical efforts of the newly liberated newspapers to legitimize the execution, in spite of headlines such as "Hoveyda Had Invited All of the World's Bandits to Pillage Iran" and "Hoveyda's Government Was the Government of Injustice," the pictures on the front page of *Kayhan*, Tehran's most popular daily newspaper, told a sad and different story. In one, Hoveyda sits in the court, glum, gaunt, and dejected, taking notes. There was about him an air of anxiety, and sad resignation. In the other, though bullet-scarred, there is a haunting tranquility on his face.

For much of his political life, Hoveyda had been caught between an opposition, dogmatic and unbending, and a king who in the autumn of his life grew more and more self-referential and despotic. With that almost beatific smile on his dead face, Hoveyda seems to say, "A plague o' both your houses."[65]

Notes

Abbreviations

AD = French Foreign Ministry, Archive Diplomatique, Serie Asie, 1944-1955

AD Carton 24 = French Foreign Ministry, Archive Diplomatique, Serie Asie, Sous-Serie Iran, 1944-1955, Serie E, Carton 24, Dossier 2, "Iran: Corps Diplomatique et Consulaire Iranien." This file is closed until 2007 but I was given special permission to look through it.

LBJ Library = LBJ Library, National Security File, Visit of PM Hoveyda of Iran, 12/5-6/68.

JFK Library = John Fitzgerald Kennedy Library and Museum, Boston, Massachusetts.

NSA = National Security Archive, Washington, D.C.

NA = National Archives, Washington, D.C.

Preface

1. For an account of these prison days, see my *Tales of Two Cities: A Persian Memoir* (Washington, D.C., 1996).

2. Sven Birkerts, "Losing Ourselves in Biography," *Harper's Magazine*, March 1995, v. 290, 24 [excerpt from "Biography and the Dissolving Self: A Note" in AGNI journal].

3. Ahmad Ashraf, "Short History of Iranian Memoirs," *Iran Nameh*, vol. XX, no. 1, Winter 1997, 3.

4. Ahmad Ashraf, "History, Memoir, and Fiction," *Iran Nameh*, vol. XIV, Fall 1996 25.

5. Alexander Popodopoli, *Islam and Muslim Art* (New York, 1979), 49.

6. For an account of the rise of portraits see *Royal Persian Painting: The Qajar Epoch*, ed. Layla Diba with Maryam Ekhtiar (London, 1998).

7. Peter Levi, *The Life and Times of William Shakespeare* (New York, 1989).

8. Cyrus Ghani, *Iran and the Rise of Reza Shah: From Qajar Collapse to Pahlavi Rule* (London, 1998).

Chapter 1: Bridge of Sighs

1. Parviz C. Radji, *In the Service of the Peacock Throne: The Diaries of the Shah's Last Ambassador to London* (London, 1983), 99.

2. Christine Ockrent, *La Memoire du Coeur* (Paris, 1998), 15.

3. Fereshteh Ensha, interviewed by author, Paris, France, 4 June 1998. Among the documents she gave me at the time of our interview were copies of Amir Abbas Hoveyda's hitherto unpublished last letters that she had smuggled out of prison (see pages 324–27).

4. I learned about Hoveyda's preference for mysteries from his brother, Fereydoun Hoveyda, who is himself a connoisseur of detective novels. See Fereydoun Hoveyda, *Petite Histoire du Roman Policier* (Paris, 1956), and his *L'Histoire du Roman Policier* (Paris, 1969).

5. Marvin Zonis, *Majestic Failure: The Fall of the Shah* (Chicago, 1991), 7–23.

6. Hoveyda's discretion regarding the tailor was described in an interview with Vajieh Ma'refat, on 20 January 1998. For twenty years, she was Hoveyda's trusted private secretary.

7. Dr. Abdol Hossein Samii, interviewed by author, 7 February 1998. Dr. Samii was one of the attending physicians when Hoveyda was brought to the hospital on the day of his car accident. In subsequent years, he remained one of Hoveyda's physicians, eventually joining the cabinet as a minister of science and higher education.

8. For a very cynical account of Hoveyda's life that mixes gossip and innuendo with an eclectic selection from Hoveyda's published memoirs, see Eskandar Doldom, *Zendegi va Khaterat-e Amir Abbas Hoveyda* [The Life and Memoirs of Amir Abbas Hoveyda] (Tehran, 1993). The fact that even this marred and altogether unreliable offering has reached a fourth edition is an indication of the growing curiosity about Hoveyda's life.

9. Samii, interview.

10. Hoveyda amassed as many as 350 pipes and 150 canes. See Dr. Mostafa Alamouti, *Iran Dar Asr-e Pahlavi* [Iran Under the Pahlavis], vol. 12 (London, 1992), 126. Fereydoun Hoveyda told me that the cane and pipe collections were not sought out by Amir Abbas himself but were mostly gifts from his colleagues. Fereydoun Hoveyda, interviewed by author, 3 August 1998.

11. For an account of the school's establishment and the role of the two clerics in its creation, see Mohsen Hashemi, ed. *Hashemi Rafsanjani: Dowran-e Mobarezeh* [Hashemi Rafsanjani: The Period of the Struggle] (Tehran, 1997), 37.

12. For an account of Rafsanjani's role in the assassination, see Mohsen Hashemi, ed. *Hashemi Rafsanjani: Dowran-e Mobarezeh*, 33.

13. Fereydoun Hoveyda, interviewed by author, 17 January 1998.

14. Bani Sadr, interviewed by author, 2 June 1998. The ayatollah's words are as Bani Sadr remembers them.

15. Bani Sadr, interview. Salar Jaf's words are as Bani Sadr remembers them.

16. The Islamic Republic kept the red, white, and green flag, omitting the lion and the sun and replacing them with Arabic verses from the Koran. For a history of the symbolism of the lion and the sun, see Ahmad Kasravi, "Tarikh-e Shir o Khorshid" [History of the Lion and the Sun] in *Karvand-e Kasravi* [The Kasravi Anthology] (Tehran, 1974), 94–109.

17. Fereshteh Ensha, interviewed by author, Paris, France, 4 June 1998. Fereshteh Ensha visited Hoveyda in the same room and provided me with an account of its layout.

18. Bani Sadr, interview. Hoveyda's general demeanor, his calm and dignified appearance, had clearly impressed Bani Sadr.

19. Ehsan Naraghi, interviewed by author, Paris, France, 2 June 1998. Naraghi, a colorful figure of the Pahlavi regime and a friend of Hoveyda, had introduced Bani Sadr to Hoveyda.

20. In his diaries, Asadollah Alam—who was for many years the shah's trusted minister of court and Hoveyda's nemesis—wrote that in April of 1973 he confided to the king that Hoveyda survives partly by "throwing money" at members of the royal family, particularly those related to the queen. According to Alam, the shah ordered an investigation. No further mention of the investigation or its results are to be found in the diaries, or in any other source for that matter. See Asadollah Alam, *Yadashtha-ye Alam* [Alam's Diaries], ed. Alinaghi Alikhani, vol. 3 (Bethesda, 1995), 23. An abridged translation of these diaries is available in English, see note 47 in this section.

21. There is disagreement over the exact amount Hoveyda provided the clerics. Some have guessed the figure to be closer to eighty million dollars a year. The eleven million dollar figure suggested by Hoveyda's brother is from the *New York Times*, 11 April 1979, sec A, p. 9. For a less reliable estimate, see David Shumer, *Yek Sanad-e Tarikhi as Efsha-ye Towte'eha-ye Bozorg* [An Important Document Exposing Big Conspiracies] (Washington, D.C., 1982), 55.

22. Bani Sadr, interview.

23. Fereshteh Ensha, interviewed by author, 4 June 1998. Hoveyda repeated the gist of this conversation to Dr. Ensha during her next visit to him in prison.

24. *Kayhan,* 27 Bahman 1357/1979, 1 and 28 Bahman 1357/17 February 1979, 1.

25. For Khomeini's defense, see *Kayhan,* 14 Farvardin, 1358/3 April 1979, 3.

26. In those days, Bani Sadr wrote and lectured widely about the virtues of the Islamic government and its new brand of power and justice. See "Hokoomat-e Eslami Hokoomat-e Aghideh Ast" [Islamic Government Is the Rule of Ideas], *Kayhan,* 30 Bahman 1357/19 February 1979.

27. Bani Sadr, interview.

28. For a subtly brilliant discussion of filicide in the *Shahnameh* of Ferdowsi, see Dick Davis, *Epic and Sedition: The Case of Ferdowsi's Shahnameh* (Fayetteville, Ar. 1992; Washington, D.C., 1998), 97–166.

29. Fereydoun Hoveyda, a formidable cultural and film critic long before he was named Iran's ambassador to the United Nations during his brother's tenure, discerned a "father-son" relationship between the shah and Hoveyda. Fereydoun Hoveyda has been writing and lecturing for some 30 years about the pervasive influence of patriarchal archetypes in Persian mythology. See in particular, Fereydoun Hoveyda, "Jomhouri Islami dar Parto-ye Mythologi-ye Iran" [The Islamic Republic in Light of Persian Mythology], *Akhtar,* 1991, No. 10, 42–55. There he writes about what he calls the "Rostam complex," as opposed to the Oedipal complex, as the key to the history of Persian culture and politics. He first articulated his views on this subject in 1959, during a psychoanalytical conference in Paris.

30. Much has been written about this agreement. Bani Sadr categorically claimed that such a list existed. He said that the list was mentioned in several meetings of the Revolutionary Council, of which he was a member. Bani Sadr, interviewed by author, 2 June 1998.

William Sullivan, the American ambassador to Iran at the time, writes in his memoirs that, before the shah's departure, he met Mehdi Bazargan, who would soon become the prime minister of the Provisional Revolutionary Government of Iran, and Ayatollah Mussavi, who "spoke for the religious element of the revolution." Using the circumspect language of a diplomat in describing the meeting, Sullivan writes, "Bazargan and I spoke in French, and then he deferentially translated the gist of the conversation into Farsi for the benefit of the ayatollah, who said very little throughout. Bazargan repeated to me what his associates had been telling embassy officers for some time. They wanted the armed forces to remain intact and to work with the new government. They had a list of designated military officers who would be requested to leave the country but would take their possessions with them and escape any retribution." See William Sullivan, *Mission to Iran* (New York, 1981), 236–37.

31. Bani Sadr, interview. When General Nematollah Nasiri was shown on television, he had been badly beaten and could hardly speak.

32. *Kayhan,* 26 Esfand 1357/17 March 1979.

33. Fereshteh Ensha, interviewed by author, Paris, France, 4 June 1998. The family had come to believe that the delay and the transfer meant the danger of execution had passed.

34. Ockrent, *La Memoire*, 30. Ladan Boroumand, the interpreter, does not remember Ockrent making any points about the Geneva Convention. She was too excited about the scoop, Boroumand says, to worry about such ethical points. Ladan Boroumand, interviewed by author, 20 May 1999.

35. All quotes from the interview, unless otherwise stated in the notes, are taken from French television's Channel Three tape. See Amir Abbas Hoveyda, interview by Christine Ockrent, Canal 3 [Channel Three], France.

36. For an account of the journalists' encounters with several of these politicians, see Ockrent, *La Memoire,* 17–27.

37. Some critics of Christine Ockrent have questioned her version of the events leading to the interview. They allege that she came to a secret, and highly unethical, agreement with Sadegh Ghotbzadeh, another one of Ayatollah Khomeini's trusted young advisors, who rose to become Iran's foreign minister and was then executed on charges of high treason. These critics, which include some of France's leading journalists, such as Edouard Sablier, suggest that in return for his help in making the interview possible, Ghotbzadeh demanded the right to decide the questions that Ockrent would ask Hoveyda. This, they say, is the only explanation for the belligerent tone of Ockrent's interview. See Ehsan Naraghi, *Khaterat* [Recollections], unpublished manuscript (Paris, 1998), 313–32.

38. Ladan Boroumand, interviewed by author, 6 January 1998.

39. Apparently in those days in Tehran, there was more than one Fouquier-Tinville look-alike. In Ockrent's account of her trip to Tehran leading up to the interview, she writes of her visit to Sadegh Khalkhali, the infamous "Hanging Judge" of the revolution and refers to him as another Fouquier-Tinville. See Ockrent, *La Memoire*, 25.

40. Ockrent, *La Memoire*, 15–16.

41. Boroumand, interview.

42. The habit of sending reporters to the Third World who are ignorant of the local culture and mute in the native tongue seems like a manifest act of colonial haughtiness. In her memoirs, Ockrent makes no reference to any discussions about translators. I learned of the discussions from Ladan Boroumand. Ladan Boroumand, interviewed by author, 6 January 1998.

43. Ockrent, too, writes of becoming "nauseated" at the sight of so much human suffering. Ockrent, *La Memoire,* 15.

44. Boroumand, interview.

45. Boroumand and Ockrent both noticed this initial joy.

46. Ockrent, *La Memoire,* 31.

47. The shah's closest confidant and his minister of court, Asadollah Alam, provides many examples of the shah's utter dismay and distress when he read any articles in the Western press critical of the Iranian regime. Behind each article he saw a conspiracy. See Asadollah Alam, *The Shah and I: The Confidential Diary of Iran's Royal Court, 1969–1977,* ed. Alinaghi Alikhani, trans. by Alinaghi Alikhani and Nicholas Vincent (London, 1992).

48. Massoud Behnoud, *Az Seyed Zia ta Bakhtiar* [From Seyyed Zia to Bakhtiar] (Tehran, 1990), 510.

49. Ockrent writes about some of this criticism. See Ockrent, *La Memoire,* 33–40.

50. If Ockrent's memoirs, written with the privilege of hindsight and with the help of editors, can be taken as a measure of her knowledge of Iranian politics and of her journalistic attention to details, then Hoveyda's charge must be true. The chapter of her memoir covering her trip to Tehran is full of glaring inaccuracies. Not only is she misinformed about such details as to where Hoveyda was educated—in Brussels, and not in France as she claims—she even uses a made-up name for Hoveyda's prison. She calls the prison "Erevan." (See Ockrent, *La Memoire,* 35.) No such prison exists in Tehran. She seems to be confusing the Evin prison with Qasr, where Hoveyda was incarcerated. Contrary to her claim, Bani Sadr was never a "theology professor." (See Ockrent, *La Memoire,* 20.) Ghotbzadeh, a man she met to solicit help in arranging the interview, was not at the time—or ever—the minister of information.

51. Radji writes at some length about Hoveyda's role in making the Red Cross visits a possibility. It was Hoveyda, he writes, who helped arrange a crucial meeting between the shah and Martin Ennals, the general secretary of Amnesty International. See Radji, *In the Service,* 55. Documents of the U.S. Embassy in Iran indicate that Hoveyda was also involved in negotiations between the shah and William J. Butler, Chairman of the executive committee of the International Commission of Jurists. Hoveyda met Butler in Shiraz on May 1, 1978. See "Summary of Discussions Between His Imperial Majesty the Shahanshah Aryamehr and William J. Butler at Shiraz on May 2, 1978." NSA, no. 644. I was a political prisoner in Iran when the Amnesty International visits to prisons took place. Our lives were perceptibly improved in both the anticipation and the aftermath of the visits. For an account of these changes, see my *Tales of Two Cities: A Persian Memoir* (Washington, D.C., 1996), 131–81.

Chapter 2: Beirut Blues

1. As a human habitat, the area where Tehran is located has an eight-thousand-year history; as a village, it dwelled for some five hundred years under the shadow of its neighbor, Rey, a grand city in medieval Iran. With the demise of Rey, and with marauding hordes of Asian tribes wandering through the landscape and pillaging all they found, Tehran developed a reputation—some say its name—for its ability to escape the danger by building houses underneath the orchards. For an overview of the city's history and evolution, see *Tehran: Capitale Bicentenaire,* ed. C. Adle and B. Hourcade (Paris, 1992).

2. Amir Abbas Hoveyda, "Yad-e Ayam-e Javani"[Memories of Days of Youth] in *Donya,* 22nd annual ed. 32, 328.

3. *Tarikh-e Moaser-e Iran* [History of Contemporary Iran] (Tehran, 1989), 171–72; Hoveyda, "Yad-e Ayam-e Javani," 328.

4. Hoveyda, "Yad-e Ayam-e Javani," 328.

5. For a discussion of this trip, the shah's memoirs of his trips, and his elective affinity with modernity, see my "Narratives of Modernity: Perspectives of an Oriental Despot" in *Challenging Boundaries,* ed. Michael Shapiro (Minneapolis, 1996), 219–32.

6. For a discussion of the historical aspects of Tehran, and the influence of European plans on the city's growth, see John D. Gurney, "The Transformation of Tehran in Late Nineteenth Century" in Adle, *Tehran: Capitale Bicentenaire,* 53–71.

7. For an encyclopedic picture of Tehran in the first two decades of the twentieth century, see Jafar Shahri, *Tarikh-e Ejtemai-ye Tehran* [The Social History of Tehran], vol. 1. (Tehran, 1990), 89–110.

8. For a description of the twelve gates, see Shahri, *Social History,* vol. 1, 89–110; also Vita Sackville-West, *Passenger to Tehran* (New York, 1990), 77, 123.

9. For an account of the creation of the school, see Bastani Parizi, *Talash-e Azadi* [Struggle

for Freedom] (Tehran, 1962), 78–84.

10. Willem Floor, "Les Premiere Regles de Police Urbaine à Tehran," in Adle, *Tehran: Capitale Bicentenaire*, 173–98.

11. Shahri provides a wonderful account of this event in his one volume history of Tehran. See Jafar Shahri, *Tehran-e Ghadim* [Old Tehran] (Tehran, 1977), 24.

12. Hoveyda, "Yad-e Ayam-e Javani," 328.

13. For a brilliant account of Nasir-al Din Shah's life and his troubled relationship with Amir Kabir, see Abbas Amanat, *Pivot of The Universe: Nasir al Din Shah Qajar and the Iranian Monarchy, 1831–1896* (Berkley, 1997), 106–68. Other historians have indicated that the princess was sixteen when she was ordered to marry the prime minister. See Fereydoun Adamiyat, *Amir Kabir va Iran* [Amir Kabir and Iran] (Tehran, 1969), 24.

14. For a history of the famous "Qajar Coffee," see Bastani Parizi, *Talash-e Azadi* [Struggle for Freedom], 118.

15. Maryam Ensha, interviewed by author, 27 July 1998. Much of the information about Hoveyda's mother's family came from an interview with Afsar al-Moluk's niece, Maryam Ensha.

16. Hoveyda, "Yad-e Ayam-e Javani," 330–33. Fereydoun Hoveyda, interviewed by author, 6 December 1997.

17. For an account of his life, and the list of books he helped translate or publish in Iran, see Sardar Asaad, *Khaterat-e Sardar Asaad Bakhtiari* [Memoirs of Sardar Asaad], ed. Iraj Afshar (Tehran, 1993), 3–7.

18. E. G. Browne, *Materials for the Study of the Babi Religion* (Cambridge, 1918), 4. Browne has provided one of the most reliable, albeit sympathetic, early accounts of the rise of the Bab and of the Bahai religion in English. See also his *A Year Among the Persians* (Cambridge, 1893).

19. E. G. Browne, *Materials,* see also E. G. Browne, *A Year Amongst.* For a more recent, scholarly treatment of the same topic, see Abbas Amanat, *Resurrection and Renewal: The Making of the Babi Movement in Iran, 1840–1850* (Ithaca, 1989).

20. The claim of Ayn-al Molk's role as a scribe can be found in Bahram Afrasyabi, *Tarikh-e Jameh-ye Bahaiyat: No Masoni* [The Complete History of Bahai Society: A New Masonic Trend] (Tehran, 1982), 72. As the title of the book indicates, the narrative is founded on the conspiracy theory of the Bahai faith's rise as a form of Masonic ideas. Very little is offered by way of evidence for most of the book's claims, including the nature of the ties between Ayn al-Molk and Efendi.

21. Hoveyda, "Yad-e Ayam-e Javani," 32.

22. Ibid., 329.

23. T. E. Lawrence, *Seven Pillars of Wisdom* (New York, 1927), 34.

24. Hoveyda, "Yad-e Ayam-e Javani," 328.

25. Ibid., 332.

26. Ibid., 328.

27. Ibid.

28. Fereydoun Hoveyda, *Les Nuits Feodales: Tribulations d'un Persan au Moyen-Orient* (Paris, 1954), 23.

29. Hoveyda, "Yad-e Ayam-e Javani," 331.

30. Ibid., 324.

31. Ibid., 337.

32. For a succinct account of the Wahhabi ideology and political structure, see Aziz Al-Azmeh, "Wahhabi Polity," in *Islam and Modernities* (London, 1993), 104–22.

33. Ibid., 337.

34. Fereydoun Hoveyda, interviewed by author, 3 September 1998.

35. Hoveyda, *Les Nuits Feodale.*

36. Frank J. Sulloway, *Born to Rebel: Birth Order, Family Dynamics, and Creative Lives* (New York, 1997), 22.

37. For a comprehensive account of Reza Shah's rise to power, see Cyrus Ghani, *Iran and the Rise of the Reza Shah: From Qajar Collapse to Pahlavi Rule* (New York, 1998).

38. Hoveyda, "Yad-e Ayam-e Javani," 330.

39. Ibid.

40. Ibid., 331.

41. Ibid., 332.

42. Ibid.

43. Ibid., 336.

44. Fereydoun Hoveyda, interviewed by author, 26 June 1998. Amir Abbas, in "Yad-e Ayam-e Javani," might be discreetly alluding to the same fact when he writes of his father's unfailing fidelity to his friends.

45. Fereydoun Hoveyda, interviewed by author, 26 June 1998.

46. Hoveyda, "Yad-e Ayam-e Javani," 336.

47. Ibid.

48. Fereydoun Hoveyda, interviewed by author, 26 June 1998.

49. Ahmad Ghoreishi, interviewed by author, 14 August 1998.

50. Amir Abbas Hoveyda, "Yad-e Ayam-e Tahsil dar Orupa" [Memories of School Days in Europe], *Donya*, 23rd annual ed. (Tehran, 1968), 337.

51. Fereydoun Hoveyda, *Les Nuits,* 171.

52. Fereydoun Hoveyda, on more than one occasion told me of his brother's affinity for the Baron de Clapique. In Malraux's memoirs (called, with the particular panache of the French, *Anti-Memoirs*) Baron de Clapique appears in the narrative as a person Malraux meets in real life. See André Malraux, *Anti-Memoirs*, trans. Terrence Kilmartin (New York, 1968), 264–334.

53. André Malraux, *Man's Fate*, trans. Haakan M. Chevalier (New York, 1934), 37.

54. Ibid.

55. Ibid., 46.

56. Ibid., 259.

57. Ibid., 279.

58. Ibid., 314.

59. Ibid., 257.

60. Sulloway, *Born to Rebel,* 316.

61. Simon Schama, *Citizens: A Chronicle of the French Revolution* (New York, 1980), 651.

62. Fereydoun Hoveyda, interviewed by author, 6 September 1998.

63. Renée Demont, interviewed by author, Brussels, Belgium, 1 June 1998.

64. For a history of the Templars, see Peter Partner, *The Murdered Magicians: The Templars and Their Myth* (Rochester, 1987), xiv–xvii. In recent years, several writers have turned the Templars into subjects for successful novels. Umberto Eco's *Foucault's Pendulum* and Lawrence Durrell's *Monsieur* are two of the most successful examples.

65. Hoveyda, "Yad-e Ayam-e Javani," 332.

66. Jean Baptiste Racine, *The Complete Plays of Jean Racine*, vol. 1, trans. Samuel Solomon (New York, 1967), 220.

67. Fereydoun Hoveyda, interviewed by author, 26 June 1998.

68. Both Renée Demont and Fereydoun Hoveyda remembered the tale of Amir Abbas in his Dandin improvisation.

69. Amir Abbas Hoveyda, private correspondence to Renée Demont (n.d.).

70. Ibid.

71. Renée Demont, interviewed by author, Brussels, Belgium, 1 June 1998.

72. Laila Emami, interviewed by author, Paris, France, 12 March 1999.

73. William Rees, ed. *French Poetry 1820–1950* (New York, 1990), 20.

74. Percy Mansell Jones, and Geoffrey Richardson, *A Book of French Verse* (London, 1964), 73–74.

Chapter 3: Paris Pilgrim

1. Fereydoun Hoveyda, interviewed by author, 7 February 1999.

2. Hoveyda, "Yad-e Ayam Tahsil dar Orupa," 336.

3. Ibid., 336.

4. Ibid., 337.

5. Ibid.

6. Claude Lévi-Strauss, *Tristes Tropiques* (Paris, 1983), 405.

7. For a more detailed discussion of the same attitudes and tendencies of the modern French intellectual tradition, or what a critic calls their "collective moral anesthesia, and infatuation with ideas at the expense of reality," see Tony Judt, *The Burden of Responsibility: Blum, Camus, Aron and the French Twentieth Century* (Chicago, 1999). Hoveyda was an avid reader of both Aron and Camus.

8. Hoveyda, "Yad-e Ayam," 337.

9. For a discussion of this debate amongst Arab intellectuals, see Fouad Ajami, *The Arab Predicament* (New York, 1992).

10. For a discussion of the special role of France in the intellectual landscape of Iran in the first half of this century, see Christophe Balay, *La Genese du Roman Persan Moderne* (Tehran, 1998).

11. Hoveyda, "Yad-e Ayam-e Tahsil dar Orupa," 337.

12. Ibid.

13. Ibid., 338.

14. Ibid.

15. Ibid.

16. Ibid.

17. Ibid.

18. For a pioneering and lucid discussion of the *fokolis*, see Seyyed Fakhraddin Shadman, *Taskhir Tamadon-e Farang* [Conquering the Western Civilization] (Tehran, 1947).

19. Hoveyda, "Yad-e Ayam-e Tahsil dar Orupa," 344.

20. Ibid., 346.

21. Amir Abbas Hoveyda, "Yad az Ayam Khedmat-e Vazifeh-ye Afsari dar Daneshkadeh-ye Afsari" [Memoirs of Service in the Officers' Academy] in *Donya*, 25th annual ed., 372.

22. Fereydoun Hoveyda, interviewed by author, 2 February 1999.

23. The information about his keen interest in white shirts is from his wife. Laila Emami, interviewed by author, Paris, France, 12 March 1999.

24. Hoveyda, "Yad-e Ayam-e Tahsil dar Orupa," 344.

25. Amir Abbas Hoveyda, private correspondence to Renée Demont, 28 April 1939.

26. Ibid.

27. Hoveyda, "Yad-e Ayam-e Tahsil dar Orupa," 345.

28. For a brief overview of some recent debates about the nature of biography as a genre and Nabokov's views, see Allison Light, "The Mighty Mongrel: Biography as a Literary Form," *New Statesmen and Society,* 17 December 1993, 65.

29. Sigmund Freud, *The Psychopathology of Everyday Life,* trans. James Strachy (New York, 1997).

30. Hoveyda, "Yad-e Ayam-e Tahsil dar Orupa," 345.

31. Amir Abbas Hoveyda, private correspondence to Renée Demont, 1939.

32. For an account of the French views of Belgian culture, see Luc Sante, *The Factory of Facts* (New York, 1998).

33. Hoveyda, "Yad-e Ayam-e Tahsil dar Orupa," 345–46.

34. In Belgium, only students and their immediate families are provided access to student records. But with the kind help of Pierre Morlett, Brussels' district attorney, and my brother Dr. Hossein Milani, who had been on the faculty of the university, the president of the university kindly agreed to provide me access to Hoveyda's transcripts.

35. For an account of the speech Hoveyda gave at the ceremony, I relied on the words of Mohammad Safa, one of Hoveyda's trusted staff who accompanied him on the Belgium trip. Mohammad Safa, interviewed by author, 21 November 1997.

36. Amir Abbas Hoveyda, "Yadashtha-ye Zaman-e Jang" [Memories of Times of War], in *Donya*, 21st annual ed., 32–33.

37. Ibid., 36.

38. Ibid.

39. Ibid., 34.

40. Ibid., 35.

41. Ibid.

42. Ibid., 36.

43. Ibid.

44. Ibid., 38.

45. Ibid., 43.

46. Ibid., 47.

47. Ibid., 55.

48. Ibid., 49.

49. Fereydoun Hoveyda, interviewed by author, 8 February 1998.

50. Ahmad Mahrad, "Iranian Jews in Europe during W.W. II," in *The History of Contemporary Iranian Jews,* Center for Iranian Jewish Oral History, vol. 3 (Beverly Hills, 1999), 59–109. For some years now, Ahmad Mahrad has done pioneering work, using Nazi archives, to document the fate of Iranian Jews in Europe. He has also published several books and essays on the subject in German, including, Ahmad Mahrad, *Das Schiksal Jüdischer Iraner im Orient* (Hamburg, 1985).

51. Mahrad, "Iranian Jews," 34.

52. Fereydoun Hoveyda, letter to the National Committee on American Foreign Policy, 1997.

53. Fereydoun Hoveyda, Letter to the National Committee, 1997.

54. Hoveyda, "Yadashtha-ye Zaman-e Jang," 50.

55. Fereydoun Hoveyda, interviewed by author, 6 December 1997.

56. Fereydoun Hoveyda, interviewed by author, 17 February 1998.

57. All information on Panait is from *Le Robert*, vol. 3 (Paris, 1984).

58. Hoveyda, "Yadashtha-ye Zaman-e Jang," 57.

Chapter 4: The Land of Oz

1. Ghani, *Iran and the Rise of Reza Shah*, 395–407.

2. Asadollah Alam, in his diaries, refers to the shah's discussion of the insult some thirty years after the event. See Alam, *Yadashtha-ye Alam* [Alam's Diaries], vol. 2, 133.

3. For a discussion of the bent twig phenomenon, see Isaiah Berlin, *The Crooked Timber of Humanity: Chapters in the History of Ideas* (New York, 1993), 133.

4. For a discussion of Britain's machinations to keep its monopoly position in Iran, see Ghani, *Iran and the Rise of Reza Shah,* chapters 1 to 5.

5. James A. Bill, *The Eagle and the Lion: The Tragedy of American-Iranian Relations* (New Haven, 1988), 28.

6. Noureddin Kia-Nouri and Ehsan Tabari have both, at different times, made this claim. See Noureddin Kia-Nouri, *Khaterat-e Noureddin Kia-Nouri* [Memoirs] (Tehran, 1992), 144. He claims that one of the party's leaders had "very close ties" with Hoveyda. Anvar Khamehi, who was for a brief period a rising star of the Tudeh Party and then was for many years its fierce critic, writes in his memoirs that Hoveyda joined a "leftist circle" in Beirut. See Anvar Khamehi, *Panja-o Se Nafar* [The Group of 53] (Tehran, 1992), 112.

7. For a discussion of some of these movements and the impact of Kasravi's ideas, see Ali Rahnema, *An Islamic Utopian: A Political Biography of Ali Shariati* (London, 1999), 1–23.

8. Ruhollah Khomeini, *Kashf al-Asrar* [Key to the Secrets] (Tehran, 1941), 104–10.

9. Ryszard Kapuscinski, *Shah of Shahs.* trans. William R. Brand and Katarzyna Mroczkowska-Brand (New York, 1992).

10. For a brilliant account of the shah's character, as well as a revealing comparison between his behavior in his last few days of power, and that of his father's last days in Iran see Kaveh Safa, "Melting Like Snow in Water: Patterns in the Collapse of a Consequential Life," a paper presented to the "Writing Lives in South Asia and Middle East" conference, held at the University of Virginia on April 22 and 23, 1999. My contribution to the conference was called "The Perils of Persian Biography: An Excursion into the Poetics of Culture." A much revised, and shortened version of that paper is now the Preface to this book.

11. *Khandaniha,* No. 28, 1326/1947, 5.

12. For a fascinating account of Cook's days in Iran, see Nesta Ramezani, "The Dance of the Rose and the Nightingale," forthcoming publication.

13. Stephen Lee McFarland, "The Crisis In Iran, 1941–1947: A Society in Change and the Peripheral Origins of the Cold War" (Ph.D. diss., University of Texas, 1988).

14. Ebrahim Golestan, personal correspondence, 22 January 2000.

15. Hoveyda, "Yad as Ayam Khedmat-e Vazifeh," 374.

16. Ibid.

17. Ibid.

18. Doldom, *Zendegi va Khaterat,* 77.

19. *Current Biography Yearbook, 1971* (New York, 1971), 200. This text indicates that Hoveyda earned a "master's degree in Political Science" at the Université Libre de Bruxelles and "a doctorate in history at the Sorbonne."

20. *Iran Almanac* (Tehran, 1966), 762.

21. Jahangir Behrouz, interviewed by author, 2 April 1999.

22. Hoveyda's having a doctorate is mentioned in Pakravan's novella, *The Arrest of Hoveyda* (Costa Mesa, 1998). When I asked her about the source of the claim, she indicated that Hoveyda had, unambiguously, told her of this "doctoral dissertation." Saideh Pakravan, interviewed by author, 15 February 1998.

23. Doldom, *Zendegi va Khaterat-e,* 77.

24. Hoveyda, "Yad as Ayam," 375.

25. Doldom, *Zendegi va Khaterat-e,* 77.

26. Hoveyda, "Yad as Ayam," 375.

27. Ibid., 374.

28. Ibid., 375.

29. Ebrahim Golestan, personal correspondence, 22 January 2000.

30. Fereydoun Hoveyda, interviewed by author, 5 June 1999.

31. In a letter to his friend, Hassan Shahid-Nourai, Hedayat seems to indicate that *Amerika* was sent by Hoveyda through an intermediary. See Sadeq Hedayat, *Nameha* [Letters], comp. Mohammad Baharlou (Tehran, 1999), 385. In another letter dated 17 November 1946, Hedayat writes that he has received two books sent by Hoveyda, one by Sartre, the other by Henry Miller. Naser Pakdaman, who is editing a collection of Hedayat's letters, was kind enough to look through galleys, and send me copies of all references to Hoveyda. See Sadeq Hedayat, *Hashtad-o Yek Nameh be Hassan Shahid Nourai* [Eighty One Letters To Hassan Shahid-Nourai] ed. Naser Pakdaman (Paris, forthcoming), 134–139.

32. In 1959, when Hoveyda was at the National Iranian Oil Company, one of his friends, Manouchehr Pirouz, asked him to find a way to provide some much needed financial help for Anjavi Shirazi. With the help of Abdollah Entezam, who was the head of the oil company, Hoveyda found a way of giving Anjavi Shirazi a regular stipend. In a meeting Hoveyda suggested that Anjavi edit the Hedayat letters which he claimed he had in a safe deposit box in Switzerland. Manouchehr Pirouz, interviewed by author, Paris, France, 14 March 1999. (Though he had been the governor of the state of Fars for many years, Pirouz, now in exile, makes his living operating a small grocery store in Paris, France. We met at his store and could only talk while there were no customers present.)

33. Few people were more critical of Hoveyda than Ardeshir Zahedi. He was refreshingly honest in articulating his forceful opinions. He spoke of Hoveyda's often embarrassing drunkenness and his "clownish dancing, with his cane dangling from his arm." Ardeshir Zahedi, interviewed by author, Montreux, Switzerland, 5 June 1998.

34. At different times, I have talked to Hoveyda's wife, Laila Emami, his chief of staff, Mohammad Safa, his brother, Fereydoun, his friend, Chubak, and they have all said the same thing about his religious views.

35. Sadeq Chubak, interviewed by author, 15 February 1998.

36. See Sadeq Hedayat, *Hashtad-o Yek Nameh be Hassan Shadid Nourai* [Eighty One Letters to Hassan Shahid-Nourai] (Paris, forthcoming), 136. I am grateful to Naser Pakdaman for his help in finding this information in the letters.

37. Jalal Al-e Ahmad, *Karnameh-ye Se Saleh* [A Three Year Record] (Tehran, 1980).

38. Chubak, interview.

Chapter 5: Paris Redux

1. AD, "Rahnema," Télégramme. Document 2.

2. Hoveyda (Fereydoun), *Les Nuits Feodales*, 270.

3. AD Carton 24, le Préfet de Police à Monsieur, no. 6511–4.

4. Numerous telegrams in the files of the French foreign ministry testify to the attempts of the embassy officials to travel to Germany. Any such trip had to be first cleared with the occupying authorities.

5. Hoveyda, "Yad as Ayam-e Khedmat-e Vazifeh," 375.

6. Fereydoun Hoveyda, interviewed by author, 5 February 1998.

7. Fatemeh Soudavar Farmanfarmaian, interviewed by author, 11 May 1999.

8. Fereydoun Hoveyda, interviewed by author, 10 May 1999.

9. For the character of Hassan-Ali Mansur, I have relied on interviews with Fereydoun Hoveyda, Nassir Assar, Zia Shadman, Fatemeh Soudavar Farmanfarmaian, and Ehsan Naraghi. Persian sources on his life and ideas are few.

10. Fereydoun Hoveyda, interviewed by author, 25 July 1999.

11. Fereydoun Hoveyda, interviewed by author, 24 May 1999.

12. Fatemeh Soudavar Farmanfarmaian, interviewed by author, 10 May 1999.

13. Edouard Sablier, interviewed by author, Paris, France, 14 March 1999.

14. Edouard Sablier, *Iran, La Poudrière: Les Secrets de la Revolution Islamique* (Paris, 1980), 146.

15. Sablier, interview.

16. Ibid.

17. Sablier, *Iran*, 146.

18. AD Carton 24, 94.

19. Ibid., 287–88.

20. AD Carton 24, "Le Ministre des Affaires Étrangères à Monsieur le Préfet de Police," 2 Août, 1945.

21. AD Carton 24, "Télégramme a l'Arrivée," 254–255. Document 73.

22. AD Carton 24, "Le Préfet de Police à Monsieur le Ministre des Affaires Étrangères: Direction d'Asie-Oceanie," No. 6511–4.

23. Ibid., 2.

24. AD Carton 24, "Le Ministre des Affaires Étrangères à Monsieur le Préfet de Police," 2 August 1945.

25. Ibid., 3.

26. Ahmad Ghoreishi, interviewed by author, 15 February 1998. Fereydoun Hoveyda also confirmed this story and added that, at this time, Amir Abbas turned in his resignation, which the shah did not accept. Fereydoun Hoveyda, interviewed by author, 24 July 1999.

27. The Islamic Republic has published much of the official correspondence between Iranian officials and Swiss authorities and attorneys. The picture that emerges is not pretty, and implicates a large number of people in both countries. See Hossein Kouchekian-Fard, "Rosvai dar Swiss: Asnadi az Darbar-e Shahanshahi dar Bareh-ye Ghachag-e Mavad-e Mokhader" [The Embarrassing Fiasco in Switzerland: Documents from the Royal Court about Smuggling Illicit Drugs] Fasl-nameh-ye Tarikh-e Moaser-e Iran [Quarterly of Contemporary Iranian History], first year, No. 4, Winter 1997, 135–208.

28. McFarland, "The Crisis in Iran," 159–60.

29. Ibid.

30. *Khandaniha*, no. 207 (12 Shahrivar 1325/3 September 1946), 2 and no. 252 (19 Bahman 1325/8 February 1946), 2–3.

31. AD Carton 24, "Télégramme a l'Arrivée," 22–25. Document 129.

32. Fereydoun Hoveyda, interviewed by author, 24 May 1999.

33. AD Carton 24, "Télégramme 00135," 26 Juillet 1946.

34. AD Carton 24, "Note pour le Cabinet du Ministre," 24 Juillet 1946. The same charges are repeated in at least two other telegrams.

35. AD Carton 24, "Télégramme a l'Arrivée," 00144. 9 Août 1946.

36. AD Carton 24, "Note pour le Secrétaire Générale," 24 Juillet 1947.

37. In a telegram from the French Embassy in Tehran, the Chargé d'Affaire declared, "We are clearly in the presence of something of a conspiracy masterminded by suspicious characters and deal-makers. They are conscious that they no longer have in Paris the facilities they once enjoyed. They clearly want to see Mr. Sepahbodi replaced with 'someone like Mr. Rahnema who has the requisite business sense (sic).' That is the real source of the current press campaign." AD Carton 24, "Télégramme a l'Arrivée," 30 Janvier 1947. Ambassade de France en Iran. Document 128.

38. Sadeq Hedayat, *Nameha* [Letters], comp. Mohammad Baharlou (Tehran, 1999), 383–84.

39. Ibid., 389.

40. Ibid., 390.

41. Hoveyda, "Yad as Ayam-e Khedmat-e Vazifeh," 375.

42. *Atash*, 26 Esfand 1325/17 March 1947.

43. Fereydoun Hoveyda, interviewed by author, 19 May 1999.

Chapter 6: The Wandering Years

1. Nassir Assar, interviewed by author, Washington, D.C., 12 May 1999.

2. My information about Hoveyda's relations with Entezam comes primarily from Fereydoun Hoveyda. Nassir Assar also provided some details. References to Hoveyda's relations with Entezam can be found in many books and articles. For example, Parviz Radji, an assistant to Hoveyda for many years, writes that Hoveyda was Entezam's "acknowledged protégé." See Radji, *In the Service of the Peacock Throne*, 4.

3. Amir Abbas Hoveyda, "Editorial," in *Kavosh*, vol. 1, no. 1, Shahrivar 1339/August 1960.

4. Fereydoun Hoveyda, interviewed by author, 12 May 1999.

5. Much of my information on Hoveyda's life in his Stuttgart days comes from Nassir Assar, who was also a young diplomat assigned to the German consular office. During this period, he befriended Hoveyda and would remain a close associate for the rest of Hoveyda's life. Nassir Assar, interviewed by author, Washington, D.C., 15 February 1999.

6. Cyrus Ghani, interviewed by author, 9 June 1999.

7. Esmail Ra'in, *Faramoush-khaneh va Faramasoneri dar Iran* [Freemasonry In Iran], vol. 3, (Tehran, 1978), 357. Hoveyda's membership in the lodge was also confirmed both by Ahmad Ghoreishi and the "High Ranking Security Official." Ahmad Ghoreishi, interviewed by author, 28 February 1997. "High Ranking Security Official," interviewed by author, 23 November 1997.

8. Persians, of course, have not been the only people inclined towards notions of an all embracing conspiracy by the Freemasons. To describe the prevalence of the same kind of proclivity amongst Americans, Richard Hofstadter, an acclaimed historian, has coined the phrase, "the paranoid style in American politics," a style that "evokes qualities of heated exaggeration, suspiciousness, and conspiratorial fantasy." In America, well into the nineteenth century, the Freemasons were thought to be the main culprits of such a conspiracy. Eventually, the Catholics, the Illuminati, the Jews, and the Communists replaced the Freemasons as the subjects of this paranoid curiosity. For a discussion of the "paranoid style," see Richard Hofstadter, *The Paranoid Style in American Politics and Other Essays* (Cambridge, 1996), 3–14.

9. SAVAK apparently closely followed the activities of the Masons in Iran. According to "High Ranking Security Official," Hoveyda never attended any meetings after his appointment as prime minister. "High Ranking Security Official," interviewed by author, 23 November 1997.

10. For an account of SAVAK's role in the collection of information, see General Manouchehr Hashemi, *Davari: Sokhani dar Bareh-ye Karnameh-ye* SAVAK [Judgment: Some Thoughts on SAVAK's Record] (London, 1994), 261–264.

11. "High Ranking Security Official," interviewed by author, 20 March 1999.

12. Ra'in, *Faramoush-khaneh*, 505. The book claims that Entezam was the grand master of the "Independent Grand Lodge of Iran." It further adds that he was "the master of the Safi Ali-Shahi branch of Dervishes."

13. Zia Shadman, interviewed by author, Montreal, Canada, 30 May 1999.

14. Ra'in, *Faramoush-khaneh*, 674.

15. For a discussion of the shah's conspiratorial proclivities, see Ahmad Ashraf, "The Appeal of Conspiracy Theories to Persians," in *Princeton Papers: Interdisciplinary Journal of Middle Eastern Studies*, vol. 5 (1996), 65–70.

16. U.S. Embassy, Tehran, Iran, "Discussion of Censorship and Former Prime Minister Ali Amini: Confidential Memorandum of Conversation," NSA, no. 710.

17. U.S. Embassy, Tehran, Iran, "Semi-annual Assessment of the Political Situation in Iran, February 20, 1969," NSA, no. 724, 19.

18. Ehsan Naraghi, who knew both men well, talked of this father-son relationship. Ehsan Naraghi, interviewed by author, Paris, France, 11 March 1999.

19. Kaplan, *The Arabists*, 202.

20. Nassir Assar, interviewed by author, 12 May 1999.

21. Nassir Assar, interviewed by author, Washington, D.C., 12 May 1999.

22. Radji, *In the Service of the Peacock Throne*, 40.

23. Laila Emami, interviewed by author, Paris, France, 10 March 1999.

24. Stuart Rockwell, interviewed by author, 23 May 1999.

25. Fatemeh Soudavar Farmanfarmaian, interviewed by author, 12 May 1999.

26. Fereydoun Hoveyda, interviewed by author, 8 June 1999.

27. Fereydoun Hoveyda, interviewed by author.

28. Fereydoun Hoveyda, interviewed by author, 10 May 1999.

29. According to Fereydoun Hoveyda, Kazemi disliked Amir Abbas primarily for two reasons. On the one hand, Kazemi considered Hoveyda a protégé of Sepahbodi, for whom he had nothing but contempt. Furthermore, Kazemi also apparently had disliked Hoveyda's father. Fereydoun Hoveyda, interviewed by author, 11 May 1999.

30. Fatemeh Soudavar Farmanfarmaian, interviewed by author, 11 May 1999.

31. For the text of the letter, see Doldom, *Zendegi va Khaterat*, 84–85.

32. Ibid., 64–90.

33. Fereydoun Hoveyda, interviewed by author, 10 June 1999.

34. Cyrus Ghani, *Iran and the West* (London, 1987), 20.

35. The account of Hoveyda's first day of work at the NIOC was provided by Sadeq Chubak, interviewed by author, 22 November 1997.

36. Sadeq Chubak, interviewed by author, 15 February 1998.

37. Sadeq Chubak, interviewed by author, 15 November 1997.

38. Sadeq Chubak, interviewed by author, 10 October 1997.

39. Radji, *In the Service of the Peacock Throne*, 6.

40. Vajieh Ma'refat, interviewed by author, 27 January 1998.

41. "High Ranking Security Official," interviewed by author, 5 January 2000.

42. One such advisor was Zia Shadman, interviewed by author, Montreal, Canada, 29 May 1999.

43. Ghodsi Chubak, interviewed by author, 27 March 1999.

44. U.S. Embassy in Tehran, "The Iranian Intellectual Community: Problems and Recommendations for U.S. Action," Confidential Airgram, U.S. Embassy in Tehran, NSA, no. 494.

45. U.S. Embassy, Tehran, Iran, "The Iranian Intellectual Community," 8.

46. Ehsan Naraghi, *Khaterat*, 313–30.

47. Manouchehr Pirouz, interviewed by author, Paris, France, 14 March 1999.

48. U.S. Department of State, Bureau of Intelligence and Research, "Studies in Political Dynamics in Iran," NSA, no. 603.

49. Abdollah Entezam, "Letter," *Kavosh*, no. 1, Shahrivar 1339/August 1960.

50. Amir Abbas Hoveyda, "Introduction," *Kavosh*, No. 4, 4.

51. Ibid.

52. Laila Emami, interviewed by author, Paris, France, 8 March 1999.

53. For a detailed account of the work of the Point 4 program in Iran, see William E. Warne, *Mission for Peace: Point 4 in Iran* (Bethesda, 1999).

54. Jean Becker, interviewed by author Napa, California 21 March 1999.

55. Ibid.

56. Laila Emami, interviewed by author, Paris, France, 8 March 1999.

57. Ibid.

58. Ibid.

Chapter 7: The White Revolution

1. CIA, "Stability of the Present Regime in Iran: Secret Special National Intelligence Estimate," 1958/08/25, NSA, no. 362; see also "The Outlook for Iran: Secret National Intelligence Estimate NIE 34–60," NSA, no. 385.

2. Qarani was given a surprisingly light sentence of three years in jail. Immediately after the Islamic government came to power, he was named the revolution's first chief of the joint staff of the armed forces, only to be assassinated by terrorists less than two months later. For a brief account of Qarani's coup attempt and the role of the American Embassy in denying the rumors that the general enjoyed the support of the American government, see Bill, *The Eagle and the Lion*, 127–28.

3. For an account of the February meeting and others, and for the text of some important official correspondence in this matter, see *Foreign Relations, 1958–1960*, vol. XII (Washington, D.C., 1993), 537–543. In *The Eagle and the Lion*, James A. Bill suggests that rumors that Qarani enjoyed American support was partly the work of the British and, more importantly, "Clearly fictitious." See Bill, *The Eagle and the Lion*, 128. Embassy documents clearly show not only that there were serious discussions with Qarani but that one of his associates, Esfandiyar Bozorgmehr, had had meetings with Assistant Secretary of State William M. Roundtree, in Athens, Greece. The shah had known of these meetings and had complained to American officials. Secretary of State Dulles, in a telegram to the American Embassy in Tehran, wrote that the shah should be reassured that Roundtree had no previous knowledge of the meeting and that Bozorgmehr had "mentioned no plans or organization." See *Foreign Relations*, 542.

4. For a sympathetic insider's account of SAVAK, see Hashemi, *Davari*.

5. Much has been written about the coup. For a summary account, see David Halberstam, *The Fifties* (New York, 1993), 366–67.

6. U.S. Department of State, "Top Secret: A Survey of U.S.-Iranian Relations, 1941–1979," NSA, no. 3556, 23.

7. Mohammad Reza Pahlavi, *Answer to History* (New York, 1980) 93–97.

8. "Stability of the Present Regime in Iran," August 26, 1958, *Foreign Relations*, vol. XII, 586.

9. CIA, "Intelligence Memorandum," in *Foreign Relations of the United States, Iran, 1964–68*, vol. XXII (Washington, D.C. 1999), 247.

10. Ibid., 564.

11. Many sources have written about this decision and its consequences for both Iranian politics and the future of the relations between the U.S. and Iran. Henry Precht, who in the early seventies was in charge of military matters and arms sales in the U.S. Embassy in Iran talks about the briefing he received before he left Washington for Iran. "I was told that Iran could purchase anything the shah wanted. As a result, there was never any objection raised by us about the sale of arms. The only attempt to curb the sales came from [Melvin] Laird, at the Department of Defense; he wanted to set a limit on the number of American advisors that could be sent to Iran; but he left his job before he could actually implement the policy." Henry Precht, interviewed by author, 12 January 2000.

12. U.S. Department of State, "The Evolution of the U.S.-Iranian Relationship," NSA, no. 3556, 26.

13. "NSC Discussion of Our Policy Towards Iran, September 9, 1958," *Foreign Relations*, vol. XII, 588–89.

14. U.S. Department of State, "Top Secret: A Survey," *Foreign Relations*, vol. XII 29–30.

15. U.S. Embassy, Tehran, Iran, "Economic Assessment of Iran: November 1960," NSA 448, 3.

16. Abdol-Madjid Madjidi, interviewed in *Ideology, Process and Politics in Iran's Development Planning*, ed. Gholam Reza Afkhami (Washington, D.C., 1999), 292.

17. CIA, "Research Study: Elites and the Distribution of Power in Iran," February 1976,

facsimile reproduced in *Asnad-e Laneh-ye Jasusi* [Documents from the Den of Spies], vol. 7 (Tehran, n.d.), 37–40.

18. Farokh Najmabadi, interviewed by author, Washington, D.C., 12 July 1999.

19. Amir Abbas Hoveyda, "Bahs-e Ruz" [Current Issues], in *Kavosh*, Esfand 1339/March 1960, 2–3.

20. Amir Abbas Hoveyda, "Sali ke Gozasht" [The Year That Passed], in *Kavosh*, Norouz 1342/March 1963, 2–3.

21. Ibid.

22. Amir Abbas Hoveyda, handwritten notes. These notes were provided courtesy of Fereydoun Hoveyda.

23. U.S. Department of State, "The Iranian Intellectual Community: Problems and Recommendations for U.S. Action," 1963/12/21, NSA 494, 5.

24. A facsimile of the SAVAK report is produced in *Jostarhai dar Tarikh-e Moaser Iran* [Investigations into the Modern History of Iran], vol. 2 (Tehran, 1991), appendix. The pages of the appendix are not numbered.

25. Ibid.

26. Khodadad Farmanfarmaian, interviewed by author, 26 June 1999. Fereydoun Hoveyda also talked at length about such claims by Mansur.

27. Gratian Yatsevitch, "Interview," Foundation for Iranian Studies: Program of Oral History, Nov. 5, 1988, January 1989. 125–26.

28. For accounts of the early meetings, I have relied on interviews with Zia Shadman and Nassir Assar. Zia Shadman, interviewed by author, Montreal, Canada, 30 May 1999. Nassir Assar, interviewed by author, Washington, D.C., 12 May 1999.

29. JFK Library, "A Review of the Problem in Iran and Recommendations for the National Security Council," May 15, 1961.

30. T. Cutler Young, "Iran in Continuing Crisis," in *Foreign Affairs* (January 1962), 275–92. For a detailed discussion of this period and the contours of U.S. relations with Iran, see also Bill, *The Eagle and the Lion*, 98–131.

31. Alam indicates that in 1961, Ardeshir Zahedi was removed as Iran's ambassador to the United States because President-elect Kennedy had requested it. Kennedy was angry because of Zahedi's meddling in the election. See Alam, *Yadashtha-ye Alam* [Alam's Diaries], vol. 1, 219. Ardeshir Zahedi denies any involvement with contributions to the Nixon campaign. Ardeshir Zahedi, interviewed by author, 3 August 1999.

32. Alam, *Yadashtha-ye Alam* [Alam's Diaries], vol. 1, 137.

33. Ibid., 41.

34. JFK Library, "Basic Facts in the Iranian Situation," n.d.

35. JFK Library, U.S. Embassy, Tehran, Iran, "Confidential Cable," May 10, 1961.

36. Ibid., 137.

37. Gratian Yatsevitch, interviews in the Foundation for Iranian Studies: Program of Oral History, November, 1988, January 1989, 63–64.

38. U.S. Embassy, Tehran, Iran, "Economic Assessment for Iran, June 1961," NSA, no. 470, 13–14.

39. Ibid., 14.

40. For an early report of the committee's work and ideas, see "Report of the Chairman, Iran Task Force," National Security Archives, doc. 428. A brief discussion of its findings is found in *Iran: The Making of U.S. Policy, 1977-1980*, vol. 1 (Washington, D.C., 1990), 241.

41. JFK Library, A Review of the Problem in Iran, 1–3.

42. JFK Library, "Memorandum for the President," 18 May 1961.

43. "Summary of Proceedings of a Meeting of the Iran Task Force," Washington, September

7, 1961, in *Foreign Relations, 1961-63,* 252.

44. Armin Meyer, interviewed by author, 5 August 1999.

45. JFK Library, "Position Paper on Iran," 24 February 1961. No author for the report is indicated. In a note attached to the file, it is indicated that "the origin of...the paper is unknown," but that the "views expressed...parallel those of Dick Bissell's shop." From other sources in the JFK Library, we learn that "Bissell's shop" is in fact the CIA.

46. Memorandum from Robert W. Komer, Ibid., 428.

47. Memorandum for the President, 1961/10/19, NSA, no. 428, 1–2.

48. Ibid., 4–5.

49. JFK Library, National Security Council, 24 February 1961.

50. Memorandum from the State Department, Foreign Relations, 516.

51. JFK Library, U.S. Embassy, Tehran, Iran, "Confidential Cable," May 13, 1961.

52. NA, "Confidential Report, U.S. Embassy in Tehran," March 1964.

53. Bill, *The Eagle and the Lion,* 134.

54. Quoted in Bill, *The Eagle and the Lion,* 134.

55. Ibid., 35.

56. Ibid., 37.

57. U.S. National Security Council, "Memorandum from Robert W. Komer of the National Security Council Staff to President Johnson," in *Foreign Relations of the United States, 1964-1968,* vol. XXII (Washington, 1999), 139.

58. William O. Douglas, *The Court Years: 1939-75* (New York, 1980), 303–4.

Chapter 8: The Progressive Circle

1. JFK Library, "Confidential Memorandum, Iran," 3 April 1961, 3.

2. *Foreign Relations, 1961-63,* Vol. XVII (Washington, D.C. 1994), 429.

3. Stuart Rockwell, interviewed by author, 23 May 1999.

4. Amir Abbas Hoveyda, "Sokhan-e Kutah" [A Brief Note], in *Kavosh,* no. 2, new series, 1–2.

5. NA, "Confidential Telegram: U.S. Embassy in Tehran," 31 October 1963.

6. NA, "Conversation with Hassan Ali Mansur," 31 October 1963.

7. For a detailed discussion of the history and results of the land reform in Iran see, Eric J. Hoogland, *Land and Revolution in Iran, 1960-1980* (Austin, 1982), 72.

8. Firouz Tofig, "Development in Iran: A Statistical Note," in *Iran: Past, Present and Future,* ed. by Jane W. Jacqz (New York, 1976), 60.

9. Hoogland, *Land and Revolution,* 138.

10. Tofig, Development in Iran, 62.

11. Hoogland, *Land and Revolution,* 138–52.

12. Alam, *Yadashtha-ye Alam* [Alam's Diaries], vol. 1, 38–39.

13. For Alam's view of the American involvement see Alam, *Yadashtha-ye Alam* [Alam's Diaries], vol. 2, 69.

14. *Foreign Relations,* vol. XVIII (Washington, D.C., 1995), 610–12.

15. Ibid., 602.

16. NA, "Confidential Telegram to the Secretary of State," U.S. Embassy in Tehran, 25 October 1963.

17. Ibid., 2.

18. Zia Shadman, interviewed by author, Montreal, Canada, 30 May 1999.

19. Alinaghi Alikhani, personal correspondence, 20 January 2000.

20. NA, "Confidential Cable, U.S. Embassy," Tehran, March 1964.

21. NA, "U.S. Department of Army: Confidential Message," February 1964.

22. Mohammad Baheri, interviewed by author, Washington, D.C., 30 May 1999.

23. Mohammad Baheri, interviewed by author, Washington, D.C., 15 February 1999.

24. Letter no. 2157/2291/18, dated 1342/11/25. The letter is on the official stationery of the foreign ministry. Copy of the letter, courtesy of Mohammad Baheri.

25. Baheri, interview.

26. Baheri, interview.

27. Mozakerat-e Majlis Sena [Senate Proceedings], session 67, number 729/1342/5/3, 23–24. Copies of the proceedings courtesy of Mohammad Baheri.

28. NA, "Confidential Report, Department of the Army," 13 October 1964.

29. Baheri, interview.

30. NA, "Confidential Report, Department of the Army," 13 October 1964.

31. NA, "Confidential Report, Department of the Army," 5 November 1964.

32. NA, "Confidential Report, Department of the Army," 13 November 1964.

33. U.S. Embassy in Tehran, Iran, "Telegram from the Embassy to the Department of State," in *Foreign Relations*, Vol. XXII, 109–110.

34. Stuart Rockwell, interviewed by author, 9 February 2000.

35. Mozakerat-e Majlis Shora-ye Meli [Proceedings of Majlis] 12 Mehr 1343/4 October 1964, 28–33. Copies of the proceedings courtesy of Mohammad Baheri.

36. Ayatollah Khomeini, *Islam and Revolution: Writings and Declarations of Imam Khomeini*, tr. Hamid Algar (Berkeley, 1981), 182. The full text of the speech can be found there.

37. NA, " Confidential Report, Department of the Army," 5 November 1964.

38. Nassir Assar, interviewed by author, Washington, D.C., 3 February 1998.

39. Seyyed Fakhraddin Shadman, "Siyasat Nameh-ye Iran" [A Discourse on Iranian Politics], in *Khandaniha*, 26 Tir 1344/17 July 1965.

40. Jay Walz, "New Premier Gives Iranians Fresh Confidence" in *The New York Times*, Tuesday, April 7, 1964, 4.

41. U.S. Embassy, Tehran, Iran, "Memorandum of Conversation: Dr. Hossein Mahdavi and William O. Miller," NSA, no. 503, 1.

42. Ibid.

43. Jamshid Garachedaghi, interviewed by author, Berkeley, California, 30 June 1999.

44. Abdol-Madjid Madjidi, interviewed in *Ideology, Process and Politics in Iran's Development Planning*, ed. Gholam Reza Afkhami (Washington, D.C., 1999), 288–93.

45. NA, "Confidential Cable: U.S. Embassy in Tehran," January 1964.

46. Jamshid Garachedaghi, interviewed by author, Berkeley, California, 30 June 1999.

47. Laila Emami, interviewed by author, Paris, France, 12 March 1999.

48. U.S. Embassy, Tehran, Iran, "Bi-Weekly Economic Review: October 22-September 4, 1964," NSA, no. 45, 3.

49. Ibid., 2.

50. Ibid., 3.

51. U.S. Embassy in Tehran, Iran, "The Iranian One Party System," NSA, no. 975, 7.

52. U.S. Embassy, Tehran, Iran, "Quarterly Economic Summary for the Fourth Quarter: 6 March 1965," NSA, no. 67, 3.

53. U.S. Embassy in Tehran, Iran, "Shah and U.S.," NSA, no. 560, 1.

54. CIA, "National Intelligence Estimate, Iran," NSA, no. 520.

55. Director of Intelligence and Research, U.S. Department of State, "Land Reform in Iran: Implications for the Shah's 'White Revolution,'" 8 February 1965, NSA, no. 548.

Chapter 9: The Winter of Discontent

1. "Premier of Iran Shot by Student," *New York Times*, 22 January 1965.

2. U.S. Embassy, Tehran, Iran, "Assassination Attempt on Iranian Prime Minister," Unclassified Cable #00762, 1/21/65. NSA, no. 545.

3. For a discussion of Fada'iyun-e Islam and its affinities with Ayatollah Khomeini, see Amir H. Ferdows, "Khomeini and Fada'iyun's Society and Politics," *International Journal of Middle East Studies* 15 (1983), 241.

4. Ahmad Kasravi, *Shii'gari* [Shiism] (Tehran, 1978). Kasravi was murdered on 30 April 1945. For a detailed account of his murder, see Naser Pakdaman, *Qatl-e Kasravi* [Murder of Kasravi] (Upssala, 1999).

5. For an account of Hashemi's role in the assassination, see *Hashemi Rafsanjani: Dowran-e Mobarezeh* [Hashemi Rafsanjani: The Period of Struggle] (Tehran, 1997), 33–37.

6. *Khandaniha*, 29 Khordad 1344/20 June 1965.

7. U.S. Embassy, Tehran, Iran, "Discussion of Various Topics Including the Mansur Assassination, the National Front, and Other Political Parties with Hedayatollah Matine-Daftary," NSA, no. 547.

8. Ibid.

9. "High Ranking Security Official," interviewed by author, 6 January 2000.

10. "High Ranking Security Official," interviewed by author, 23 November 1997.

11. Ibid.

12. Laila Emami, interviewed by author, Paris, France, 8 March 1999.

13. "Premier of Iran Shot by Student," *New York Times*, 22 January 1965.

14. "Iran, The 18th Premier," *Time*, 20 March 1964, 36.

15. Laila Emami, interviewed by author, Paris, France, 10 March 1999.

16. For information about these visits, I have relied on Iranian newspaper and magazine accounts of the time, particularly those in *Kayhan* and *Sepid va Siah*, as well as the recollections of Dr. Abdol Hossein Samii, interviewed by author, 7 February 1998. For a brief discussion of Dr. Samii's relations with Hoveyda, see chapter one, note 7.

17. Laila Emami, interviewed by author, Paris, France, 12 March 1999.

18. U.S. Department of State, "Information Memorandum," in *Foreign Relations of the United States, 1964-1968*, Vol. XXII (Washington, 1999), 138.

19. My account of Hoveyda's meeting with the shah is based on what he told several of his friends. In separate interviews, Sadeq Chubak, Ahmad Ghoreishi, and Fereydoun Hoveyda told me the same stories about the meeting, and they had each heard the story from Hoveyda himself. The only difference was in the kind of emphasis each placed on the elements of the story itself.

20. Abdol-Majid Madjidi, interviewed by author, Washington, D.C., 15 February 1999.

21. For an account of Reza Shah's treatment of his ministers, see Abbasgholi Golshayan, "Khaterat" [Memoirs], *Vahid*, December 1997, 2–17.

22. "High Ranking Security Official," interviewed by author, 6 January 2000.

23. Sadeq Chubak, interviewed by author, 25 November 1997.

24. According to Mostafa Alamouti, Hoveyda told him the gist of his discussion with the shah only hours afterwards. Hoveyda insisted that he had told the shah he did not feel he could shoulder the responsibilities of prime minister. See Alamouti, *Iran Dar Asr-e Pahlavi*, 98.

25. Abdol-Majid Madjidi, interviewed by author, 15 February 1999.

26. *Khandaniha*, 12 Tir 1344/3 July 1965. The same magazine claimed that Jamshid Amouzegar would be the next prime minister. Amouzegar was eventually appointed prime minister, but in June 1977, a good twelve years later!

27. NA, U.S. Embassy, Tehran, Iran, "Short-Term Trends in the Political Situation in Iran," March 18, 1965, A-483.

28. Sadeq Chubak, interviewed by author, 25 November 1997. Ahmad Ghoreishi also recounted hearing Hoveyda say that the shah told him those words. Ahmad Ghoreishi, interviewed by author, 14 August 1998. The tone of what the shah said is very similar to a conversation he had with Mehdi Samii. When there were rumors about Samii taking over the job of Hoveyda as prime minister, he went to see the shah to tell him that he thought he did not "have the mettle" to become a prime minister, and furthermore he considered himself a close friend of Hoveyda. "All of this is of no importance," the shah said, adding, "if we want to make someone a prime minister, all we have to do is decide." He then pointed to a small path that ran by the stream in the palace compound. "You see that path," the shah said by way of reassuring the reluctant candidate for the prime minister's job, "you see how narrow it is; that is how much independence our prime minister has." Mehdi Samii, interviewed by author, Los Angeles, 11 June 1998.

29. Bureau of Intelligence and Research, Department of State, "Studies in Political Dynamics in Iran," Secret Intelligence Report # 13, NSA, no. 603.

30. For a discussion of the relationships between kings and viziers, see Amanat, *The Pivot of the Universe.*

31. Bureau of Intelligence and Research, "Studies in Political Dynamics of Iran," 14.

32. Samii, interview.

33. Samii, interview.

34. In his angry public pronouncement, the shah was rather circumspect, and indirect, in his reference to the possible role of the British. In private, however, he seems to have attacked, and accused Britain, much more openly. "High Ranking Security Official," interviewed by author, 27 November 1999.

35. I heard the account of the story from Ahmad Ghoreishi and the "High Ranking Security Official."

36. "High Ranking Security Official," interviewed by author, 12 January 2000.

37. *Bamshad*, 5 Bahaman 1343/25 February 1965.

38. *New York Times*, 28 January 1965, 6.

39. Zia Shadman, interviewed by author, Montreal, Canada, 29 May 1999.

40. Shadman, interview.

41. U.S. Embassy, Tehran, Iran, "Discussion of Various Topics, including the Mansur Assassination, the National Front, and Other Political Parties with Hedayatollah Matine-Daftary," NSA, no. 547, 4.

42. NA, U.S. Embassy, Tehran, Iran, "Confidential Cable," 25 March 1969.

43. *Khandaniha*, 5 Azar 1345/26 November 1966.

44. *Khandaniha*, 11 Bahman 1345/31 January 1967.

45. Laila Emami, interviewed by author, Paris, France, 12 March 1999. The text of the resolution is in Alamouti, *Iran dar Asr-e Pahlavi*, 103.

46. In a secret cable, the American Embassy provides an "illustrative, not exhaustive" list of "well-known U.S. companies" that are, "to the embassy's certain knowledge, buying the influence of the persons listed." The list is as follows: "General Electric—Fathollah Mahvi; Northrop Corporation—Fathollah Mahvi; Boeing Aircraft Company—Fathollah [Abolfath] Mahvi; Cities Service—Khosrow Eghbal; McDonald Douglas Corporation—Fathollah [Abolfath] Mahvi; Radio Corporation of America—Reza Razmara; Merill[sic]-Price—Shapour Reporter." See "American Companies and Influence Peddlers," Secret List (Documents from U.S. Espionage Den. V, 17–70), NSA, no. 781.

47. For an account of Reporter's life and role in Iran, see "Iranian Affairs: Caught Reporter," *Private Eye*, 19 March 1976. Quoted and briefly described in Cyrus Ghani, *Iran and The West* (London, 1987), 877.

48. Laila Emami, interviewed by author, Paris, France, 12 March 1999.

49. Emami, interview.

50. Emami, interview.

51. NA, U.S. Embassy, Tehran, Iran, "Confidential Cable," March 1965.

52. *Khandaniha*, 1 Mordad 1345/23 July 1966, 6.

53. Ibid., 50.

54. Eskandar Doldom, *Zendegi va Khaterat-e Amir Abbas Hoveyda* [The Life and Memoirs of Amir Abbas Hoveyda] (Tehran, 1998), 63–66.

55. Laila Emami, interviewed by author, Paris, France, 12 March 1999.

56. Laila Emami, interviewed by author, Paris, France, 19 July 1999.

57. Edouard Sablier, interviewed by author, Paris, France, 12 March 1999.

Chapter 10: Notes from a Time of War

1. Hoveyda, "Yadashtha-ye Zaman-e Jang," 33.

2. In the early 1960s, several people helped Hoveyda write and polish his Persian material. They included his chief of staff, Mohammad Safa, his friends, Sadeq Chubak, Anjavi Shirazi, and Parviz Radji; Safa, Chubak, and Radji, each indicated that they had no part in the translation of the journals. They also did not know who helped with the translation.

3. Fereshteh Ensha, interviewed by author, Paris, France, 11 March 1999.

4. Amir Abbas Hoveyda, "Moraje'at be Iran" [Return to Iran] in *Donya*, 24th annual edition (Tehran, 1971), 376.

5. For an overview of the history of biography and memoir in Iran, see Ahmad Ashraf, "Short History of Iranian Memoirs" in *Iran Nameh* vol. XX, no. 1 (1997).

6. For a discussion of the idea of "equivocation," see Austin Fagothey, *Right and Reason: Ethics in Theory and Practice* (St. Louis, 1953), 319–21.

7. Isaiah Berlin, *Russian Thinkers*, ed. Henry Hardy and Aileen Kelly (London, 1986), 22.

8. Walter Benjamin, *Charles Baudelaire: A Lyric Poet in the Era of High Capitalism*, tr. Harry Zohn (London, 1969), 36–40.

9. Reza Baraheni, interviewed by author, 12 June 1999.

10. Quoted in *Bamshad*, 21 Esfand 1345/12 March 1967.

11. Both Baraheni and Sa'edi concur on the elements of this discussion. See Baraheni, *Zel Allah*, 14–27; and Gholam Hossein Sa'edi, Iran's Oral History Project at Harvard University, in *Alefba*, (Paris), no. 7, 139–170.

12. At this time, Mohammad Safa had been hired by Hoveyda to manage the daily affairs of the magazine. Safa had been a follower of Mosaddeq, and in the footnotes he prepared for an interview the magazine had conducted with Ali Amini, Safa had included a savory comment about Mosaddeq. According to Safa, Asadollah Alam made sure the shah saw a copy of the interview, and the shah was so angered by the reference to Mosaddeq that he ordered the magazine closed for a while. Mohammad Safa, interviewed by author, 21 November 1997.

13. For Al-e Ahmad's comments, I have relied on Reza Baraheni, interviewed by author, 12 June 1999.

14. Sa'edi, *Alefba*, 100.

15. Jalal Al-e Ahmad and Parviz Darius, *Ma'edeha-ye Zamini* (Tehran, 1965).

16. Reza Baraheni, interviewed by author, 12 June 1999.

17. See Ebrahim Golestan, *Gofteha* [Sayings] (New Jersey, 1999).

18. Ebrahim Golestan recounts his regular visits to Fereydoun's house in Tehran where a wide assortment of intellectuals often gathered. Ebrahim Golestan, Forough Farokhzad, and Sadeq Chubak were among the regular visitors. Ebrahim Golestan, interviewed by author, 15 September 1999.

19. In the introduction to the Persian edition of his *Crowned Cannibals*, Reza Baraheni provides a sense of the intellectual flavor of the time. See Baraheni, *Zel Allah* [Crowned Cannibals], 14–27. For Al-e Ahmad's views on the two Hoveyda brothers, see Al-e Ahmad, *Karnameh-ye Se Saleh* [A Three-Year Report], 223–25.

20. Khalil Maleki, *Do Nameh* [Two Letters] (Tehran, 1978). Maleki's letters are addressed to Mosaddeq. In the letters, Maleki complains about the leaders of the National Front, who in his words have become allies of reactionary clerics. Even the shah, Maleki suggests, is preferable to the mullahs. The shah and SAVAK also turned out to be incapable of accepting the opposition as serious negotiating partners. Ironically, as the shah's power grew, his tolerance for dissent and mild opposition diminished.

21. Ehsan Naraghi, interviewed by author, Paris, France, 12 March 1999.

22. "Karnameh-ye Dowlat-e Hoveyda" [The Record of the Hoveyda Cabinet] in *Socialism*, Farvardin 1345/April 1966, 1–16.

23. Mohammad Safa, interviewed by author, 21 November 1997.

24. Safa, interview.

25. U.S. Embassy, Tehran, Iran, "Confidential Memorandum of Conversation: Prime Minster Hoveyda's Meeting with Nation of Iran Party Leader Foruhar," 1968/05/09, NSA, no. 664.

26. Amir Abbas Hoveyda, "Notes for a Talk," courtesy of Fereydoun Hoveyda.

27. Ibid.

28. For an account of Hoveyda's role in the negotiations to legalize the Tudeh Party and return its leaders to Iran, see Iraj Eskandari, *Khaterat* [Memoirs] (Tehran, 1983), 417.

29. U.S. Embassy, Tehran, Iran, "Confidential Memorandum of Conversation," NSA, no. 835. Vladimir Vlasov, first secretary of the Soviet Embassy in Tehran, suggests that "the Tudeh would like to return to Iran and operate openly as a legitimate political party but the shah will not accept it."

30. U.S. Embassy, Tehran, Iran, "Discussion about Vienna Convention, Military Assistance, the Mansur Government and Land Reform: Memorandum of Conversation," National Security Archive, doc. 542.

31. U.S. Embassy, Tehran, Iran, "Discussion with Shapour Bakhtiar about the National Front, the Shah, Communism and Prime Minister Hoveyda: Memorandum of Conversation," NSA, no. 552.

32. Seifeddin Vahidnia, editor of a magazine called *Vahid*, who was a proponent of Hoveyda's, provided a published account of these payments. With Hoveyda's help, the editor became a member of parliament. He wrote, "It has often happened that [Hoveyda] has helped scholars and intellectuals of this country who have been forced to sit at home....When he heard about their plight, with no pretense and no expectation [of gratitude] he has tried to alleviate their difficulties. Recently, we have heard that he has sent some money to one of the most capable of poets who was stranded in Europe." See *Vahid*, Aban 1349/November 1970, 636. Ahmad Ghoreishi, who in the mid-1970s was named president of the National University, suggested that soon after his appointment, he was called by the prime minister and told to place Karim Sanjabi, one of the leaders of the National Front, on the university payroll as a consultant. Ahmad Ghoreishi, interviewed by author, 28 November 1997. In another report to the American Embassy, it is claimed that "Sanjabi has long been on the NIOC payroll at a salary of...about $3,220." U.S. Embassy, "Secret Intelligence Report," NSA, no. 2142.

33. Mostafa Alamouti indicated that while he was the majority whip in the Majlis, he visited Hoveyda and told him of Eslaminia's reputation for financial corruption. Hoveyda is supposed to have responded, "I know, I receive reports on these things regularly...Eslaminia, however, is very close to Ayatollah Ahmad Khonsari...Any problems we have with the clergy or with

people in the bazaar, he can solve." Mostafa Alamouti, *Iran dar Asr-e Pahlavi* [Iran under the Pahlavis] (London, 1992), 117–18.

34. On June 21, 1978, Eslaminia carried the message to the shah, through Hoveyda, that he "would no longer cooperate with Khomeini, because Khomeini is against the shah." U.S. Embassy, Tehran, Iran, "Latest Developments on the Religious Front: Confidential Memorandum of Conversation," NSA, no. 1427.

35. Nassir Assar, interviewed by author, Washington, D.C., 15 February 1999. There was, of course, always a perception among the public that the Oghaf's wealth was notoriously ill-managed.

36. Nassir Assar, interview.

37. According to Nassir Assar, the million toman budget was the largest, and the only regular, payment made to the clerics through his office. Nassir Assar, interviewed by author. He believes that not only SAVAK and the ministry of court paid out sums to clerics but that the NIOC also had a special fund set aside for this purpose. Only when the archives of these institutions are opened for public scrutiny can the details of these charges be sorted out.

38. Daryoush Homayoun, interviewed by author, Belmont, California, 6 June 1999.

39. Quoted in James A. Bill, *The Eagle and the Lion: The Tragedy of American-Iranian Relations* (New Haven, 1988), 166.

40. Fatemeh Soudavar Farmanfarmaian, Cyrus Ghani, and Jahangir Behrouz each recounted an experience along the same lines.

41. Hoveyda, "Yadashtha-ye Zaman-e Jang," 34.

42. Ibid., 38.

43. Ibid., 39.

44. Ibid., 53.

45. Ibid.

46. Alam, *The Shah and I*, 133.

47. Ibid., 223.

48. Hoveyda, "Yadashtha-ye Zaman-e Jang," 39.

49. Ibid., 53.

50. CIA Board of National Estimates, "Secret Special Memorandum, #9–68: The Shah's Increasing Assurance," NSA, no. 448.

51. Ibid., 1–3.

52. I had many conversations with Chubak about his friendship with Hedayat in the mid-1990s. On more than one occasion, he indicated that Hedayat, by his own admission, was inspired by *Ninotchka* in writing *The Islamic Pilgrimage to the Land of the Franks*. It is not clear whether he had in fact seen the film or simply read about it in one of the European magazines he avidly read. Ebrahim Golestan, personal correspondence, 26 January 2000.

53. Hoveyda, "Yadashtha-ye Zaman-e Jang," 34.

54. Laila Emami, interviewed by author, Paris, France, 12 March 1999.

55. Eskandar Doldom's book repeats all of these allegations without offering any evidence. See Doldom, *Zendegi va Khaterat* [Life and Memoirs].

56. A center generally acknowledged in Iran to be an arm of the Islamic Republics' intelligence agencies published the document. See *Jostarha-i dar Tarikh Moaser-e Iran* [Investigations into the Modern History of Iran], vol. 2 (Tehran, 1991), 396–97. Doldom repeats the charge in his book, see Doldom, *Zendegi va Khaterat*, 66–68.

57. Laila Emami, interviewed by author.

58. "High Ranking Security Official," interviewed by author, 22 November 1997.

59. Hoveyda, "Yadashtha-ye Zaman-e Jang," 47.

60. Mohammad Reza Pahlavi, *Mission for My Country* (New York, 1961). The book includes

numerous allusions to mystic experiences. As the shah later told an incredulous Oriana Fallaci, he always felt like he received "a kind of revelation, or messages from above." See Oriana Fallaci, *Goftogouha* [Interviews] (Tehran, 1998), 145–153.

61. Quoted in *The Nation*, 7 October 1978, 329.

62. Amir Abbas Hoveyda, "The Future of Iran" in *Iran: Past, Present and Future*, ed. Jane W. Jacqs (New York, 1975), 448.

Chapter 11: Politics in Petro-Pompeii

1. Laila Emami, interviewed by author, Paris, France, 12 March 1999.

2. Jean Becker, interviewed by author, Napa, California, 21 March 1999.

3. Abdol-Madjid Madjidi, "Interview with Abdol-Madjid Madjidi," Foundation for Iranian Studies: Program of Oral History, April-October 1982, 47.

4. Afsaneh Jahanbani, interviewed by author, Paris, France, 3 June 1998.

5. Mohammad Safa, interviewed by author, 21 November 1997.

6. Vajieh Ma'refat, interviewed by author, 27 January 1997.

7. NA, U.S. Embassy, Tehran, Iran, "Bi-Weekly Economic Review, December 25, 1965-January 7, 1966," A-462.

8. U.S. Embassy, Tehran, Iran, "Memorandum of Conversation," 1/21/78, NSA, no. 2142.

9. Fereydoun Hoveyda, interviewed by author, 1 August 1999.

10. Vajieh Ma'refat, interviewed by author, 27 January 1998.

11. Radji, *In the Service of the Peacock Throne*, 236.

12. The facsimile of the SAVAK report can be found in *Jostarhai dar Tarikh Moaser–e Iran* [Inquiries in Modern History of Iran] (Tehran, 1991), vol. 2. The document is the next to the last reproduced in the book as part of the appendix. The whole section of the indexes has no page numbers.

13. Ibid.

14. *Khandaniha*, 3 Mehr 1343/25 September 1964.

15. Laila Emami, interviewed by author, Paris, France, 26 July 1999.

16. Radji, *In the Service of the Peacock Throne*, 8.

17. Ahmad Ghoreishi, interviewed by author, 24 November 1997.

18. Ahmad Ghoreishi, interview.

19. Fereydoun Hoveyda, interviewed by author, 6 December 1997.

20. LBJ Library, "Profile of the Prime Minister" in *Visit of the PM Hoveyda of Iran*, 12/5-6/68.

21. Jahansouz Bahrami was the head of Hoveyda's security detachment. Bahrami, interviewed by author, Los Angeles, California, 23 April 1998.

22. Alam, *Yadashtha-ye Alam* [Alam's Diaries], vol. 3.

23. U.S. Embassy, Tehran, Iran, "Washburn's Views and Thoughts on Iran upon Leaving," August 11, 1973, NSA, no. 830.

24. Fereydoun Hoveyda, interviewed by author, 23 July 1999.

25. Mohammad Safa, interviewed by author, 21 November 1997.

26. Alinaghi Alikhani, interviewed by author, 4 August 1999.

27. NA, U.S. Embassy, Tehran, Iran, "Bi-Weekly Economic Review, May 29-June 11 1965," A-667.

28. U.S. Embassy, Tehran, Iran, "Bi-Weekly Economic Review, March 6-19, 1965," NSA, A-489.

29. NA, U.S. Embassy, Tehran, Iran, "Semi-Annual Assessment of the Political Situation in Iran," February 19, 1966, A-104, 2.

30. NA, U.S. Department of the Army, "Confidential Cable," March 1965.

31. Fereydoun Mahdavi, interviewed by author, 8 August 1999.

32. Mahdavi, interview.

33. NA, "Confidential Cable, Department of the Army," February 1965.

34. U.S. Embassy, Tehran, Iran, "Bi-Weekly Economic Review, January 23-February 5, 1965," NSA, no. A-415.

35. NA, U.S. Embassy, Tehran, Iran, "Death of Former Prime Minister Mohammed Mosaddeq," 9 March 1967, A-493. Fereydoun Hoveyda confirms the embassy story; Fereydoun further adds that it was Mosaddeq's son, Gholam Hossein, who approached Amir Abbas as a friend and asked for help in receiving permission for the funeral.

36. NA, U.S. Embassy, Tehran, Iran, "Aftermath of Mosaddeq Death," 8 March 1967.

37. NA, U.S. Embassy, Tehran, Iran, "Semi-Annual Assessment of the Political Situation in Iran," August 1965, A-105.

38. Mehdi Pirasteh, interviewed by author, 8 August 1999.

39. Pirasteh, interview.

40. U.S. Department of State, "Memorandum from the Director of the Bureau of Intelligence and Research (Hughes) to Secretary of State Rusk," in *Foreign Relations*, Vol. XXII, 127.

41. U.S. Embassy, Semi-Annual Assessment, 5.

42. Quoted in Mahmoud Toloui, *Bazigaran-e Asr-e Pahlavi* [Players in the Pahlavi Regime], vol. 1 (Tehran, 1994), 516-18. I have used the English translation of the letter in *Islam and Revolution: Writings and Declarations of Imam Khomeini*, tr. Hamid Algar (Berkeley, 1981), 189–193.

43. NA, American Consulate, Tabriz, Iran "Prime Minister Hoveyda Cracks the Whip," A-5, 31 August 1967.

44. Abdol-Madjid Madjidi, interviewed by author, Washington, D.C., 15 February 1999.

45. Fereydoun Hoveyda, interviewed by author, 6 December 1997.

46. The Islamic Republic's version of SAVAK, SAVAMA, has claimed that Hoveyda joined the ranks of the secret police not long after the formation of SAVAK. The claim is based on an alleged employment list and a notation on Hoveyda's file in SAVAK. In conversations with the "High Ranking Security Official," he not only denied the story of Hoveyda's employment but also argued that the document referred to must be a fabrication. The department it claims Hoveyda belonged to did not begin its operation until long after the date of the incriminating list. "High Ranking Security Official," interviewed by author, 23 November 1998. For the Islamic Republic's version of the story, see *Jostarhai dar Tarikh Moaser-e Iran* [Inquiries in Modern History of Iran], 372–75.

47. "High Ranking Security Official," interviewed by author, 24 November 1997. He provided examples of cases where the shah had to personally approve the text of a declaration of repentance by one of the opponents of the regime. The case of Bahram Molai, one of the arrested members of the Tudeh Party, was an example of such royal micro-managment of the SAVAK.

48. Pahlavi, *Answer to History*, 158.

49. "High Ranking Security Official," interview.

50. "High Ranking Security Official," interview.

51. "High Ranking Security Official," interview.

52. Farokh Najmabadi, interviewed by author, Washington, D.C., 12 July 1999.

53. Homayoun, interview.

54. Jahangir Behrouz, interviewed by author, 2 April 1999. The story is confirmed in its most important details by Dariush Homayoun. "Maybe he is right and I should have stood up for him," said Homayoun when I told him about Behrouz's criticism of his inaction.

55. NA, U.S. Embassy, Tehran, Iran, "Changes in Ministry of Information," 22 June 1971, A-178. Some observers have suggested that Mansur's downfall was primarily the result of his refusal to agree to a bill that would have granted independence to the country's radio and television organization. Iraj Aryanpour, personal correspondence, 13 January 2000.

56. U.S. Embassy, Tehran, Iran, "Confidential Telegram," 1968/02/27, NSA, no. 649.

57. Homayoun, interview.

58. Homayoun, interview.

59. U.S. Embassy, Tehran, Iran, "Traditional Iranian Politics," 10/25/78, NSA, no. 1617.

60. Mostafa Mesbahzadeh, letter to author, 24 August 1998.

61. Alam, *Yadashtha-ye Alam* [Diaries], vol. 3, 316–17.

62. Such views can be found among both Hoveyda's friends and foes. Of the latter group, Houshang Nahavandi believes that toward the end of his tenure, Hoveyda had amassed more power than the shah, and that in fact the king had grown concerned about the whole issue. Jamshid Garachedaghi, a seasoned technocrat, opines that Hoveyda often manipulated the shah. In his view, Hoveyda did not flaunt his power but indeed worked hard to feign powerlessness, which was a key to his success.

63. U.S. Embassy, Tehran, Iran, "Ali Amini, 28 February 1968," NSA, no. 652. After 1965, when the shah first attacked Amini, the U.S. Embassy apparently kept in touch with Amini through an intermediary. Invariably, messages to the embassy from Amini, including the one quoted here, were delivered by Rahmatollah Moghadam. See also NA, U.S. Embassy, Tehran, Iran, "The Public Attack on Former Prime Minister Ali Amini," 2 March 1968, A-465.

64. Iradj Amini, interviewed by author, 4 August 1999.

65. Iradj Amini, interview.

66. Alinaghi Alikhani, interviewed by author, 5 August 1999.

67. NA, U.S. Embassy, Tehran, Iran, "Prime Minister Hoveyda: Recommendation for an Official Visit to the United States," 14 December 1967, Airgram, A-332.

68. LBJ Library, Harold H. Saunders, "Memorandum for Walt Rostow," 13 November 1968.

69. LBJ Library, "Suggestions on Approaching Iranians and Topics of Conversation."

70. LBJ Library, Memorandum for the President, 4 December 1968.

71. LBJ Library, "Checklist of Talking Points," 4 December 1968.

72. LBJ Library, "Wife of the Prime Minister of Iran," 1–2.

73. LBJ Library, "Cyrus Ghani, Advisor to the Prime Minister."

74. Cyrus Ghani, interviewed by author, 25 July 1999.

75. Cyrus Ghani, interviewed by author, 9 July 1999.

76. LBJ Library, "Visit of PM Hoveyda, Gift Suggestions."

77. Ibid., 1.

78. Ibid., 2.

79. U.S. Embassy, Tehran, Iran, "Telegram from the Embassy in Iran to the Department of State," *Foreign Relations,* Vol. XXII, 190.

80. CIA, The Shah of Iran's Current Outlook, *Foreign Relations,* vol. XXII, 227.

81. CIA, Secret Special Memorandum #9-68, "The Shah's Increasing Assurance," 1968/05/07, NSA, no. 663.

82. Radji, *In the Service of the Peacock Throne,* 6.

83. LBJ Library, Memorandum, 4.

84. U.S. State Department, "The Evolution of the U.S.-Iranian Relations," NSA, no. 3555, 20.

85. Radji, *In the Service of the Peacock Throne,* 97.

86. Madjidi, "Interview with Abdol-Madjid Madjidi," 7.

87. NA, "Secret Cable, British and Iranian Relations in the Persian Gulf," June 1970.

88. NA, "Secret Cable, Iran-UK relations Re Gulf," July 1970.

89. NA, U.S. Embassy, Tehran, Iran, "Secret Cable, Possible Iran-British Crisis Brewing," June 1971.

90. NA, "Secret Cable, Oil-Consortium/GOI Negotiations," January 1973.

91. LBJ Library, Memorandum, 2.

92. LBJ Library, "Checklist of Talking Points."

93. Ibid., 6.

94. LBJ Library, "President's Toast."

95. NA, State Department, "Secret Cable to Mr. Rostow," 18 December 1968.

96. I heard the most articulate rendition of this wager from Farokh Najmabadi. Najmabadi, interview. Madjidi, too, in his "Oral History Interview" makes much the same point.

97. Ghani, interview.

98. Akbar Etemad, *Iran's Atomic Energy Program: Mission, Structures, Politics,* ed. Gholam Reza Afkhami (Bethesda, 1997), 15.

99. Ibid., 85.

100. Ibid., 65.

101. Ibid.

102. Ibid., 29.

103. *New York Times,* 29 May 1976.

104. LBJ Library, Office of the White House Press Secretary, "Joint Statement," 5 December 1968.

105. NA, "State Department, Secret Cable to Mr. Rostow," 18 December 1968. According to Fereydoun Hoveyda, there was a reason for the snub. "On the one hand, Nixon had received money from the shah for his campaign and by meeting with Hoveyda he might have thought this would attract attention." On the other hand, "many of Nixon's advisors were close to Zahedi who, through his machinations, was able to get them to snub Hoveyda." Fereydoun Hoveyda, interviewed by author, 11 October 1999.

Chapter 12: The Ghost Valley

1. He is mentioned in a rather strange list of the Iranian political elite, before and after the revolution, prepared by the United States Department of State. NSA, no. 3510.

2. Alam, *Yadashtha-ye Alam* [Alam's Diaries], vol. 1, 378.

3. Many of his ministers, including Farokh Najmabadi, Abdol-Madjid Madjidi, and Mahnaz Afkhami, told me about this problem. Afkhami also told me that on the day of her appointment as the minister of women's affairs, Hoveyda mentioned that she should not try to contact the shah directly. Mahnaz Afkhami, interviewed by author, San Francisco, 26 October 1997.

4. CIA, "Elites and the Distribution of Power in Iran," February 1976, NSA, no. 1012, 37.

5. Zahedi, interview.

6. Zahedi, interview.

7. Zahedi, interview.

8. NA, U.S. Embassy, Tehran, Iran, "The Style of the New Foreign Minister," 13 February 1967, A-431.

9. Ibid., 2.

10. Zahedi, interview.

11. Zahedi, interview.

12. For an account of this meeting, I have relied on Alikhani (interview by author, 12 January 2000) and Zahedi (interviewed by author, 11 January 2000).

13. For a brief overview of the Bahrain developments, see Rouhollah K. Ramazani, *Iran's Foreign Policy 1941-1973: A Study of Foreign Policy in Modernizing Nations* (Charlottesville, 1975), 410–23.

14. Fereydoun Hoveyda, who was a member of the committee, told me about the long hours spent pondering the question and their shock at hearing the news of the shah's secret agreement. Fereydoun Hoveyda, interviewed by author, 6 December 1997. According to Fereydoun, when Amir Abbas Hoveyda heard of the shah's agreement, he suggested to the shah that the prime minister should claim responsibility for the deal, lest there be a public uproar against it. The shah refused the offer.

15. Zahedi, interview.

16. Several reports from the American Embassy in Tehran refer to the Pan Iranist Party as one whose leadership was controlled by the government. For example, one report indicated that "Pan Iranist deputies elected…to Majlis can be expected to serve primarily as a propaganda instrument." National Archive, "Confidential Airgram: Pan Iranist Party, August 30, 1967." In another dispatch called "the Noisy Pan Iranists in Parliament" the embassy reports that "it should be emphasized that for many of these men—particularly the older ones—membership in the party has brought tangible rewards. Largely because of its close SAVAK connections, the party has been able to advance the careers of its members." NA, "The Noisy Pan Iranists in the Parliament, January 27, 1968."

17. Zahedi, interview.

18. Alam, *Yadashtha-ye Alam* [Alam's Diaries], vol. 2, 88.

19. Ibid., 88–89.

20. Zahedi, interview.

21. NA, U.S. Embassy, Tehran, Iran, "Confidential Cable, GOI Cabinet Changes," September 1971.

22. Zahedi, interview.

23. Sally Quinn, *The Party: A Guide to Adventurous Entertaining* (New York, 1997), 206

24. Alam, *Yadashtha-ye Alam* [Alam's Diaries], vol. 3, 366.

25. Several cabinet ministers, including Madjidi and Shadman, told me about the story. Ahmad Kashefian, in charge of the discretionary fund, explained the process to me.

26. Laila Emami, interviewed by author, Paris, France, 9 March 1999.

27. Laila Emami, interviewed by author, Paris, France, 8 March 1999.

28. Laila Emami, interviewed by author, Paris, France, 8 March 1999.

29. Mohammad Safa, interviewed by author, 21 November 1997.

30. Laila Emami, interviewed by author, Paris, France, 26 July 1999.

31. Laila Emami, interviewed by author, Paris, France, 26 July 1999.

32. Laila Emami, interviewed by author, Paris, France, 11 March 1999.

33. Laila Emami letter to Jean Brumett, 22 April 1971. After her marriage, Brumett chose her husband's last name of Becker. Letter courtesy of Jean Becker.

34. Jean Crooker to Jean Brumett, private correspondence, Monday, 1972 [sic]. Letter courtesy of Jean Becker.

35. Parviz C. Radji, letter to author, 7 November 1997.

36. Abdol-Majid Madjidi, "Interview with Abdol-Majid Madjidi," Foundation for Iranian Studies: Program of Oral History, April-October 1982, 49.

37. Ibid.

38. Abbas Tofiq, interviewed by author, Los Angeles, California, 14 October 1998.

39. "High Ranking Security Official," interviewed by author, 23 November 1998.

40. Ebrahim Golestan, personal correspondence, 20 January 2000.

41. Ibid.

42. Ibid.

43. Ebrahim Golestan, *Az Ruzegar-e Rafteh Hekayat* [Tales of Old Times] in *Mad o Meh* [High Tide and the Fog] (Tehran, 1969), 65.

44. Ebrahim Golestan, interviewed by author, 12 September 1999.

45. Ebrahim Golestan, *Asrar-e Ganj-e Dareh-ye Jeni* [Mysteries of the Treasure at the Ghost Valley] (Tehran, 1974), 154.

46. Ibid., 139.

47. Ibid., 114–115.

48. Ibid., 158.

49. Ebrahim Golestan, interviewed by author, 12 September 1999.

50. "High Ranking Security Official," interviewed by author, 28 September 1999.

51. For an account of the incident, I have relied on interviews with Fereydoun Hoveyda and Ebrahim Golestan. The quoted words are from Ebrahim Golestan, personal correspondence, 20 January 2000.

52. Ibid.

53. Several sources, including Parviz Radji and Cyrus Ghani, have recounted this conversation. Here I have quoted Ebrahim Golestan, personal correspondence, 20 January 2000.

Chapter 13: The Fall of Pompeii

1. *New York Times*, 24 July 1999, 16.

2. Alam, *Yadashtha-ye Alam* [Alam's Diaries], vol. 3, 61.

3. Cyrus Ghani, interviewed by author, Lake Tahoe, Nevada, 20 August 1999.

4. For an account of the creation and work of this group, I have relied on Cyrus Ghani and Fereydoun Mahdavi. Cyrus Ghani, interview. Fereydoun Mahdavi, interviewed by author, 3 September 1999.

5. I have relied on Cyrus Ghani and Fereydoun Mahdavi for an account of these meetings.

6. Alam reports that early in 1973 he told the shah that he had received information that "the prime minister has paid off many of those around the queen and other servants." He claims the shah ordered an investigation. See Alam, *Yadashtha-ye Alam* [Alam's Diaries], vol. 3, 22.

7. Houshang Nahavandi, interviewed by Shahrokh Meskoob, 29 May 1985, Paris, France, tape no. 5, Iranian Oral History Collection, Harvard University.

8. Farokh Najmabadi, personal correspondence, 24 January 2000.

9. Ghani, interview.

10. CIA, "Elites, and the Distribution of Power in Iran," NSA, no. 1012, 66.

11. "High Ranking Security Official," interviewed by author, 18 September 1999.

12. U.S. Embassy, Tehran, Iran, "Representative List of Intermediaries and Influence Peddlers," NSA, no. 780.

13. CIA, "Elites and the Distribution of Power in Iran," NSA, no. 1012.

14. U.S. Embassy, Tehran, Iran, "Corruption in Iran," 15 December 1978, in *Documents from the U.S. Espionage Den*, vol. 13 (Tehran, n.d.), 12.

15. U.S. Embassy, Tehran, Iran, "Shah-Harriman Talk," in *Foreign Relations of the United States, 1964-1968*, Vol. XXII (Washington, 1999), 329.

16. Hossein Razavi and Firouz Vakil, *The Political Environment of Economic Planning in Iran, 1971-1983: From Monarchy to Islamic Republic* (Boulder, 1984), 67.

17. Ibid.

18. Several people, including Fereydoun Hoveyda, Laila Emami, and Abdol-Madjid Madjidi, told me about Hoveyda's reaction to his China trip.

19. Razavi and Vakil, *The Political Environment*, 69.

20. Abdol-Madjid Madjidi, interviewed by author, Washington, D.C., 15 February 1999.

21. Ahmad Ashraf, personal correspondence, 14 February 2000.

22. Razavi and Vakil, *The Political Environment*, 72.

23. *Foreign Relations*, 338.

24. Ahmad Ashraf, personal correspondence, 14 February 2000.

25. Ibid., 80.

26. Amir Abbas Hoveyda, "The Future of Iran," in *Iran: Past, Present and Future*, ed. Jane W. Jacqs (New York, 1976), 440–50.

27. Farokh Najmabadi, "Strategies of Industrial Development in Iran," in *Iran: Past, Present and Future*, 105.

28. Firouz Tofig, "Development of Iran: A Statistical Note," in Iran, *Past, Present and Future*, 63.

29. Amir Abbas Hoveyda, "The Future of Iran," 444–50.

30. Abdol-Madjid Madjidi, "Interview with Abdol-Madjid Madjidi," Oral History Project, Foundation for Iranian Studies, interviewed by Sima Dabir Ashtiani in Washington, D.C. on 21 April 1982, and by Dr. Akbar Etemad, in Paris on 12 October 1982, 54.

31. U.S. State Department, "Visit of the Shah of Iran," 1967, NSA, no. 639.

32. U.S. Embassy, Tehran, Iran, "Telegram," in *Foreign Relations*, 10.

33. For an account of these reforms, see U.S. Embassy, Tehran, Iran, "Movement toward a Welfare State," February 20, 1975, in *Documents From the U.S. Espionage Den*, vol. 61 (Tehran, n.d.), 12–22.

34. U.S. State Department, "Telegram from the Department of State to the Embassy in Iran," in *Foreign Relations*, 364.

35. U.S. State Department, "Visit of the Shah," 3.

36. Alam, *Yadashtha-ye Alam* [Alam's Diaries], vol. 3, 265.

37. "Telegram from Secretary of State Dulles," January 25, 1958, in *Foreign Relations of the United States, 1958-60*, vol. XII (Washington, D.C., 1993), 534.

38. U.S. Embassy, Tehran, Iran, "Summary of Shah's Current Concerns," NSA, no. 523.

39. NA, "Memorandum for the President," August 15, 1967.

40. U.S., Department of State, Bureau of Intelligence and Research, "Secret Report # 704," 1977/1/78, NSA, no. 1144.

41. U.S. Embassy, Tehran, Iran, "Decision-Making in Iran," n.d., NSA, no. 1066.

42. Ibid.

43. U.S. Embassy, Tehran, Iran, "Iran's Modernizing Monarchy: A Political Assessment," 1 January 1971, NSA, no. 1060, 5.

44. U.S. Embassy, Tehran, Iran, "The Recent Evolution of Power in Iran," April 15, 1975, NSA, no. 947, 3.

45. For the story of the Iran Novin Party's early days and the shah's influence in deciding its leadership, see U.S. Embassy, Tehran, Iran, "New Iran Party Celebrates 5 Anniversary with a Party Purge," January 9, 1968.

46. Fereydoun Mahdavi, interviewed by author, 3 September 1999.

47. Gholam Reza Afkhami, *The Iranian Revolution: Thanatos on a National Scale* (Washington, D.C., 1985), 70. I tried to interview Gholam Reza Afkhami about his role in shaping the Resurgence idea. He refused to talk on record, indicating only that he would prefer to let his book speak for itself.

48. Ahmad Ghoreishi, interviewed by author, 22 September 1999.

49. U.S. Embassy, "New Iran Party Celebrates," 3.

50. Afkhami, *The Iranian Revolution*, 70.

51. Amin Alimard, interviewed by author, 22 September 1999.

52. Alimard, interview.

53. Several people, including "High Ranking Security Official," Ahmad Ghoreishi and Abdol-Madjid Madjidi have suggested the Sadat connection.

54. Madjidi, Program for Oral History, 9. Amin Alimard, interview.

55. The volumes of *Yadashtha-ye Alam* [Alam's Diaries] dealing with the announcement of the new party system have not yet been published. The editor, Alinaghi Alikhani, kindly looked through the manuscripts of the forthcoming volumes and informed me of Alam's ignorance of the announcement. Furthermore, in conversations with Alam, Alikhani had learned that Alam had no advance warning of the party. Some six months before the day the new party structure was announced, in response to Alam's complaint, the shah enigmatically told him, "Next week I will have something to say about the minority party." But, as far as we know, there was to be no further conversation on that topic.

56. When the announcement of the news conference was made, General Nasiri called Sabeti and asked whether he knew what was going to be decreed. "High Ranking Security Official," interviewed by author, 23 November 1997.

57. Madjidi, Program for Oral History, 9. Amin Alimard, interview.

58. Parviz C. Radji, "Amir Abbas Hoveyda," in http// WWW. Hoveyda. Org/radji/html, Hoveyda Web Site.

59. U.S. Embassy, Tehran, Iran, "The Iranian One-Party State," 10 July 1976, NSA, no. 975, 1.

60. Afkhami, *The Iranian Revolution*, 70.

61. Parviz C. Radji, interviewed by author, 12 October 1997.

62. Afkhami, *The Iranian Revolution*, 55.

63. Radji, *In the Service of the Peacock Throne*, 97.

64. U.S. Department of State, "Research Memorandum from the Director of the Bureau of Intelligence and Research (Hughes) to Secretary of State Rusk," in *Foreign Affairs*, Vol XXII, 492.

65. Mohsen Milani, *The Making of Iran's Islamic Revolution: From Monarchy to Islamic Republic* (Boulder, 1994), 97.

66. William H. Sullivan, *Mission to Iran* (New York, 1981), 26.

67. Ibid., 59.

68. Ibid., 71–72.

69. Ali Asghar Hadj-Seyyed-Djavadi, *Do Nameh* [Two Letters] (Tehran, 1978), 7–14.

70. Ali Asghar Hadj-Seyyed-Djavadi, interviewed by author, 2 September 1999.

71. Radji, *In the Service of the Peacock Throne*, 69.

72. Abdol-Madjid Madjidi, interviewed by author, Washington, D.C., 15 February 1999.

Chapter 14: Le Bouc Émissaire

1. Edouard Sablier, interviewed by author, Paris, France, March 1999.

2. Radji, *In the Service of the Peacock Throne*, 98.

3. Ahmad Ghoreishi, interviewed by author, 12 January 2000.

4. CIA, Tehran, Iran, "New Political Activity: Making a Silk Purse out of Shah's Ear," Confidential Report # 77-046, NSA, no. 1213.

5. Entries covering this period have not been published yet. I was provided with a copy of the handwritten note, courtesy of *Alam Diaries'* editor, Alinaghi Alikhani.

6. Radji, *In the Service of the Peacock Throne*, 93.

7. I heard of Amouzegar's belief and Hoveyda's and Sabeti's response from two sources. Ahmad Ghoreishi described in detail his own role in the affair. The "High Ranking Security Official" confirmed Sabeti's response.

8. "High Ranking Security Official," interview.

9. Daryoush Homayoun, interviewed by author, Belmont, California, 6 June 1999.

10. Homayoun, interview.

11. Joseph Kraft, "Letter from Tehran," *New Yorker*, 18 December 1978.

12. Ibid., 153–54.

13. General [Abbas] Gharabaghi, *Vérités sur les Crises Iraniene* (Paris, 1985), 20–27.

14. Ibid., 24.

15. U.S. Embassy, Tehran, Iran, "Memorandum of Conversation, Internal Politics, 1978/11/01." NSA, no. 1653.

16. Iranian newspapers were soon replete with stories about Sharif-Emami's role in Freemasonry. In Ra'in's storied book about Freemasonry, Sharif-Emami figures prominently as a grand master.

17. U.S. Embassy, Tehran, Iran, "Increased Religious Pressure on the Government," Secret Cable # 07890, 19/78/08, NSA, no. 1475.

18. U.S. Embassy, Tehran, Iran, "Ex-Prime Minister Reenters the Political Lists," 1978/08.03, NSA, no. 1462.

19. Fereydoun Mahdavi, interviewed by author, 16 September 1999.

20. Mahdavi, interview.

21. Milani, *The Making of Iran's Islamic Revolution*, 117.

22. In his diaries, Alam claims to have repeatedly tried to get the shah to consent to the creation of a small coterie of advisors. For example, see Alam, *Yadashtha-ye Alam* [Alam's Diaries], vol. 1, 309.

23. Mehdi Pirasteh, interviewed by author, 4 August 1999.

24. U.S. Embassy, Tehran, Iran, "Memorandum of Conversation: Mehdi Pirasteh," 11 October 1978, NSA, no. 1591. It is a measure of the convoluted context of Iranian politics that while Pirasteh is convinced that it was the British who masterminded the revolution—"I don't know what the shah did to anger them, but I am sure it was their work," he told me—the U.S. Embassy official ends his report of their conversation by adding, "incidentally, the word among some embassy officers is that he [Pirasteh] is a British agent."

25. Ehsan Naraghi, interviewed by author, Paris, France, 22 October 1998.

26. Radji, *In the Service of the Peacock Throne*, 173.

27. "High Ranking Security Official," interview.

28. Mohammad Reza Pahlavi, *Answer to History* (New York, 1980), 167.

29. U.S. Department of State, The Evolution of U.S.-Iranian Relationship, NSA, no. 3556, 65. Sir Anthony Parsons' memoirs also makes the British position clear. See Anthony Parsons, *The Pride and the Fall* (London, 1984). Finally, the shah's own *Answer to History* clearly indicates the nature of advice he was getting from his two allies. He talks of trying to organize a "huge show of force and strength for the crown" in the aftermath of the Black Friday, and how the British and the American envoys "shrugged and said what is the point in that? The next day the opposition will have double that number opposing you. It is a race you can not win." The shah further declares that the French President Valéry Giscard d'Estaing sent a "personal envoy to Tehran, a man very close to him. He too advocated a 'political' solution to the crisis, a euphemism for accommodation and abstention from the use of force." See Pahlavi, *Answer to History*, 164, 172. What the shah's declarations do not make clear is why he felt he needed the approval, or the permission of the "two envoys" to organize a "huge show of force... for the crown?"

30. U.S. Embassy, Tehran, Iran, "Why the Sudden Quiet," Confidential Cable # 05131, NSA, no. 1401.

31. "High Ranking Security Official," interview.

32. Fereydoun Mahdavi, interviewed by author, 14 September 1999.

33. Quoted in Mohsen Milani, *The Making of Iran's Islamic Revolution*, 123.

34. Pahlavi, *Answer to History*, 166.

35. Laila Emami, interviewed by author, Paris, France, 11 March 1998.

36. Claude de Peyron, interviewed by author, Paris, France, 23 October 1998.

37. Claude de Peyron, interview.

38. For an account of the meeting, see Gharabaghi, *Vérités sur les Crises Iraniene*, 48–49.
Aside from talking to the general in Paris, France, on 10 March 1999, I also learned of the
meeting's discussions from an interview with him in Washington, D.C., on 24 April 1999.

39. Shahin Aghayan, interviewed by author, Paris, France, 12 March 1998.

40. Ardeshir Zahedi, interview.

41. Ardeshir Zahedi, interviewed by author, 12 January 2000.

42. U.S. Embassy, Tehran, Iran, "Iran, Situation," 9 November 1978, NSA, no. 1708.

43. Mehdi Samii, interviewed by author, Los Angeles, 11 June 1998.

44. U.S. Embassy, Tehran, Iran, "The Political Middle Stripes," 1978/09/19, NSA, no. 1532.

45. Mehdi Pirasteh, interviewed by author, 4 August 1999.

46. Mehdi Pirasteh, interview. A fictionalized account of this meeting has been published.
Fatemeh Pakravan in her memoirs and Saideh Pakravan in her fictionalized account of the
meeting suggest that General Pakravan was adamantly against the idea of arresting Hoveyda.
For Fatemeh Pakravan's account, see Fatemeh Pakravan, *Khaterat* [Memoir] trans., Esmail
Salemi (Tehran, 1999), 98–191. This is in fact a translation of *Memoirs of Fatemeh Pakravan*
(Cambridge, 1998), ed. Habib Ladjevardi. See also Saideh Pakravan, *The Arrest of Hoveyda*. In
this rendition, some of those present in the meeting voice their objection to the decision to
arrest Hoveyda.

47. Houshang Nahavandi, interviewed by Shahrokh Meskoob, 29 May 1985, Paris, France,
tape no. 5, Iranian Oral History Collection, Harvard University.

48. Ibid.

49. Fereshteh Ensha, interviewed by author, 3 September 1999.

50. Several people, including Maryam and Fereshteh Ensha, as well as Ahmad Kashefi have
told me of the conversation. Ahmad Kashefi, interviewed by author, 31 October 1997.

51. I was told of this de facto house arrest by both Maryam and Fereshteh Ensha and by
Jahansouz Bahrami who was in charge of Hoveyda's security detail. Jahansouz Bahrami,
interviewed by author, Los Angeles, California, 3 April 1998. Bahrami talked fondly of
Hoveyda; he suggested that had he known that they were going to keep Hoveyda in prison, he
and other officers who had worked on the security detail for many years "would certainly have
risked our lives to try and save him."

52. Maryam Ensha, interviewed by author, Los Angeles, California, 15 February 1998.

53. Fereshteh Ensha, interviewed by author, 3 September 1999.

54. Several people, including Laila Emami herself, have told me of the conversation.

55. Maryam Ensha, interview.

56. Fereshteh Ensha, interviewed by author, 3 September 1999.

57. Fereshteh Ensha, interviewed by author, 13 March 1999.

58. U.S. Embassy, Tehran, Iran, "Israeli Operations in Iran," 2 April 1965. NSA, no. 549.

59. Afsaneh Jahanbani, interviewed by author, Paris, France, 3 June 1998.

60. Uri Lubrani, interviewed by author, 8 July 1999.

61. Fereshteh Ensha, interviewed by author, Paris, 3 September 1999.

62. Fereshteh Ensha, interviewed by author, Paris, France, 12 March 1999.

63. Fereshteh Ensha, interviewed by author, 3 September 1999.

64. U.S. Embassy, Tehran, Iran, "Recommendation for President to Shah Letter," 08/02/77.
NSA, no. 1493.

65. U.S. Department of State, "The Evolution of the U.S.-Iranian Relationship," NSA, no. 3556, 65.

66. Ibid., 68.

67. Ibid., 66.

68. U.S. Embassy, Tehran, Iran, "Understanding the Shiite Islamic Movement," NSA, no. 1298.

69. U.S. Embassy, Tehran, Iran, "Political Security Report, Feb. 12, 1979," NSA, no. 2292. In his many books and tracts explaining the armed forces decision to declare neutrality, General Gharabaghi has persistently denied that prior to the meeting of the commanders, any decision had been made. The U.S. Embassy report clearly contradicts his claim.

70. Sullivan, *Mission to Iran*, 342. Sullivan claims to have sent back a "colorful but unprintable" reply.

71. Much has been written about General Robert Huyser's mission. See Robert Huyser, *Mission to Tehran* (New York, 1986).

72. Fereshteh Ensha, interviewed by author, 3 September 1999.

73. Laila Emami, interview.

74. Fereshteh Ensha, interviewed by author, Paris, France, 12 March 1999.

75. Ensha, interview.

Chapter 15: The Hanging Judge

1. Sadegh Khalkhali, "Khaterat" [Memoirs] in *Salam*, 8 Mehr 1371, 30 September 1992, 6.

2. For an account of the Ayatollah's lecture, and his early activities, see Seyyed Hamid Rouhani, *Baresi va Tahlil-e Nehzat-e Imam Khomeini* [An Analysis of Imam Khomeini's Movement] (Tehran, 1978), 336.

3. Sadegh Khalkhali, *Kourosh-e Dorughin va Jenayat-kar* [The False and Criminal Cyrus] (Tehran, 1981).

4. Ensha, interview.

5. *Kayhan,* 14 February 1979, 8.

6. Fereshteh Ensha, interviewed by author, Paris, France, 4 June 1998.

7. *Kayhan,* 14 March 1979, 6.

8. Ibid., 6.

9. Ibid., 1.

10. Ibid., 6.

11. *Kayhan,* 14 March 1979, 6.

12. *Kayhan,* 14 March 1979, 6.

13. Ali-Asghar Hadj-Seyyed-Djavadi, interviewed by author, 2 September 1999.

14. The handwritten copy of the original, titled, "The Claims of the Iranian People Against Mr. Hoveyda, the Prime Minister, and All Past and Current Ministers in his Cabinets," was provided to me courtesy of Ali-Asghar Hadj-Seyyed-Djavadi.

15. Ibid., 9.

16. Radji, *In the Service of the Peacock Throne*, 96.

17. Hadj-Seyyed-Djavadi, interview.

18. *Kayhan,* 13 February 1979, 8.

19. *Kayhan,* 14 March 1979, 8.

20. Ibid., 8.

21. Ibid.

22. Ensha, interview.

23. *Kayhan,* 14 March 1979, 8.

24. Ibid., 8.

25. Khalkhali, "Khaterat," 7.

26. *Kayhan,* 13 February 1979, 8.

27. Khosrow Moatazed, Hoveyda: *Siyasatmadar-e peep, asa va orkid* [Hoveyda: The Politician of Pipe, Cane and Orchid] (Tehran, 1999), 1019.

28. Ibid., 1019.

29. Ibid., 1010.

30. *Kayhan,* 14 March 1979, 8.

31. Ibid.

32. Edouard Sablier, interviewed by author, Paris, France, 14 March 1998.

33. Radji, *In the Service of the Peacock Throne,* 224.

34. Alinaghi Alikhani, the editor of *Alam's Diaries,* provided me with a copy of the letter. Alam offers no analysis of the nature of the problem. Instead, he places great emphasis on the recent shortages of electricity in Iran and asks the shah to remedy the situation as soon as possible.

35. Manouchehr Eghbal's brother, Khosrow, reported the contents of the letter to the American Embassy. See U.S. Embassy, Tehran, Iran, "Memorandum of Conversation, October 11, 1978," NSA, no. 1586.

36. *Kayhan,* 14 March 1979, 8.

37. Ibid., 8.

38. Ibid., 8.

39. Ibid., 8.

Chapter 16: The Frozen Lake of Cocytus

1. Khalkhali, "Khaterat" [Memoirs], *Salam,* 7 Mehr 1371 / 30 September 1992, 7.

2. Khalkhali, "Khaterat," 8 Mehr 1371/1 October 1992.

3. Khalkhali, "Khaterat," Mehr 1371/30 September 1992, 7.

4. Ibid.

5. Fereydoun Hoveyda and Fereshteh Ensha have during numerous interviews told me of their efforts. For an account of Kosinski's involvement with Hoveyda, see James Park Sloan, *Jerzy Kosinski: A Biography* (New York: 1996), 317 & 363.

6. Fereshteh Ensha, interviewed by author, Paris, France, 2 June 1998.

7. I learned of the existence of this note, and its contents not just from my interview with Bani Sadr but also from a conversation with Mahmoud Rafie. He was a close confidant of Mobasheri's and had learned of the note in that capacity. By the time I began writing the book, Mobasheri was already dead. Mahmoud Rafie, interviewed by author, 17 August 1998.

8. Bani Sadr, interviewed by author, Versailles, France, 3 June 1998.

9. Bani Sadr, interview.

10. Bani Sadr, interview. In all details, Bani Sadr's account matches that provided by Mahmoud Rafie, a prominent member of the Iranian opposition to the shah, and for the last twenty years a tireless leader in the cause of human rights in Iran.

11. Bani Sadr, interview.

12. See John F. Burns, "Former Hanging Judge of Iran Upheaval Now Backs Reformers," *New York Times,* 23 October 1999.

13. Bani Sadr, interview.

14. Bani Sadr, interview. In two books and many articles, Bani Sadr has written about these dealings. He is also of the opinion that the Reagan election team did in fact reach a secret agreement with Ayatollah Khomeini to delay the release of the American hostages until after

the November elections of 1980. For his views on the "October Surprise," shared, in many important details, by Gary Sick who was one of President Carter's national security advisors, see Abol Hassan Bani Sadr, *My Turn to Speak: Iran, the Revolution and Secret Deals with the U.S.* (New York, 1991). For Gary Sick's version of events, see Gary Sick, *The October Surprise* (New York, 1991).

15. Maryam Ensha, interviewed by author, Los Angeles, California, 15 February 1998.

16. Fereshteh Ensha, interviewed by author, Paris, France, 2 June 1998.

17. Khalkhali, "Khaterat," 30 September 1992. For a journalist's account of the trial, see *Kayhan*, 19 Farvardin 1358/10 April 1979.

18. Khalkhali, "Khaterat," 30 September 1992.

19. Henry Precht, interviewed by author, 10 January 2000.

20. Charles Naas, interviewed by author, 11 January 2000.

21. Naas, interview.

22. Moatazed, *Hoveyda*, 1032–40.

23. Khalkhali, "Khaterat," 30 September 1992, 7.

24. Moatazed, *Hoveyda*, 1041.

25. *Kayhan*, 19 Farvardin 1358/10 April 1979, 2.

26. Ibid.

27. Moatazed, *Hoveyda*, 1042.

28. Ehsan Naraghi, interviewed by author, Paris, France, 2 June 1998.

29. *Kayhan*, 19 Farvardin 1358 / 10 April 1979, 1.

30. Ibid.

31. Ibid., 2.

32. Moatazed, *Hoveyda*, 1047.

33. Khalkhali, "Khaterat," 30 September 1992, 7.

34. Khalkhali was not only aware of this reputation but seemed, by then, to relish it. See his "Khaterat," 1 October 1992, 6.

35. Ibid., 7.

36. In anticipation of his trial, Hoveyda had asked his family to collect statistics for him. He wanted figures on everything from the number of students in high school to the total production of steel in the country. The family found and provided him the data he had requested, but it would all turn out to be of no avail. Fereshteh Ensha, interviewed by author, Paris, France, 4 June 1998.

37. *Kayhan*, 19 Farvardin 1358/10 April 1979, 3.

38. Khalkhali, "Khaterat," 30 September 1992, 7.

39. *Kayhan*, 10 April 1979.

40. Khalkhali, "Khaterat," 8 Mehr 1371/1 October 1992, 6.

41. Khalkhali, "Khaterat," 30 September 1992, 7.

42. Fereydoun Hoveyda, interviewed by author, 17 January 1999.

43. Karimi told the incident to Ehsan Naraghi. Ehsan Naraghi, interviewed by author, Paris, France, 2 June 1998.

44. This account of Hoveyda's last minutes was provided by Karimi, the man who fired the coup de grâce. He told of his role in a conversation with Ehsan Naraghi. Apparently a videotape of the execution was secretly made by a journalist who now resides in France. Dr. Ensha has, so far unsuccessfully, tried to purchase a copy. Ehsan Naraghi, interviewed by author, Paris, France, 3 June 1998. Also, Fereshteh Ensha, interviewed by author, Paris, France, 4 June 1998.

45. Fereshteh Ensha, interviewed by author, Paris, France, 4 June 1998.

46. V. S. Naipal, *Among the Believers: An Islamic Journey* (New York: 1981), 56.

47. Khalkhali, "Khaterat," 8 Mehr 1371/1 October 1992, 6.

48. For the use of "the machine" in the French Revolution, see Schama, *Citizens*, 619–22.

49. Maryam Ensha, interviewed by author, Los Angeles, California, 15 February 1998.

50. Fereshteh Ensha, interviewed by author, Paris, France, 4 June 1998.

51. Fereshteh Ensha, interviewed by author, Paris, France, 4 June 1998.

52. Fereshteh Ensha, interview.

53. Fereshteh Ensha, interview.

54. Maryam Ensha, interviewed by author, Los Angeles, California, 15 February 1998.

55. Homer *Odyssey*, tr. Robert Fagels (New York, 1998), 252.

56. Ibid., 125.

57. Fereshteh Ensha, interviewed by author, Paris, France, 4 June 1998.

58. Maryam Ensha, interview.

59. Fereshteh Ensha, interviewed by author. I have confirmed the story about Dr. Garman's role in the whole affair from another source as well.

60. Ensha, interview.

61. Khalkhali, "Khaterat," 8 Mehr 1371/1 October 1992, 6.

62. Fereshteh Ensha, interviewed by author, Paris, France, 4 June 1998.

63. Maryam Ensha, interviewed by author, Los Angeles, California, 11 June 1998.

64. Ensha, interview.

65. William Shakespeare, *Romeo and Juliet*, in *The Collected Works of Shakespeare*, ed. David Bevington (New York, 1992), act 3, scene 1, 1000.

Index

About the Author

ABBAS MILANI is Chair of the Department of History and Political Science at the College of Notre Dame in Belmont, California. He has written and published extensively on Iran's encounter with modernity. His books include, *Tales of Two Cities: A Persian Memoir,* and a translation of *King of the Benighted,* a novella by Manuchehr Irani.